When my wife is out with our daughter,
apparently people ask her frequently if
her husband is a foreign guy.
I couldn't be more Japanese.

—*Yūki Tabata*, 20

YŪKI TABATA

was born in Fukuoka Prefecture
and got his big break in the 2011
Shonen Jump Golden Future Cup
with his winning entry, *Hungry
Joker*. He started the magical fantasy
series *Black Clover* in 2015.

BLACK CLOVER
VOLUME 26
SHONEN JUMP Manga Edition

Story and Art by YŪKI TABATA

Translation ✱ TAYLOR ENGEL,
HC LANGUAGE SOLUTIONS, INC.

Touch-Up Art & Lettering ✱ ANNALIESE "ACE" CHRISTMAN

Design ✱ KAM LI

Editor ✱ ALEXIS KIRSCH

Printed in Canada

Published by VIZ Media, LLC
P.O. Box 77010
San Francisco, CA 94107

10 9 8 7 6 5 4 3 2 1
First printing, August 2021

ratings.viz.com RATED T TEEN

PARENTAL ADVISORY
BLACK CLOVER is rated T for Teen and is recommended for ages 13 and up. This volume contains realistic and fantasy violence.

VIZ MEDIA
viz.com

SHONEN JUMP

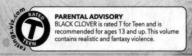

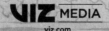

Noelle

Vanica

Lolopechka

Black ✦ Clover

YŪKI TABATA **26** BLACK OATH

Yuno

Member of:
The Golden Dawn   Magic: Wind

Asta's best friend, and a good rival who's also been working to become the Wizard King. He controls Sylph, the spirit of wind.

Asta

Member of: The Black Bulls
Magic: None (Anti-Magic)

He has no magic, but he's working to become the Wizard King through sheer guts and his well-trained body. He fights with anti-magic swords.

Finral Roulacase

Member of:
The Black Bulls
Magic: Spatial

A playboy who immediately chats up any woman he sees. He can't attack, but he has high-level abilities.

Yami Sukehiro

Member of:
The Black Bulls
Magic: Dark

A captain who looks fierce, but is very popular with his brigade, which has a deep-rooted confidence in him. Heavy smoker.

Gauche Adlai

Member of:
The Black Bulls
Magic: Mirror

A former convict with a blind, pathological love for his little sister. He has a magic item in his left eye socket.

Noelle Silva

Member of:
The Black Bulls
Magic: Water

A royal. She feels inferior to her brilliant siblings. Her latent abilities are an unknown quantity.

Grey

Member of:
The Black Bulls
Magic: Transformation

She has a shy personality, and always acts timid. She can transform to look like whoever she's with.

Vanessa Enoteca

Member of:
The Black Bulls
Magic: Thread

She has an unparalle[led] love of liquor, but it sometimes gets the b[etter of] her. During battle, sh[e uses] her magic to manipu[late] fate, changing the fu[ture.]

Gaja

Magic: Lightning

Lolopechka's close adviser. He has Zero Stage magic and is one of the Heart Kingdom's spirit guardians.

Lolopechka

Magic: Water

The princess of the [] Heart Kingdom. She[] fundamentally klutzy [and] clueless. She's been c[ursed] by the devil Megicula.

Vanica Zogratis

Magic: ??

A member of the Dark Triad and host of Megicula, a devil with whom Lolopechka and Noelle have a score to settle.

Dante Zogratis

Magic: Gravity

The leader of the Da[rk] Triad, the rulers of the Spade Kingdom. He believes that malice is supreme.

STORY

In a world where magic is everything, Asta and Yuno are both found abandoned on the same day at a church in the remote village of Hage. Both dream of becoming the Wizard King, the highest of all mages, and they spend their days working toward that dream.

The year they turn 15, both receive grimoires, magic books that amplify their bearer's magic. They take the entrance exam for the Magic Knights, nine groups of mages under the direct control of the Wizard King. Yuno, whose magic is strong, joins the Golden Dawn, an elite group, while Asta, who has no magic at all, joins the Black Bulls, a group of misfits. With this, the two finally take their first step toward becoming the Wizard King…

The Dark Disciples, the vanguard of the Spade Kingdom, appear all over the Heart Kingdom. As ferocious fighting breaks out, Dante of the Dark Triad attacks the Black Bulls. He plans to use Yami and Vangeance as the keys to form a link to the underworld and summon devils into the human world…but Yami isn't about to let him get away with it!!

CONTENTS

BLACK ❉ CLOVER

26

Page 251: The Curse Devil

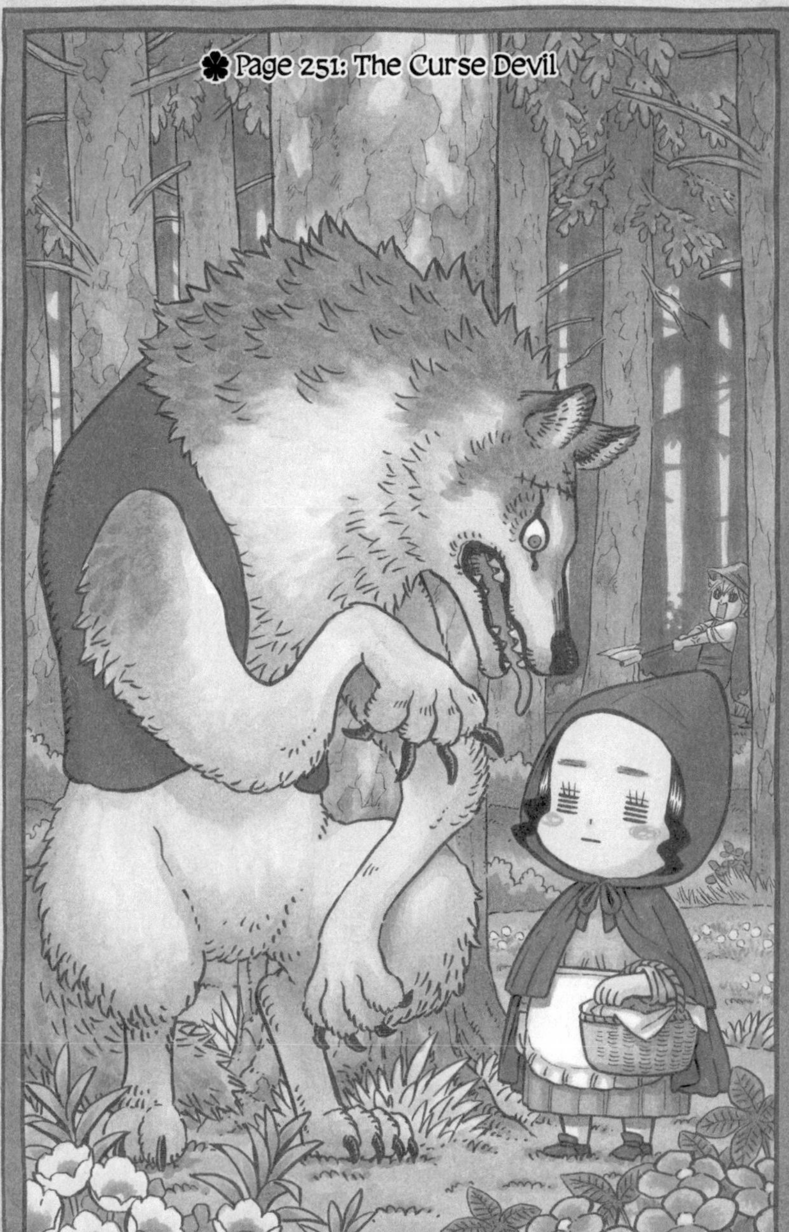

What will
I get to eat
today?!

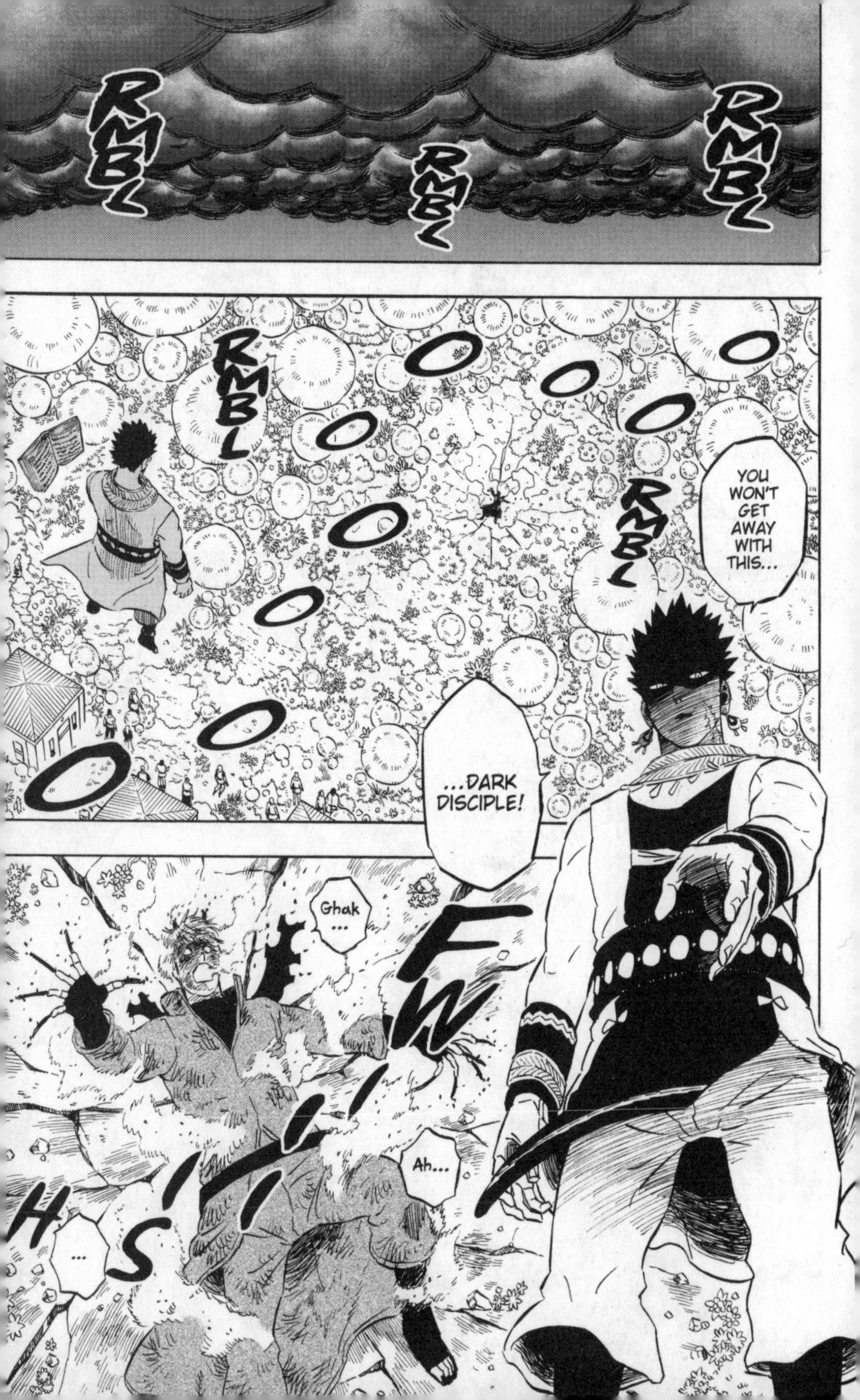
RMBL
RMBL
RMBL
RMBL
OOOOOOOOO
RMBL
YOU WON'T GET AWAY WITH THIS...
...DARK DISCIPLE!
FWISH
Ghak...
Ah...
...

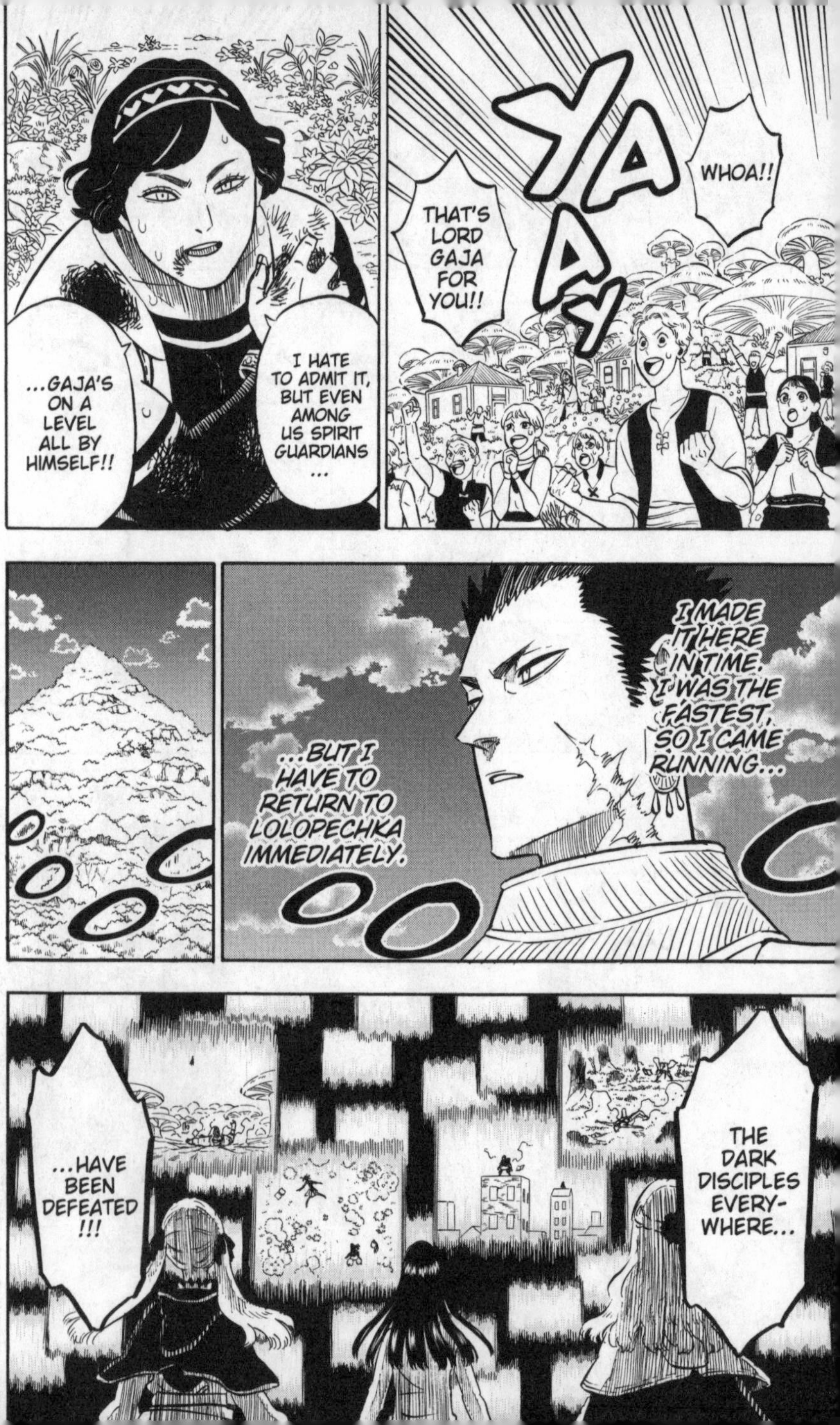
YAAY
WHOA!!
THAT'S LORD GAJA FOR YOU!!
I HATE TO ADMIT IT, BUT EVEN AMONG US SPIRIT GUARDIANS...
...GAJA'S ON A LEVEL ALL BY HIMSELF!!
I MADE IT HERE IN TIME. I WAS THE FASTEST, SO I CAME RUNNING...
...BUT I HAVE TO RETURN TO LOLOPECHKA IMMEDIATELY.
THE DARK DISCIPLES EVERYWHERE...
...HAVE BEEN DEFEATED!!!

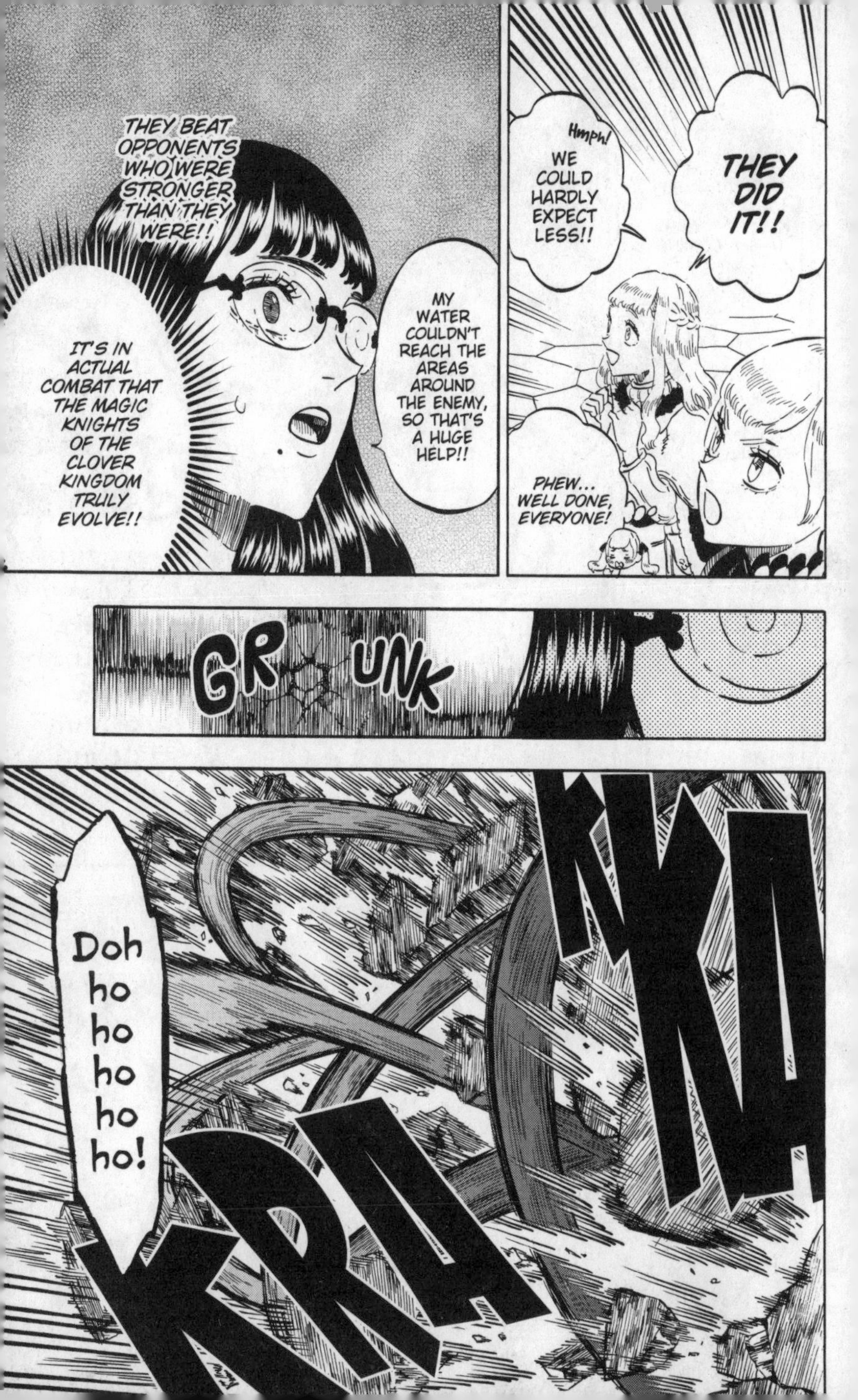
THEY DID IT!!
Hmph! WE COULD HARDLY EXPECT LESS!!
PHEW... WELL DONE, EVERYONE!
MY WATER COULDN'T REACH THE AREAS AROUND THE ENEMY, SO THAT'S A HUGE HELP!!
THEY BEAT OPPONENTS WHO WERE STRONGER THAN THEY WERE!!
IT'S IN ACTUAL COMBAT THAT THE MAGIC KNIGHTS OF THE CLOVER KINGDOM TRULY EVOLVE!!
GRUNK
KRAKKA
Doh ho ho ho ho ho!

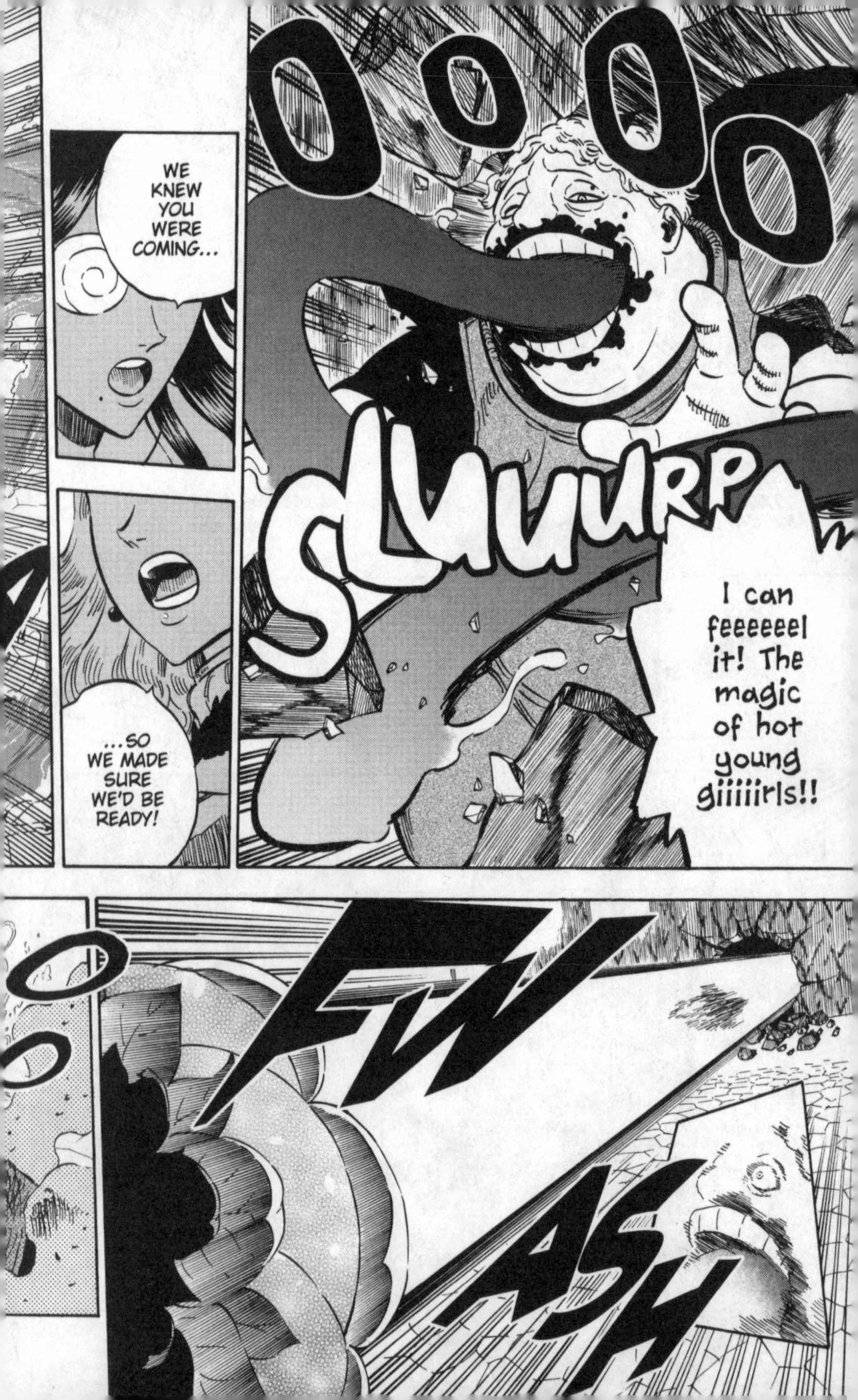
OOOOO
SLUUURP
I can feeeeeel it! The magic of hot young giiiiirls!!
WE KNEW YOU WERE COMING...
...SO WE MADE SURE WE'D BE READY!
FWASH

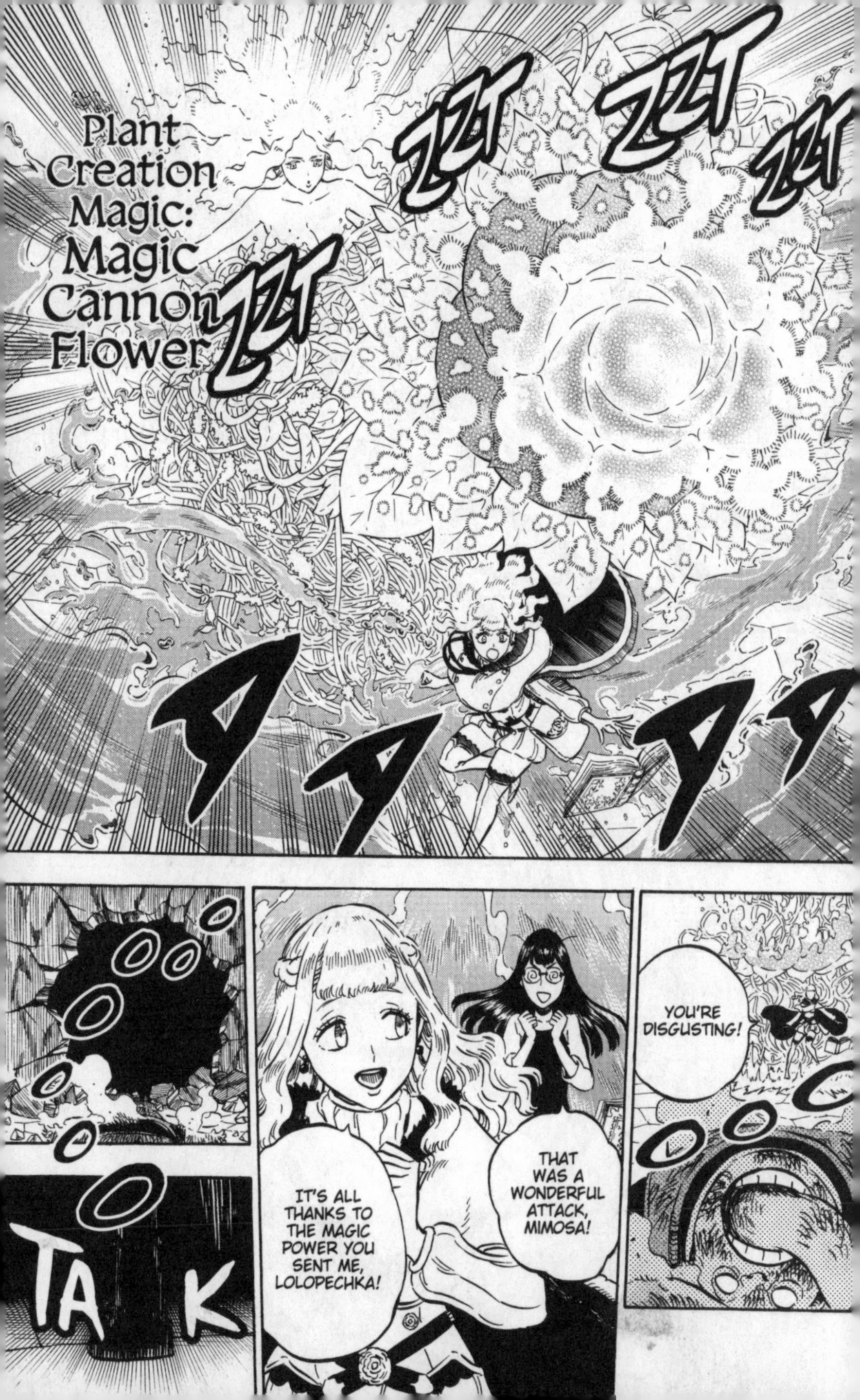
Plant Creation Magic: Magic Cannon Flower
ZZT
ZZT
ZZT
ZZT
YOU'RE DISGUSTING!
THAT WAS A WONDERFUL ATTACK, MIMOSA!
IT'S ALL THANKS TO THE MAGIC POWER YOU SENT ME, LOLOPECHKA!
TA K

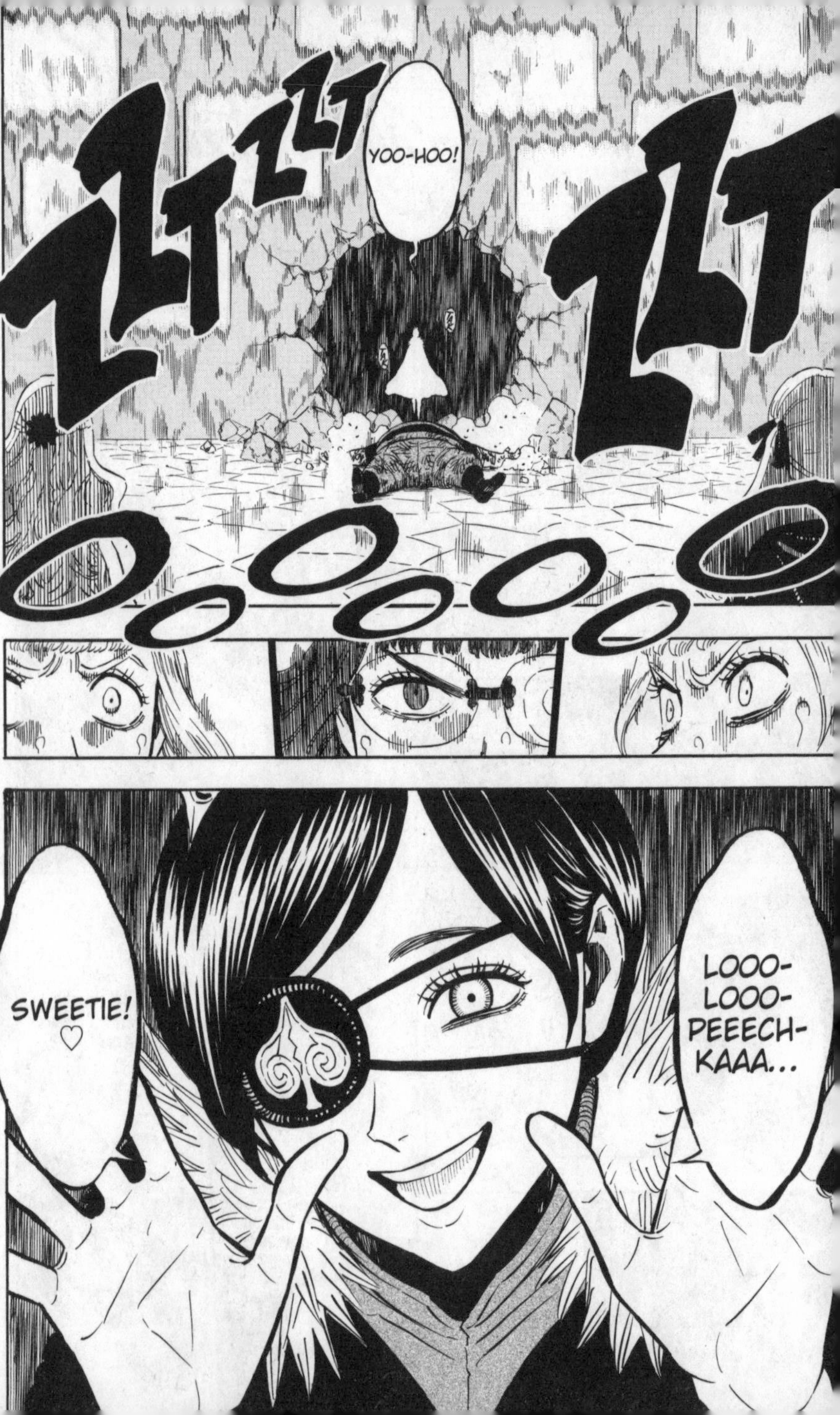
ZZT
YOO-HOO!
ZZZZT
LOOO-LOOO-PEEECH-KAAA...
SWEETIE! ♡

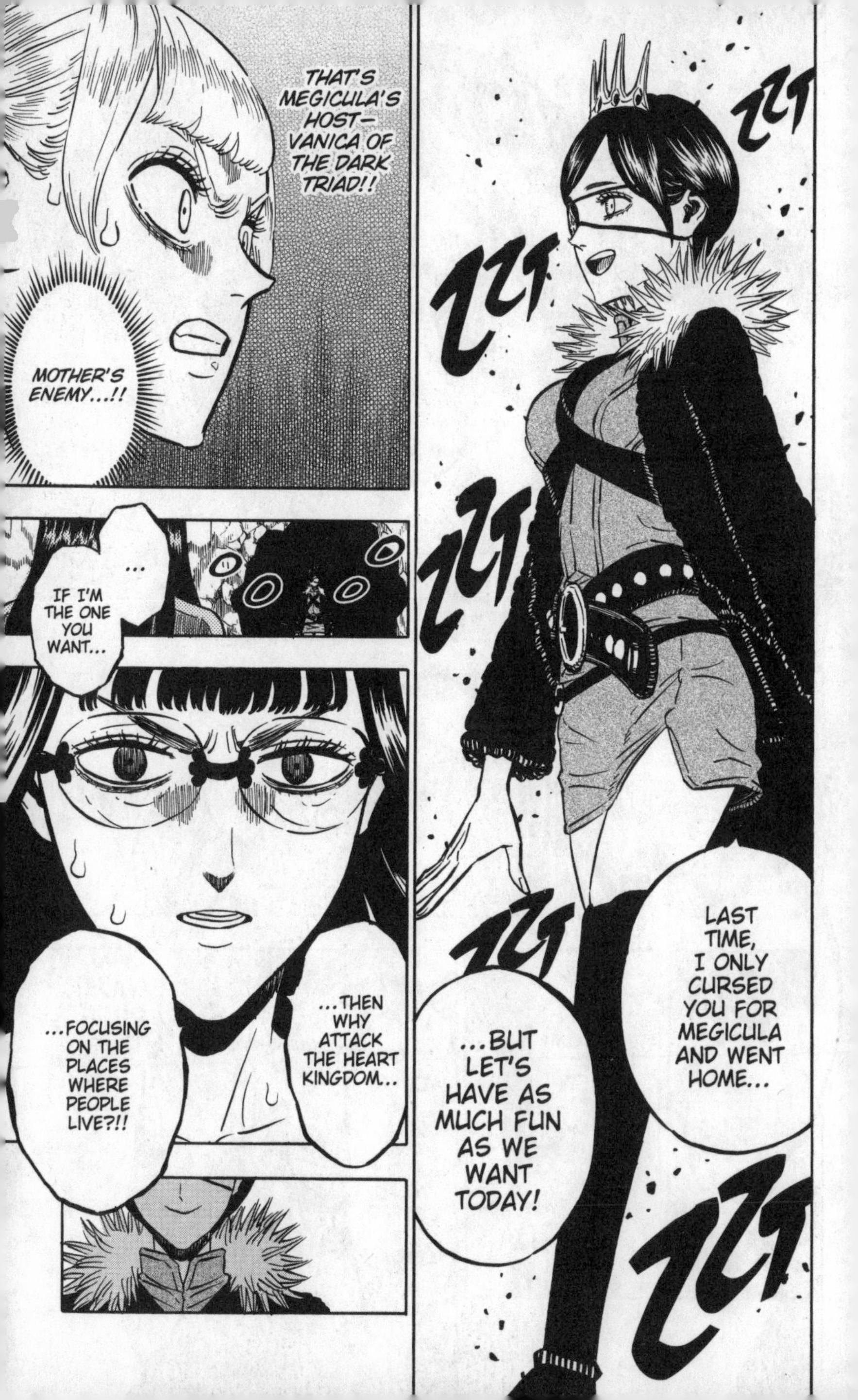
ZZT
ZZT
ZZT
ZZT
LAST TIME, I ONLY CURSED YOU FOR MEGICULA AND WENT HOME...
...BUT LET'S HAVE AS MUCH FUN AS WE WANT TODAY!
ZZT
THAT'S MEGICULA'S HOST—VANICA OF THE DARK TRIAD!!
MOTHER'S ENEMY...!!
...
IF I'M THE ONE YOU WANT...
...THEN WHY ATTACK THE HEART KINGDOM...
...FOCUSING ON THE PLACES WHERE PEOPLE LIVE?!!

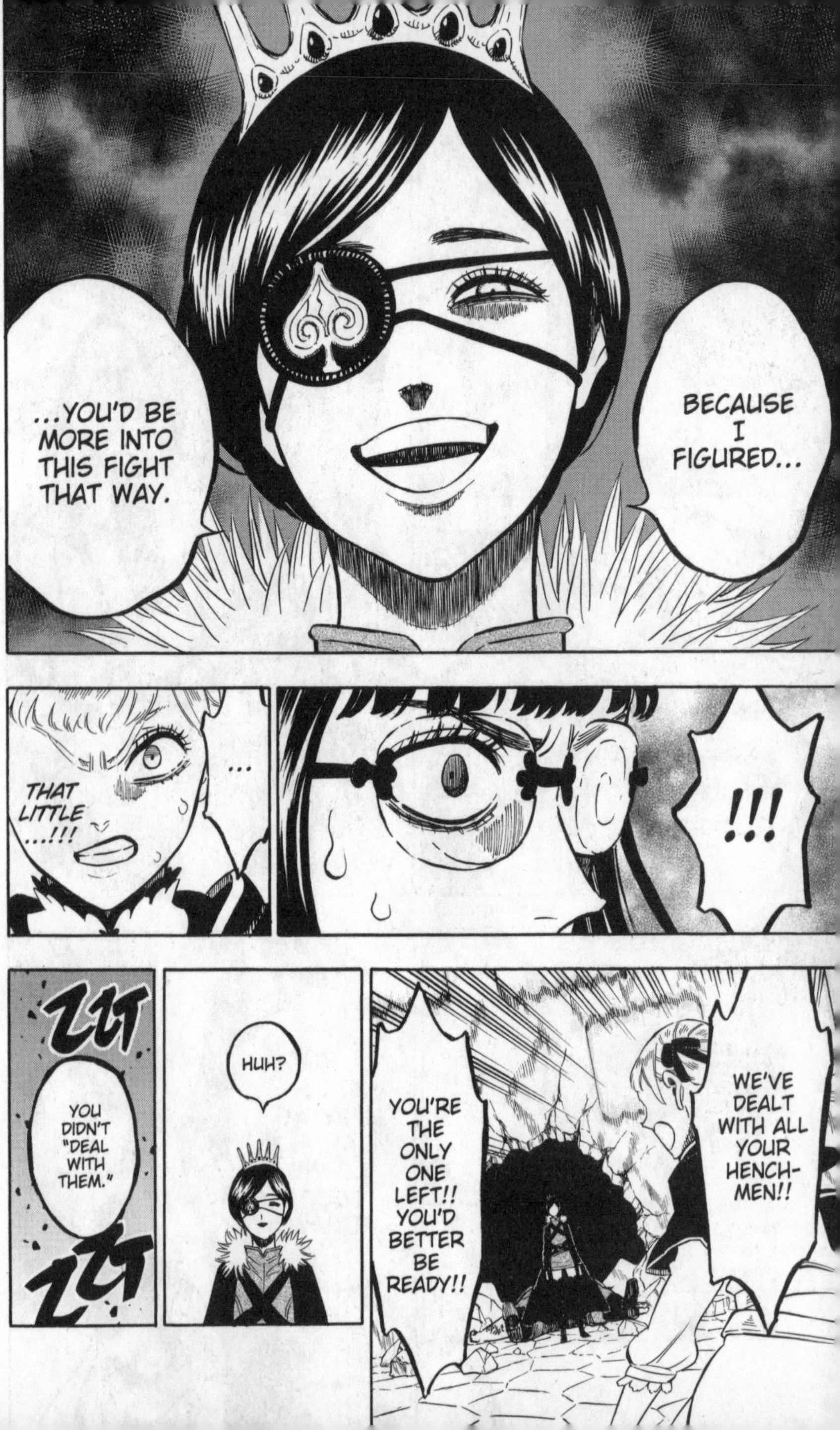
BECAUSE I FIGURED...
...YOU'D BE MORE INTO THIS FIGHT THAT WAY.
!!!
...
THAT LITTLE ...!!!
WE'VE DEALT WITH ALL YOUR HENCH-MEN!!
YOU'RE THE ONLY ONE LEFT!! YOU'D BETTER BE READY!!
HUH?
ZZT
YOU DIDN'T "DEAL WITH THEM."
ZZT

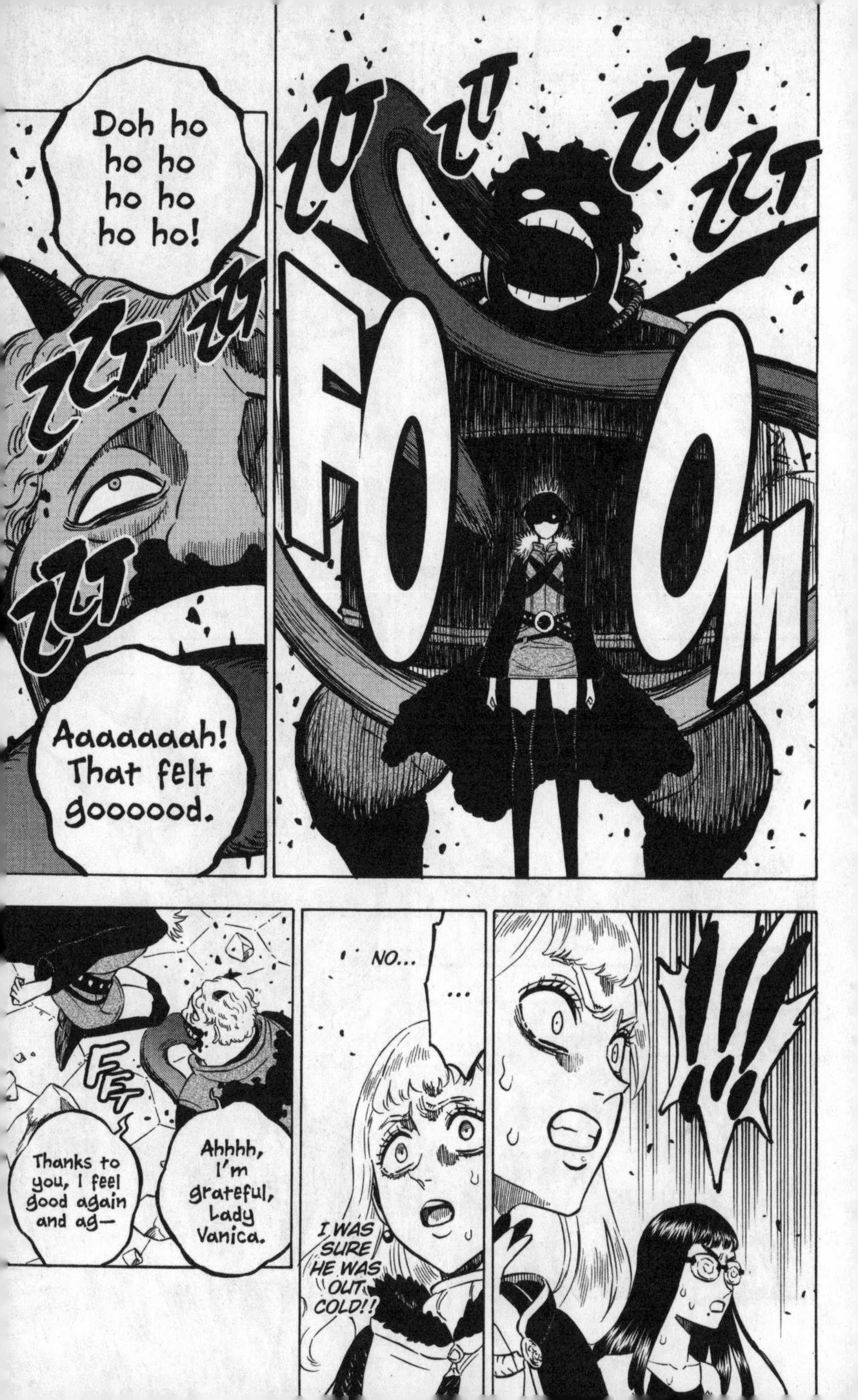
ZZT ZZT ZZT ZZT
BOOM
Doh ho ho ho ho ho ho ho!
ZZT ZZT ZZT
Aaaaaaah! That felt graaaaad.
!!
NO...
...
I WAS SURE HE WAS OUT COLD!!
FFT
Ahhhh, I'm grateful, Lady Vanica.
Thanks to you, I feel good again and ag—

?!!

SHUT YOUR MOUTH.

SHUNK

JUST HURRY UP...

...AND TAKE CARE OF THE LOSERS WHO AREN'T LOLOPECHKA.

FWISH

BLORCH

BLORCH

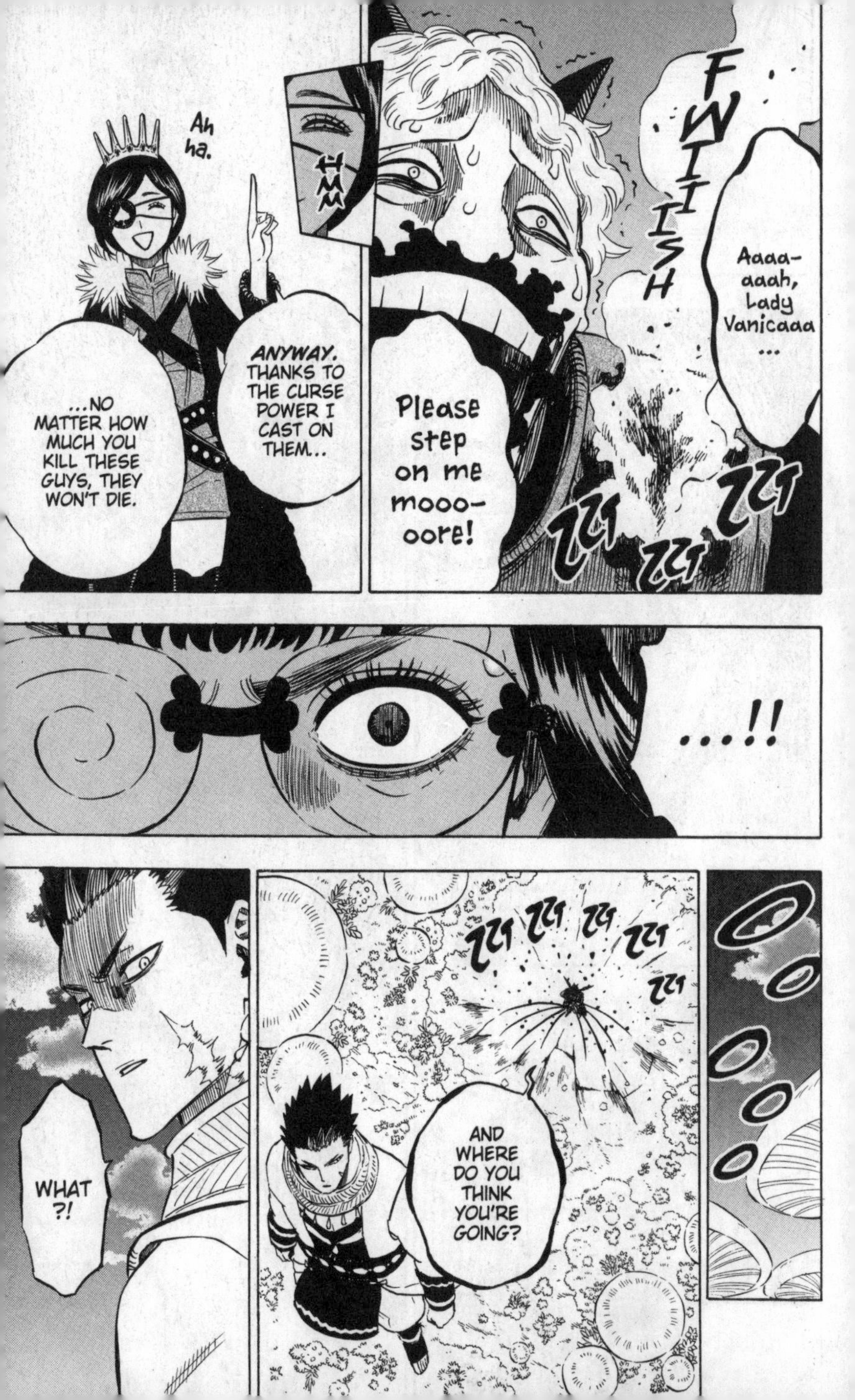
FWIIISH
Aaaa-aaah, Lady Vanicaaa...
Please step on me mooo-oore!
ZZT
ZZT
ZZT
HMM
Ah ha.
ANYWAY. THANKS TO THE CURSE POWER I CAST ON THEM...
...NO MATTER HOW MUCH YOU KILL THESE GUYS, THEY WON'T DIE.
...!!
ZZT ZZT ZZT ZZT ZZT
AND WHERE DO YOU THINK YOU'RE GOING?
WHAT?!

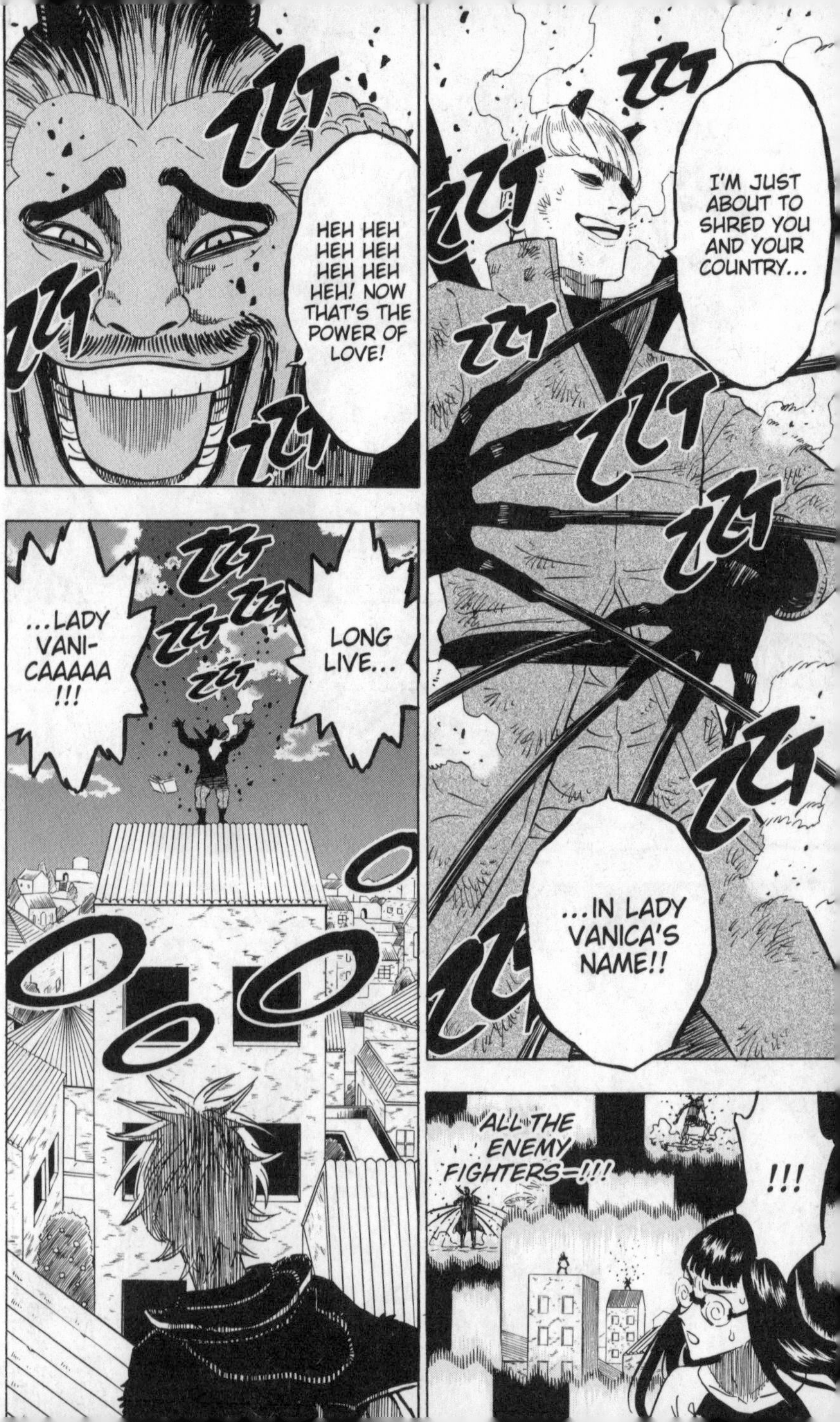
I'M JUST ABOUT TO SHRED YOU AND YOUR COUNTRY...
...IN LADY VANICA'S NAME!!
HEH HEH HEH HEH HEH HEH HEH! NOW THAT'S THE POWER OF LOVE!
LONG LIVE...
...LADY VANI-CAAAAA!!!
ALL THE ENEMY FIGHTERS—!!!
!!!

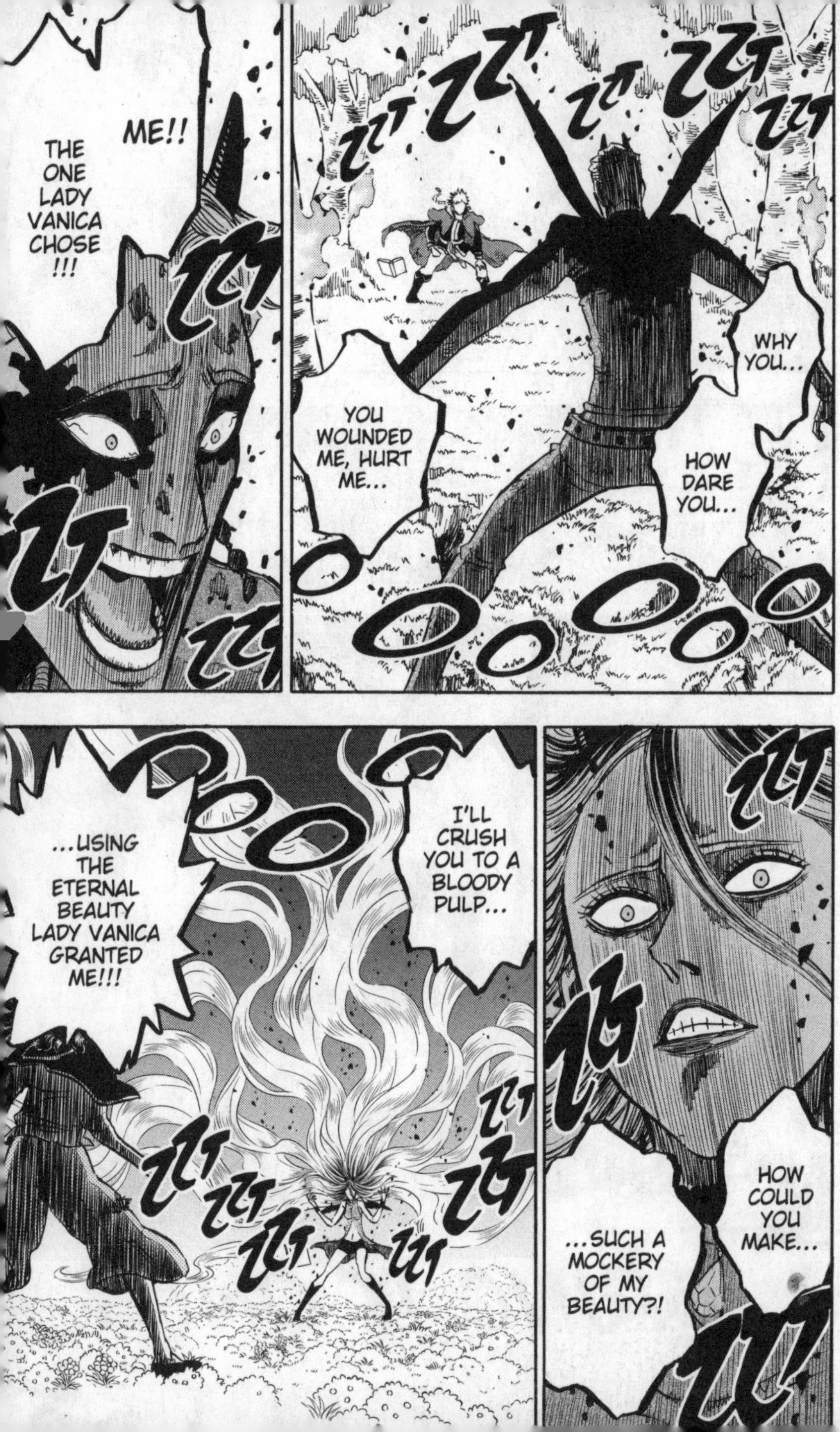
WHY YOU...
HOW DARE YOU...
YOU WOUNDED ME, HURT ME...
ME!!
THE ONE LADY VANICA CHOSE!!!
HOW COULD YOU MAKE...
...SUCH A MOCKERY OF MY BEAUTY?!
I'LL CRUSH YOU TO A BLOODY PULP...
...USING THE ETERNAL BEAUTY LADY VANICA GRANTED ME!!!

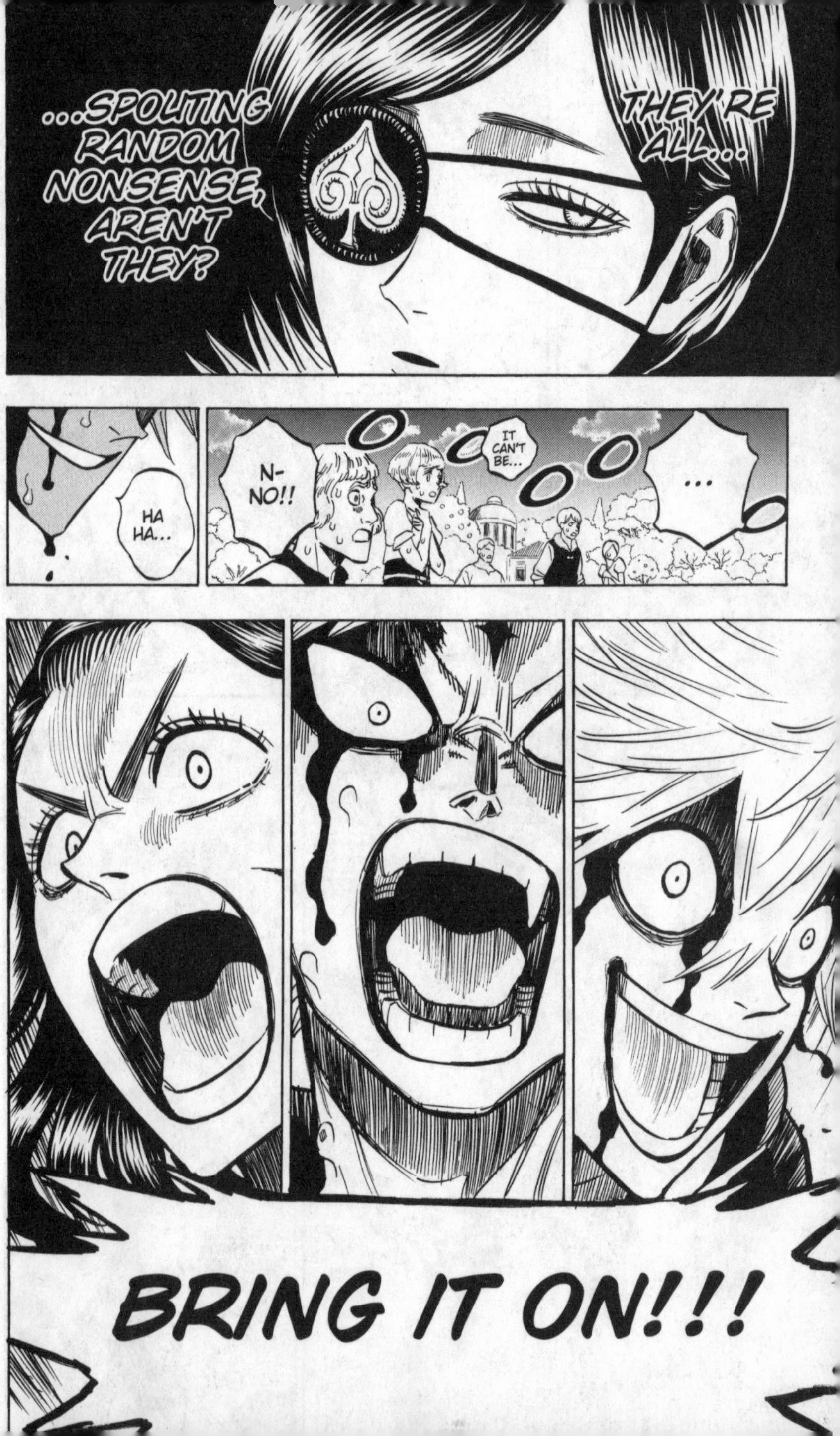
THEY'RE ALL..!
...SPOUTING RANDOM NONSENSE, AREN'T THEY?
...
IT CAN'T BE...
N-NO!!
HA HA...
BRING IT ON!!!

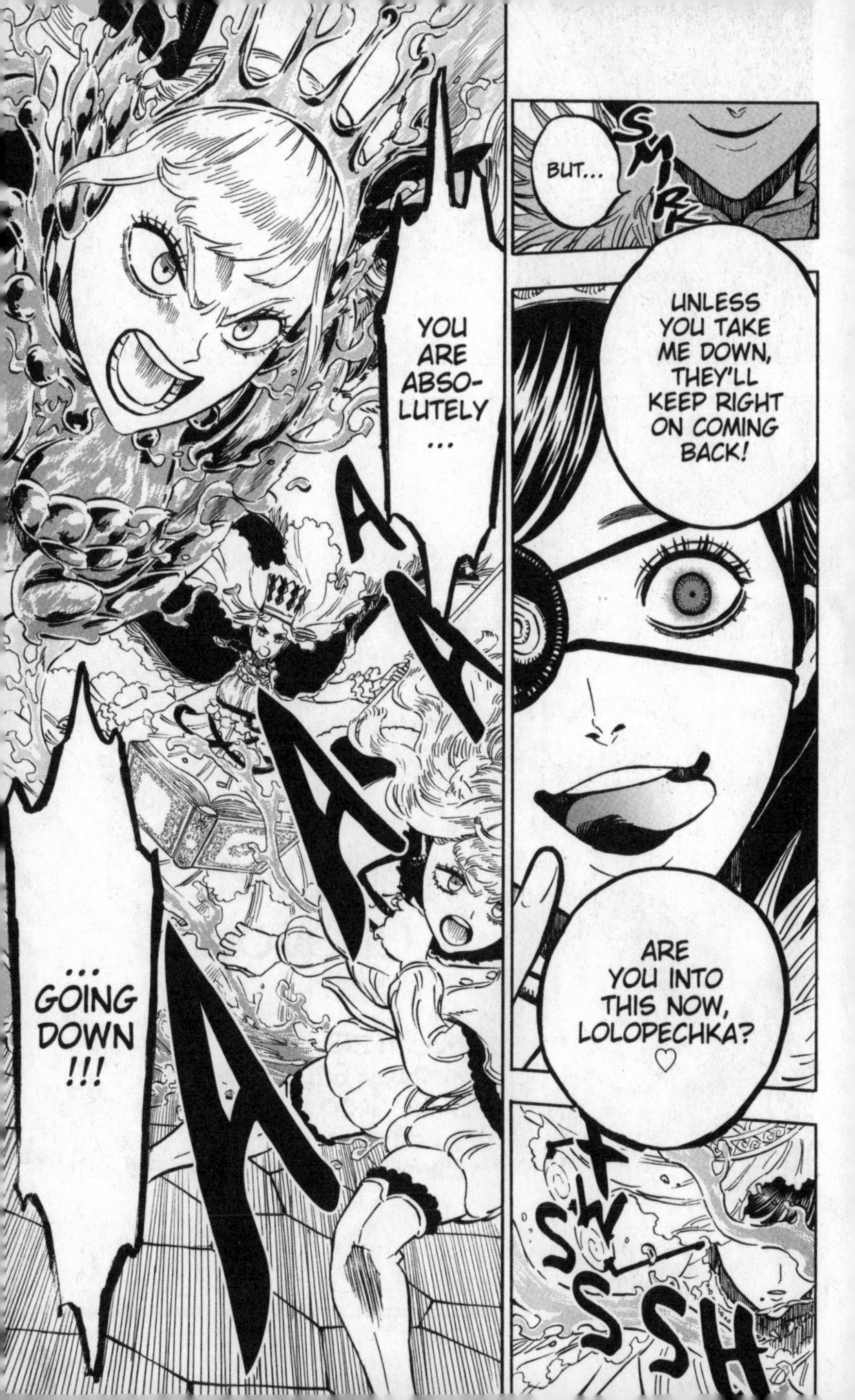
BUT...
SMIRK
UNLESS YOU TAKE ME DOWN, THEY'LL KEEP RIGHT ON COMING BACK!
ARE YOU INTO THIS NOW, LOLOPECHKA? ♡
YOU ARE ABSOLUTELY ...
... GOING DOWN !!!

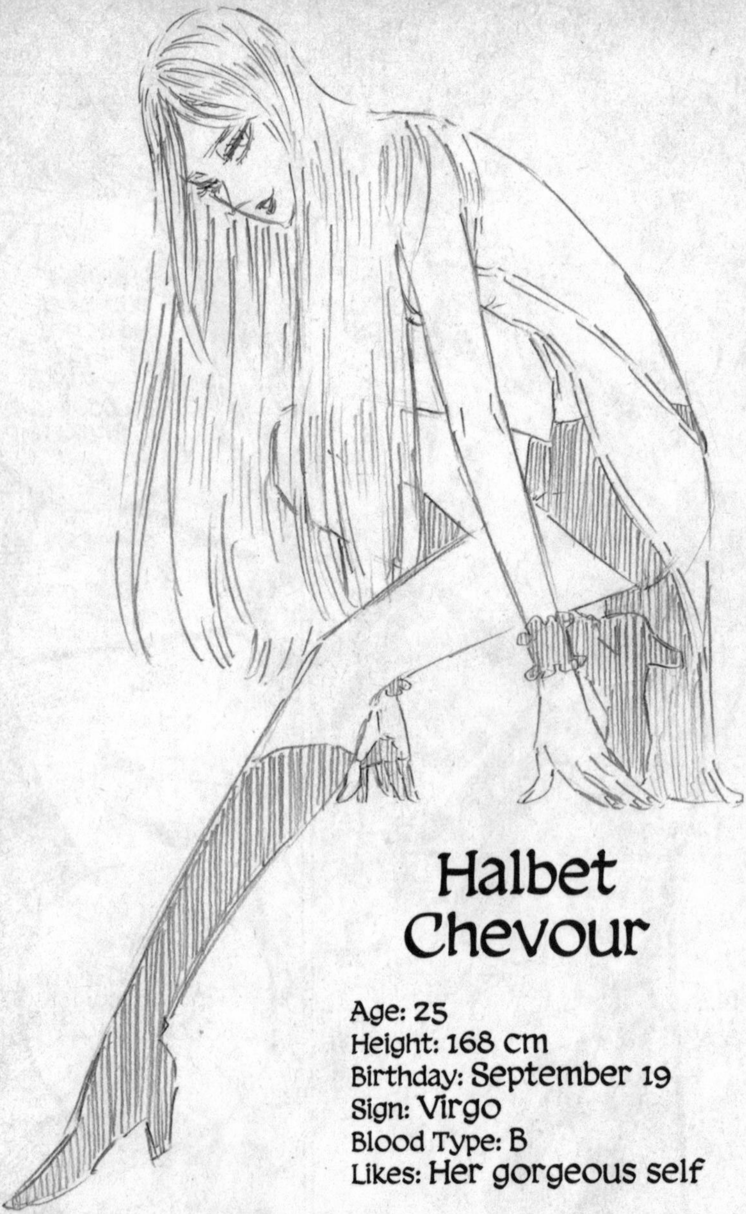

Halbet Chevour

Age: 25
Height: 168 cm
Birthday: September 19
Sign: Virgo
Blood Type: B
Likes: Her gorgeous self

Character Profile

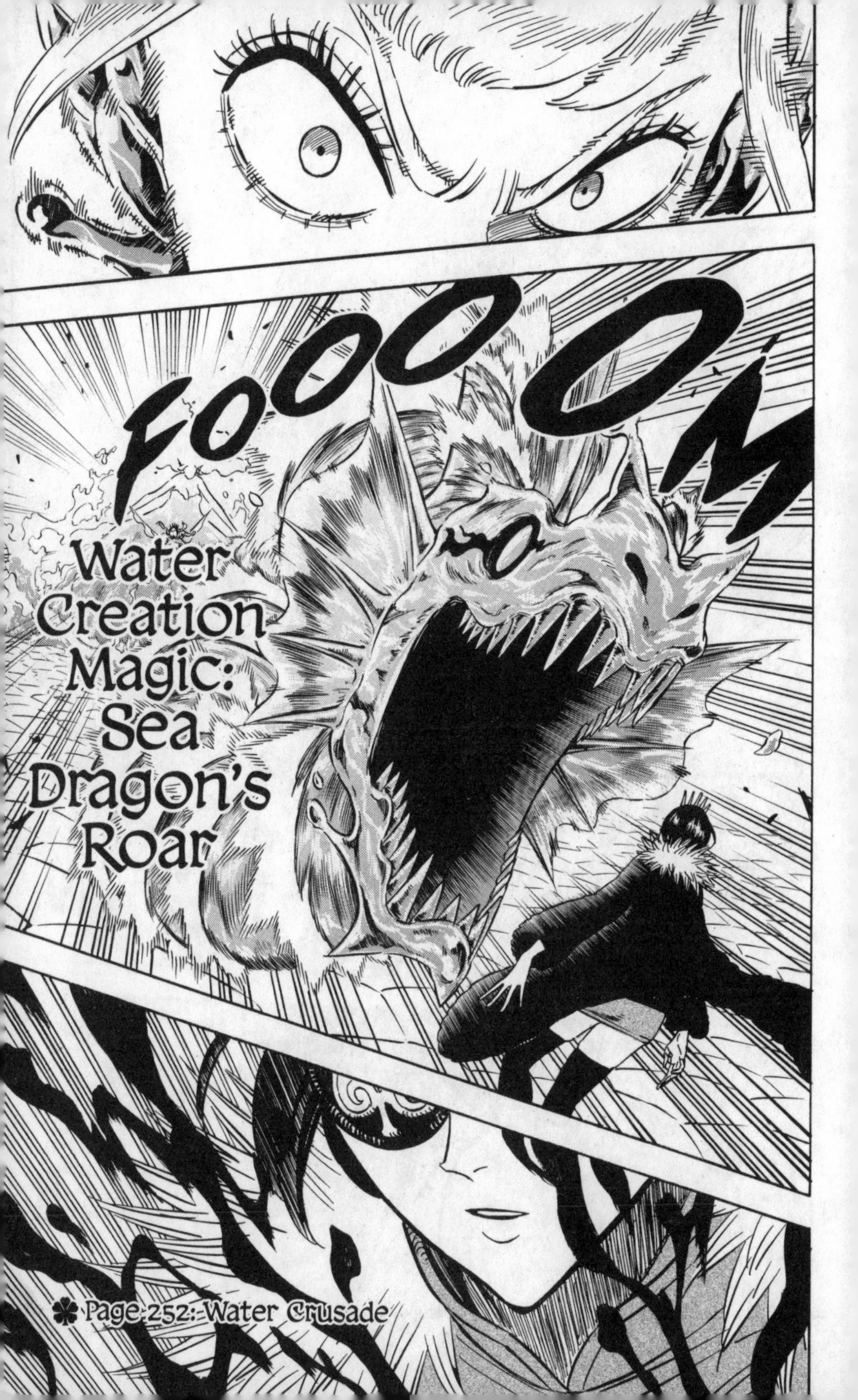
FOOOOM
Water Creation Magic: Sea Dragon's Roar
Page 252: Water Crusade

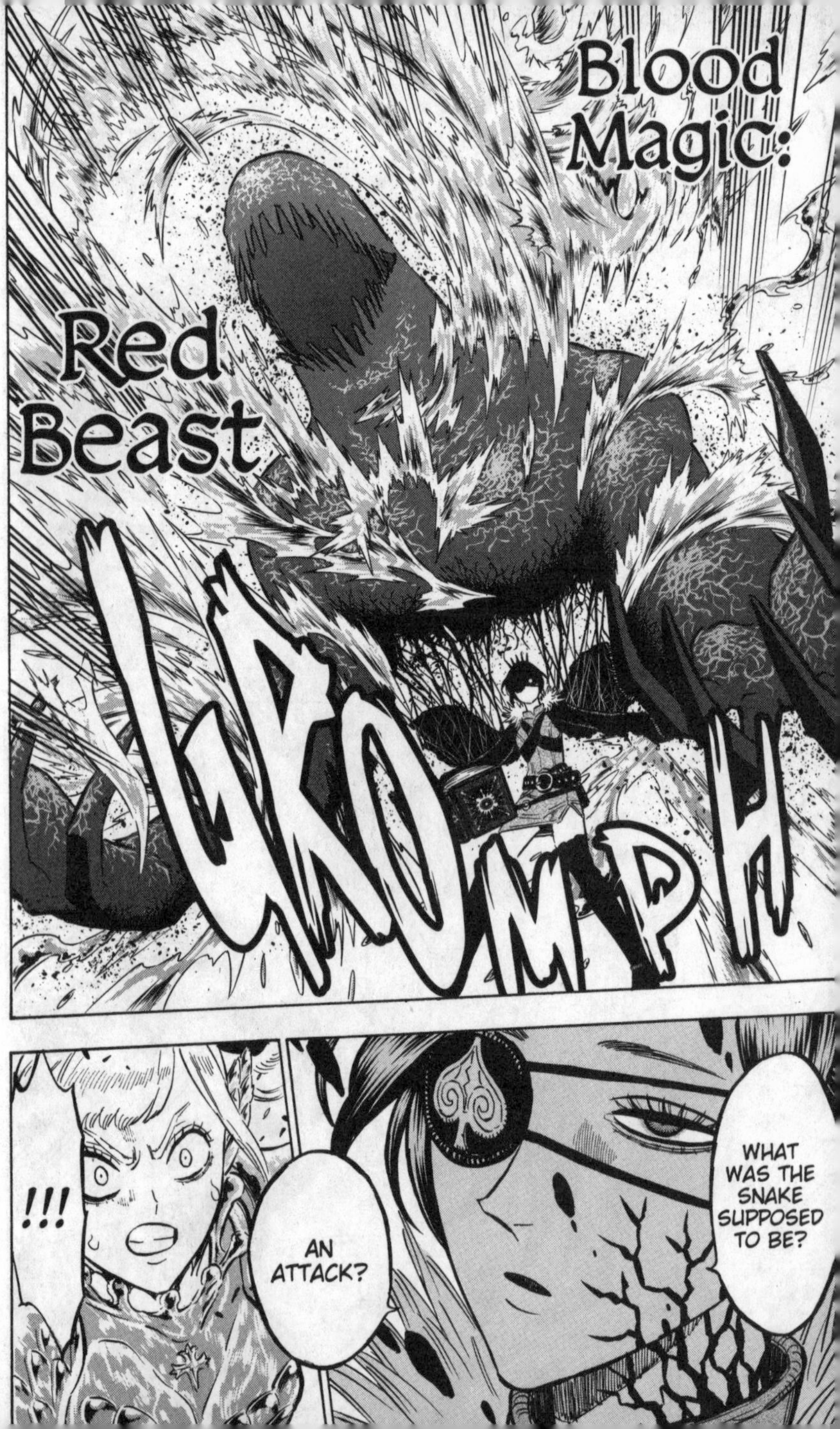
Blood Magic:
Red Beast
GROOMPH
WHAT WAS THE SNAKE SUPPOSED TO BE?
AN ATTACK?
!!!

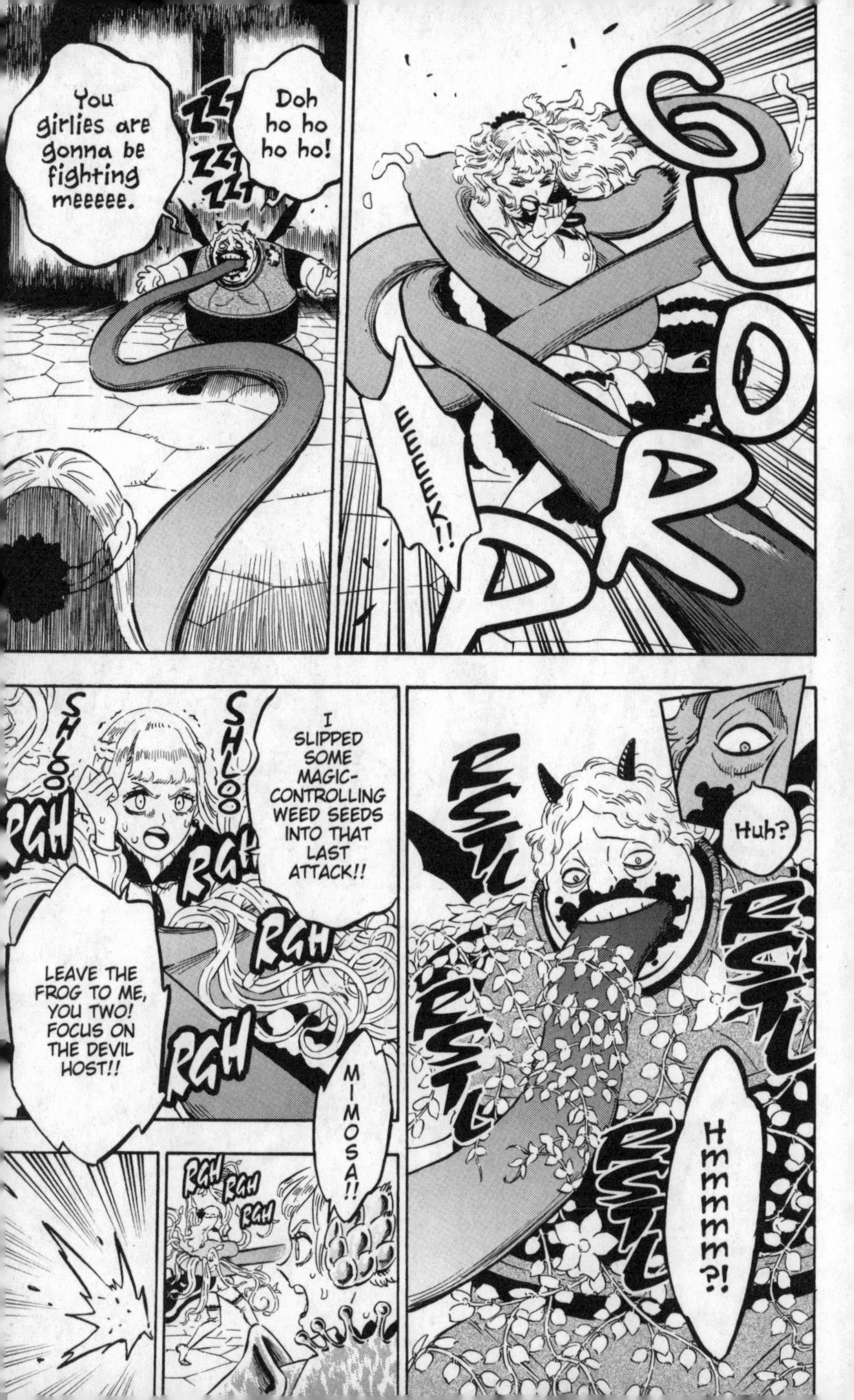
EEEEEK!!
Doh ho ho ho!
You girlies are gonna be fighting meeeee.
Huh?
Hmmmmm?!
I SLIPPED SOME MAGIC-CONTROLLING WEED SEEDS INTO THAT LAST ATTACK!!
SHLOORGH
SHLOORGH
RGH
LEAVE THE FROG TO ME, YOU TWO! FOCUS ON THE DEVIL HOST!!
MIMOSA!!
RGH RGH RGH

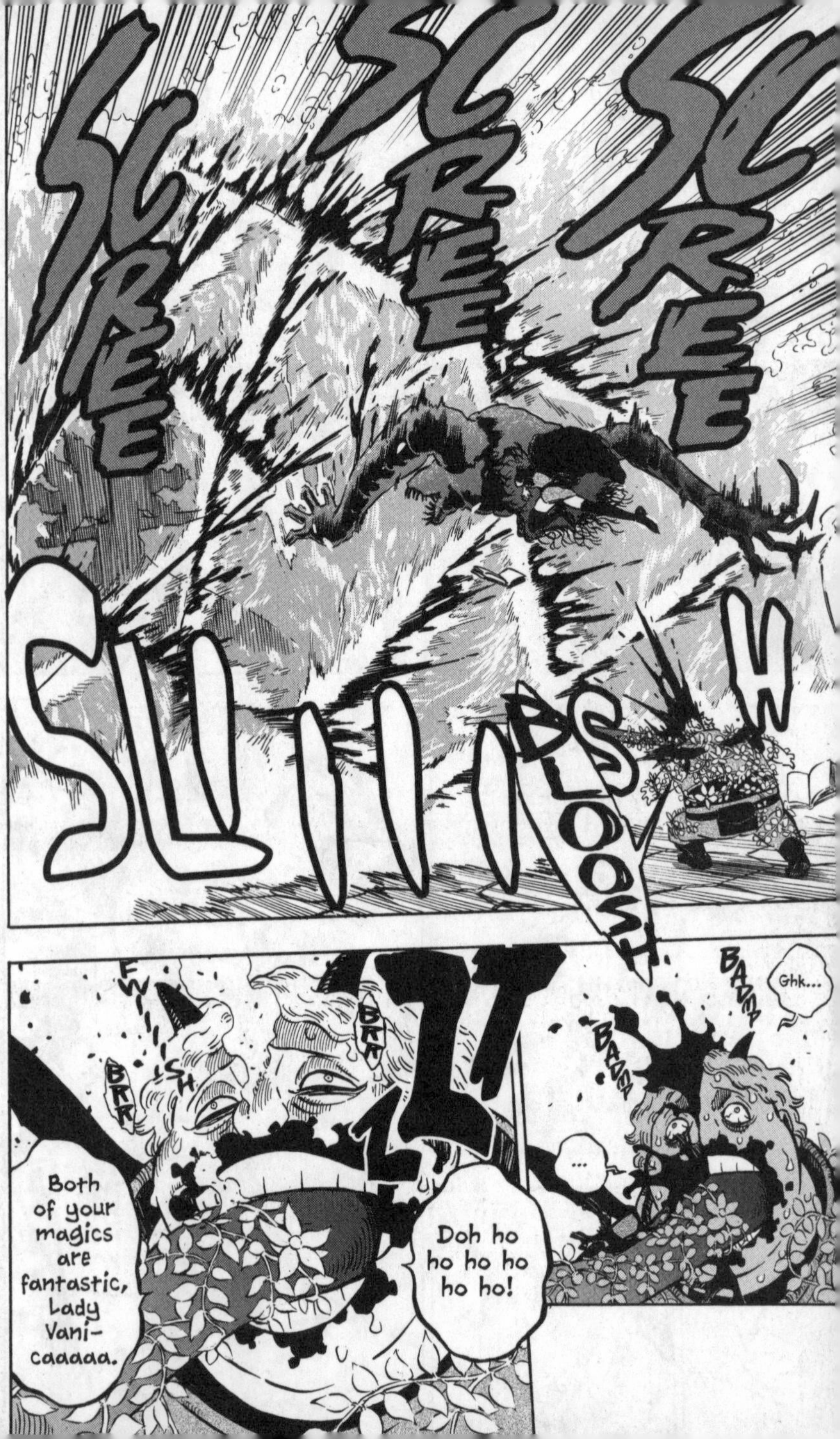
SCREE
SCREE
SCREE
SLIIIIISH
BLOOOSH
BADMP
BADMP
Ghk...
...
BRR
Doh ho ho ho ho ho ho!
FWIIISH
BRR
Both of your magics are fantastic, Lady Vani-caaaaa.

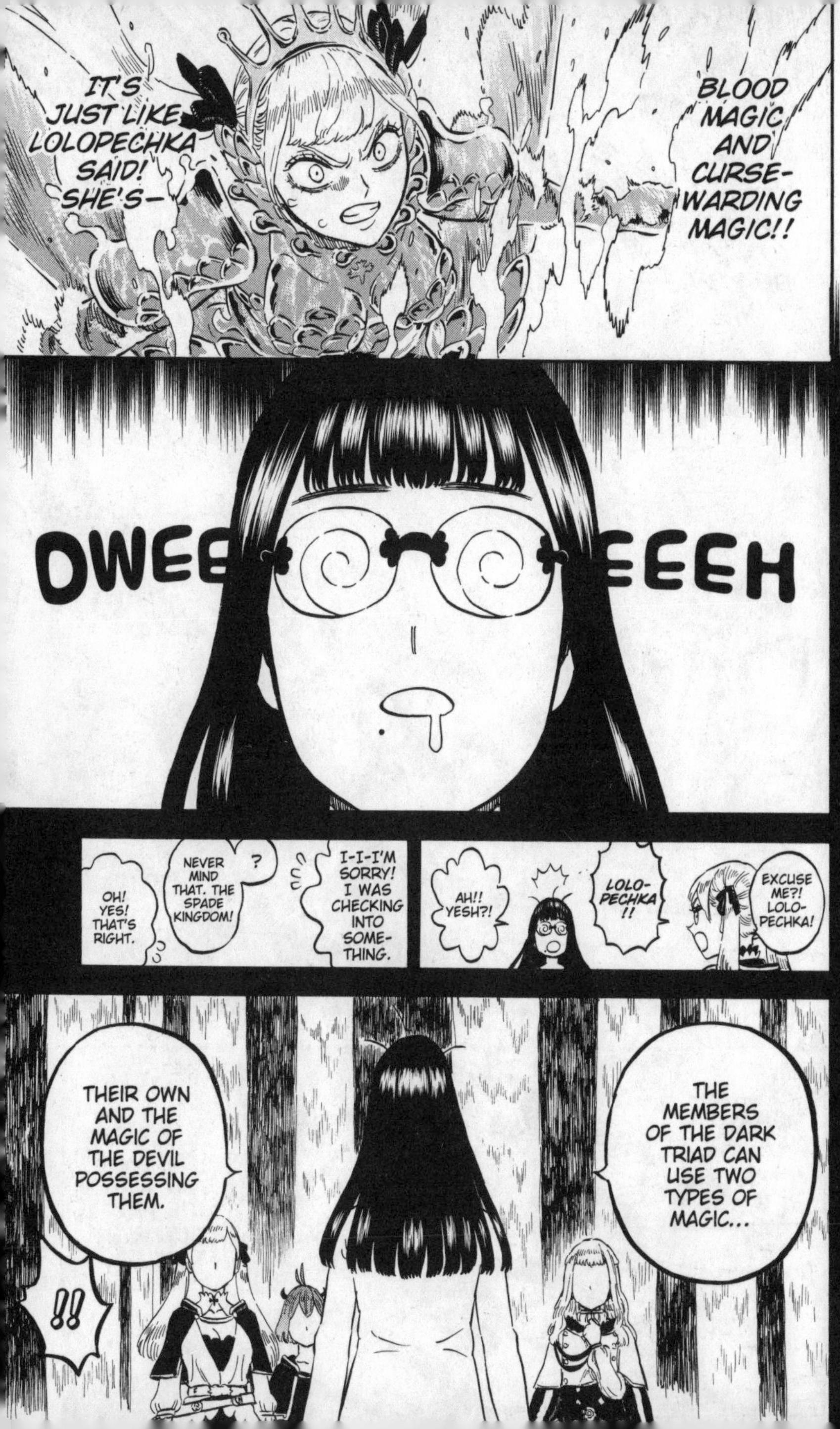
BLOOD MAGIC AND CURSE-WARDING MAGIC!!
IT'S JUST LIKE LOLOPECHKA SAID! SHE'S—
DWEEEEEEH
EXCUSE ME?! LOLO-PECHKA!
LOLO-PECHKA!!
AH!! YESH?!
I-I-I'M SORRY! I WAS CHECKING INTO SOME-THING.
?
NEVER MIND THAT. THE SPADE KINGDOM!
OH! YES! THAT'S RIGHT.
THE MEMBERS OF THE DARK TRIAD CAN USE TWO TYPES OF MAGIC...
THEIR OWN AND THE MAGIC OF THE DEVIL POSSESSING THEM.
!!

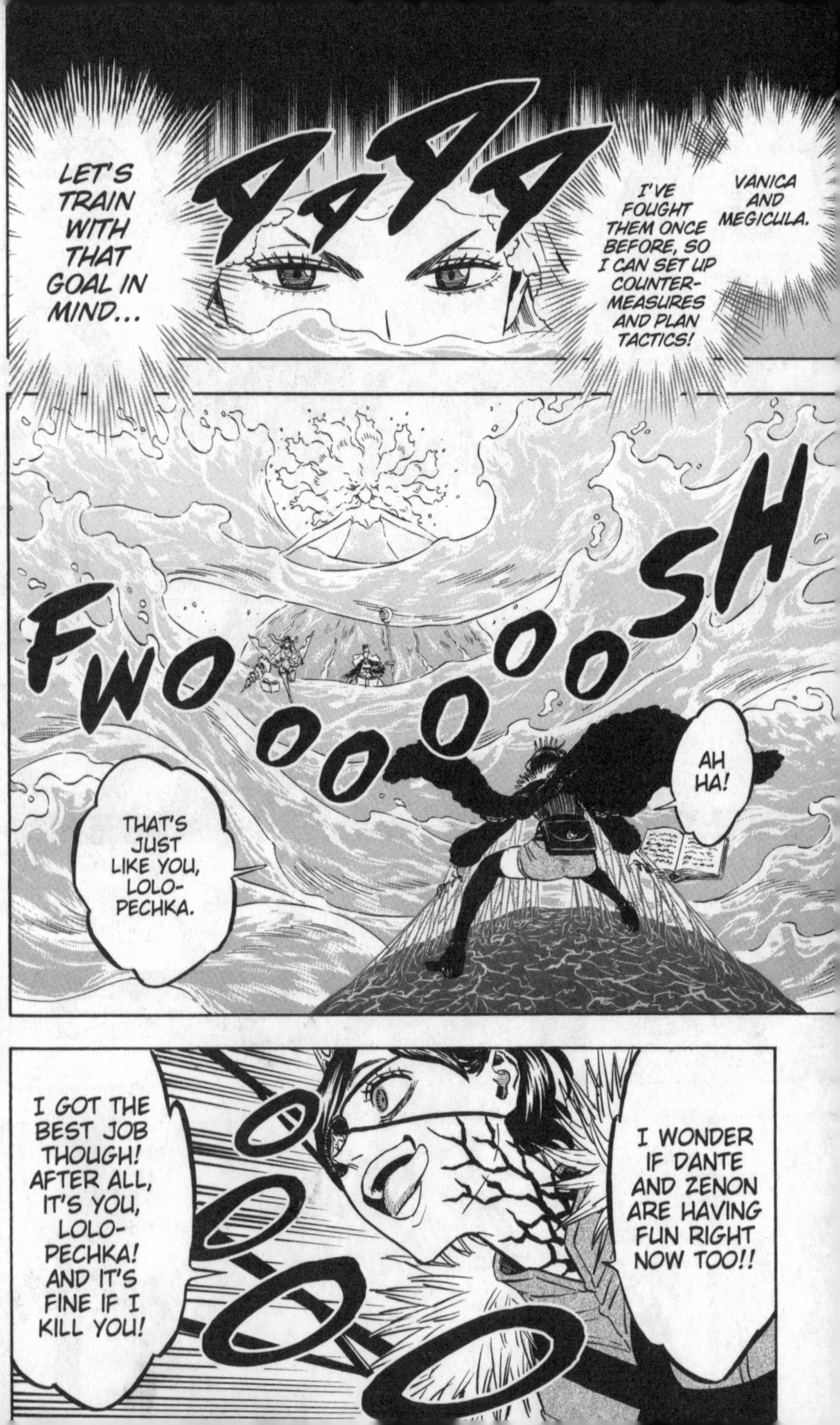
VANICA AND MEGICULA.
I'VE FOUGHT THEM ONCE BEFORE, SO I CAN SET UP COUNTER-MEASURES AND PLAN TACTICS!
LET'S TRAIN WITH THAT GOAL IN MIND...
FWOOOOOOOSH
AH HA!
THAT'S JUST LIKE YOU, LOLO-PECHKA.
I WONDER IF DANTE AND ZENON ARE HAVING FUN RIGHT NOW TOO!!
I GOT THE BEST JOB THOUGH! AFTER ALL, IT'S YOU, LOLO-PECHKA! AND IT'S FINE IF I KILL YOU!

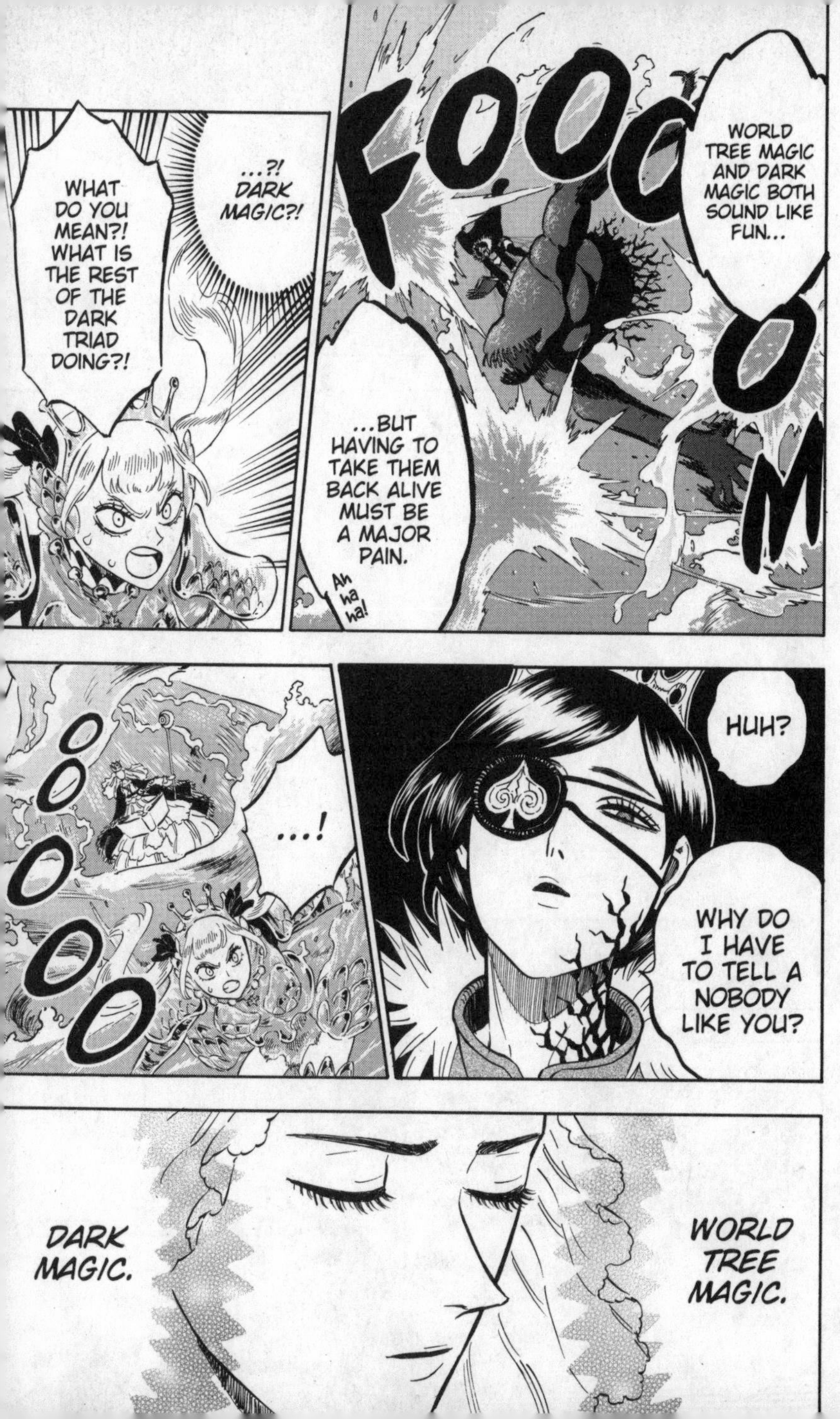
WORLD TREE MAGIC AND DARK MAGIC BOTH SOUND LIKE FUN...
FOOOOOM
...BUT HAVING TO TAKE THEM BACK ALIVE MUST BE A MAJOR PAIN.
Ah ha ha!
...?! DARK MAGIC?!
WHAT DO YOU MEAN?! WHAT IS THE REST OF THE DARK TRIAD DOING?!
HUH?
WHY DO I HAVE TO TELL A NOBODY LIKE YOU?
...!
OOOOO
WORLD TREE MAGIC.
DARK MAGIC.

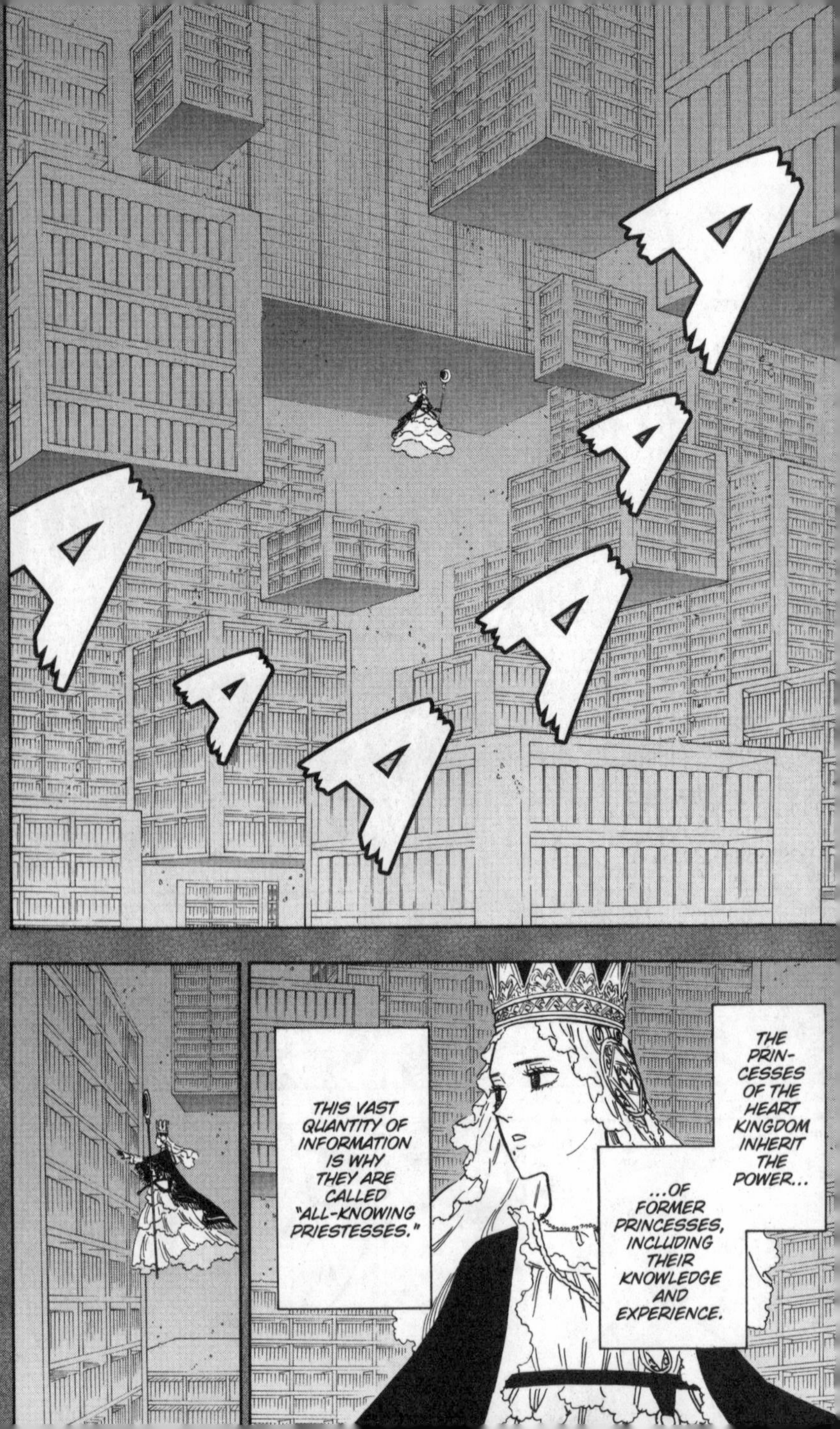
AAAAAA
THE PRINCESSES OF THE HEART KINGDOM INHERIT THE POWER...
...OF FORMER PRINCESSES, INCLUDING THEIR KNOWLEDGE AND EXPERIENCE.
THIS VAST QUANTITY OF INFORMATION IS WHY THEY ARE CALLED "ALL-KNOWING PRIESTESSES."

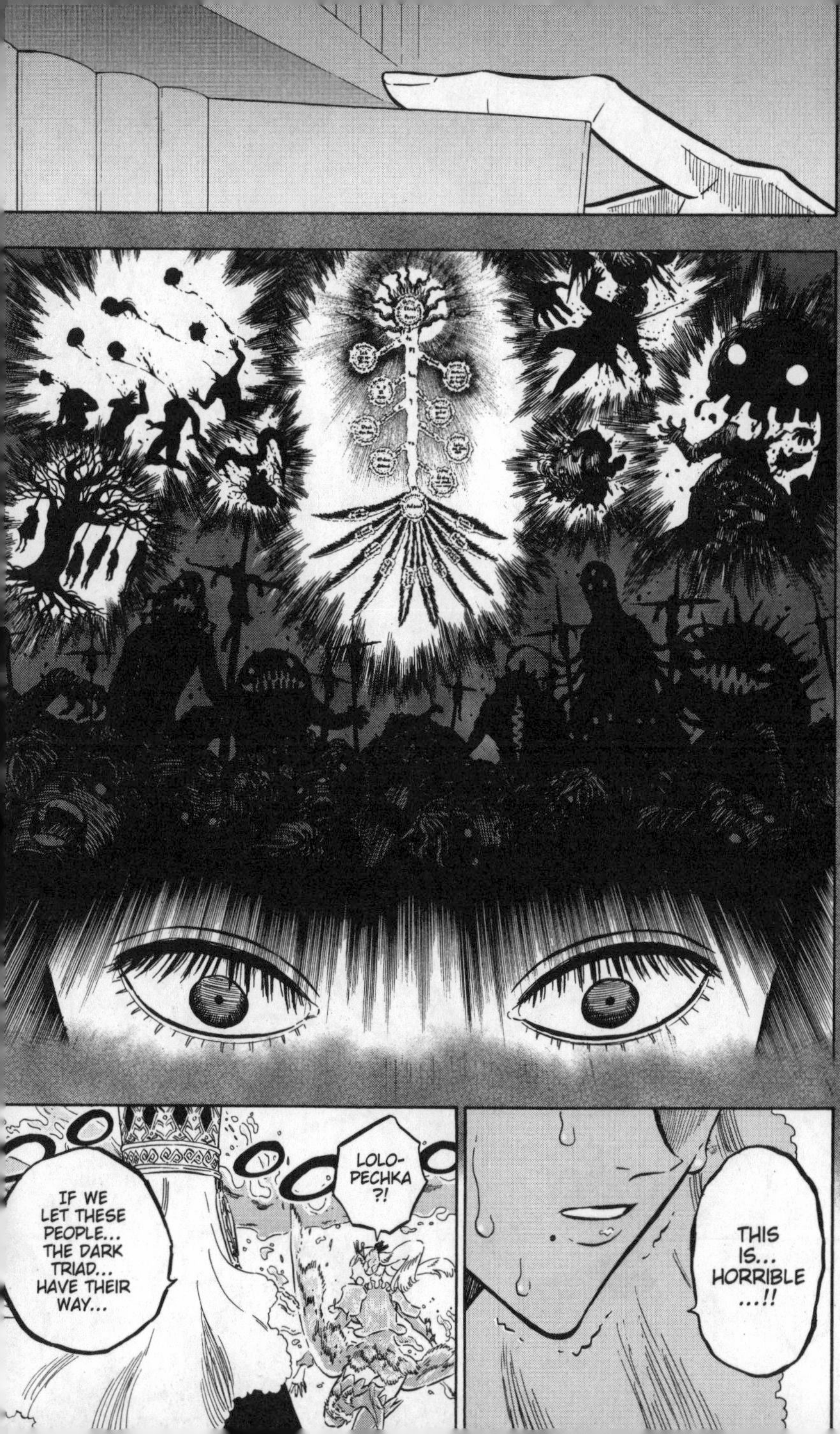
THIS IS... HORRIBLE ...!!
LOLO-PECHKA ?!
IF WE LET THESE PEOPLE... THE DARK TRIAD... HAVE THEIR WAY...

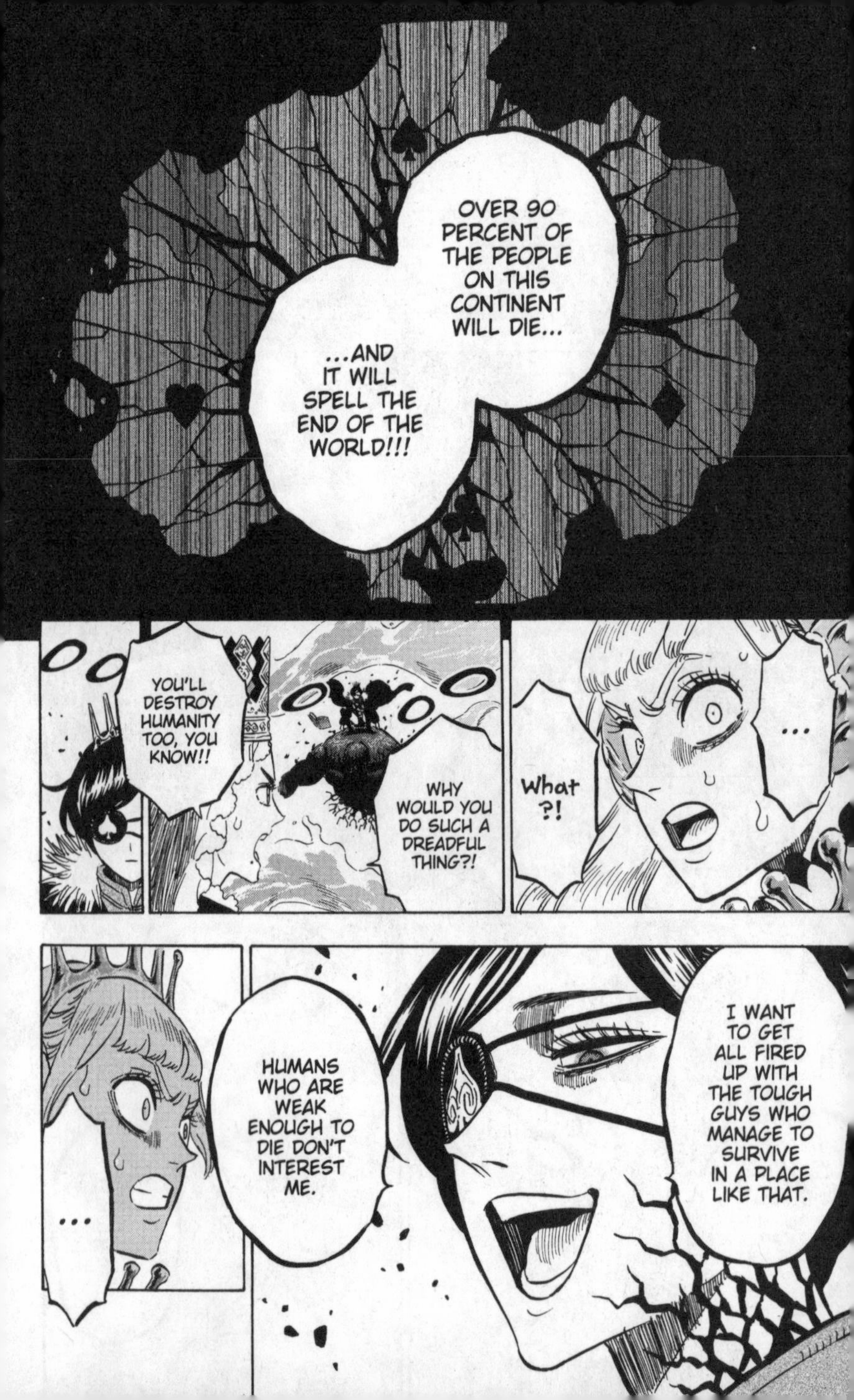
OVER 90 PERCENT OF THE PEOPLE ON THIS CONTINENT WILL DIE...
...AND IT WILL SPELL THE END OF THE WORLD!!!
...
What ?!
WHY WOULD YOU DO SUCH A DREADFUL THING?!
YOU'LL DESTROY HUMANITY TOO, YOU KNOW!!
I WANT TO GET ALL FIRED UP WITH THE TOUGH GUYS WHO MANAGE TO SURVIVE IN A PLACE LIKE THAT.
HUMANS WHO ARE WEAK ENOUGH TO DIE DON'T INTEREST ME.
...

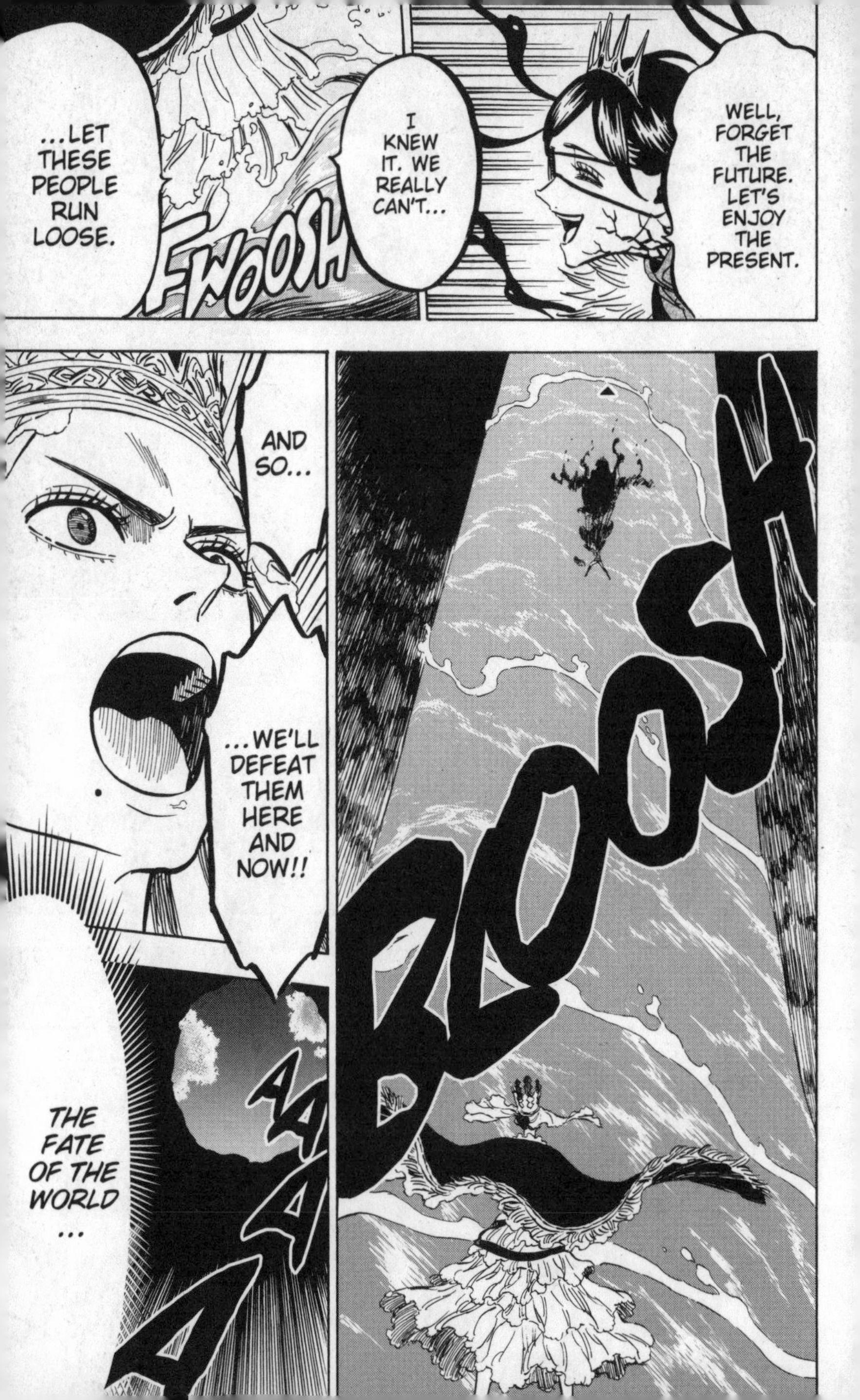
WELL, FORGET THE FUTURE. LET'S ENJOY THE PRESENT.
I KNEW IT. WE REALLY CAN'T...
FWOOSH
...LET THESE PEOPLE RUN LOOSE.
BROOOSH
AND SO...
...WE'LL DEFEAT THEM HERE AND NOW!!
AAAAA
THE FATE OF THE WORLD ...

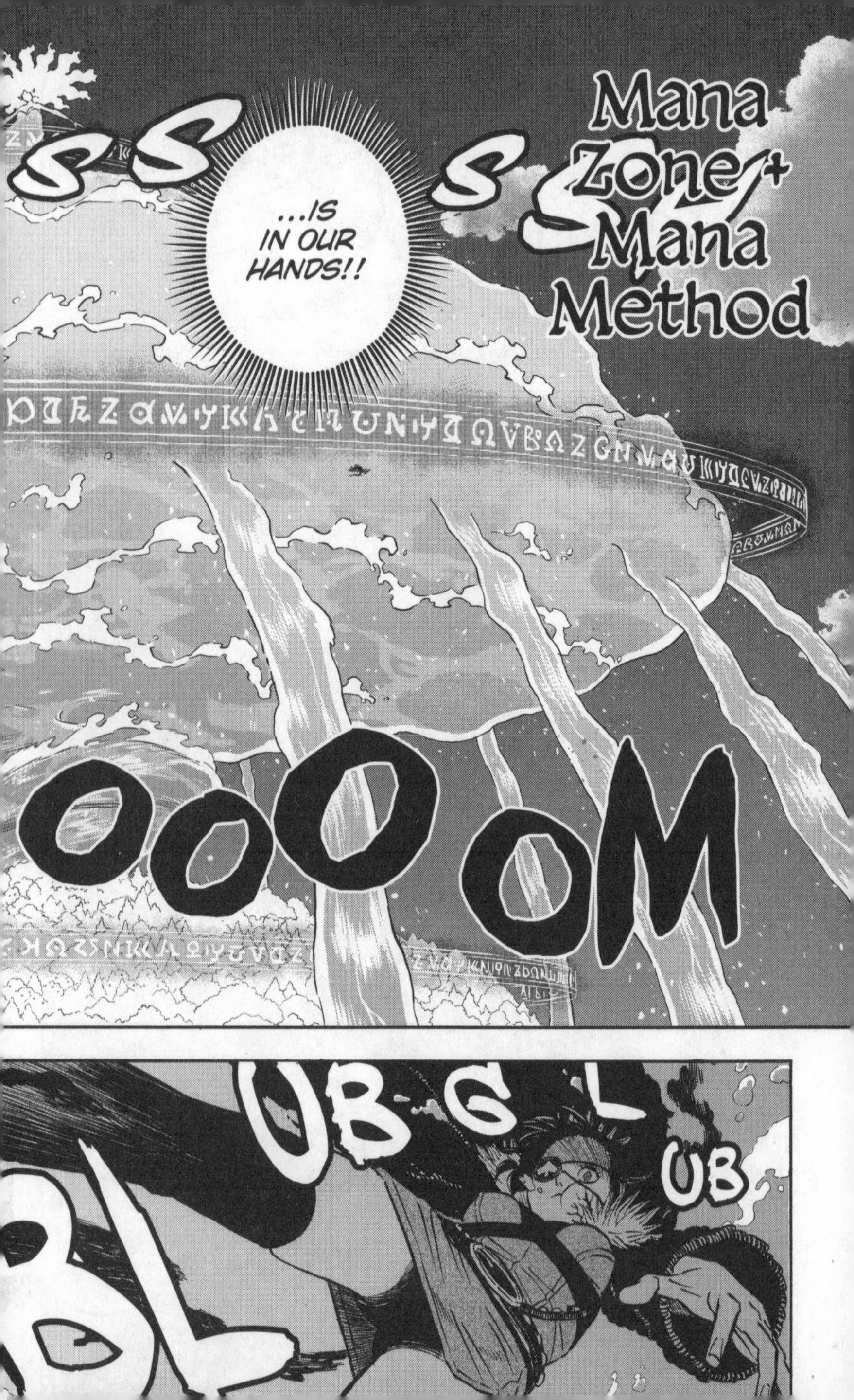
Mana Zone + Mana Method
...IS IN OUR HANDS!!
SS S S
OOO OM
UB-G L
UB
BL

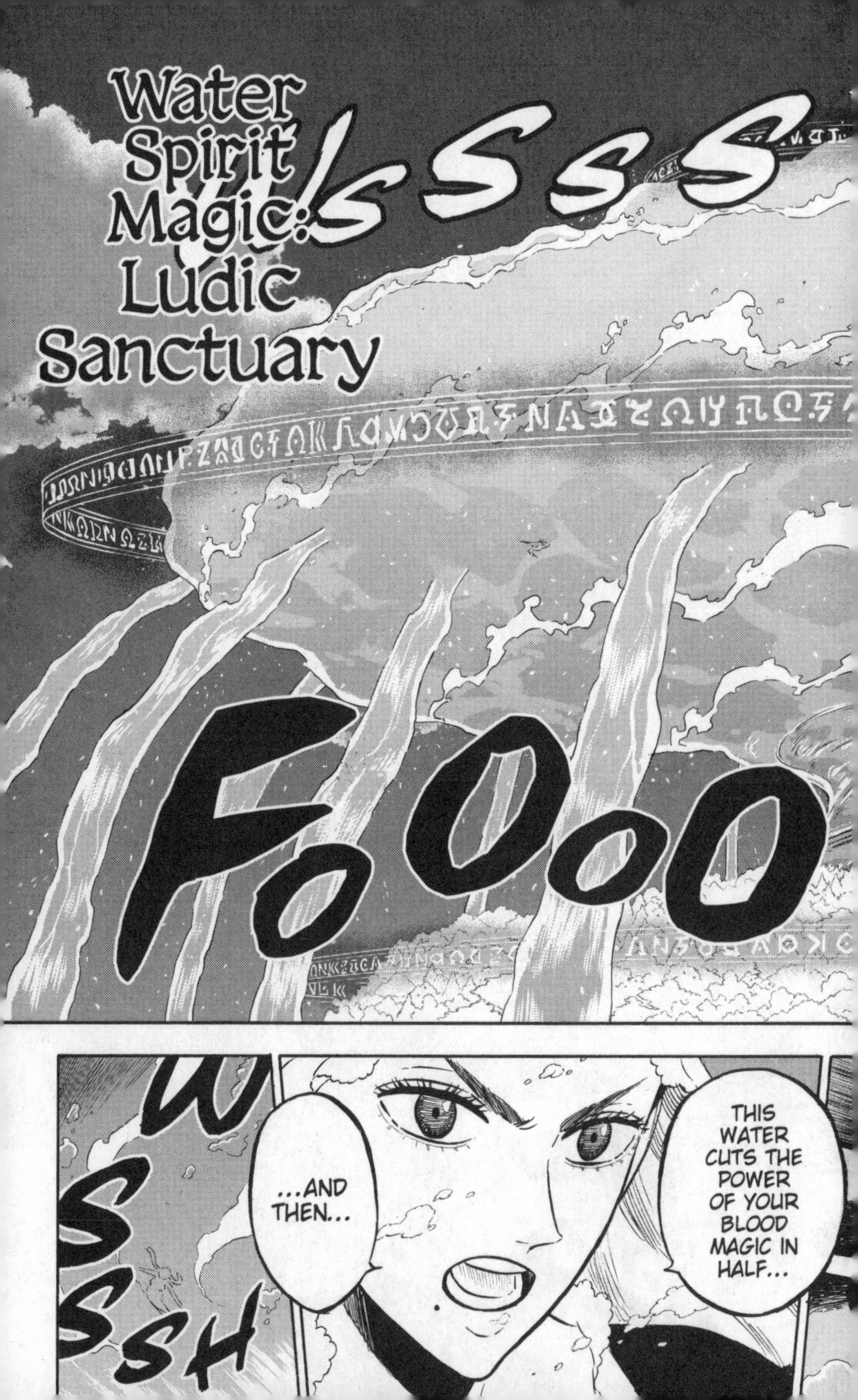
Water Spirit Magic: Ludic Sanctuary
FOOO
THIS WATER CUTS THE POWER OF YOUR BLOOD MAGIC IN HALF...
...AND THEN...
WSSSH

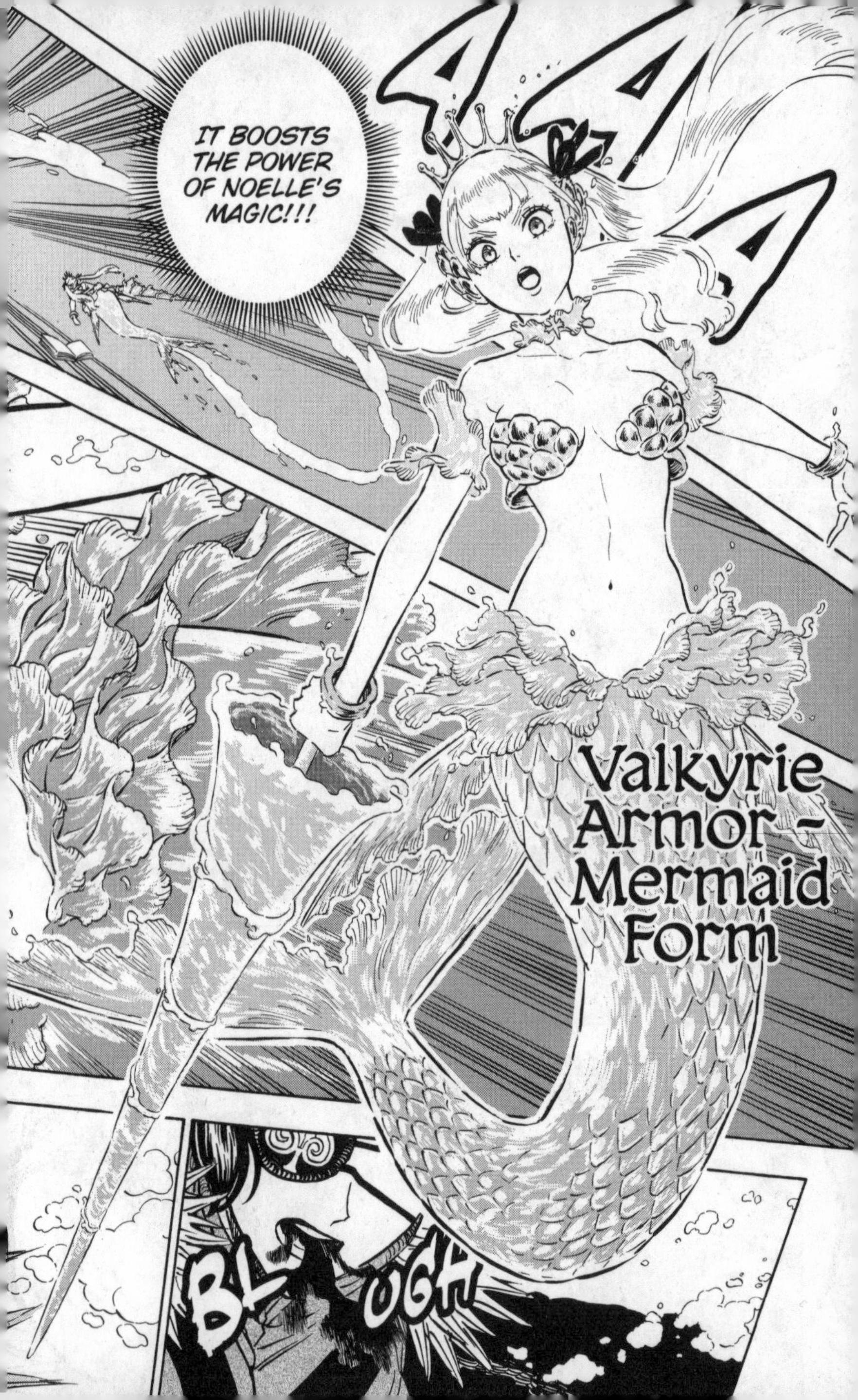
AAA
IT BOOSTS THE POWER OF NOELLE'S MAGIC!!!
Valkyrie Armor - Mermaid Form
BLOGH

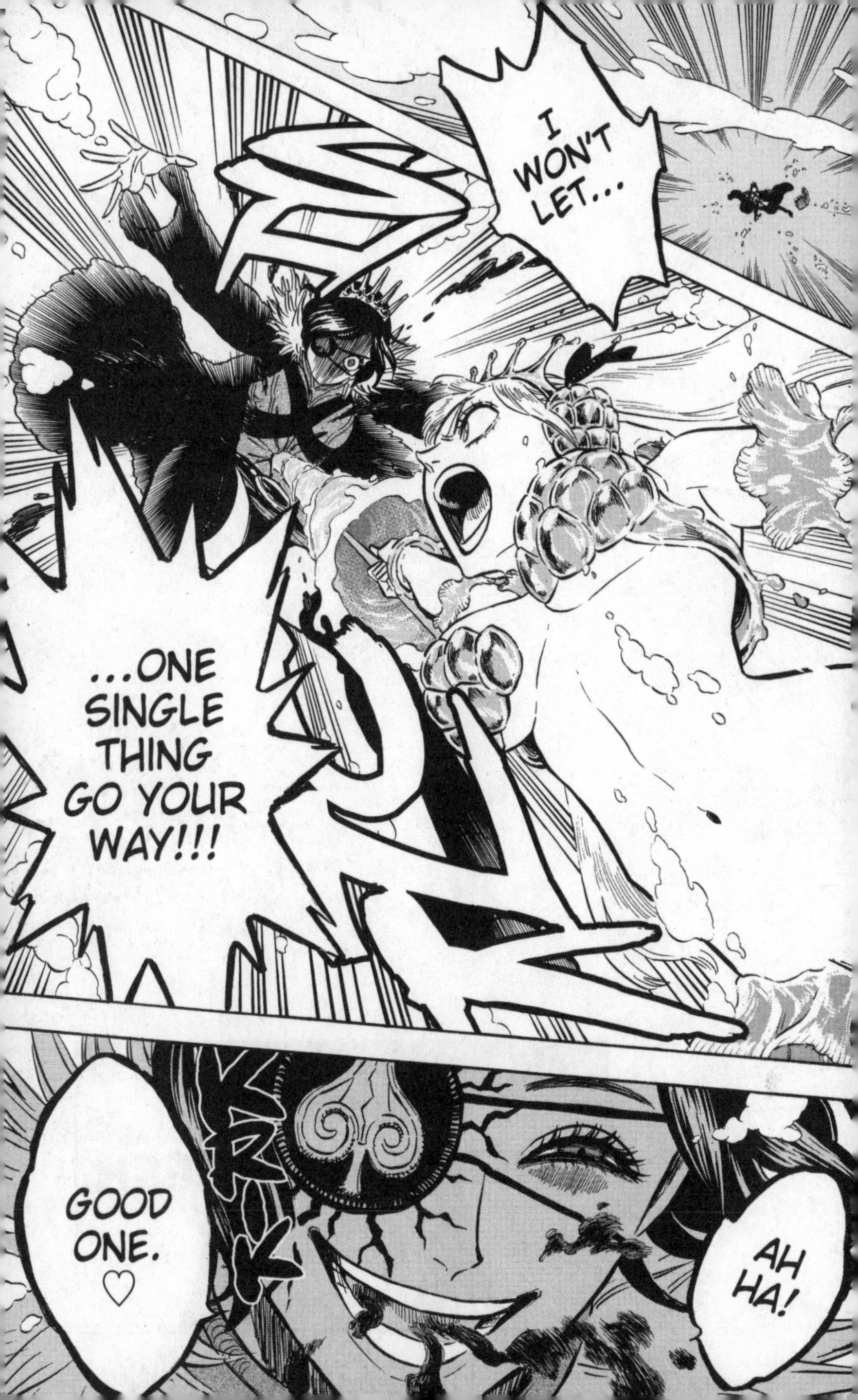
I WON'T LET...
...ONE SINGLE THING GO YOUR WAY!!!
AH HA!
GOOD ONE. ♡

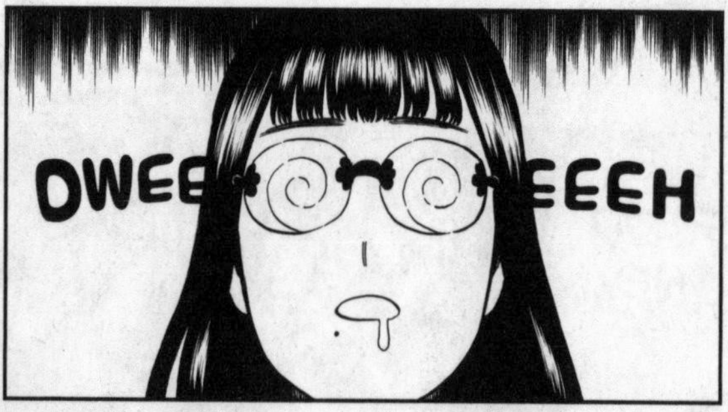
DWEE EEEH

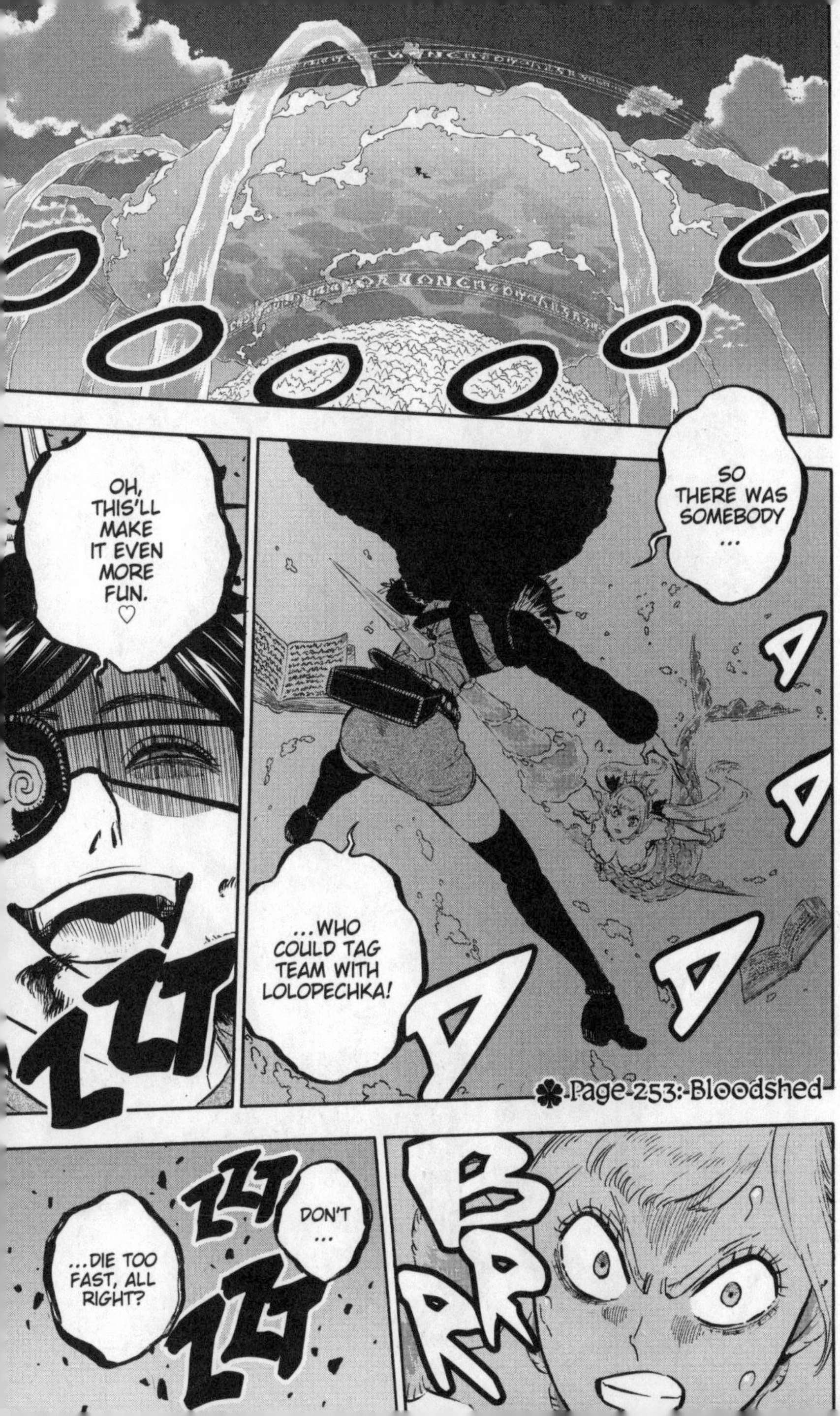
OOOOOO
SO THERE WAS SOMEBODY ...
...WHO COULD TAG TEAM WITH LOLOPECHKA!
AAAAA
OH, THIS'LL MAKE IT EVEN MORE FUN. ♡
ZZT
BRRO
DON'T ...
...DIE TOO FAST, ALL RIGHT?
ZZT
ZZT

Page 253: Bloodshed

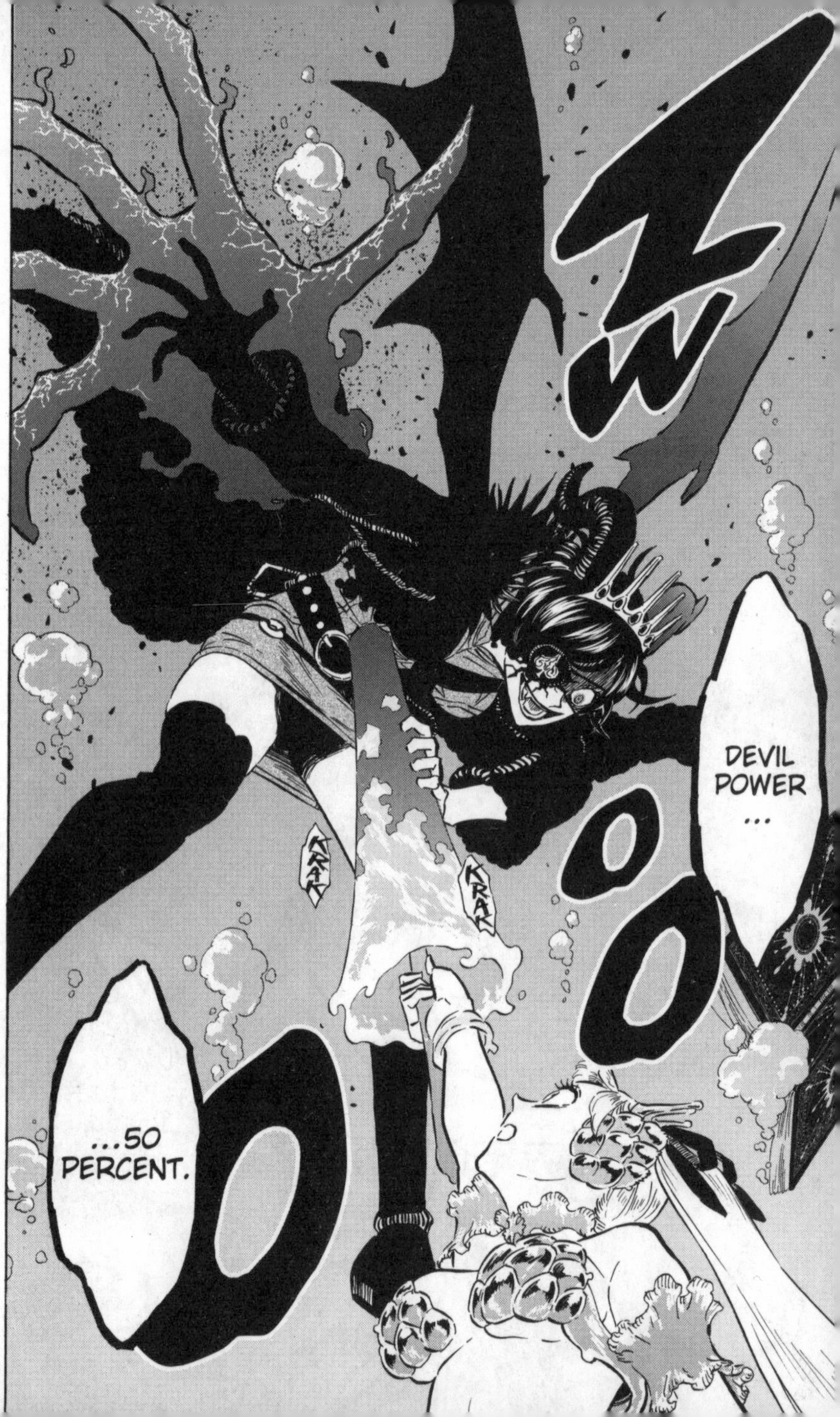
DEVIL POWER
...
...50 PERCENT.
KRAK
KRAK

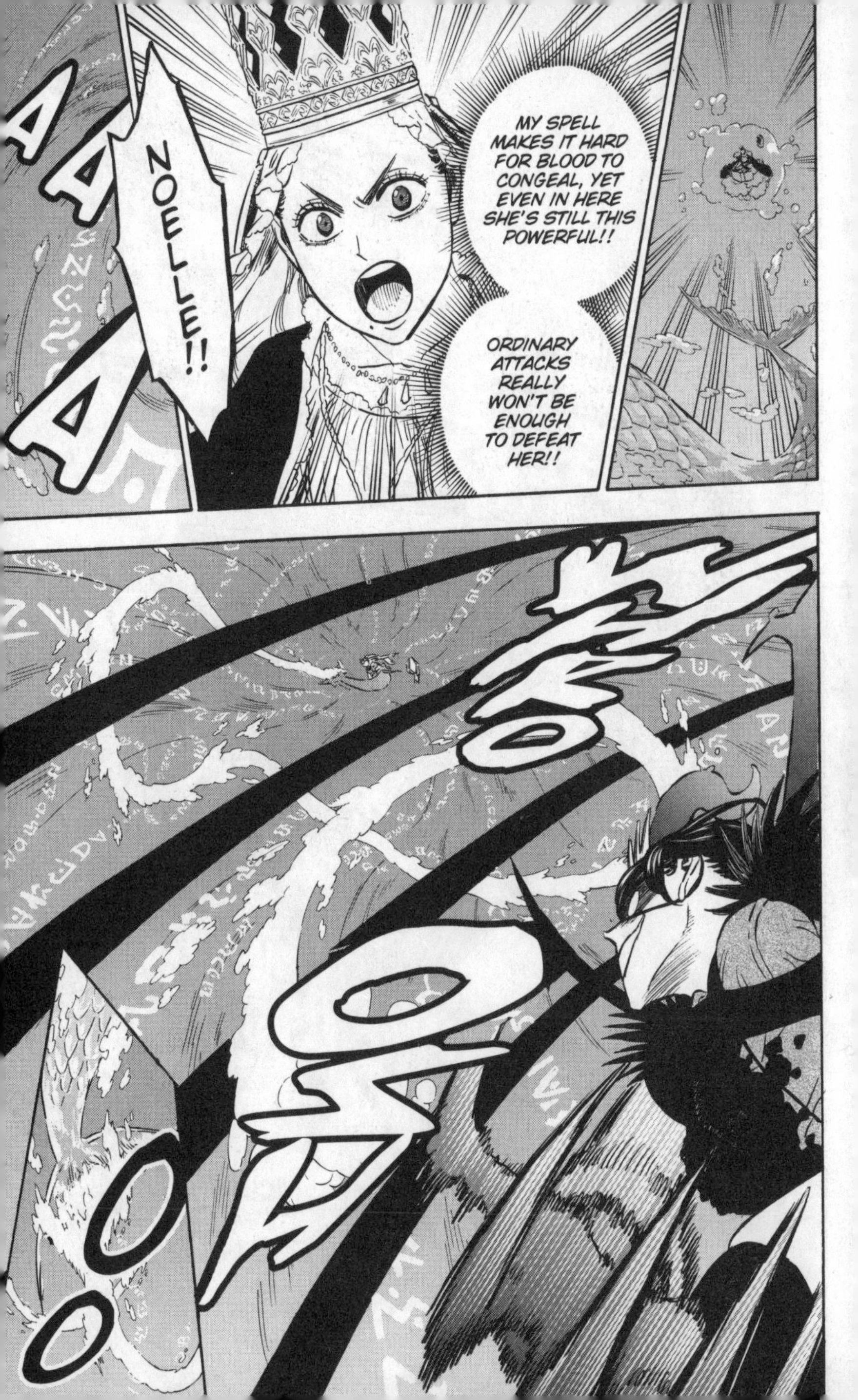
MY SPELL MAKES IT HARD FOR BLOOD TO CONGEAL, YET EVEN IN HERE SHE'S STILL THIS POWERFUL!!
ORDINARY ATTACKS REALLY WON'T BE ENOUGH TO DEFEAT HER!!
NOELLE!!
AAA

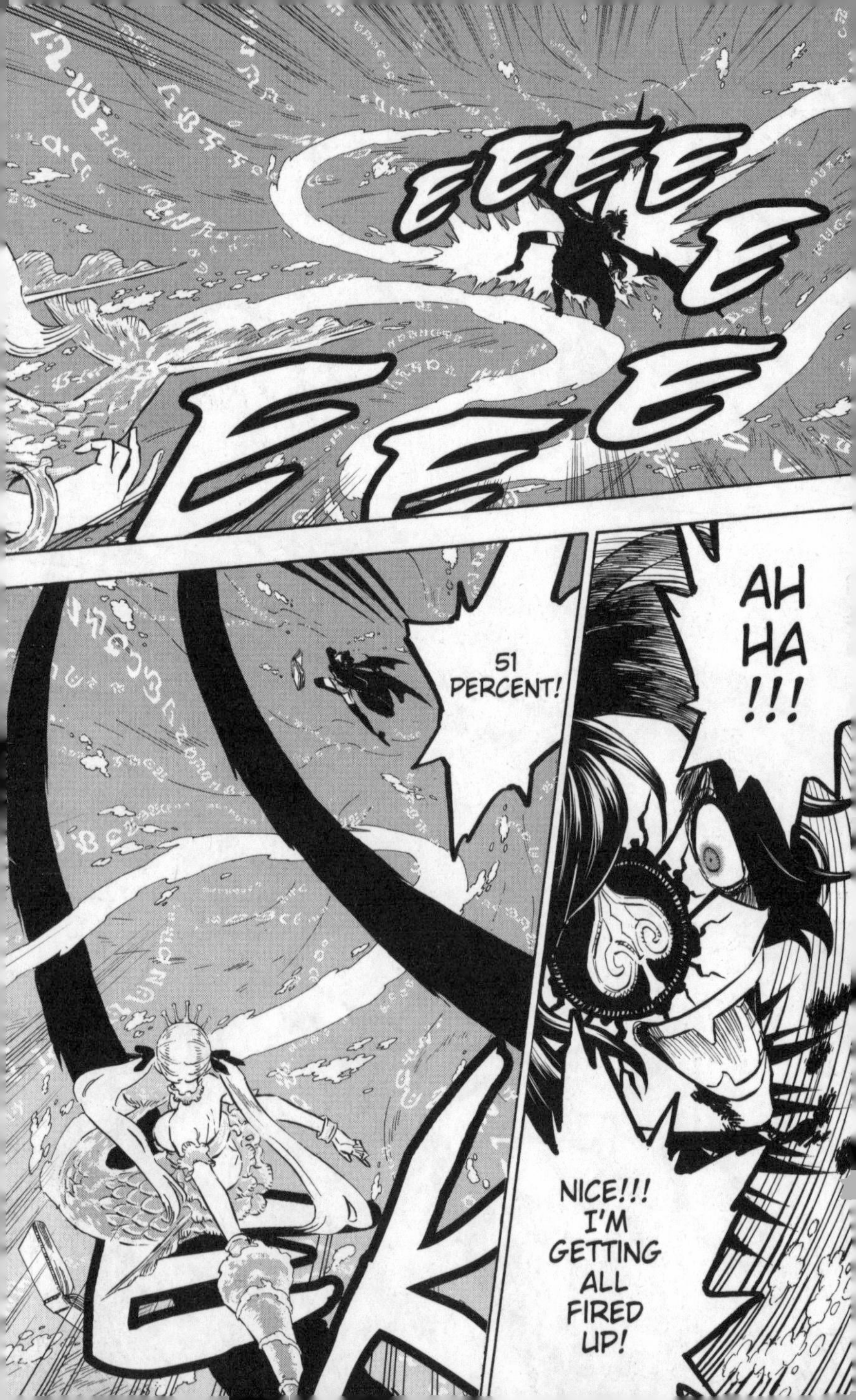
EEEEEE
EEEE
AH HA!!!
NICE!!! I'M GETTING ALL FIRED UP!
51 PERCENT!

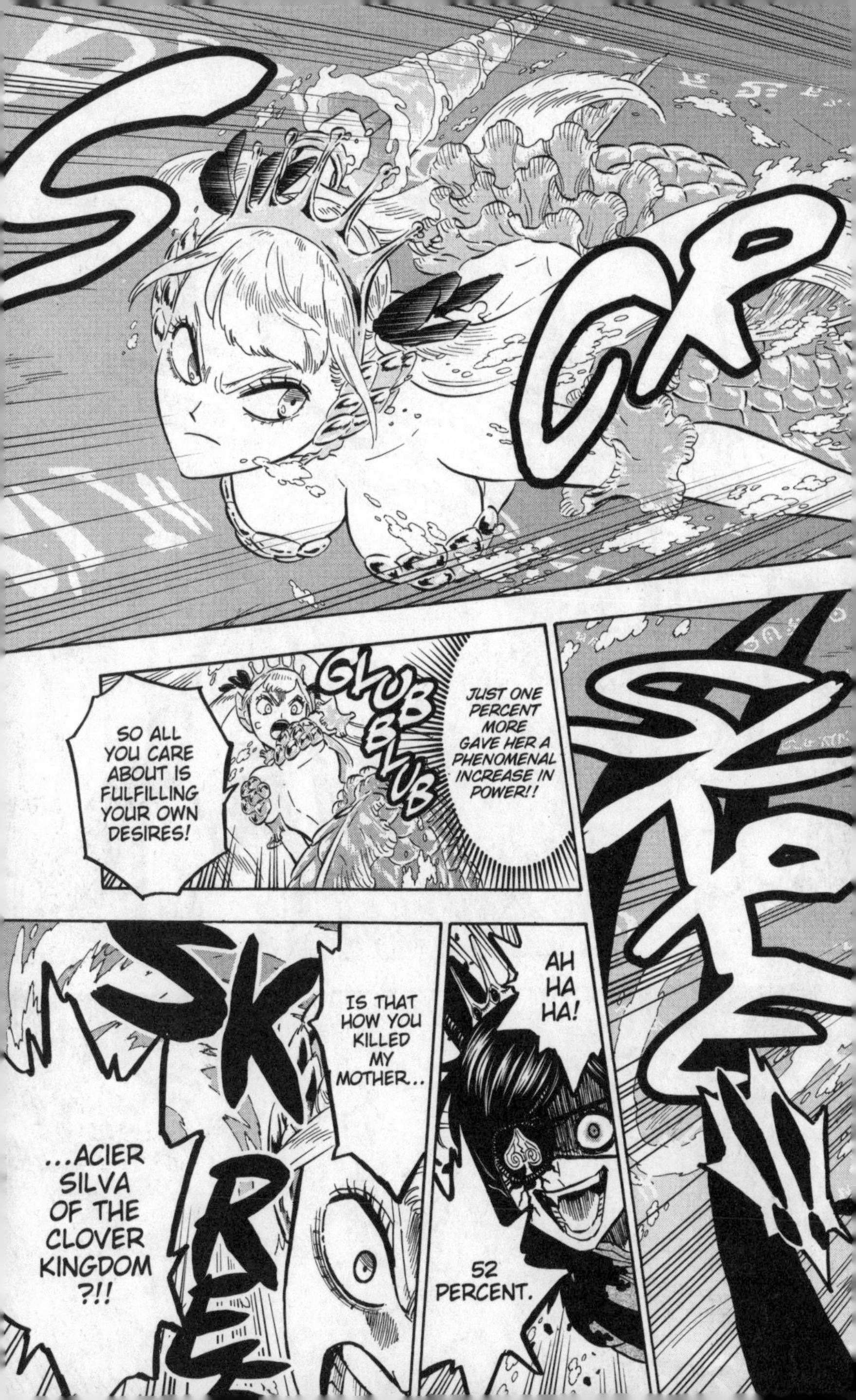
JUST ONE PERCENT MORE GAVE HER A PHENOMENAL INCREASE IN POWER!!
GLUB BLUB
SO ALL YOU CARE ABOUT IS FULFILLING YOUR OWN DESIRES!
AH HA HA!
52 PERCENT.
IS THAT HOW YOU KILLED MY MOTHER...
...ACIER SILVA OF THE CLOVER KINGDOM ?!!

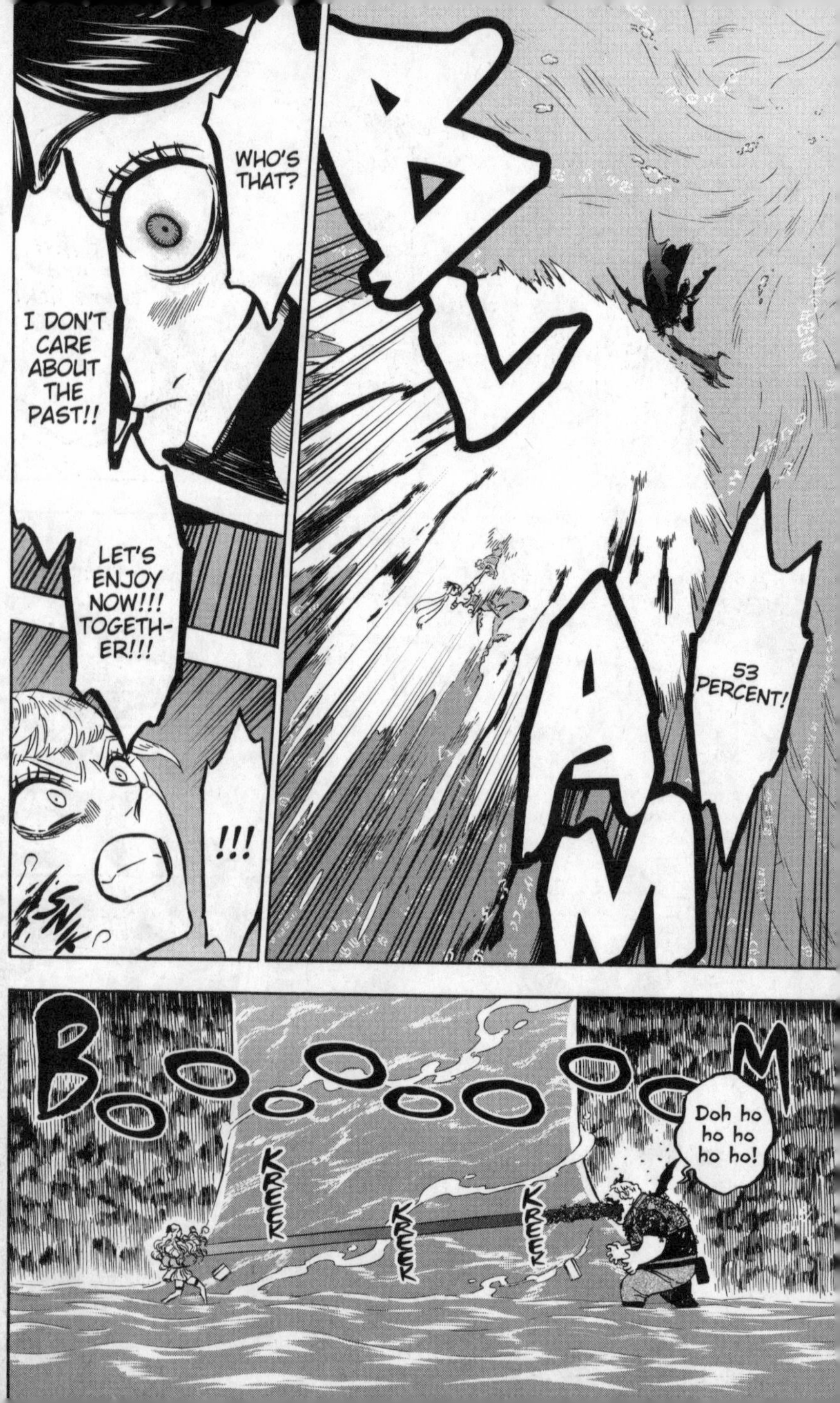
BLAM
53 PERCENT!
WHO'S THAT?
I DON'T CARE ABOUT THE PAST!!
LET'S ENJOY NOW!!! TOGETHER!!!
!!!
SNK
BOOOOOOOOM
Doh ho ho ho ho ho!
KREEK
KREEK
KREEK

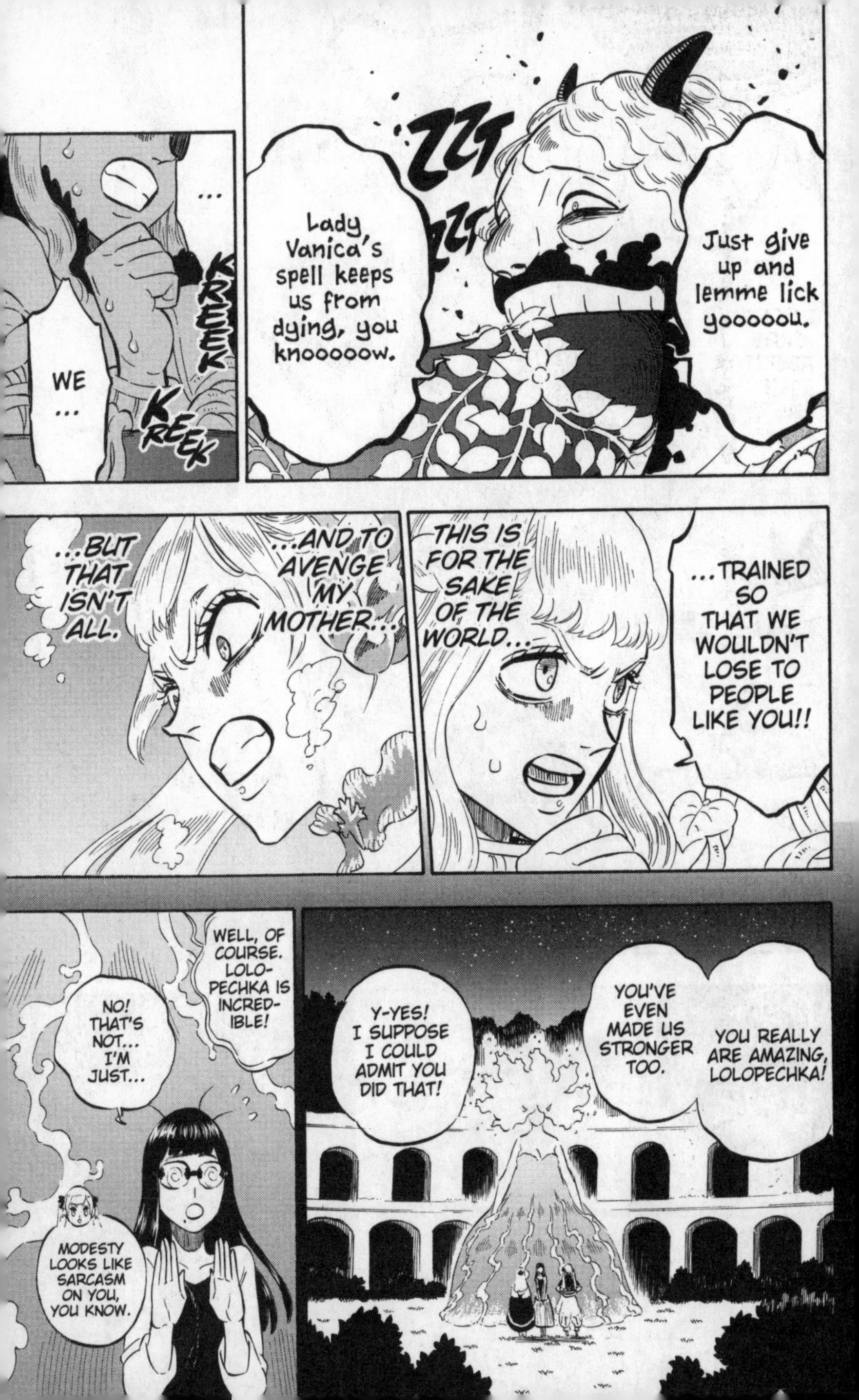
ZZZT
ZZZT
Lady Vanica's spell keeps us from dying, you knoooooow.
Just give up and lemme lick yoooou.
...
KREEK
KREEK
WE ...
...TRAINED SO THAT WE WOULDN'T LOSE TO PEOPLE LIKE YOU!!
THIS IS FOR THE SAKE OF THE WORLD...
...AND TO AVENGE MY MOTHER...
...BUT THAT ISN'T ALL.
YOU REALLY ARE AMAZING, LOLOPECHKA!
YOU'VE EVEN MADE US STRONGER TOO.
Y-YES! I SUPPOSE I COULD ADMIT YOU DID THAT!
WELL, OF COURSE. LOLOPECHKA IS INCREDIBLE!
NO! THAT'S NOT... I'M JUST...
MODESTY LOOKS LIKE SARCASM ON YOU, YOU KNOW.

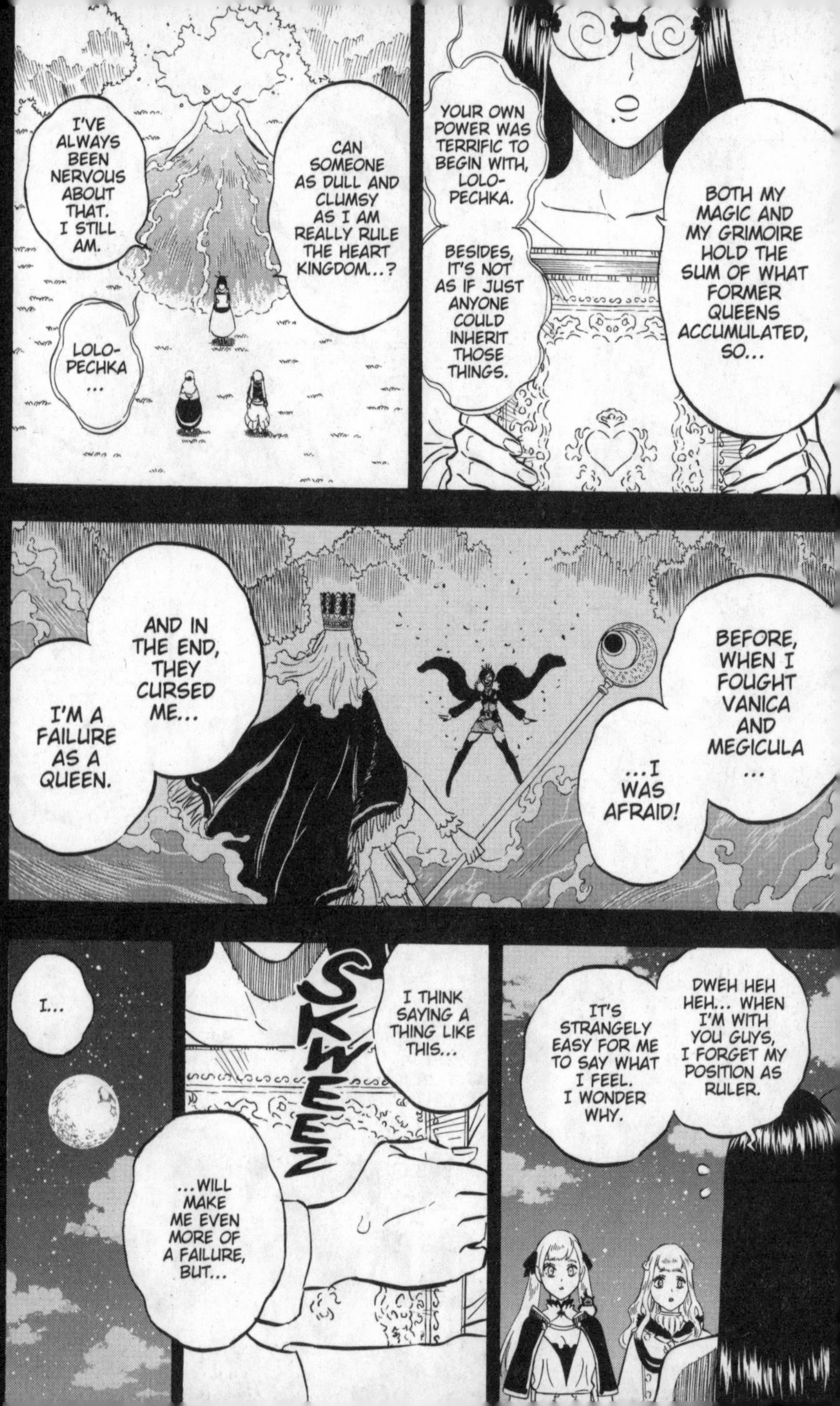
BOTH MY MAGIC AND MY GRIMOIRE HOLD THE SUM OF WHAT FORMER QUEENS ACCUMULATED, SO...
YOUR OWN POWER WAS TERRIFIC TO BEGIN WITH, LOLO-PECHKA.
BESIDES, IT'S NOT AS IF JUST ANYONE COULD INHERIT THOSE THINGS.
CAN SOMEONE AS DULL AND CLUMSY AS I AM REALLY RULE THE HEART KINGDOM...?
I'VE ALWAYS BEEN NERVOUS ABOUT THAT. I STILL AM.
LOLO-PECHKA...
BEFORE, WHEN I FOUGHT VANICA AND MEGICULA...
...I WAS AFRAID!
AND IN THE END, THEY CURSED ME...
I'M A FAILURE AS A QUEEN.
DWEH HEH HEH... WHEN I'M WITH YOU GUYS, I FORGET MY POSITION AS RULER.
IT'S STRANGELY EASY FOR ME TO SAY WHAT I FEEL. I WONDER WHY.
I THINK SAYING A THING LIKE THIS...
SKWEEZ
...WILL MAKE ME EVEN MORE OF A FAILURE, BUT...
I...

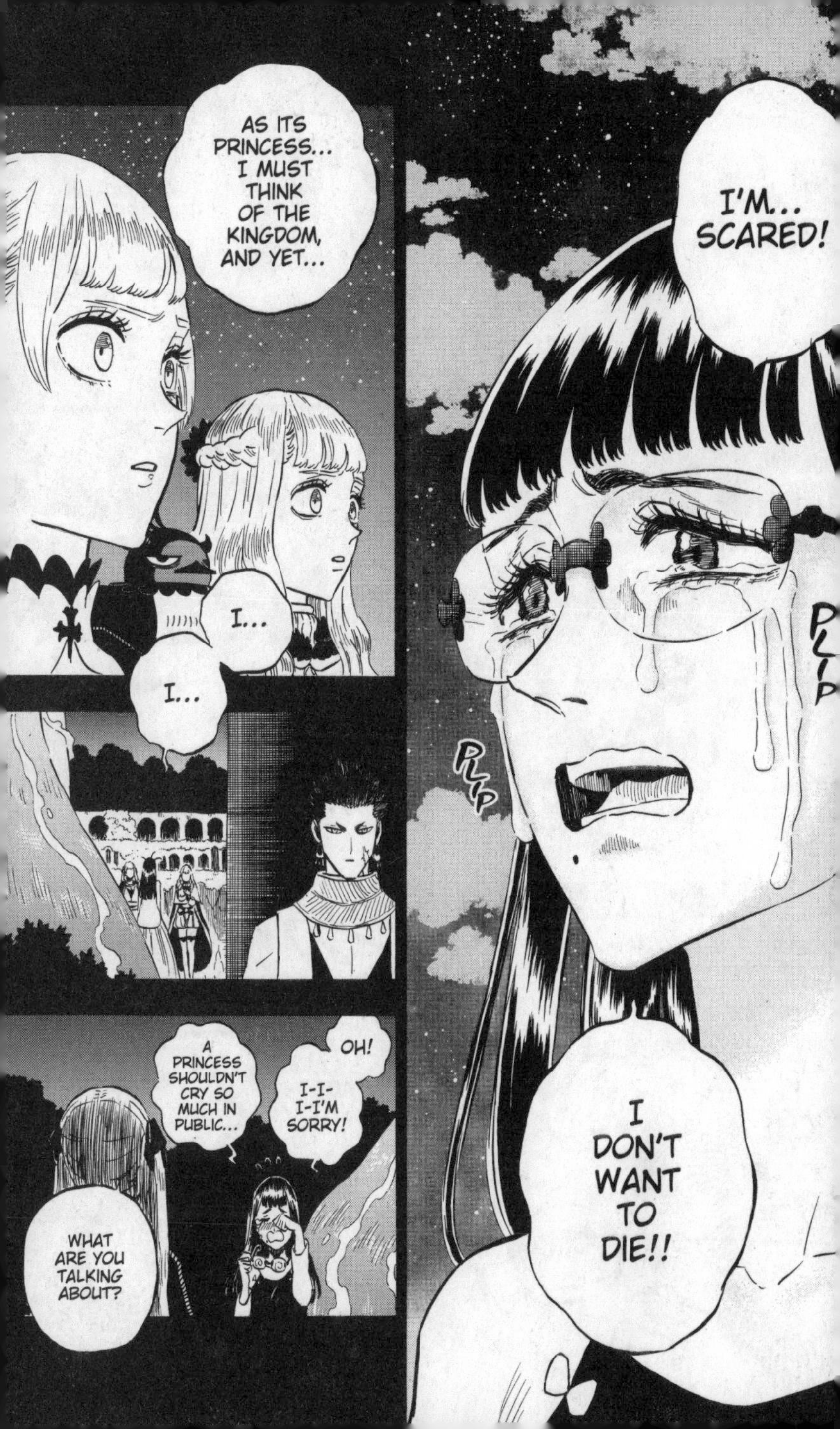
I'M... SCARED!
PLIP
PLIP
I DON'T WANT TO DIE!!
AS ITS PRINCESS... I MUST THINK OF THE KINGDOM, AND YET...
I...
I...
OH!
I-I-I-I'M SORRY!
A PRINCESS SHOULDN'T CRY SO MUCH IN PUBLIC...
WHAT ARE YOU TALKING ABOUT?

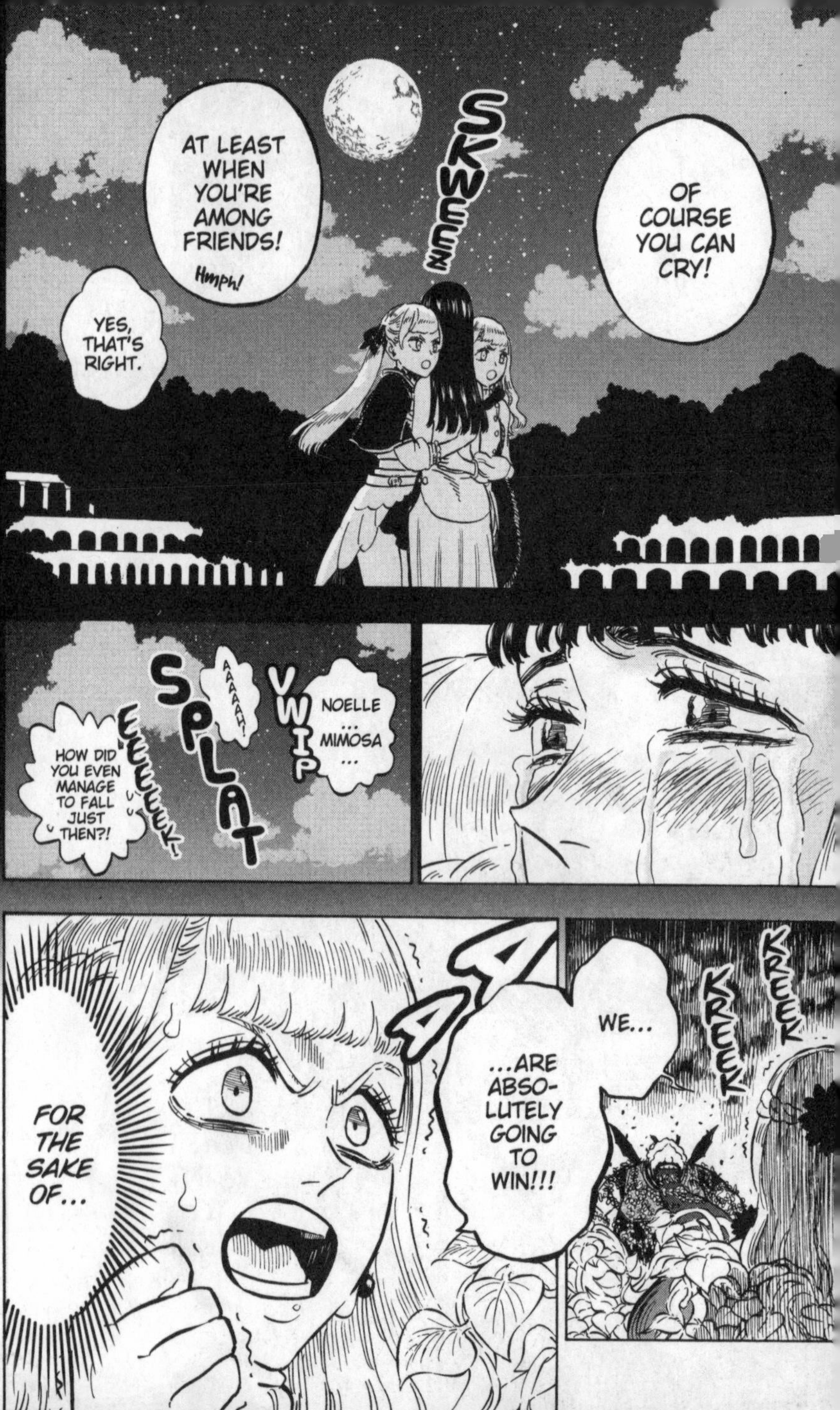
OF COURSE YOU CAN CRY!
SKWEEZ
AT LEAST WHEN YOU'RE AMONG FRIENDS!
Hmph!
YES, THAT'S RIGHT.
NOELLE ... MIMOSA ...
VWIP
AAAAAH!
SPLAT
EEEEEEK!
HOW DID YOU EVEN MANAGE TO FALL JUST THEN?!
KREEK
KREEK
WE...
...ARE ABSOLUTELY GOING TO WIN!!!
AA
FOR THE SAKE OF...

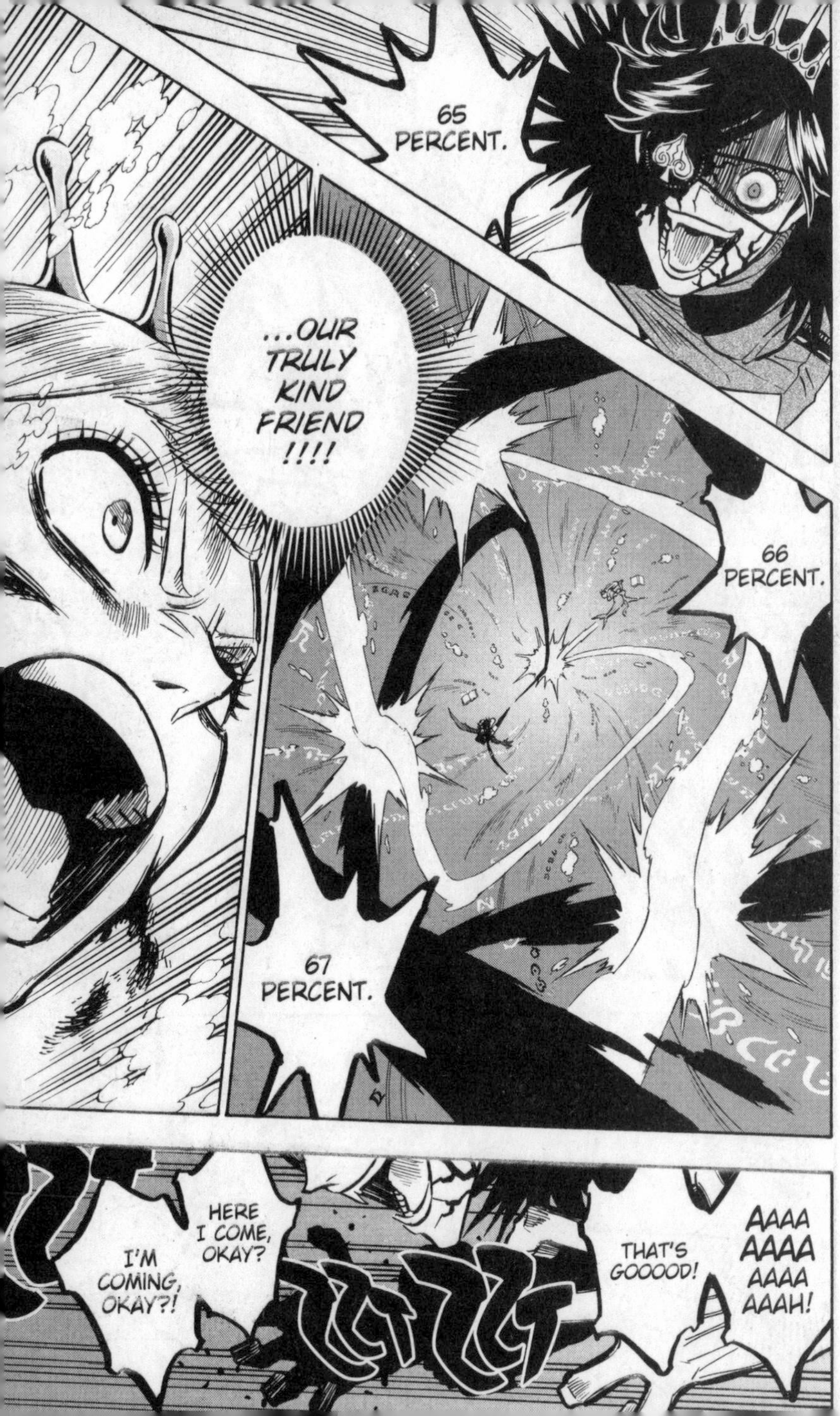
65 PERCENT.
66 PERCENT.
67 PERCENT.
...OUR TRULY KIND FRIEND!!!!
AAAA AAAA AAAA AAAH!
THAT'S GOOOOD!
HERE I COME, OKAY?
I'M COMING, OKAY?!

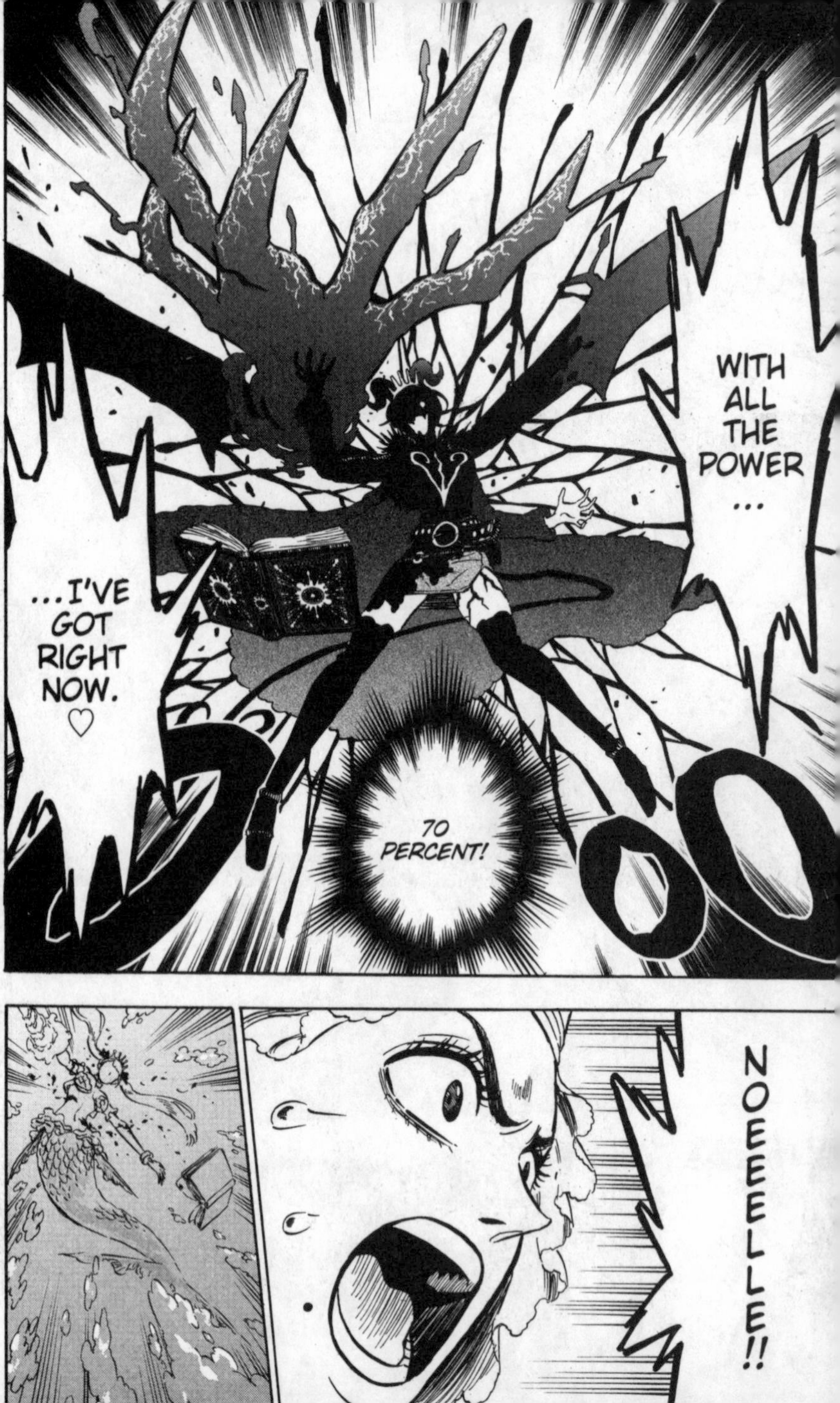
WITH ALL THE POWER...
...I'VE GOT RIGHT NOW. ♡
70 PERCENT!
NOEEELLE!!

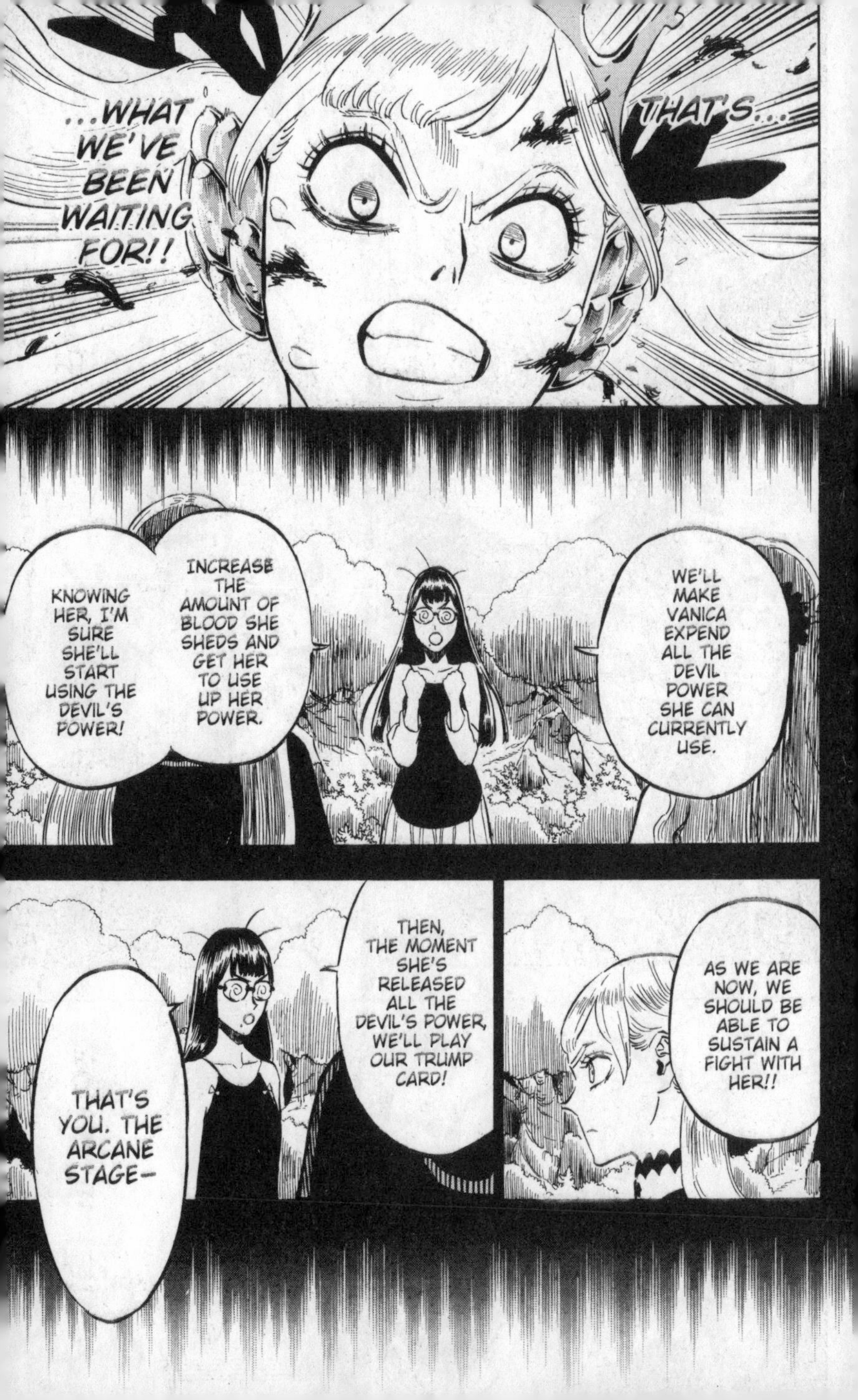
THAT'S...
...WHAT WE'VE BEEN WAITING FOR!!
WE'LL MAKE VANICA EXPEND ALL THE DEVIL POWER SHE CAN CURRENTLY USE.
INCREASE THE AMOUNT OF BLOOD SHE SHEDS AND GET HER TO USE UP HER POWER.
KNOWING HER, I'M SURE SHE'LL START USING THE DEVIL'S POWER!
AS WE ARE NOW, WE SHOULD BE ABLE TO SUSTAIN A FIGHT WITH HER!!
THEN, THE MOMENT SHE'S RELEASED ALL THE DEVIL'S POWER, WE'LL PLAY OUR TRUMP CARD!
THAT'S YOU. THE ARCANE STAGE—

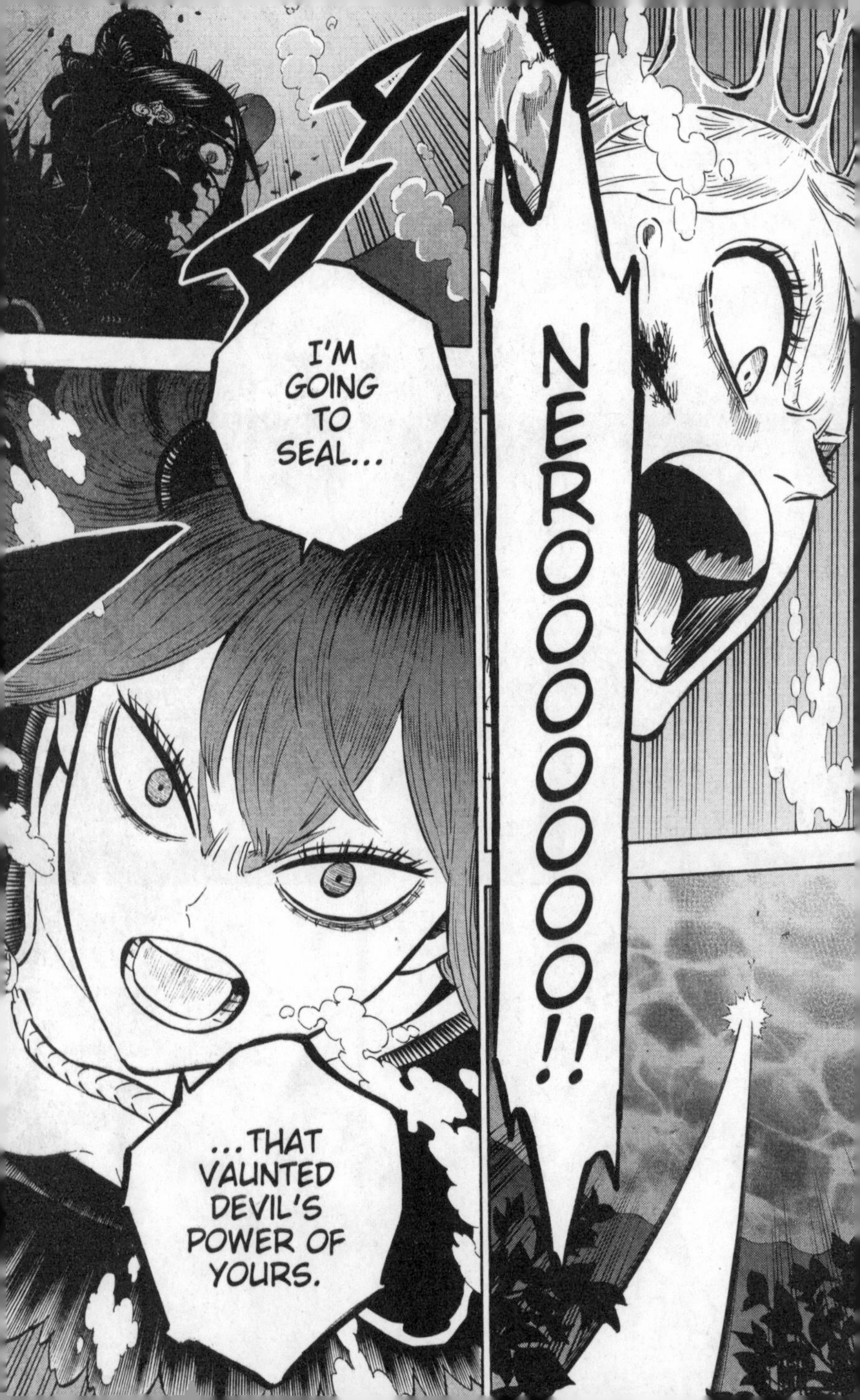
NEROOOOOOO!!
I'M GOING TO SEAL...
...THAT VAUNTED DEVIL'S POWER OF YOURS.

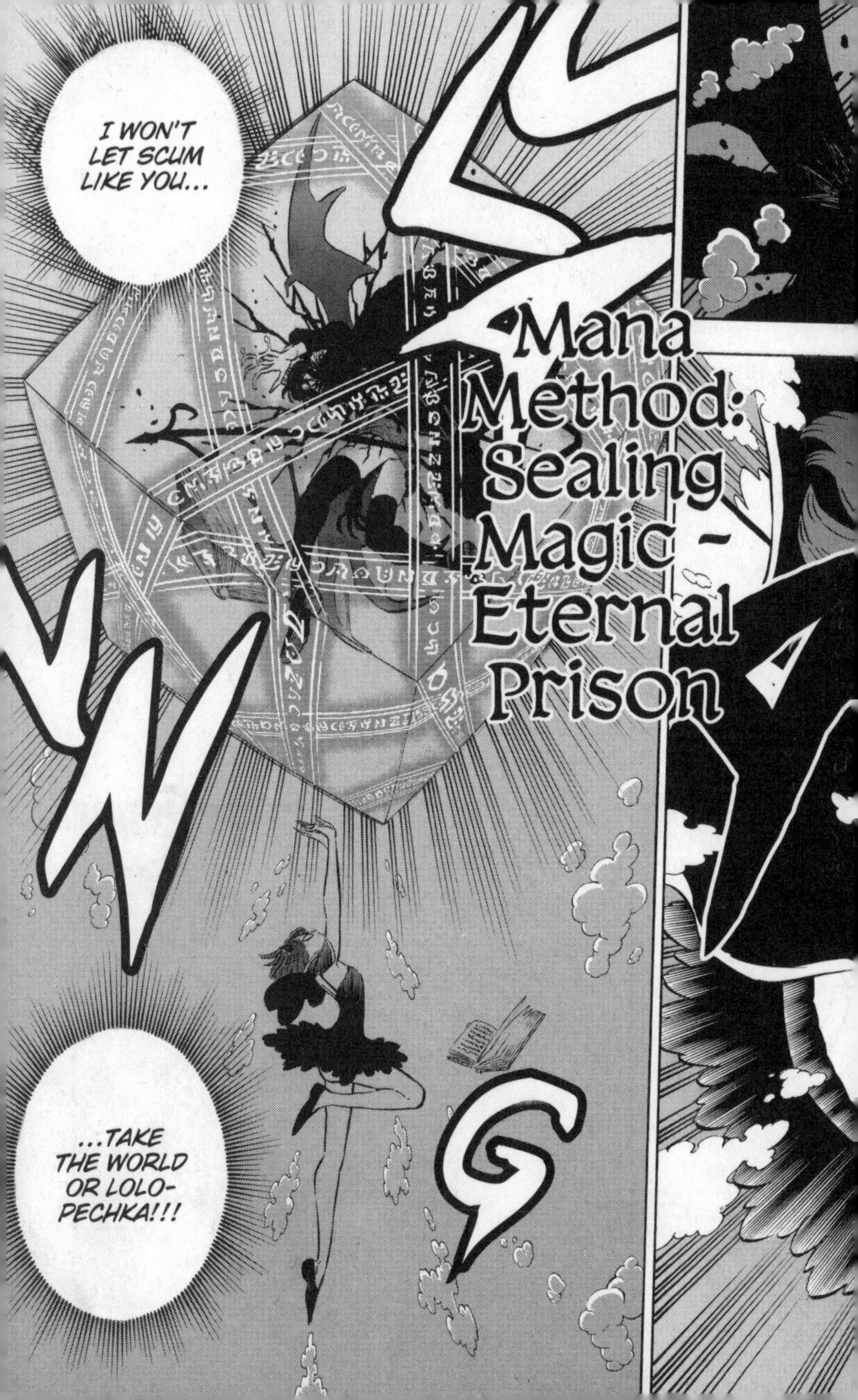
I WON'T LET SCUM LIKE YOU...
Mana Method: Sealing Magic - Eternal Prison
...TAKE THE WORLD OR LOLO-PECHKA!!!

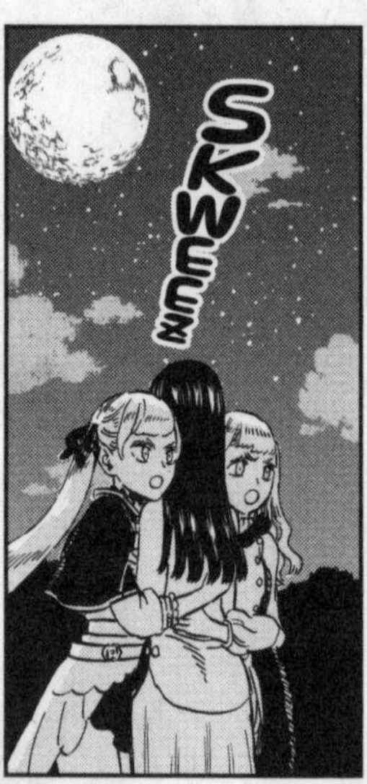
SKWEEZ

Page 254: Power Differential

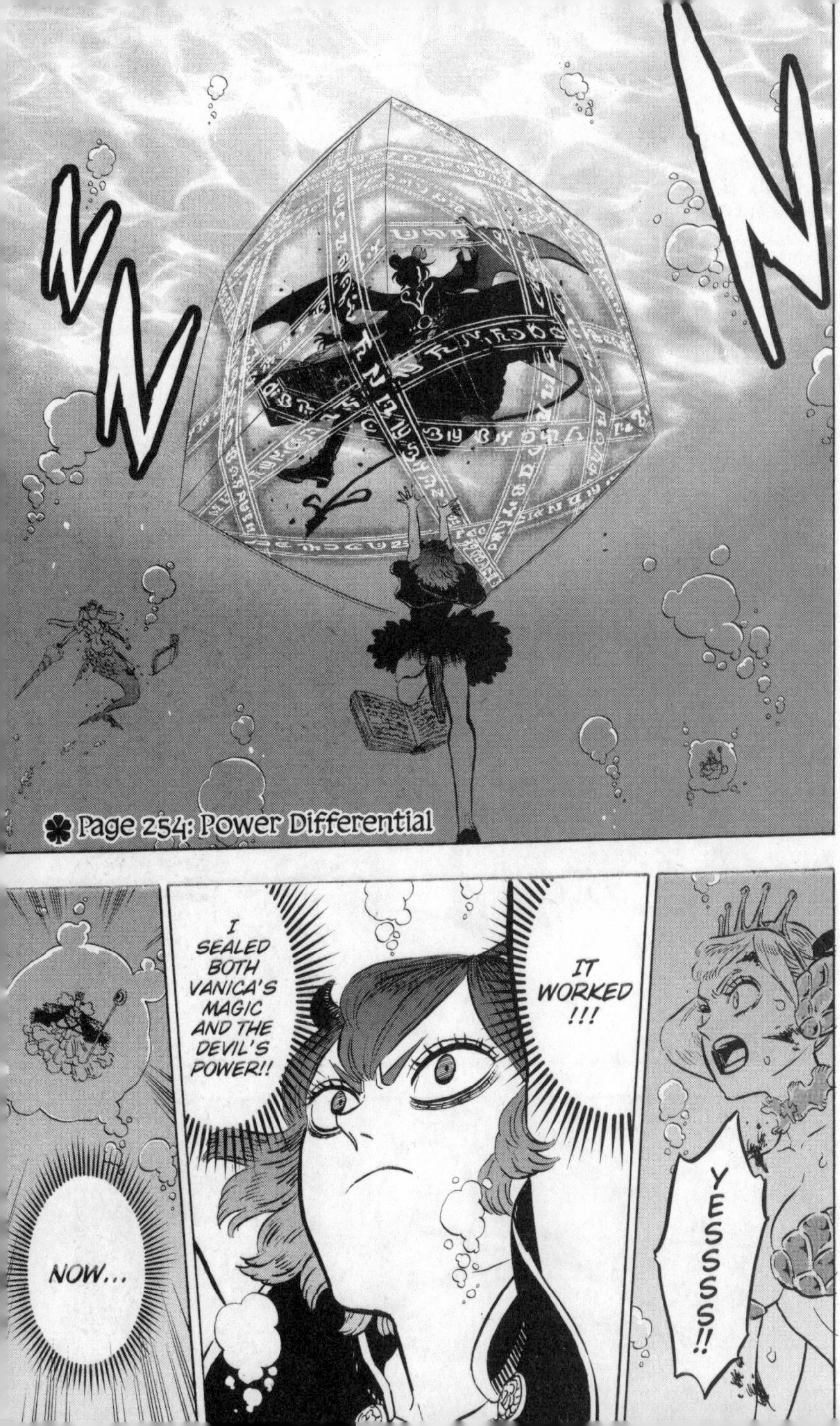
YESSSS!!
IT WORKED!!!
I SEALED BOTH VANICA'S MAGIC AND THE DEVIL'S POWER!!
NOW...

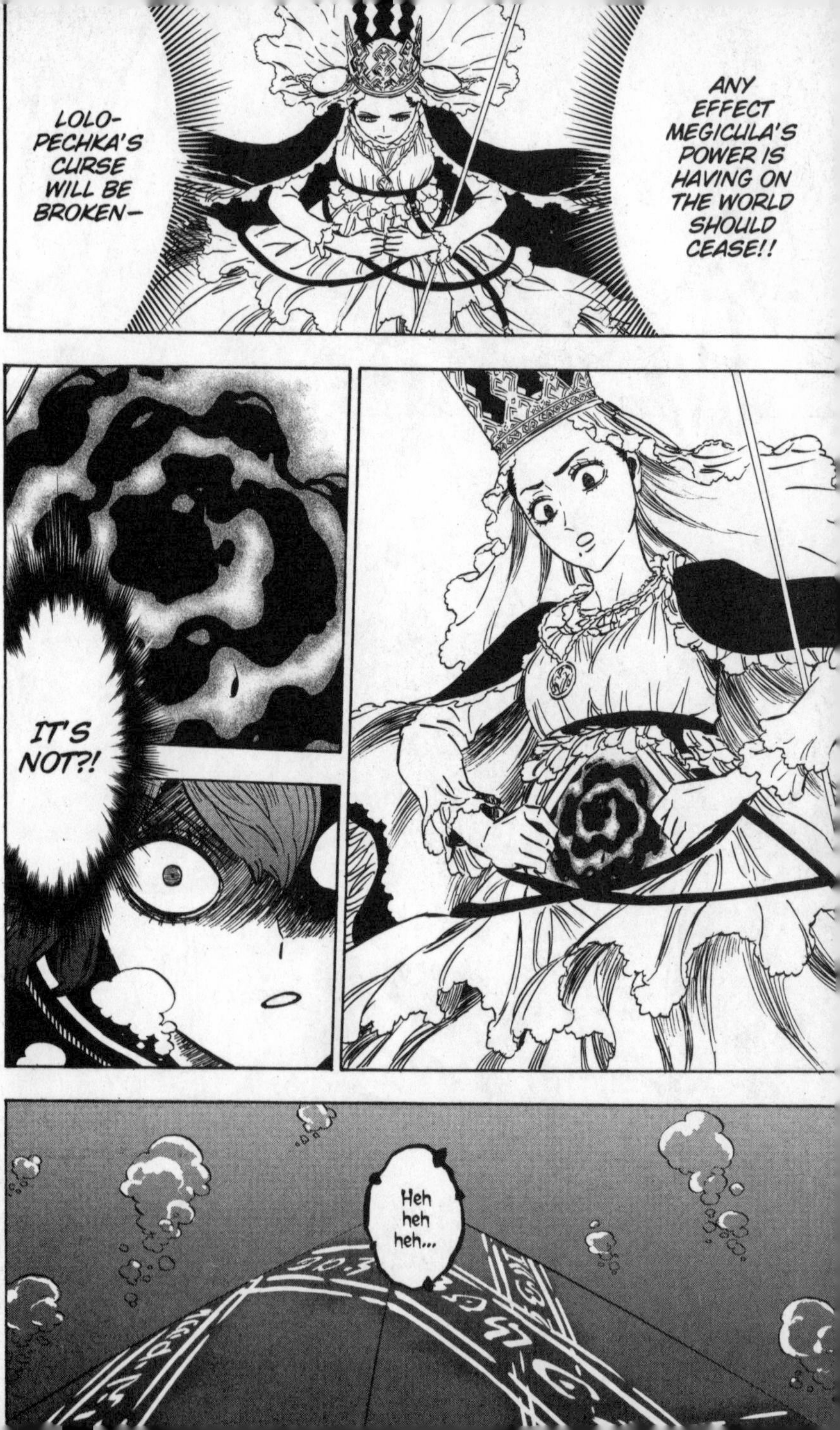
ANY EFFECT MEGICULA'S POWER IS HAVING ON THE WORLD SHOULD CEASE!!
LOLO-PECHKA'S CURSE WILL BE BROKEN—
IT'S NOT?!
Heh heh heh...

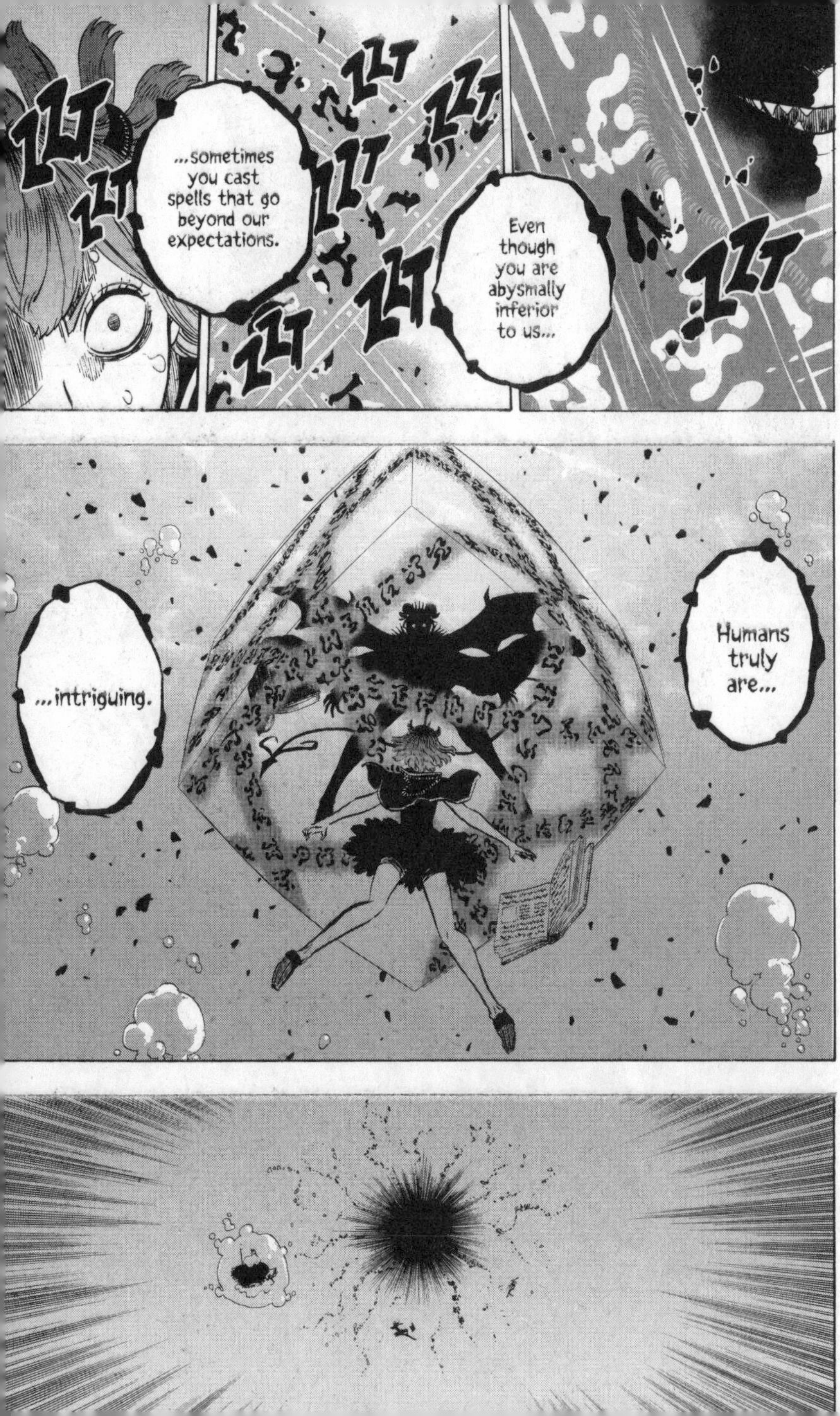
ZZT
Even though you are abysmally inferior to us...
ZZT
ZZT
...sometimes you cast spells that go beyond our expectations.
ZZT
Humans truly are...
...intriguing.

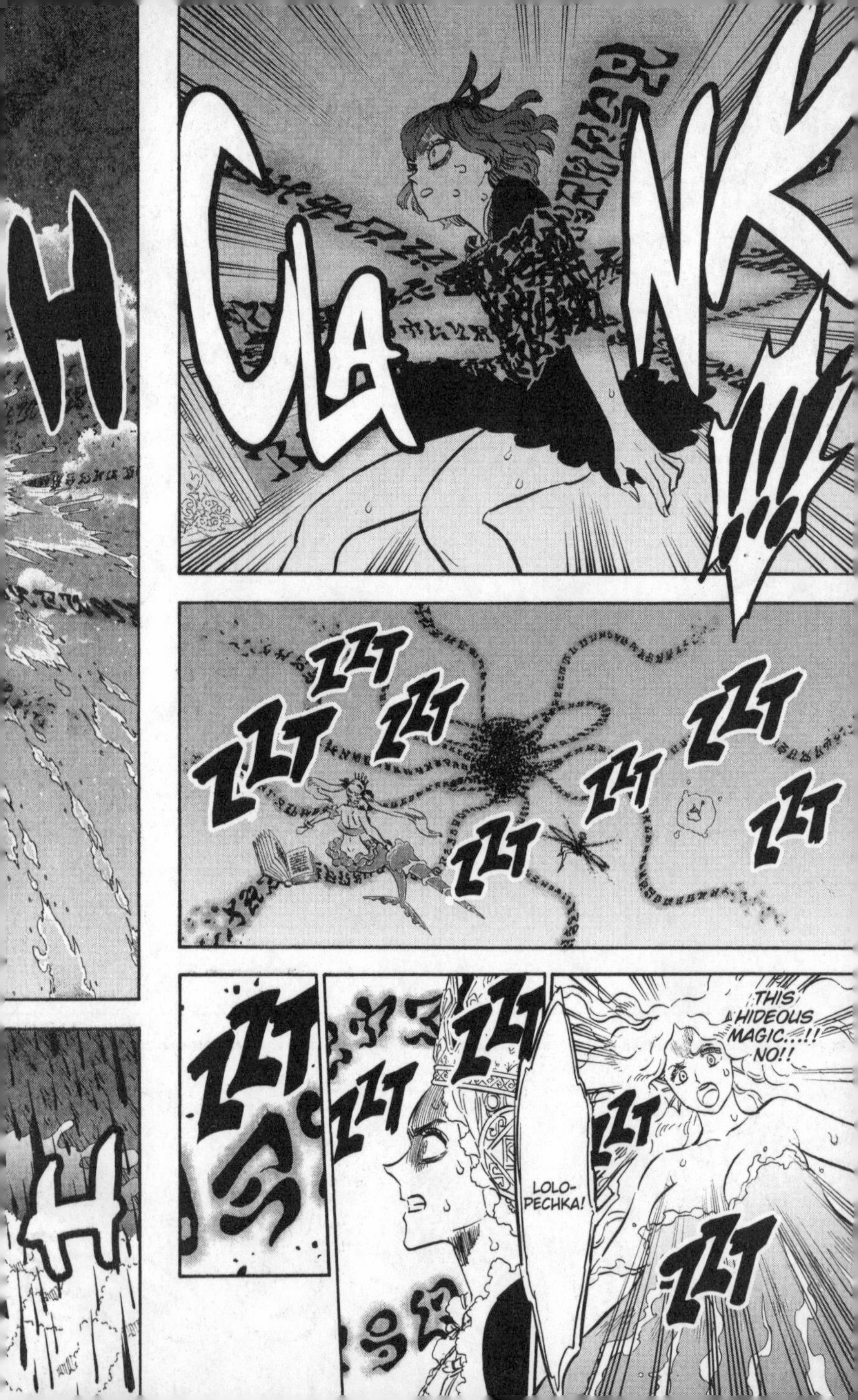
CLANK!!!
ZZZT
ZZZT
ZZZT
ZZZT
ZZZT
ZZZT
ZZZT
THIS HIDEOUS MAGIC...!! NO!!
ZZZT
ZZZT
LOLO-PECHKA!
ZZZT
ZZZT
ZZZT
H
H

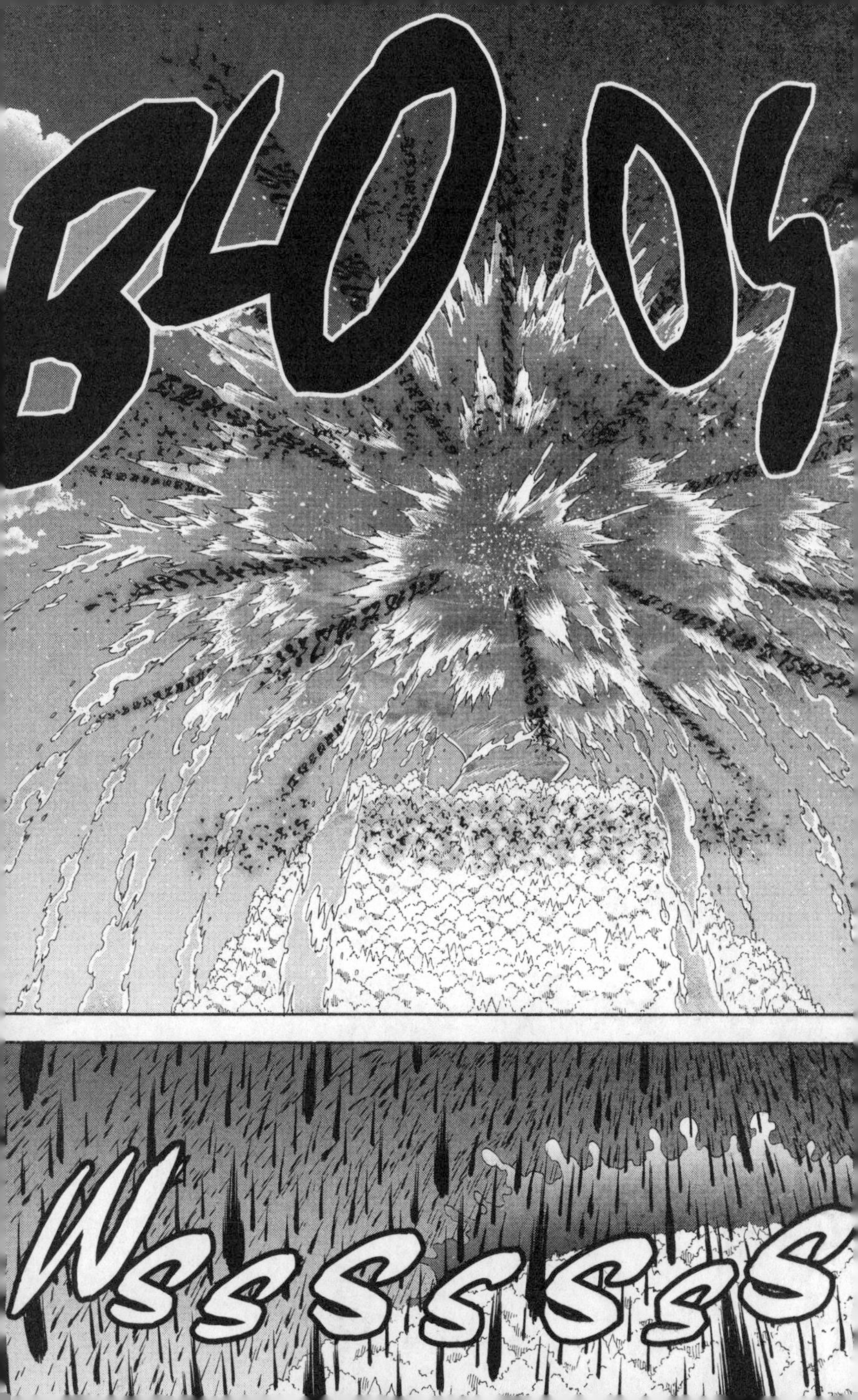
BLOOS
WSSSSSS

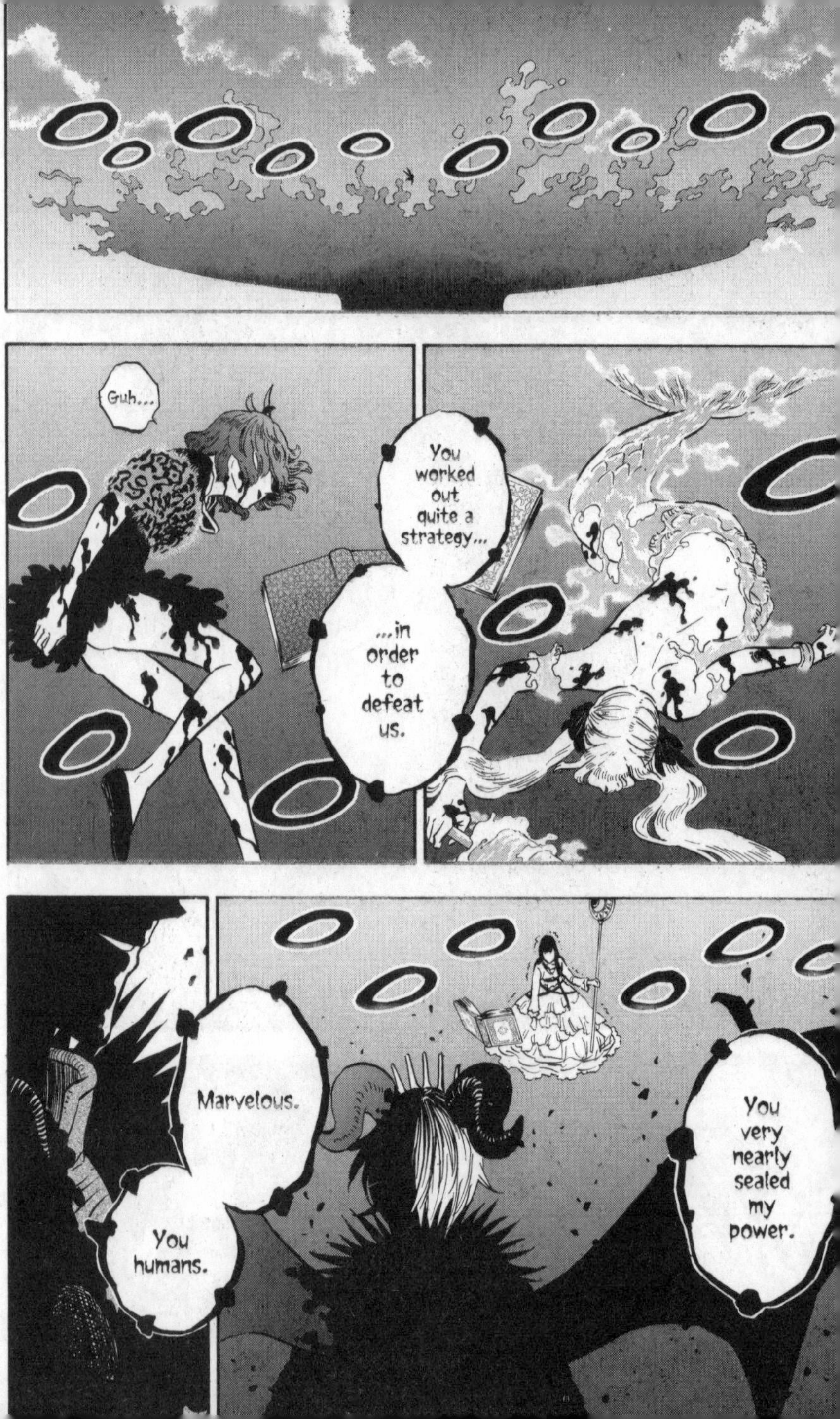
You worked out quite a strategy...
...in order to defeat us.
Guh...
You very nearly sealed my power.
Marvelous.
You humans.

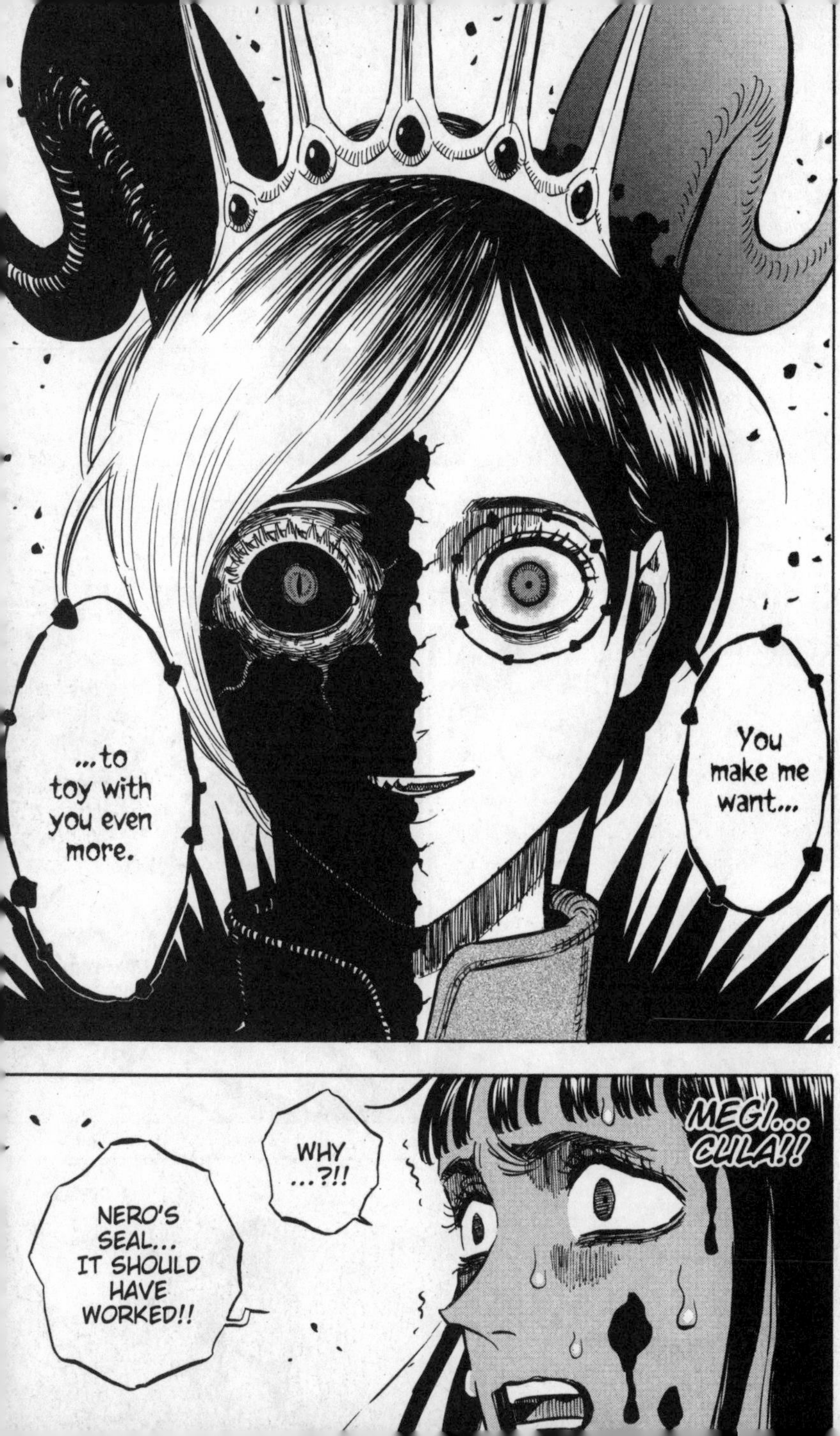
You make me want...
...to toy with you even more.
MEGI... CULA!!
WHY ...?!!
NERO'S SEAL... IT SHOULD HAVE WORKED!!

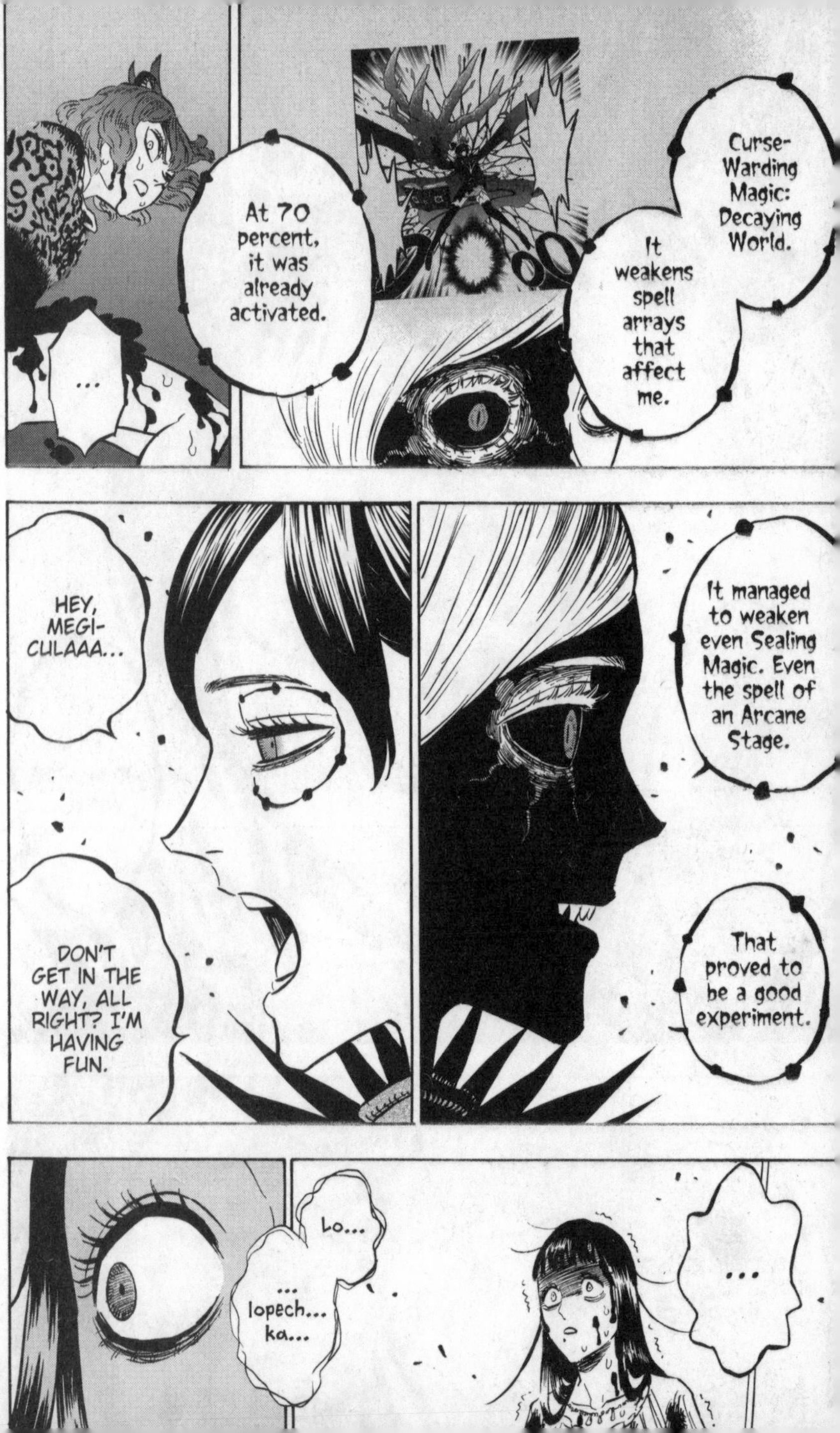
Curse-Warding Magic: Decaying World.
It weakens spell arrays that affect me.
At 70 percent, it was already activated.
...
It managed to weaken even Sealing Magic. Even the spell of an Arcane Stage.
That proved to be a good experiment.
HEY, MEGI-CULAAA...
DON'T GET IN THE WAY, ALL RIGHT? I'M HAVING FUN.
...
Lo...
...lopech... ka...

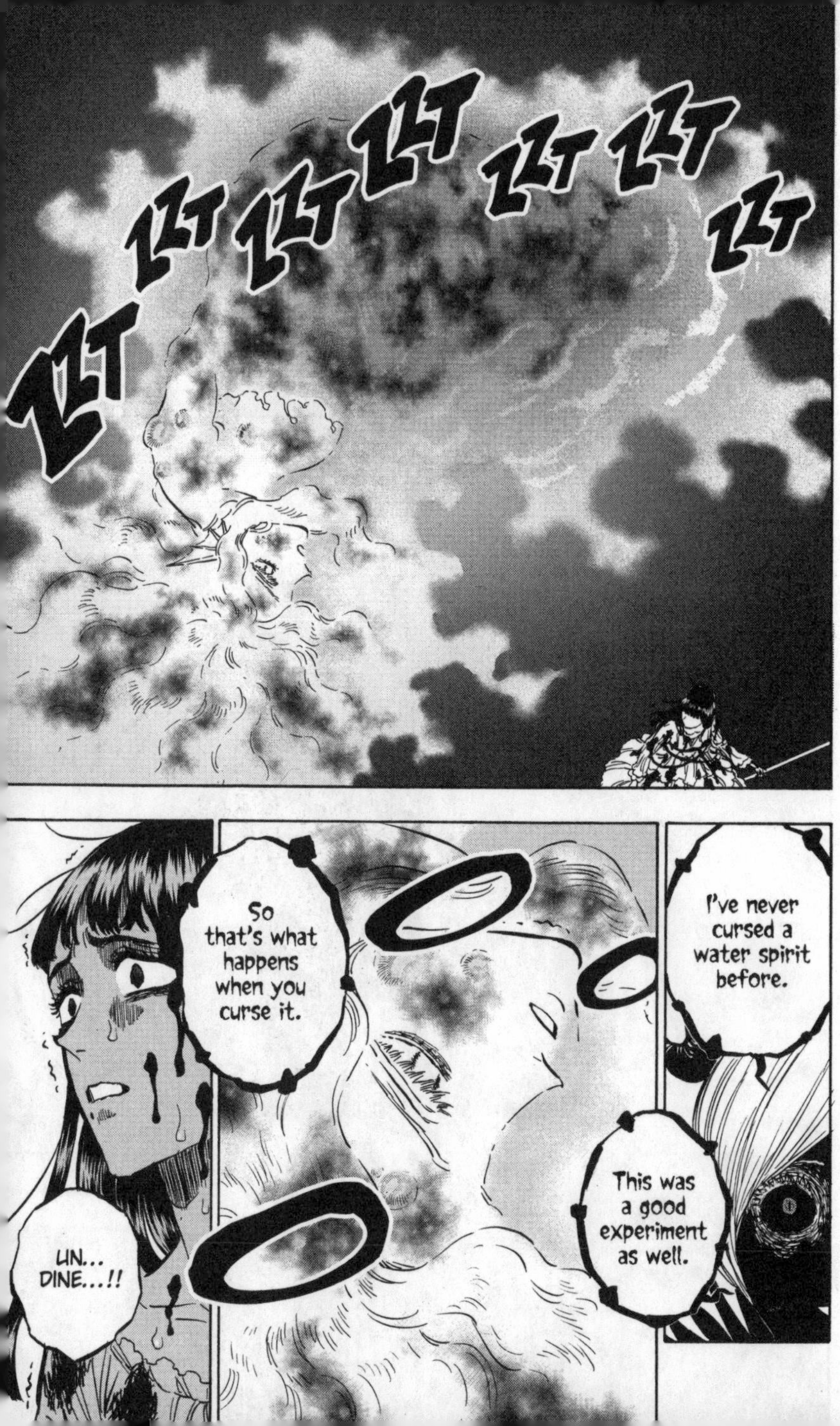
ZZT ZZT ZZT ZZT ZZT ZZT ZZT
I've never cursed a water spirit before.
This was a good experiment as well.
So that's what happens when you curse it.
UN... DINE...!!

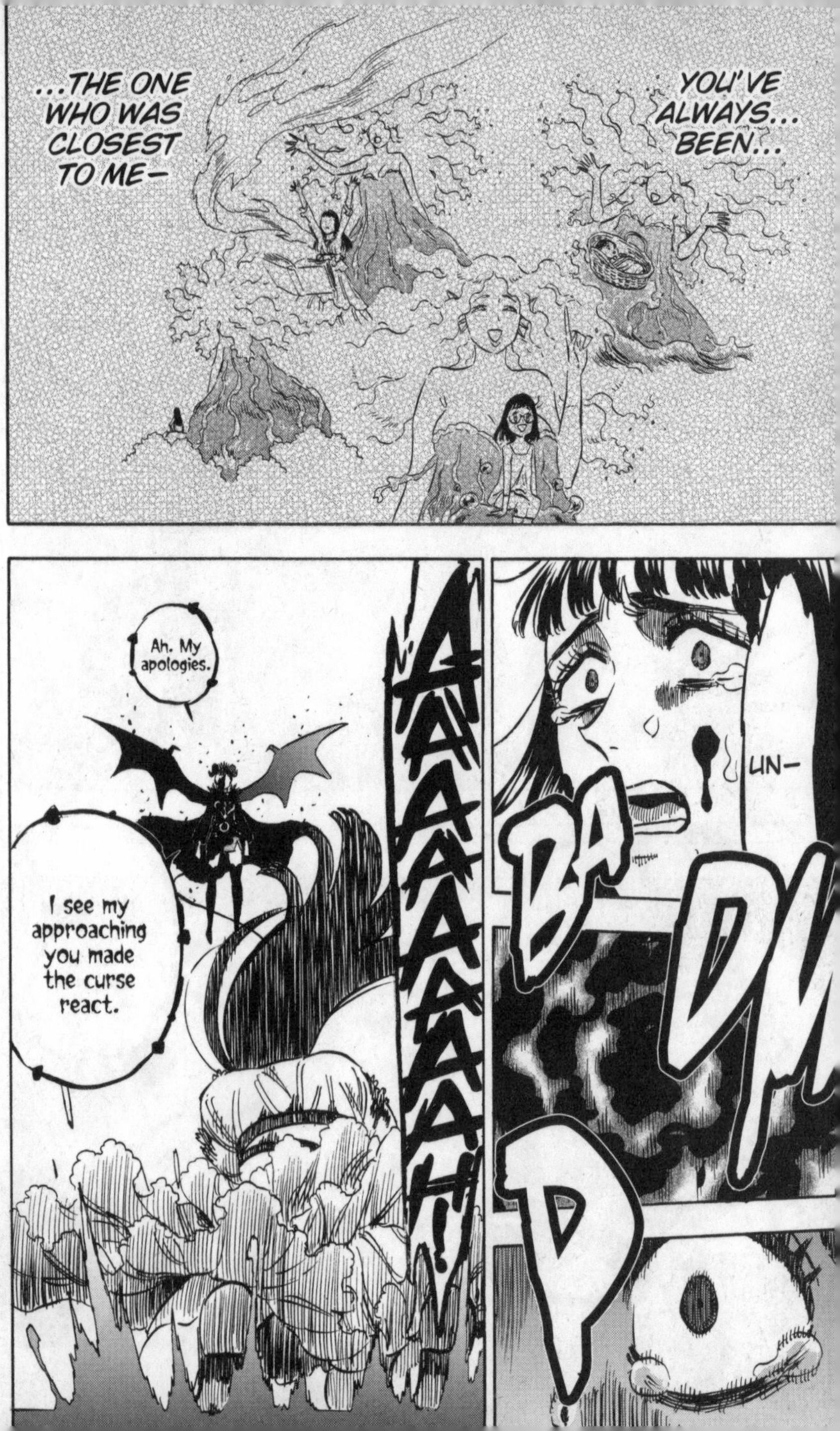
YOU'VE ALWAYS... BEEN...
...THE ONE WHO WAS CLOSEST TO ME–
UN–
BA
AAAAAAAAAAAAH!
Ah. My apologies.
I see my approaching you made the curse react.

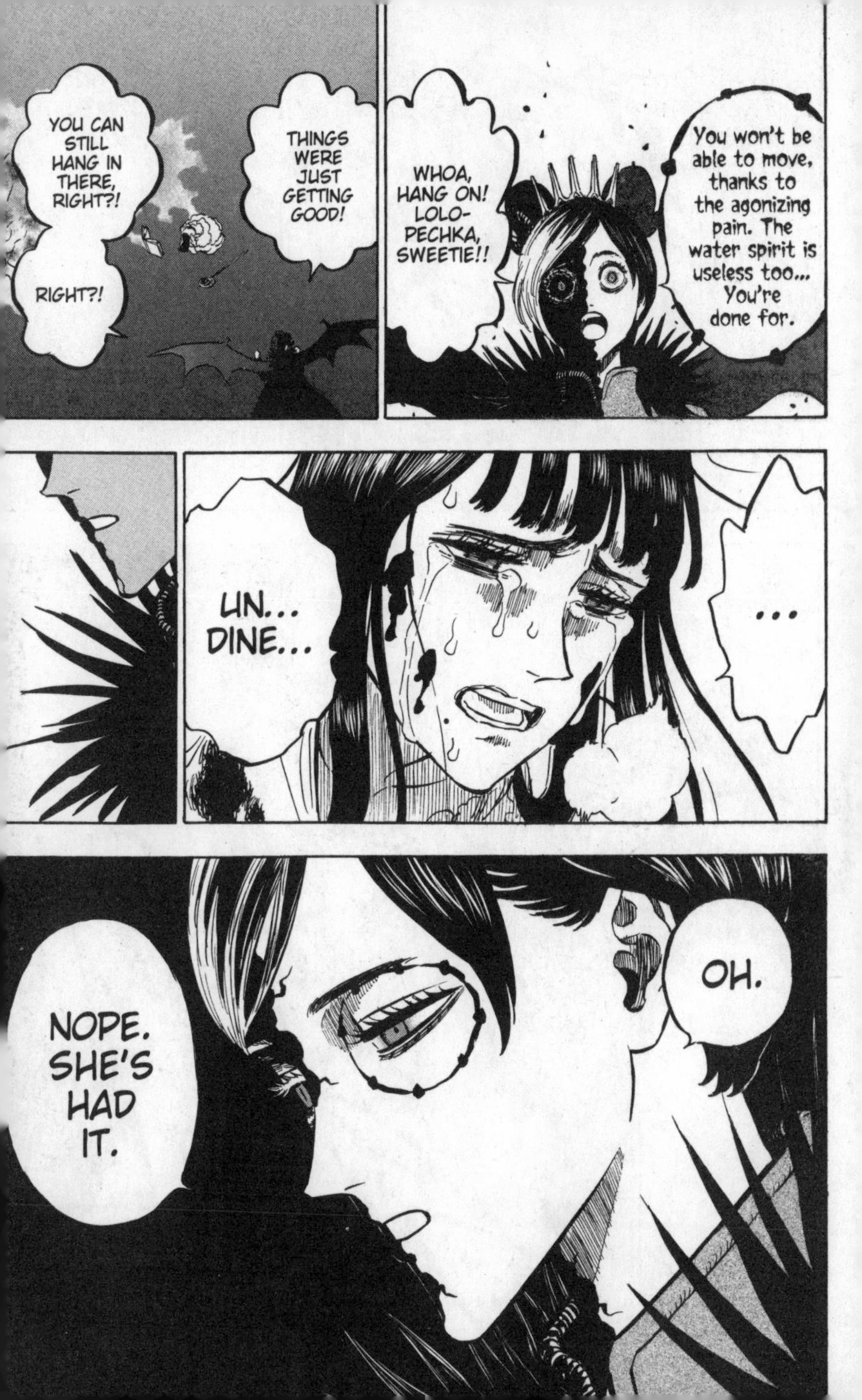
You won't be able to move, thanks to the agonizing pain. The water spirit is useless too... You're done for.
WHOA, HANG ON! LOLOPECHKA, SWEETIE!!
THINGS WERE JUST GETTING GOOD!
YOU CAN STILL HANG IN THERE, RIGHT?!
RIGHT?!
...
UN... DINE...
OH.
NOPE. SHE'S HAD IT.

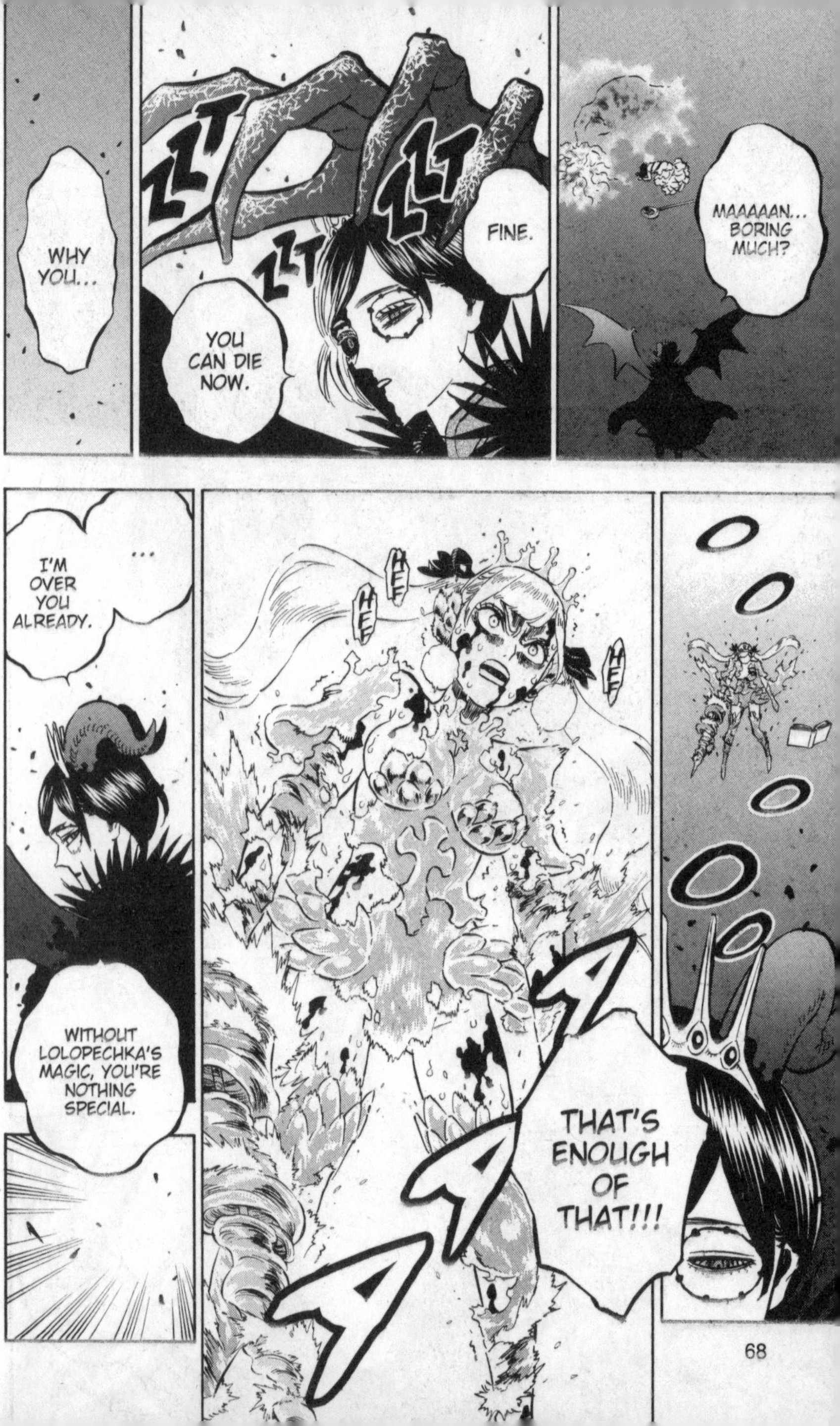
MAAAAAN... BORING MUCH?
ZZZT
ZZZT
ZZZT
FINE.
YOU CAN DIE NOW.
WHY YOU...
THAT'S ENOUGH OF THAT!!!
HEF
HEF
HEF
...
I'M OVER YOU ALREADY.
WITHOUT LOLOPECHKA'S MAGIC, YOU'RE NOTHING SPECIAL.

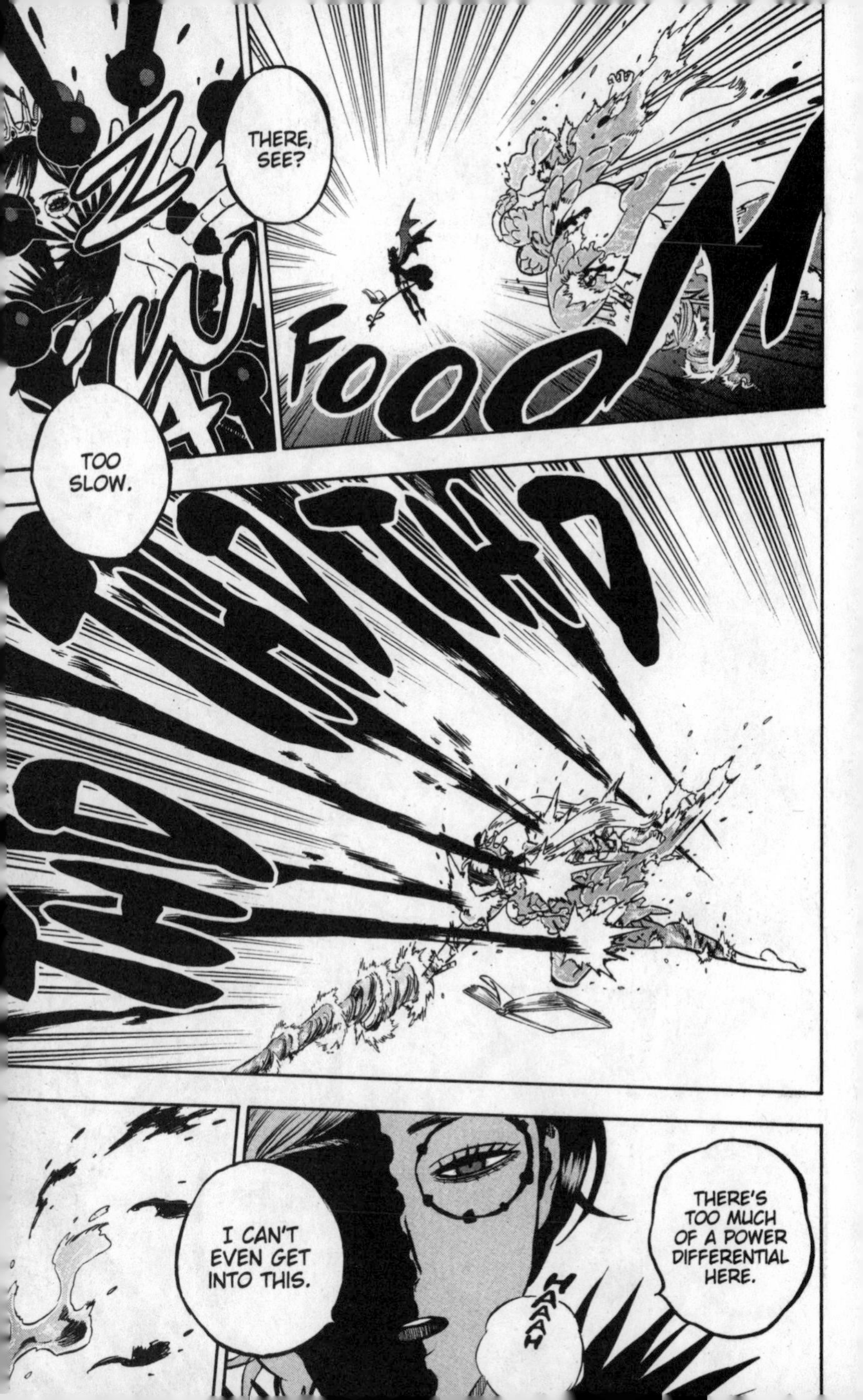
FOOOM
THERE, SEE?
TOO SLOW.
THERE'S TOO MUCH OF A POWER DIFFERENTIAL HERE.
I CAN'T EVEN GET INTO THIS.

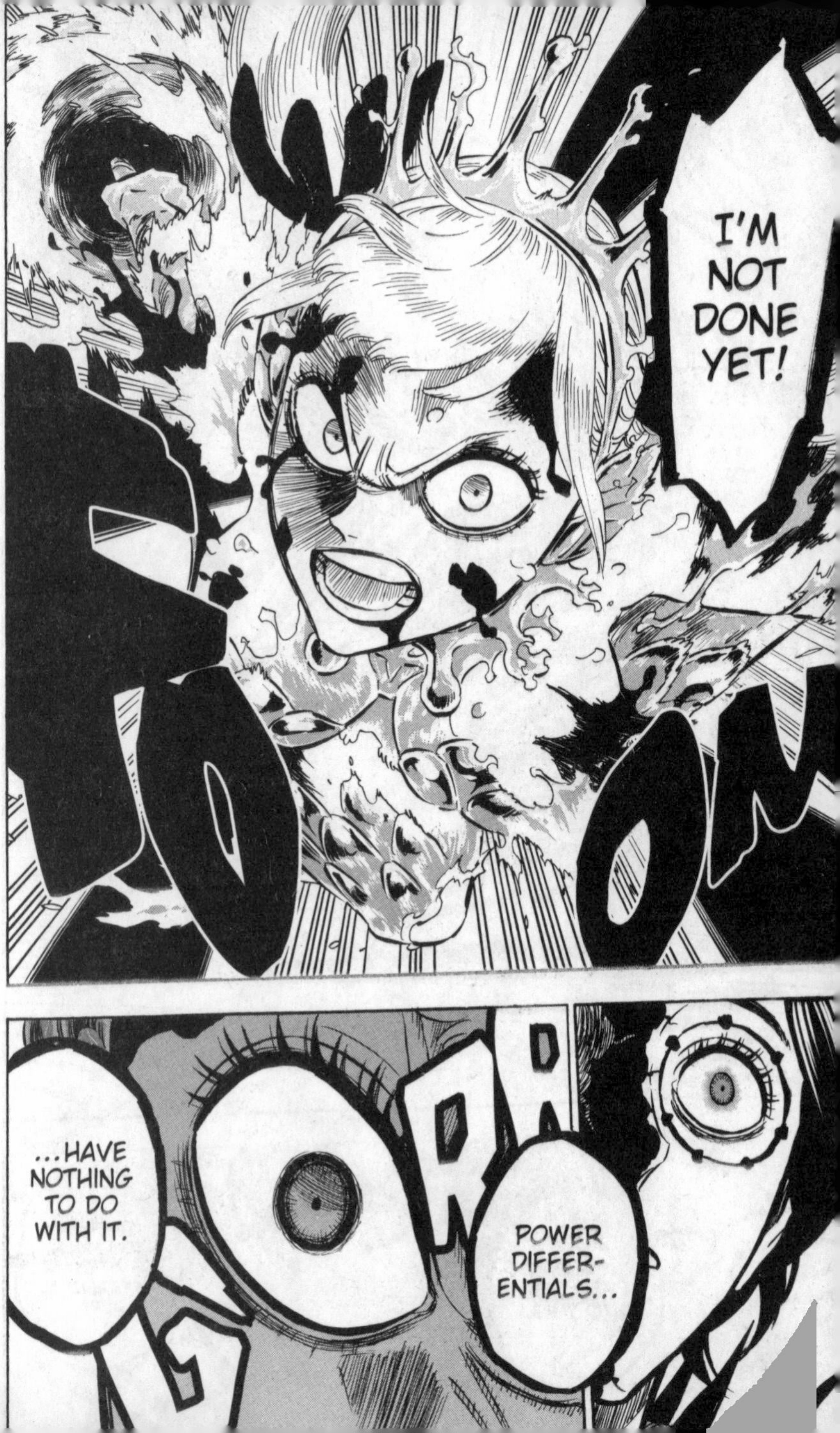
I'M NOT DONE YET!
POWER DIFFER-
ENTIALS...
...HAVE NOTHING TO DO WITH IT.

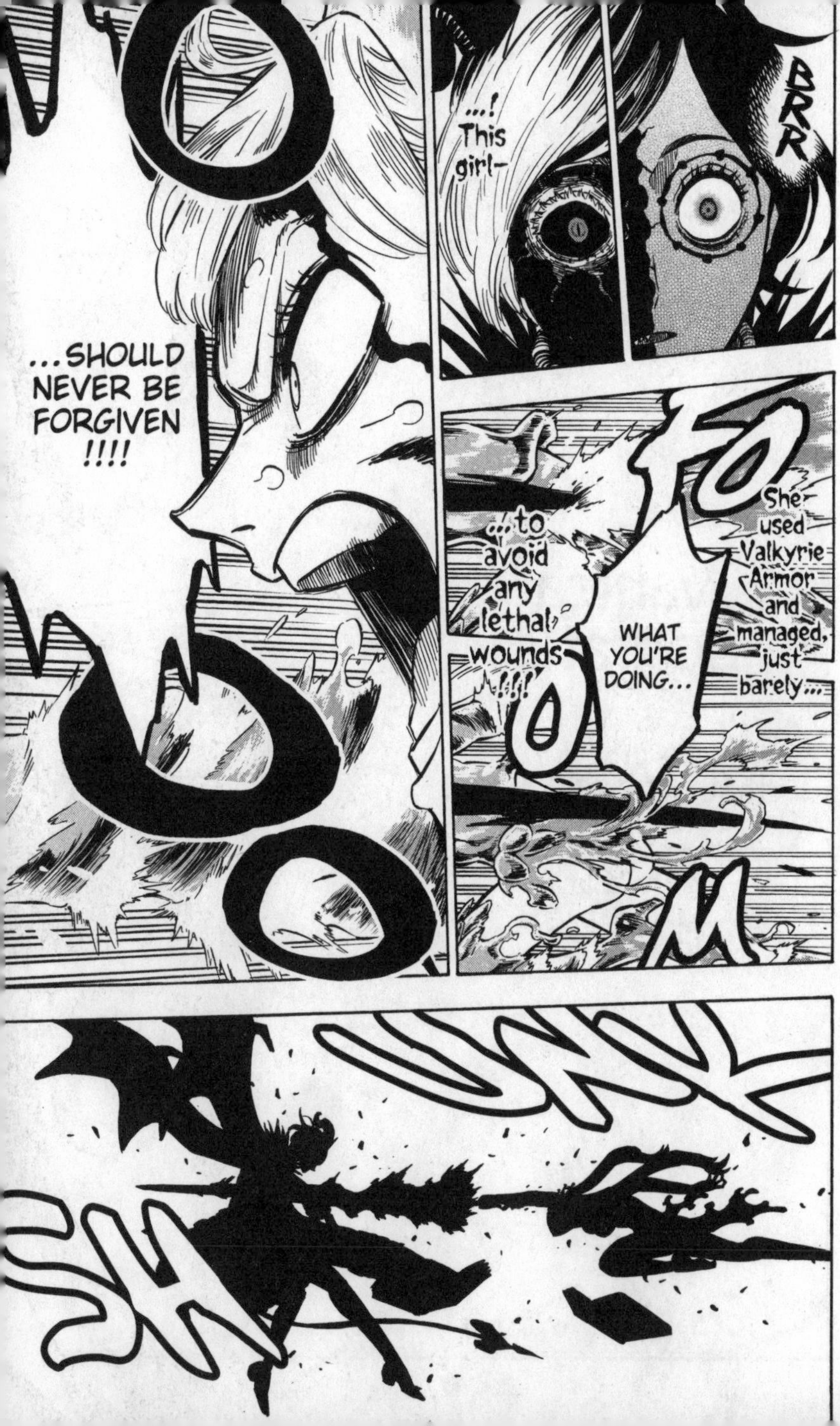
BRR
...! This girl—
FOOM
She used Valkyrie Armor and managed, just barely...
...to avoid any lethal wounds!!!!
WHAT YOU'RE DOING...
...SHOULD NEVER BE FORGIVEN!!!!

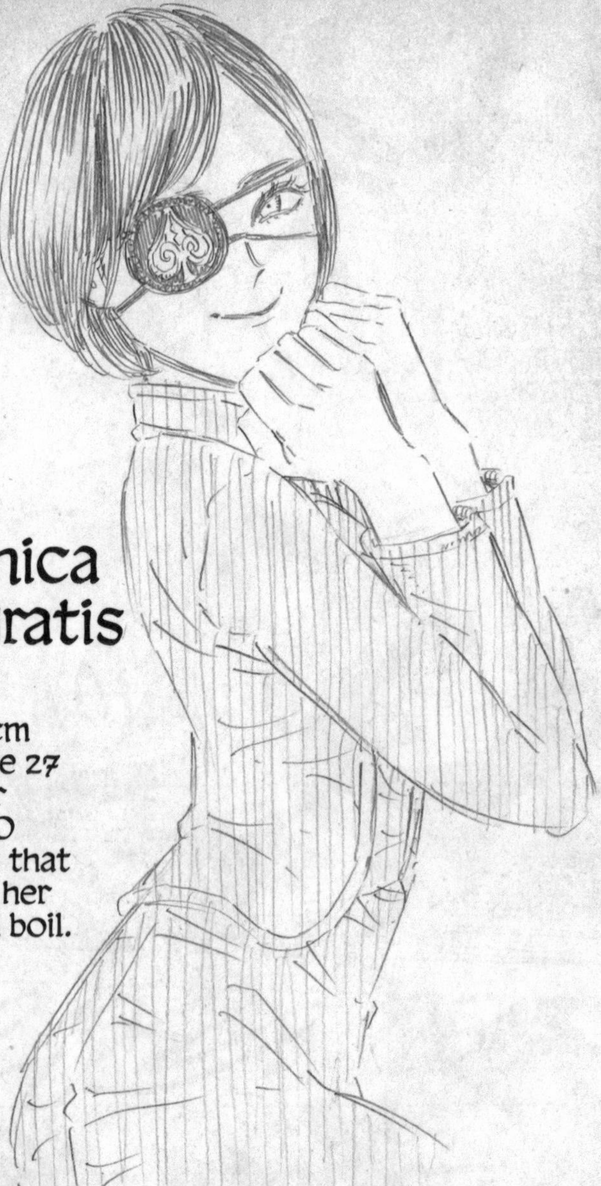

Vanica Zogratis

Age: —
Height: 166 cm
Birthday: June 27
Sign: Cancer
Blood Type: O
Likes: Fights that make her blood boil.

Page 255: Exploding Life

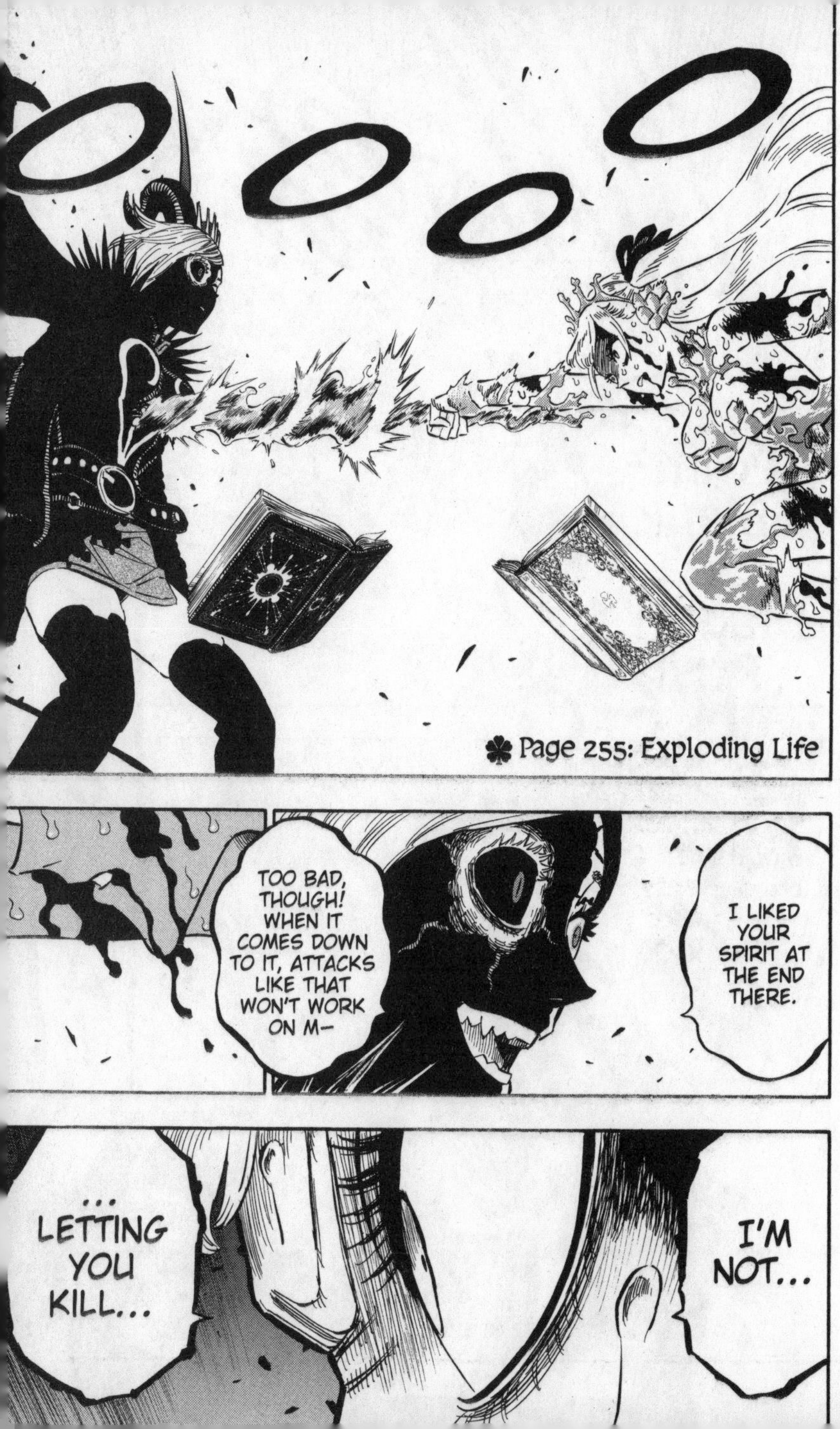
I LIKED YOUR SPIRIT AT THE END THERE.
TOO BAD, THOUGH! WHEN IT COMES DOWN TO IT, ATTACKS LIKE THAT WON'T WORK ON M—
I'M NOT...
...LETTING YOU KILL...

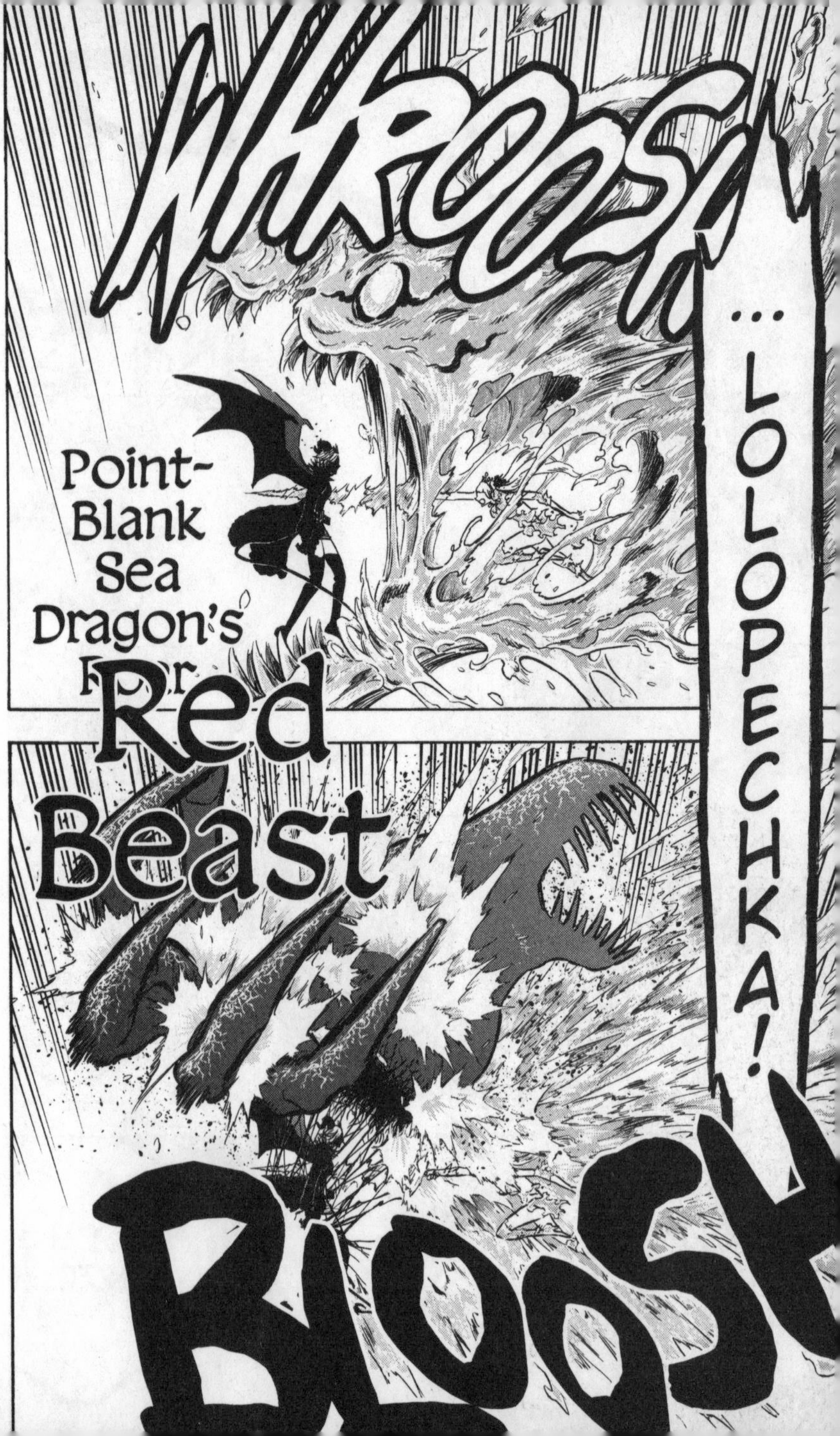
...LOLOPECHKA!
WHOOSH
Point-Blank Sea Dragon's
Red Beast
BOOSH

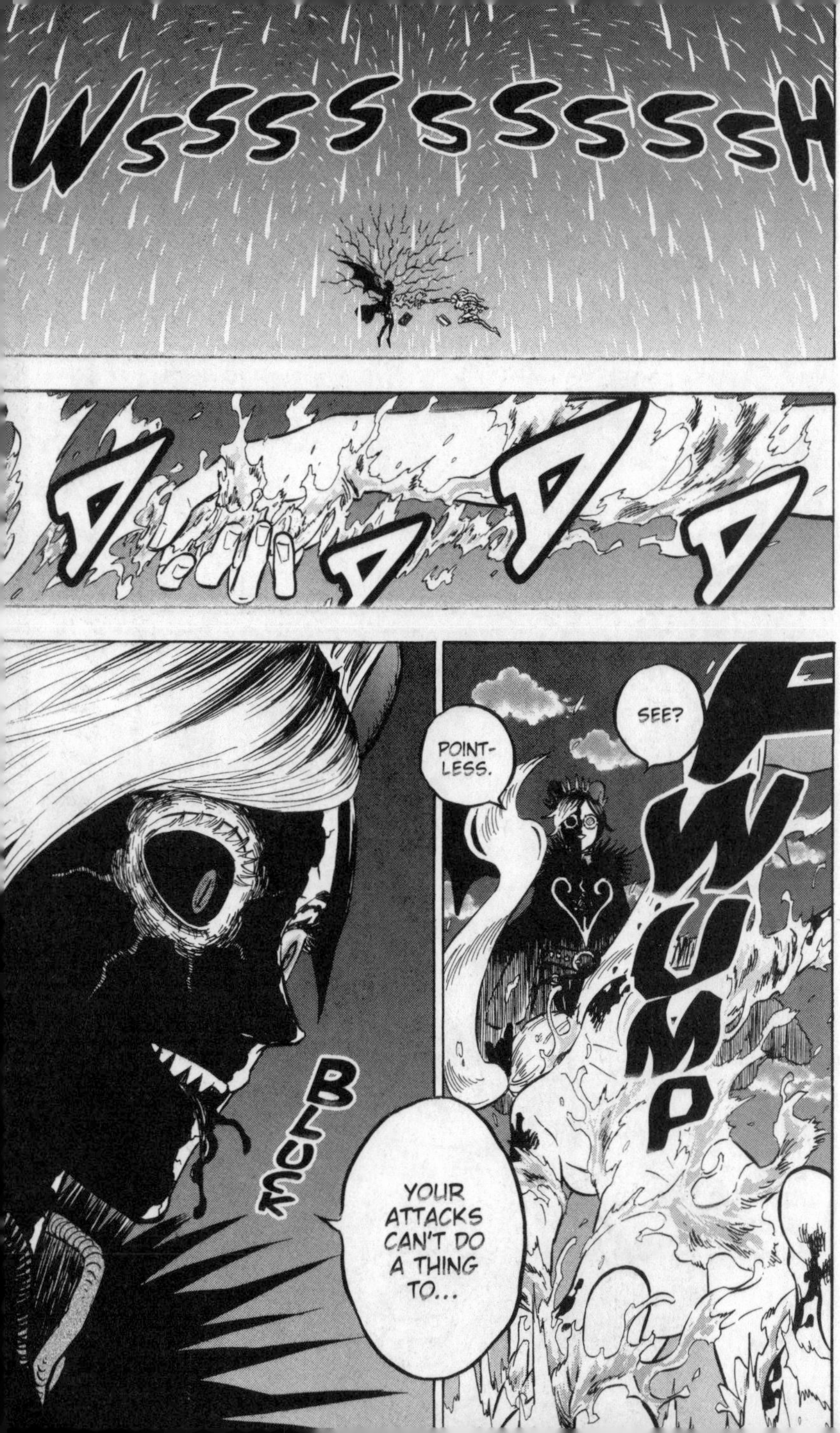
WSSSSSSSSSH
DDDD
SEE?
POINT-LESS.
WUMP
BLUCK
YOUR ATTACKS CAN'T DO A THING TO...

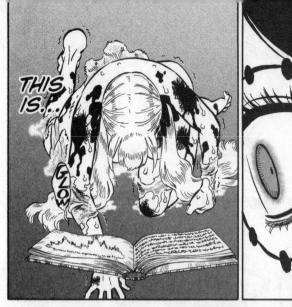

THIS IS...

GLOW

HUH?

WHAT WAS YOUR NAME AGAIN?

GIRL...

A CLOVER KINGDOM ROYAL!!

AND A MAGIC KNIGHT WITH THE BLACK BULLS!!

NOELLE SILVA!!

BRR

BRR

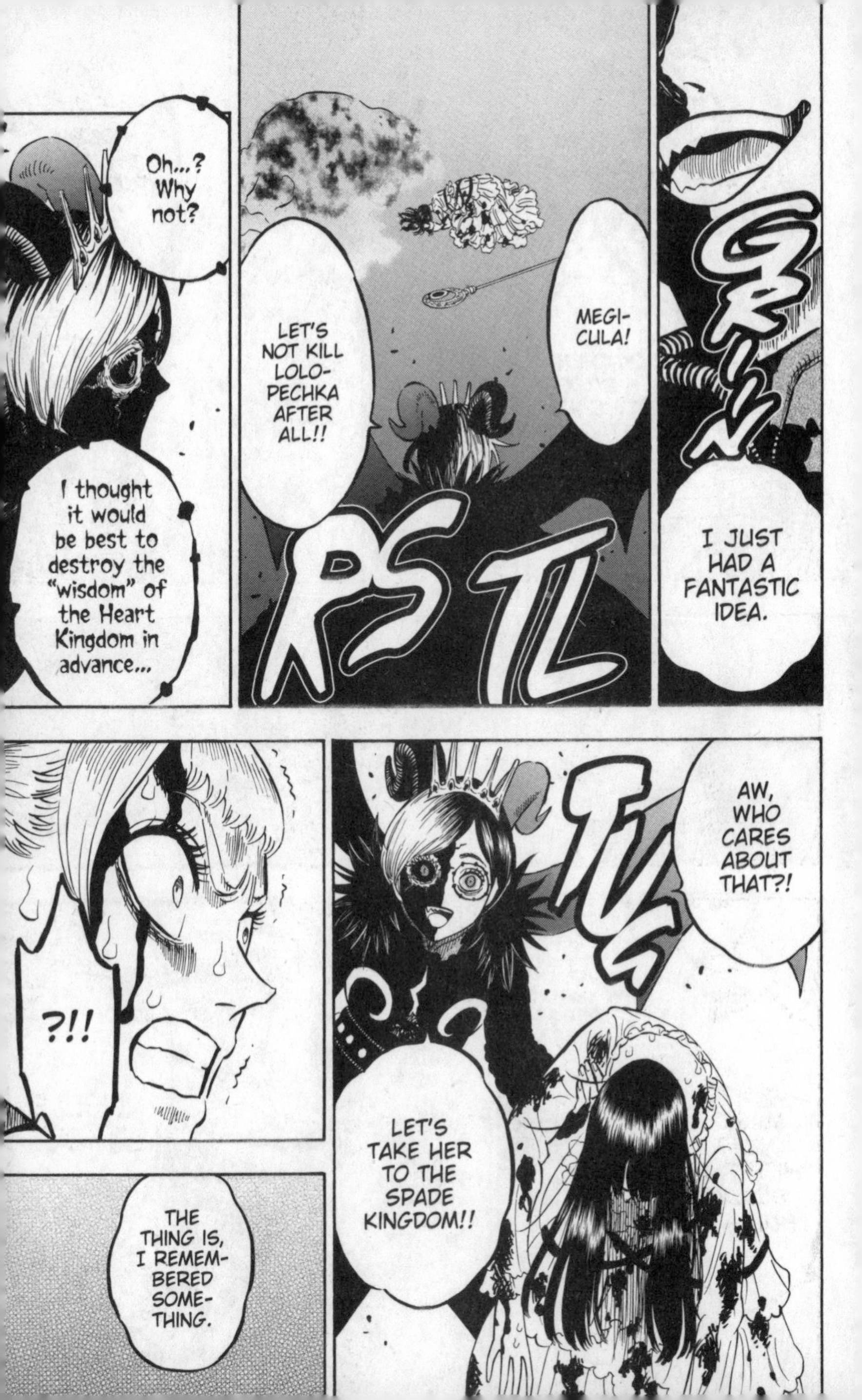
GRIN
I JUST HAD A FANTASTIC IDEA.
MEGI-CULA!
LET'S NOT KILL LOLO-PECHKA AFTER ALL!!
RSTL
Oh...? Why not?
I thought it would be best to destroy the "wisdom" of the Heart Kingdom in advance...
AW, WHO CARES ABOUT THAT?!
TU
LET'S TAKE HER TO THE SPADE KINGDOM!!
?!!
THE THING IS, I REMEMBERED SOMETHING.

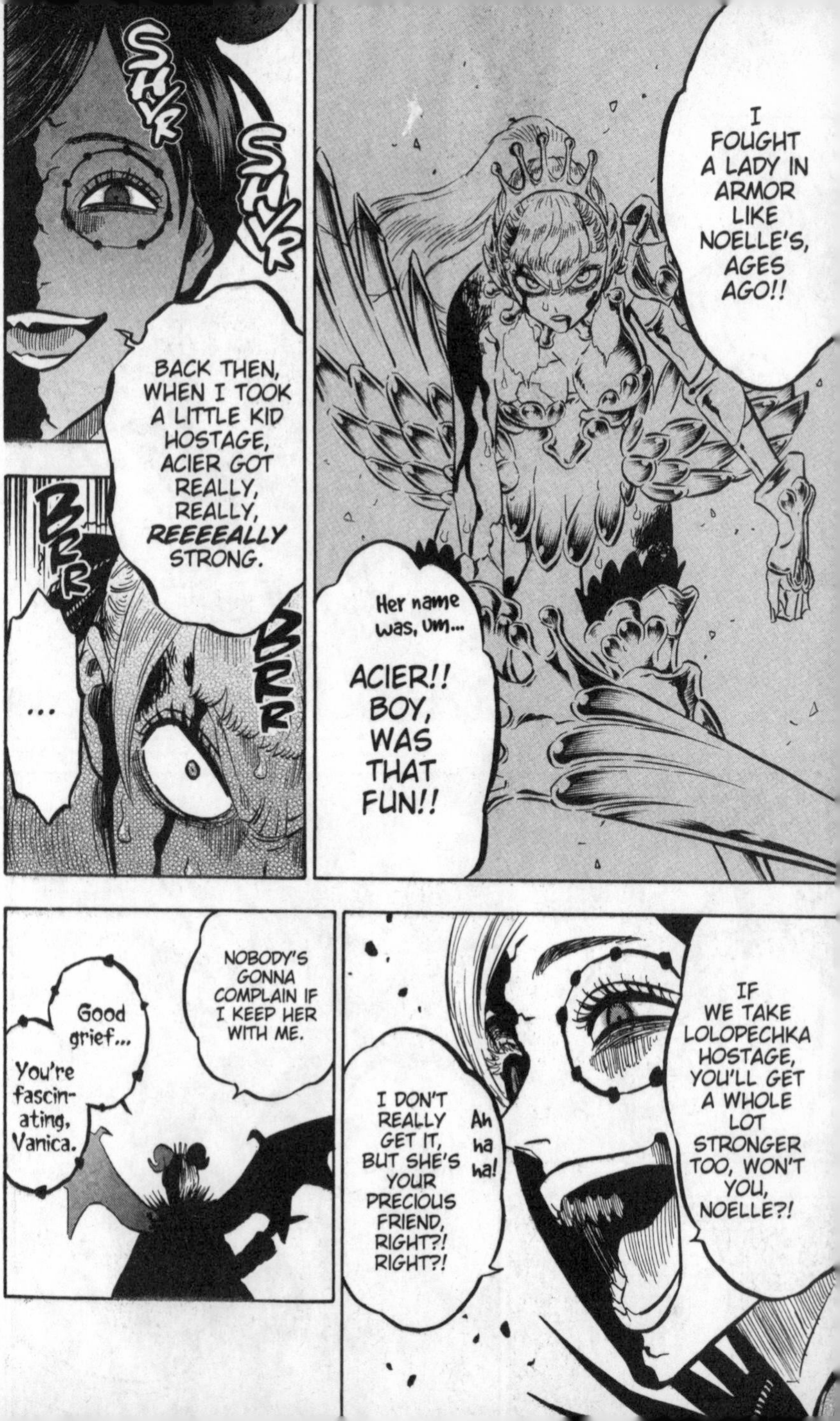
I FOUGHT A LADY IN ARMOR LIKE NOELLE'S, AGES AGO!!
Her name was, um...
ACIER!! BOY, WAS THAT FUN!!
SHVR SHVR
BACK THEN, WHEN I TOOK A LITTLE KID HOSTAGE, ACIER GOT REALLY, REALLY, *REEEEALLY* STRONG.
BRR BRR
...
IF WE TAKE LOLOPECHKA HOSTAGE, YOU'LL GET A WHOLE LOT STRONGER TOO, WON'T YOU, NOELLE?!
Ah ha ha!
I DON'T REALLY GET IT, BUT SHE'S YOUR PRECIOUS FRIEND, RIGHT?! RIGHT?!
NOBODY'S GONNA COMPLAIN IF I KEEP HER WITH ME.
Good grief...
You're fascinating, Vanica.

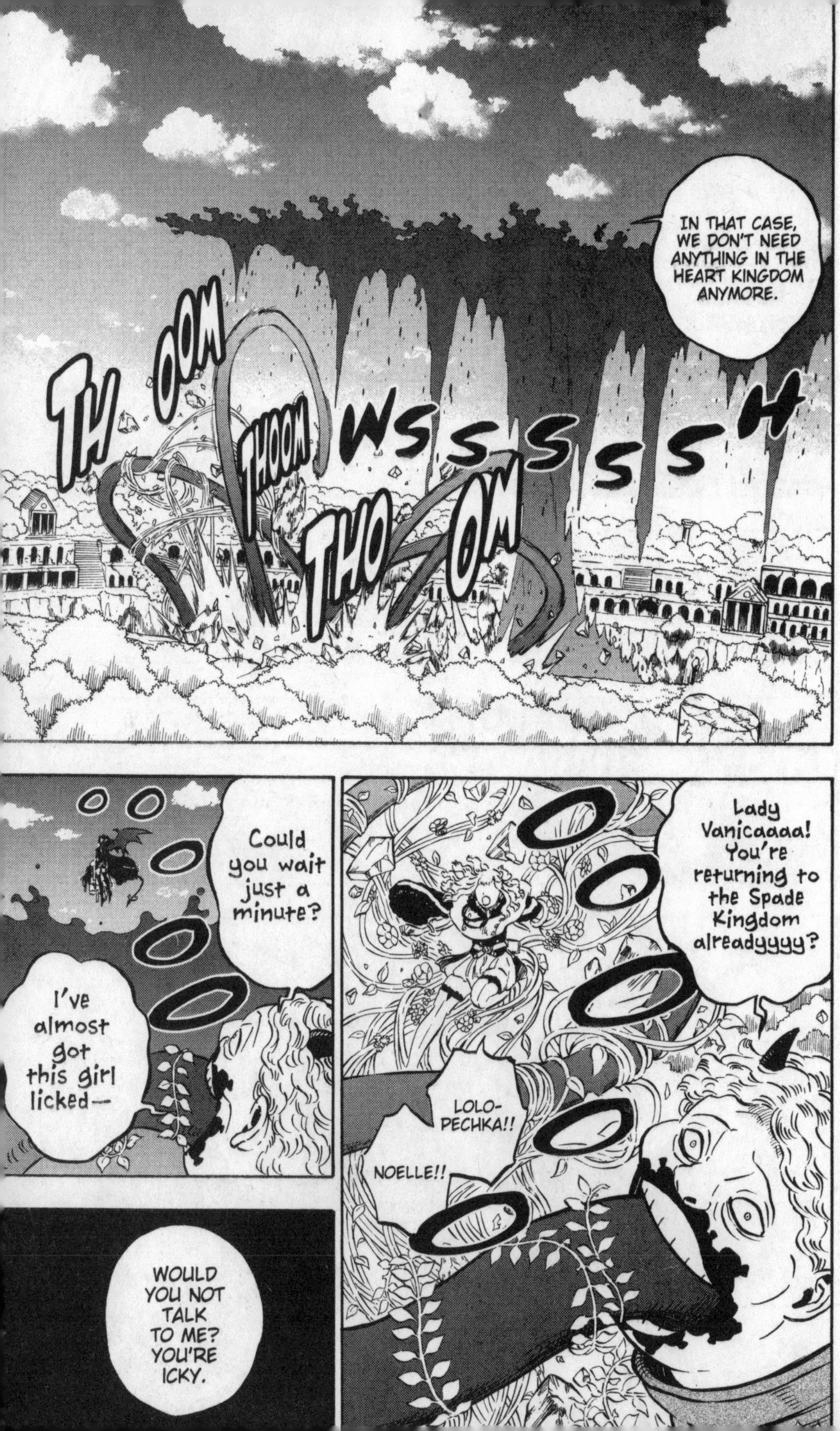
IN THAT CASE, WE DON'T NEED ANYTHING IN THE HEART KINGDOM ANYMORE.
THOOM
THOOM
WSSSSSSH
THOOM
Lady Vanicaaaa! You're returning to the Spade Kingdom alreadyyyy?
LOLO-PECHKA!!
NOELLE!!
Could you wait just a minute?
I've almost got this girl licked—
WOULD YOU NOT TALK TO ME? YOU'RE ICKY.

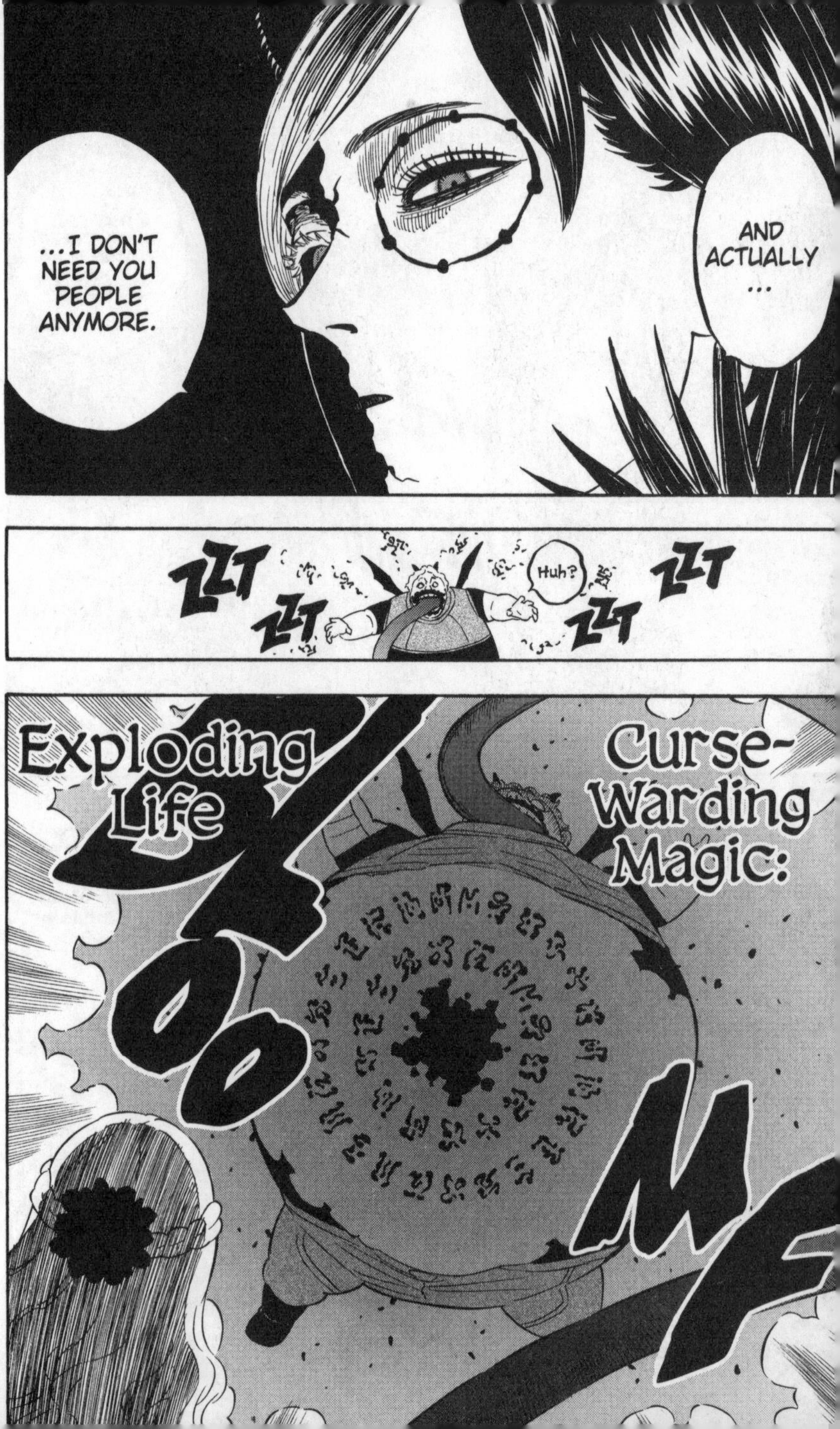
AND ACTUALLY ...
...I DON'T NEED YOU PEOPLE ANYMORE.
ZZT
Huh?
ZZT
ZZT
ZZT
Curse-Warding Magic:
Exploding Life
DOOM

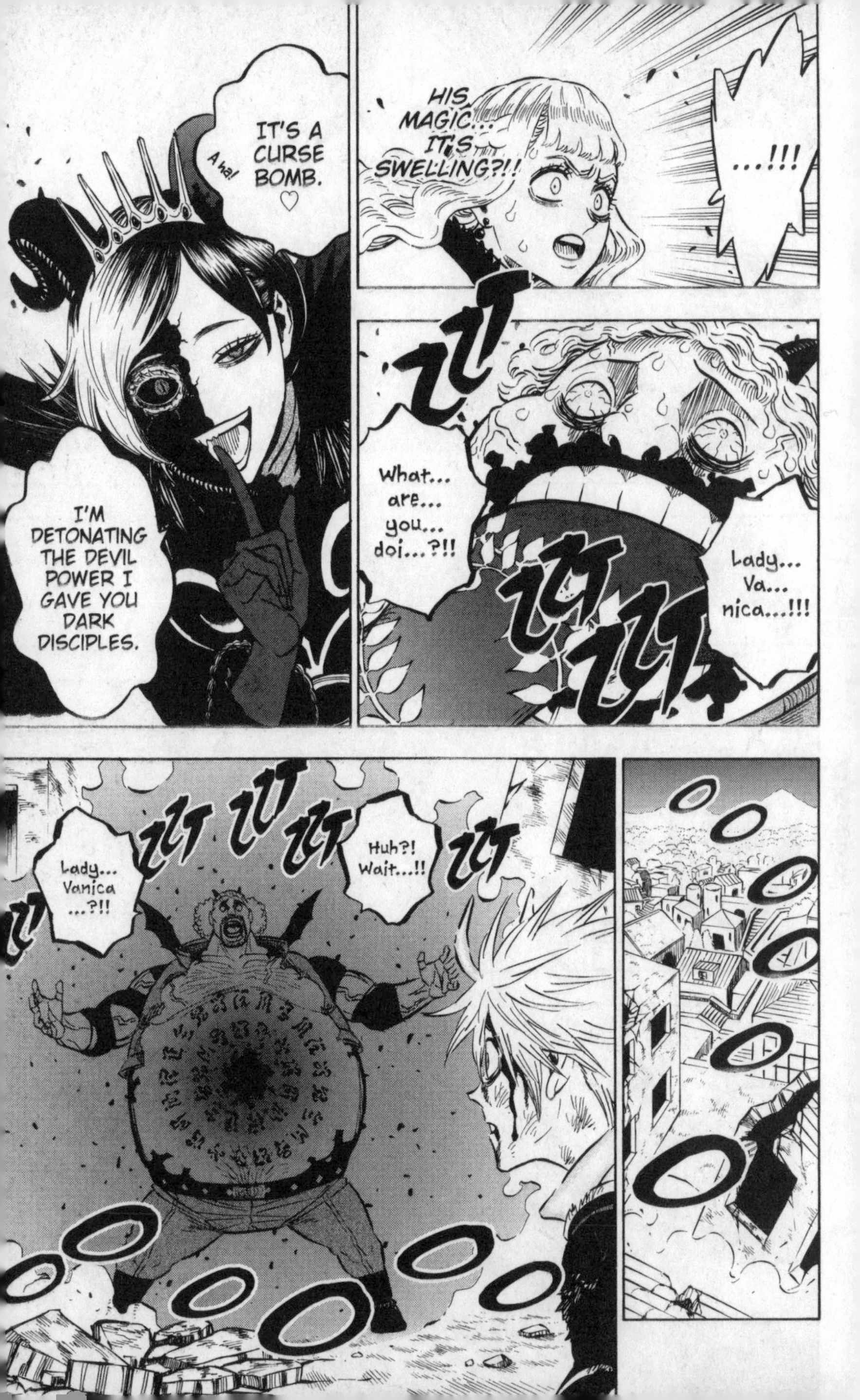

...!!!
HIS MAGIC... IT'S SWELLING?!!
Lady... Va... nica...!!!
What... are... you... doi...?!!
A ha!
IT'S A CURSE BOMB. ♡
I'M DETONATING THE DEVIL POWER I GAVE YOU DARK DISCIPLES.
Huh?! Wait...!!
Lady... Vanica...?!!

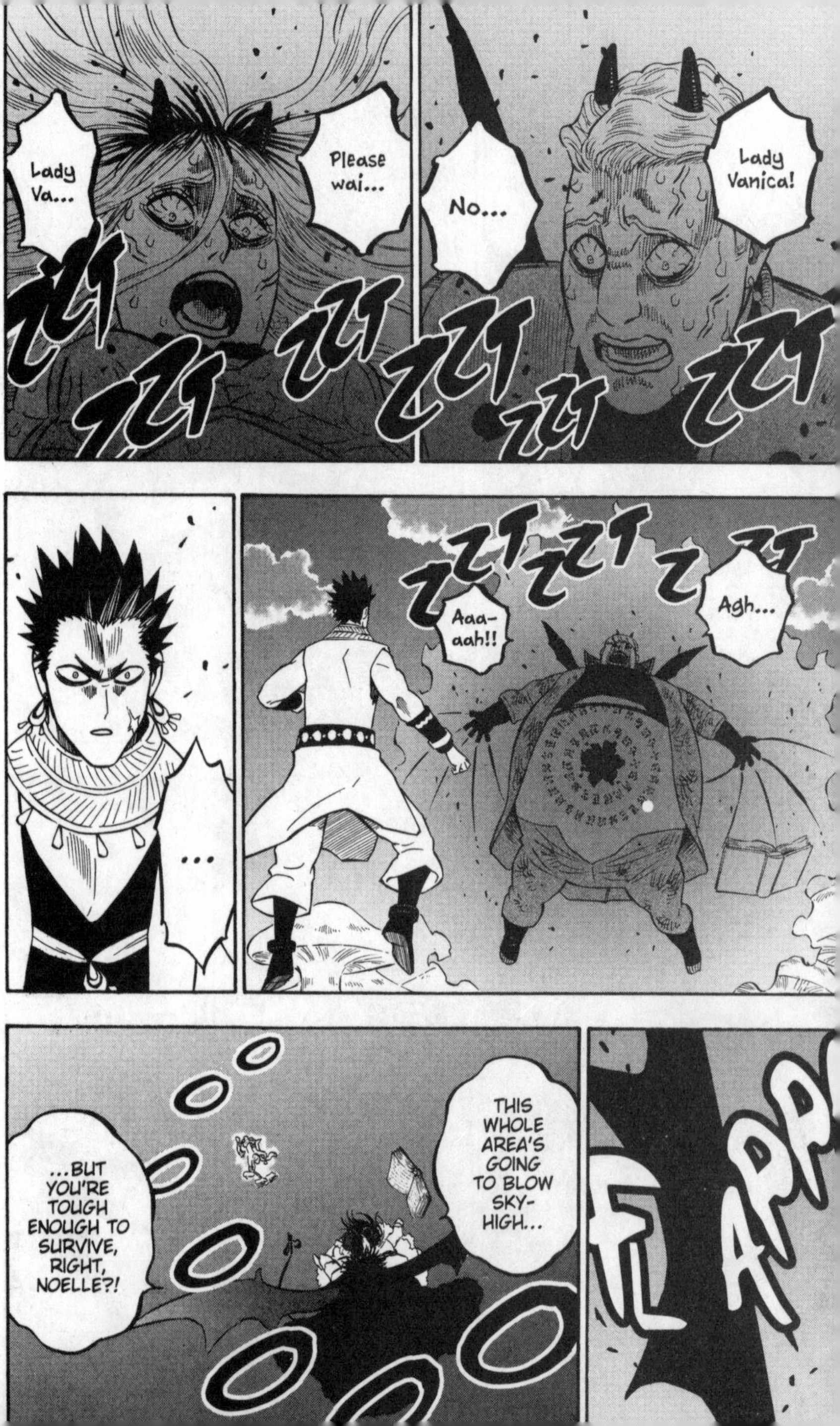

Lady Vanica!
No...
Please wai...
Lady Va...
Agh...
Aaa-aah!!
...
FLAPP
THIS WHOLE AREA'S GOING TO BLOW SKY-HIGH...
...BUT YOU'RE TOUGH ENOUGH TO SURVIVE, RIGHT, NOELLE?!

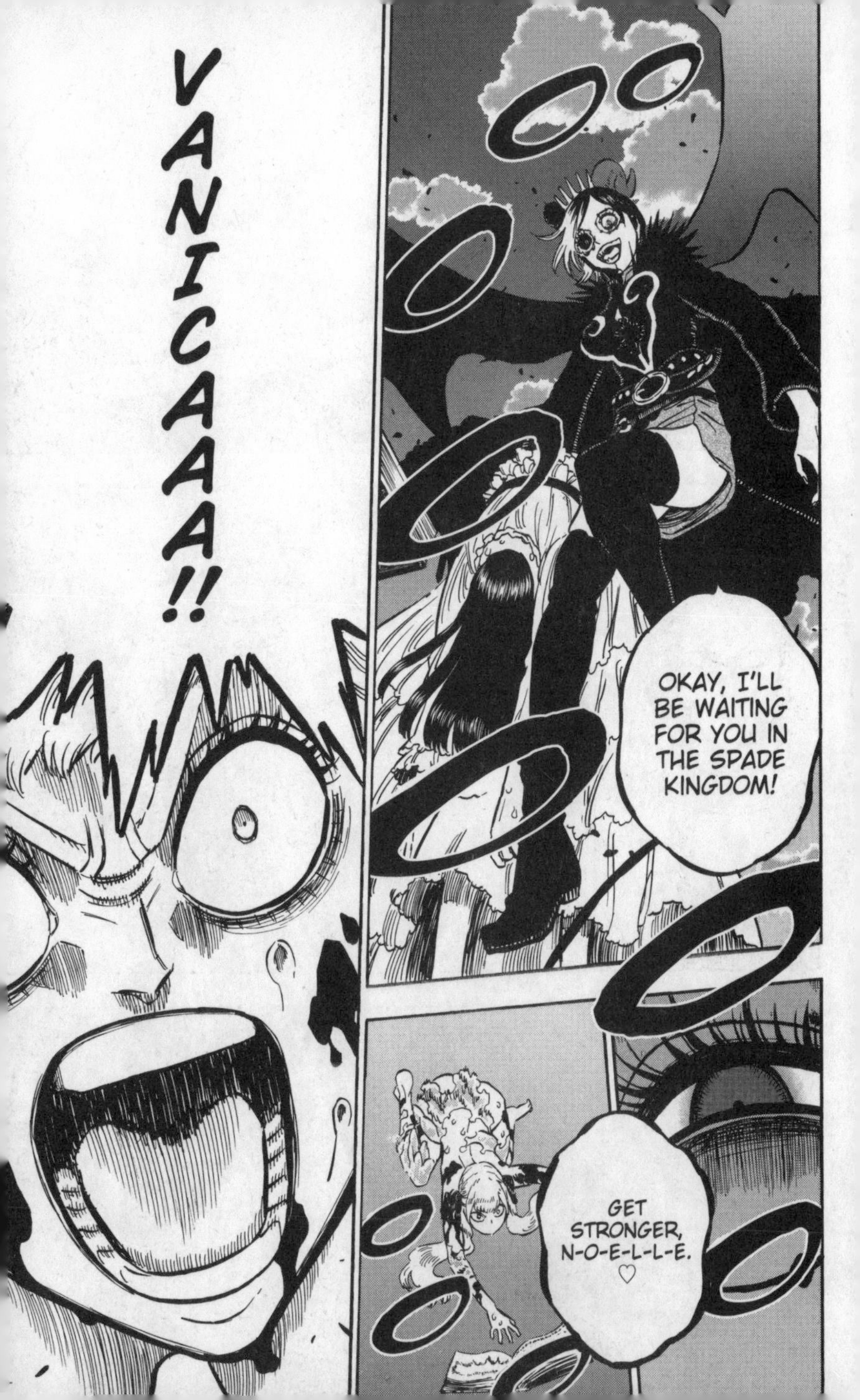
OKAY, I'LL BE WAITING FOR YOU IN THE SPADE KINGDOM!
GET STRONGER, N-O-E-L-L-E. ♡
VANICAAA!!

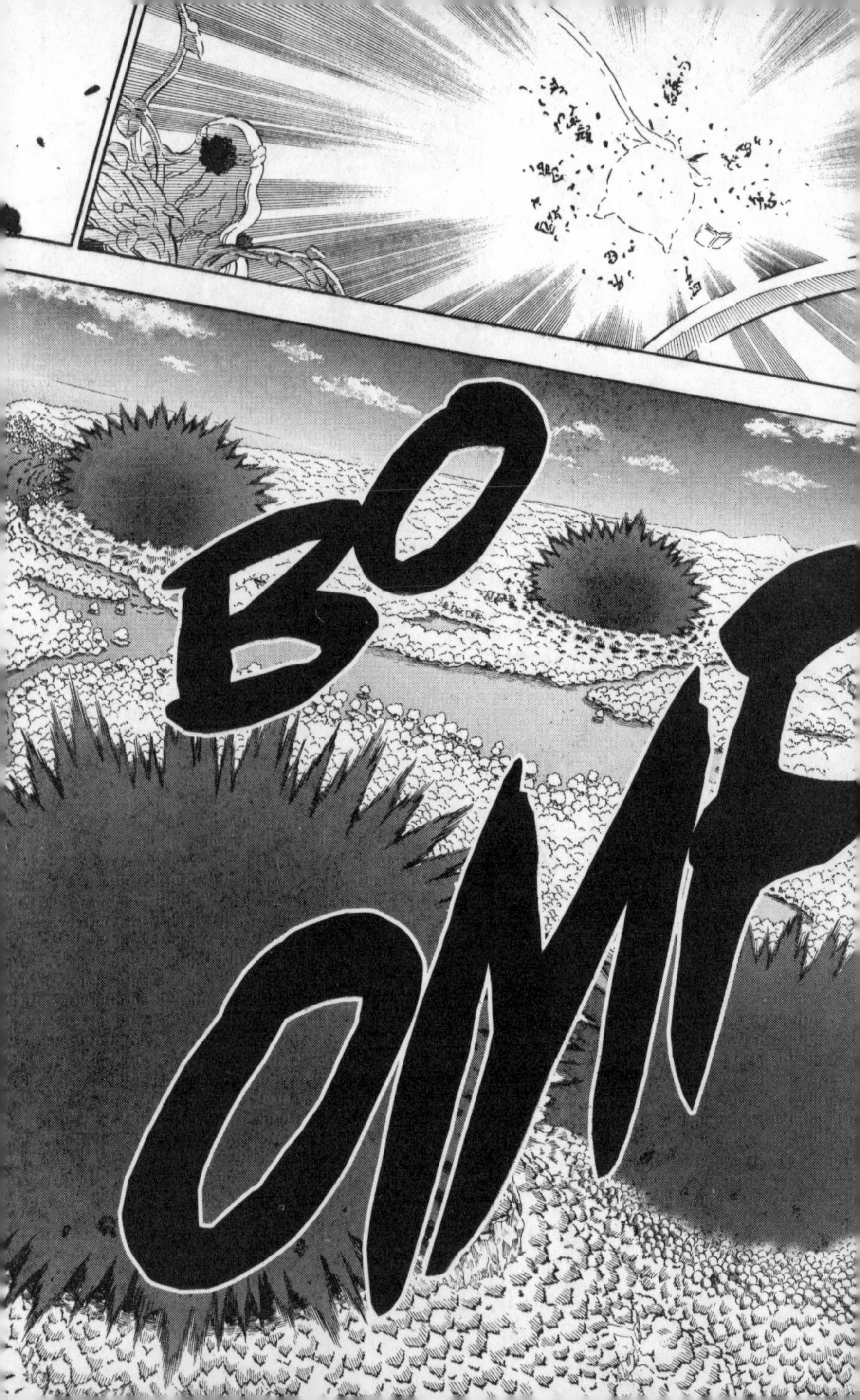
BOOM

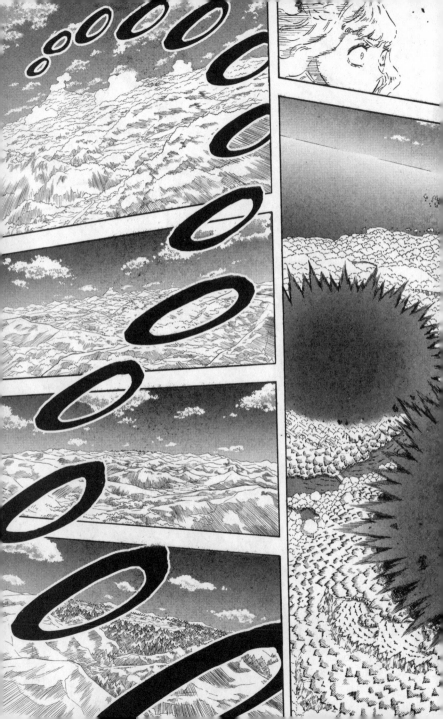

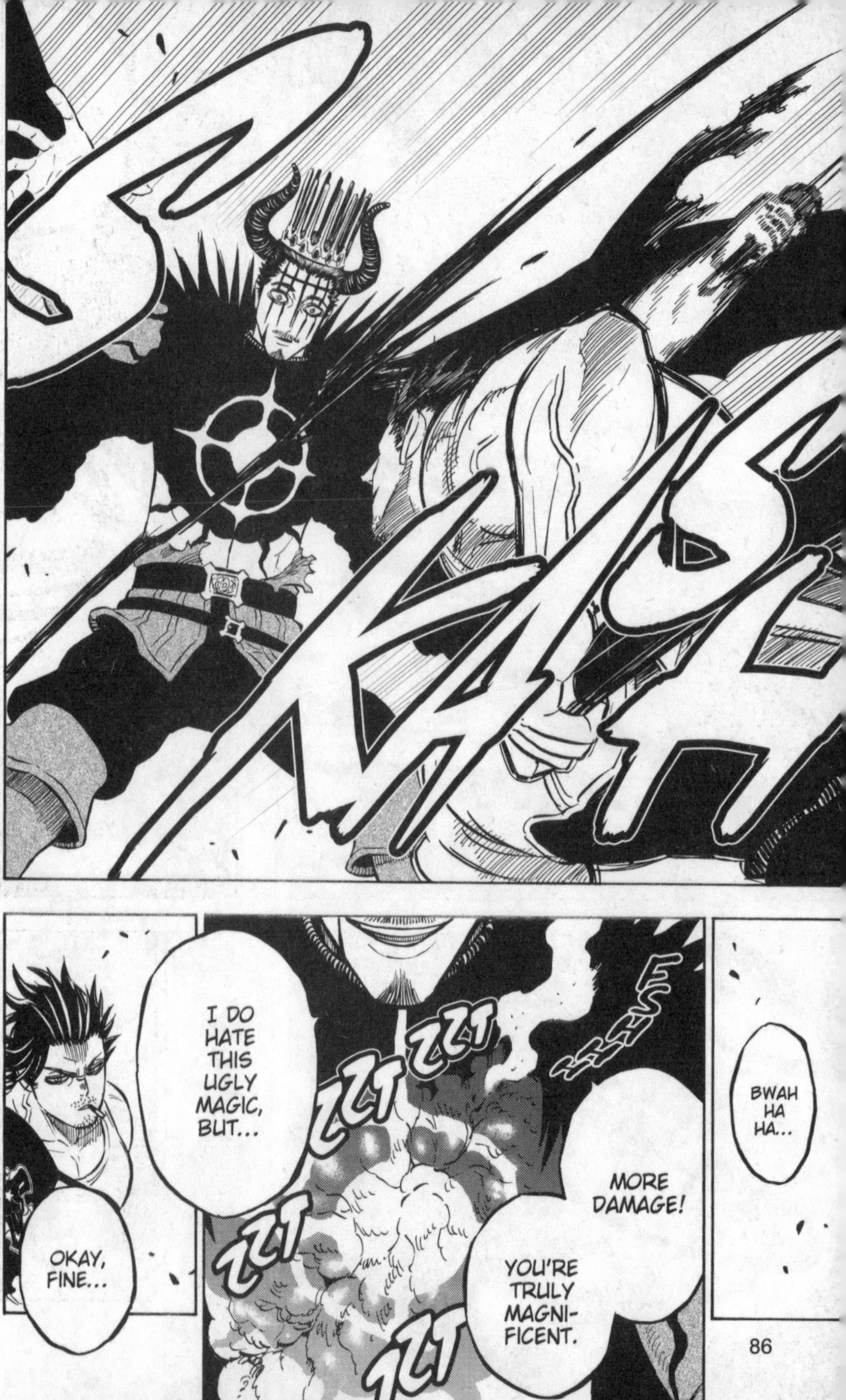
BWAH HA HA...
MORE DAMAGE!
YOU'RE TRULY MAGNIFICENT.
ZZZT
ZZZT
I DO HATE THIS UGLY MAGIC, BUT...
OKAY, FINE...

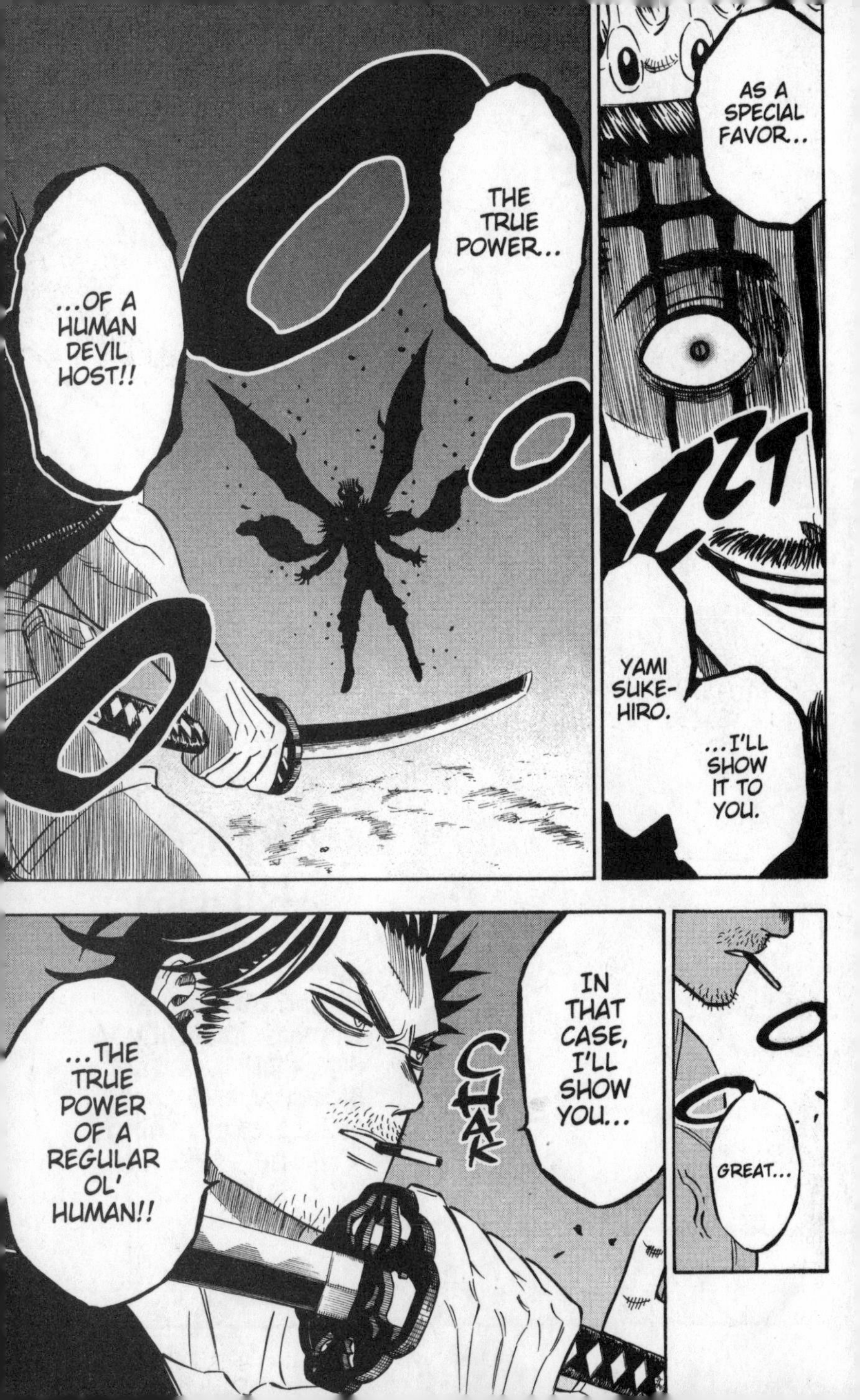
AS A SPECIAL FAVOR...
YAMI SUKE-HIRO.
...I'LL SHOW IT TO YOU.
THE TRUE POWER...
...OF A HUMAN DEVIL HOST!!
GREAT...
IN THAT CASE, I'LL SHOW YOU...
CHAK
...THE TRUE POWER OF A REGULAR OL' HUMAN!!

Hischer Ongg

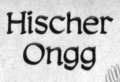

Age: 24
Height: 191 cm
Birthday: April 26
Sign: Taurus
Blood Type: O
Likes: He's gotten
      really into
      cooking lately.

Robero Ringert

Age: 24
Height: 210 cm
Birthday: Janurary 18
Sign: Capricorn
Blood Type: O
Likes: Licking things
      he's taken a
      shine to.

C h a r a c t e r   P r o f i l e

✤

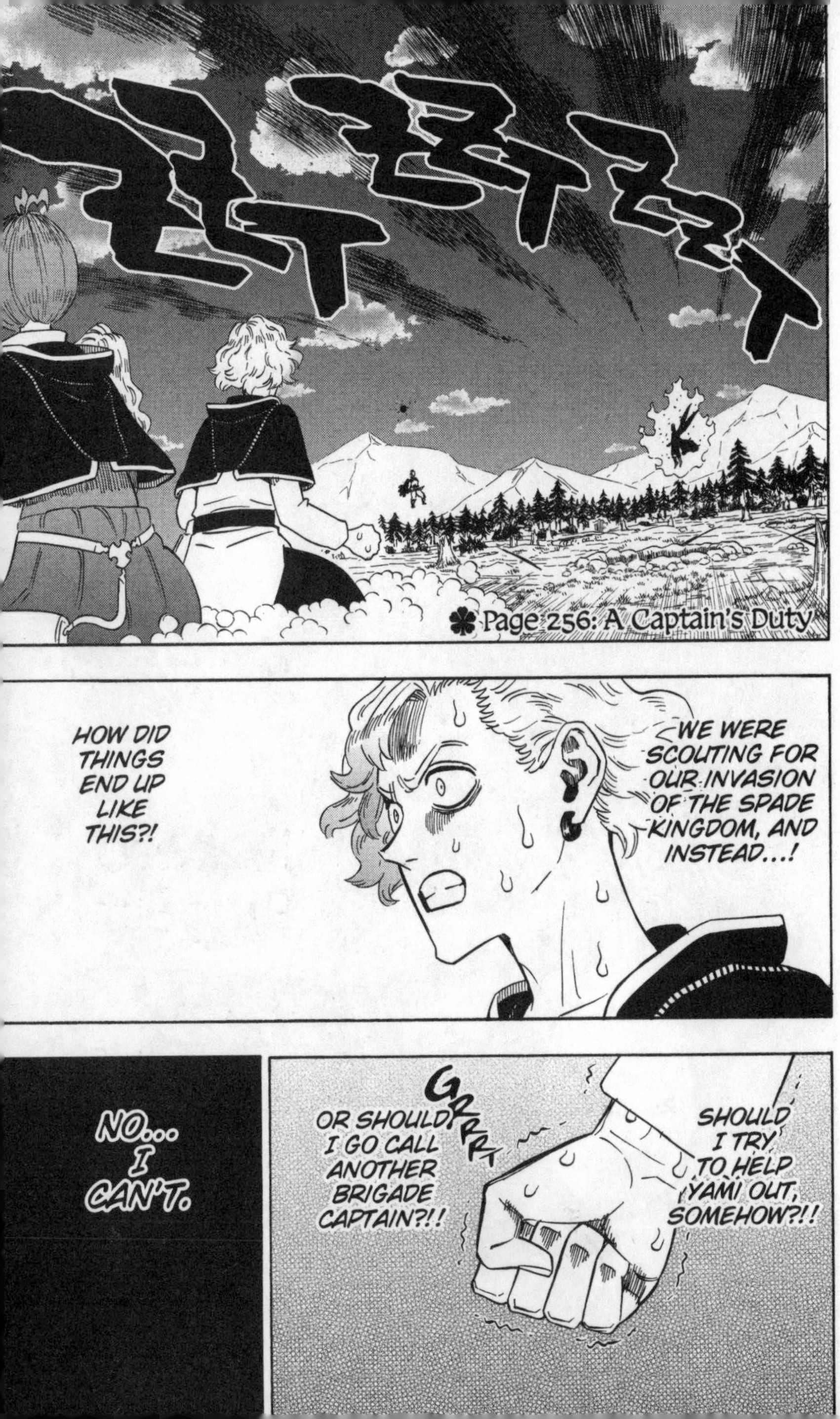
Page 256: A Captain's Duty
WE WERE SCOUTING FOR OUR INVASION OF THE SPADE KINGDOM, AND INSTEAD...!
HOW DID THINGS END UP LIKE THIS?!
SHOULD I TRY TO HELP YAMI OUT, SOMEHOW?!!
GRRRT
OR SHOULD I GO CALL ANOTHER BRIGADE CAPTAIN?!!
NO... I CAN'T.

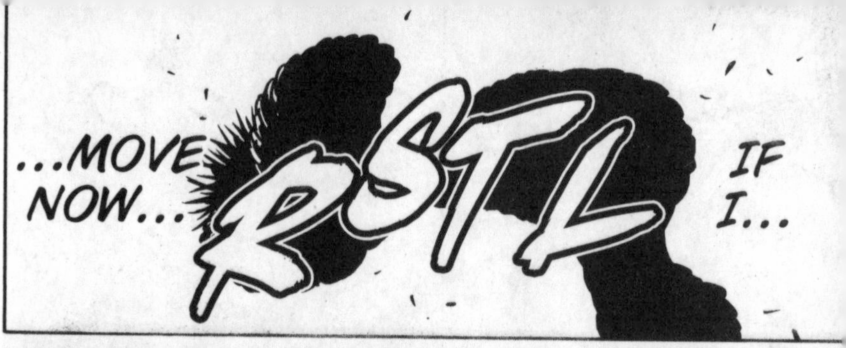
IF I...
RSTL
...MOVE NOW...

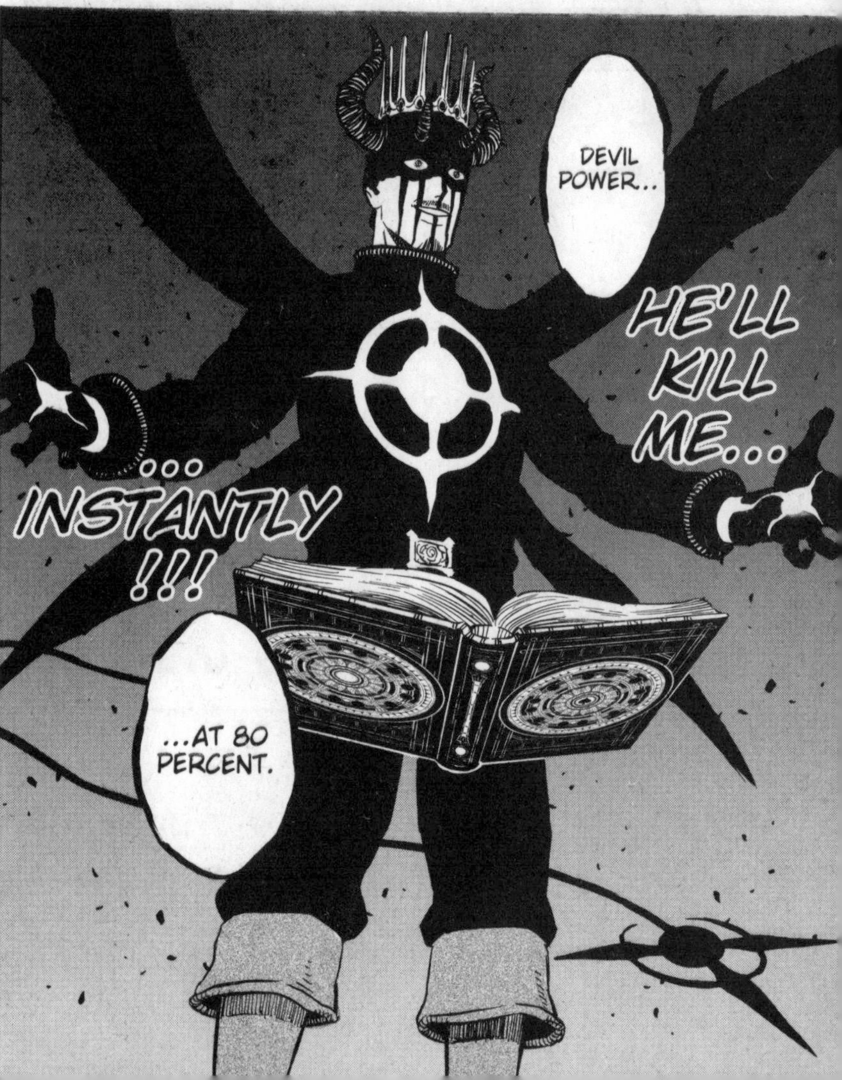
DEVIL POWER..
HE'LL KILL ME...
...INSTANTLY !!!
...AT 80 PERCENT.

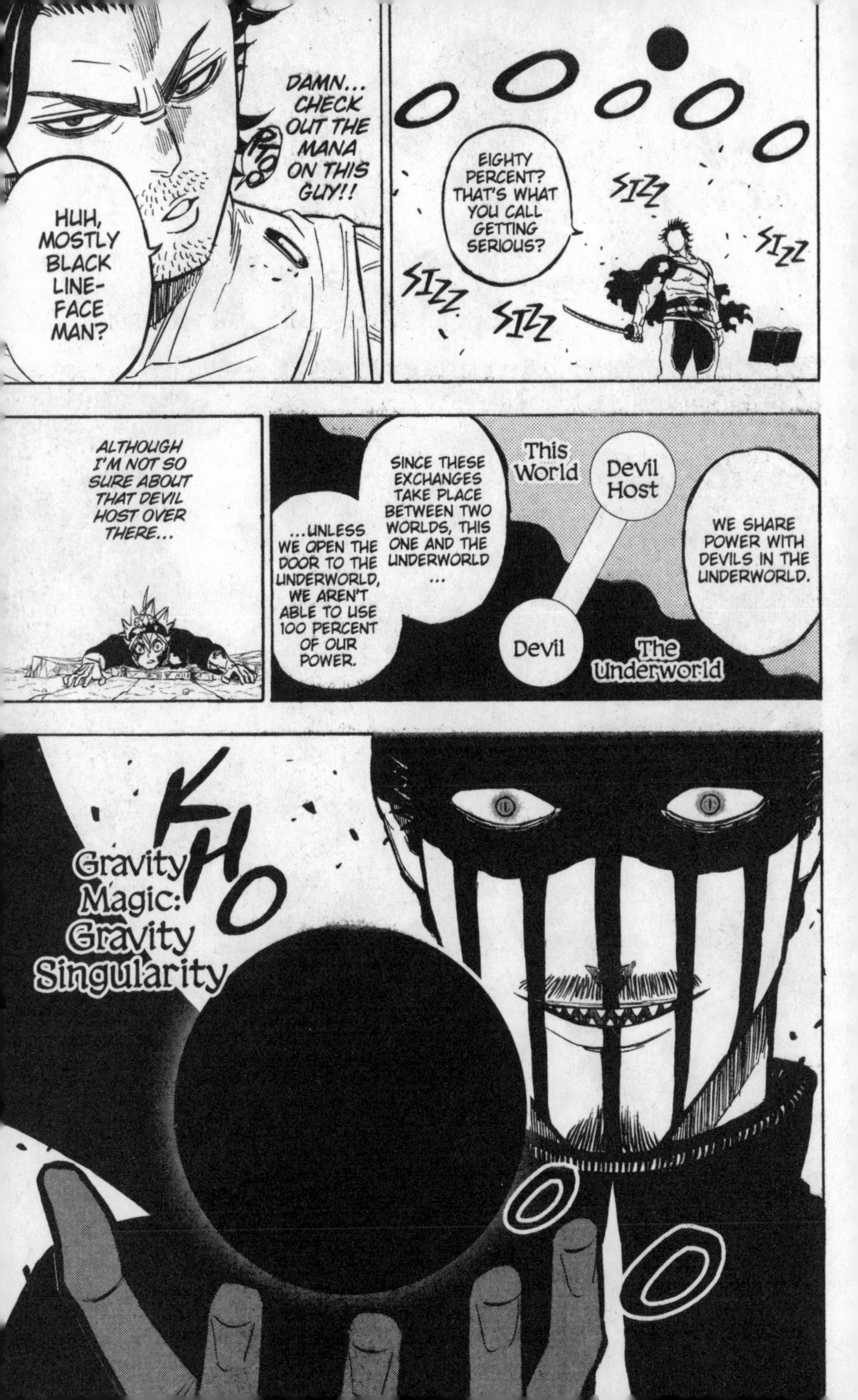
EIGHTY PERCENT? THAT'S WHAT YOU CALL GETTING SERIOUS?
SIZZ
SIZZ
SIZZ
SIZZ
DAMN... CHECK OUT THE MANA ON THIS GUY!!
HUH, MOSTLY BLACK LINE-FACE MAN?
WE SHARE POWER WITH DEVILS IN THE UNDERWORLD.
This World
Devil Host
Devil
The Underworld
SINCE THESE EXCHANGES TAKE PLACE BETWEEN TWO WORLDS, THIS ONE AND THE UNDERWORLD ...
...UNLESS WE OPEN THE DOOR TO THE UNDERWORLD, WE AREN'T ABLE TO USE 100 PERCENT OF OUR POWER.
ALTHOUGH I'M NOT SO SURE ABOUT THAT DEVIL HOST OVER THERE...
KHO
Gravity Magic: Gravity Singularity

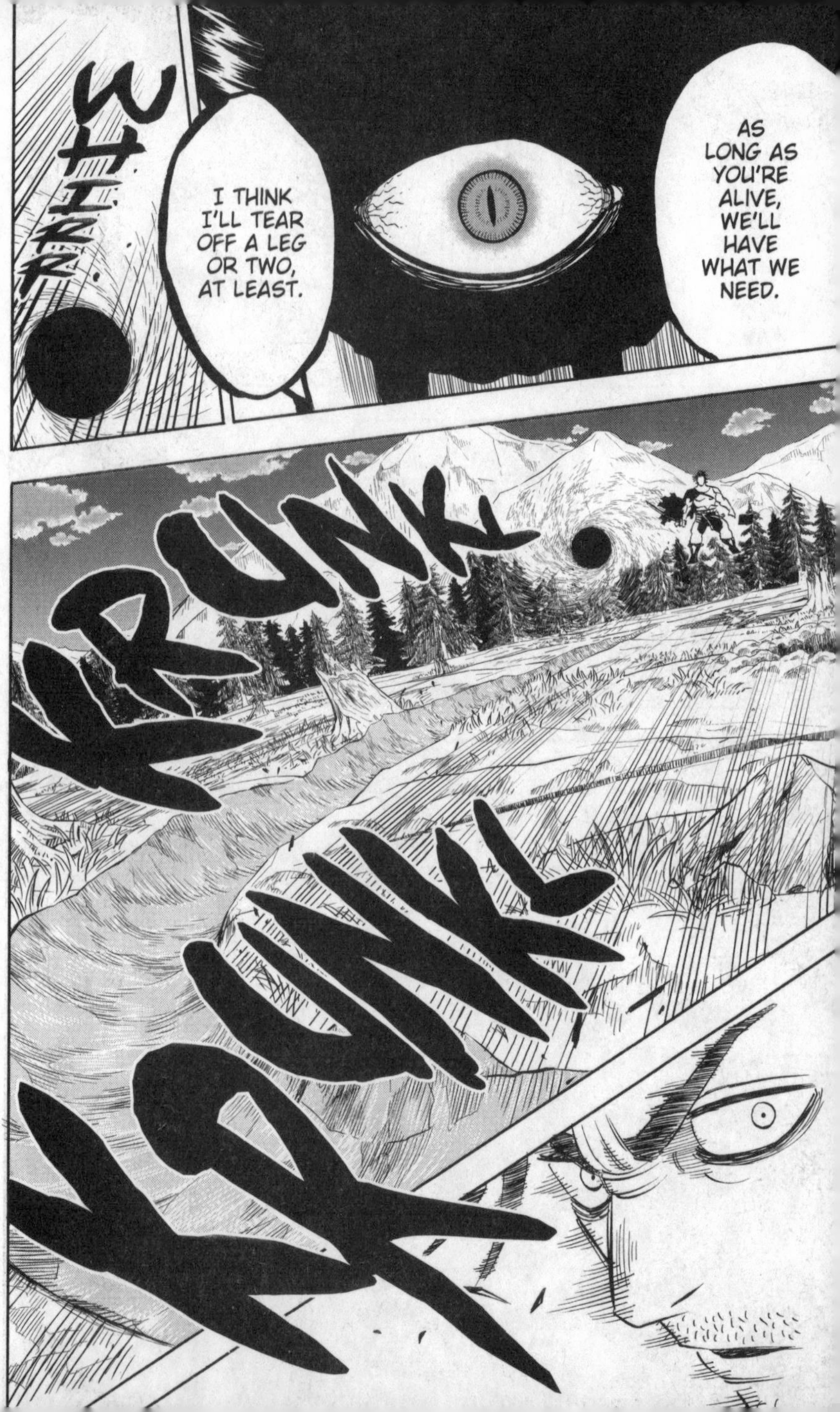
AS LONG AS YOU'RE ALIVE, WE'LL HAVE WHAT WE NEED.
I THINK I'LL TEAR OFF A LEG OR TWO, AT LEAST.
WHIRR

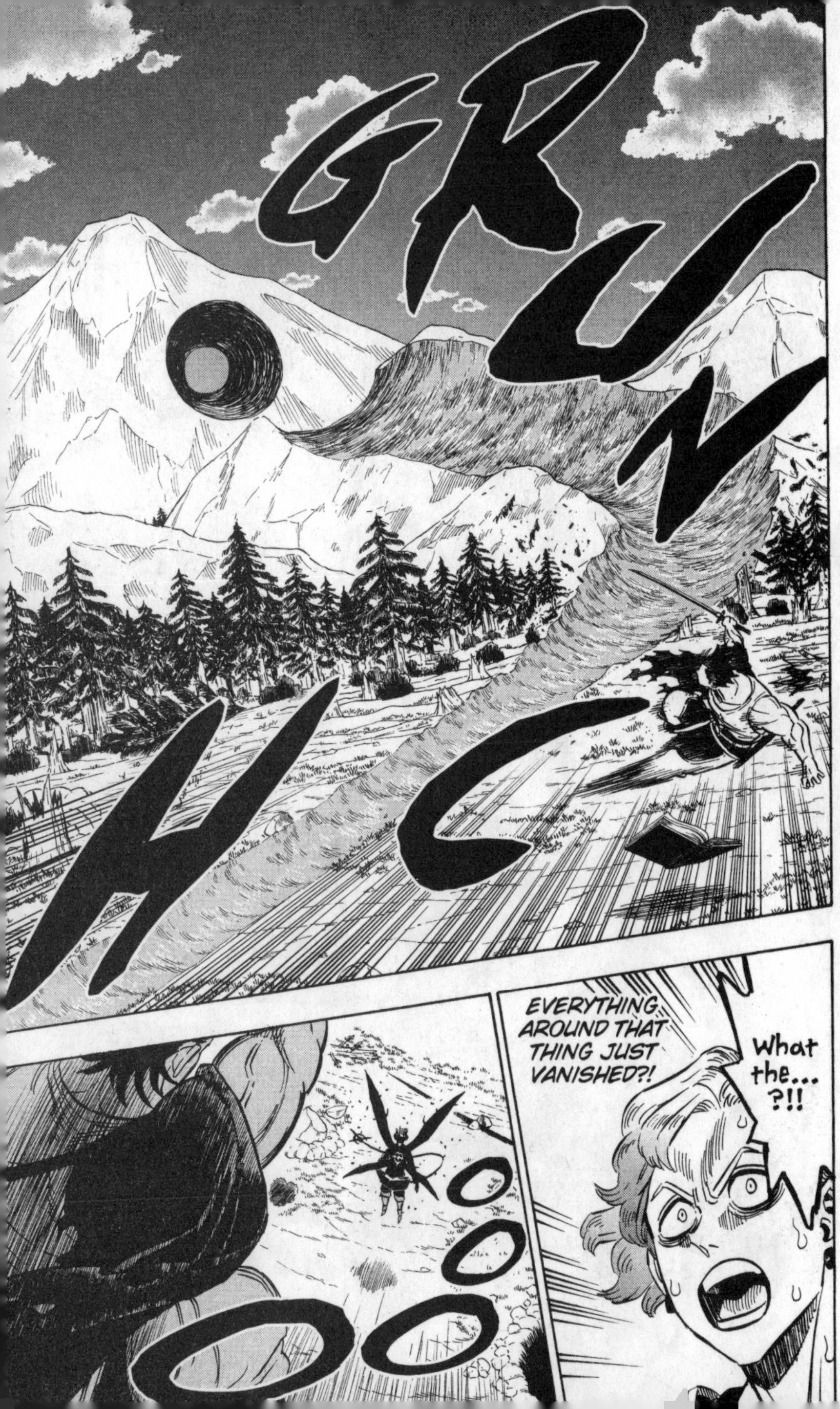
GRUNCH
What the... ?!!
EVERYTHING AROUND THAT THING JUST VANISHED?!
OOOOO

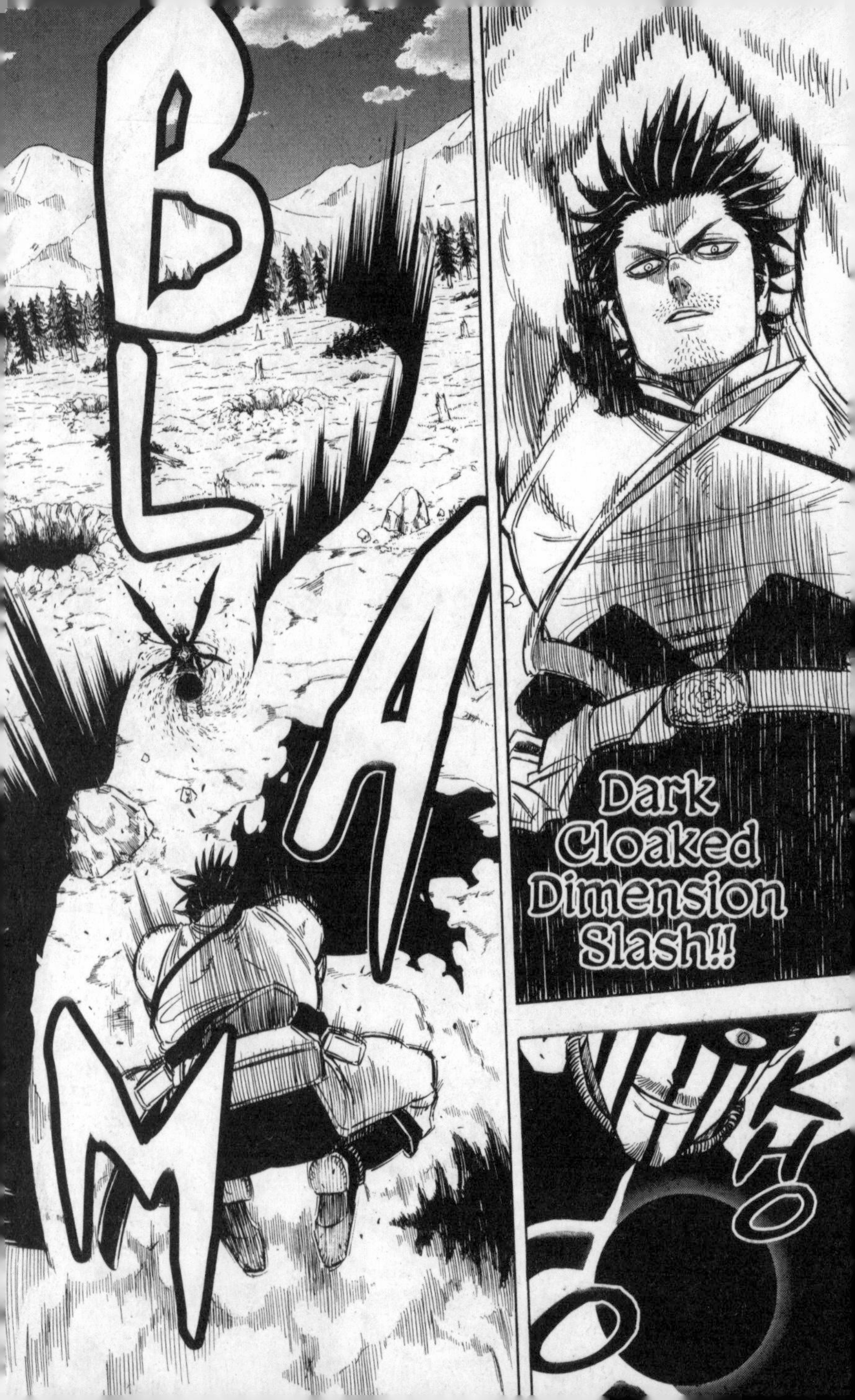
Dark Cloaked Dimension Slash!!
BLAM

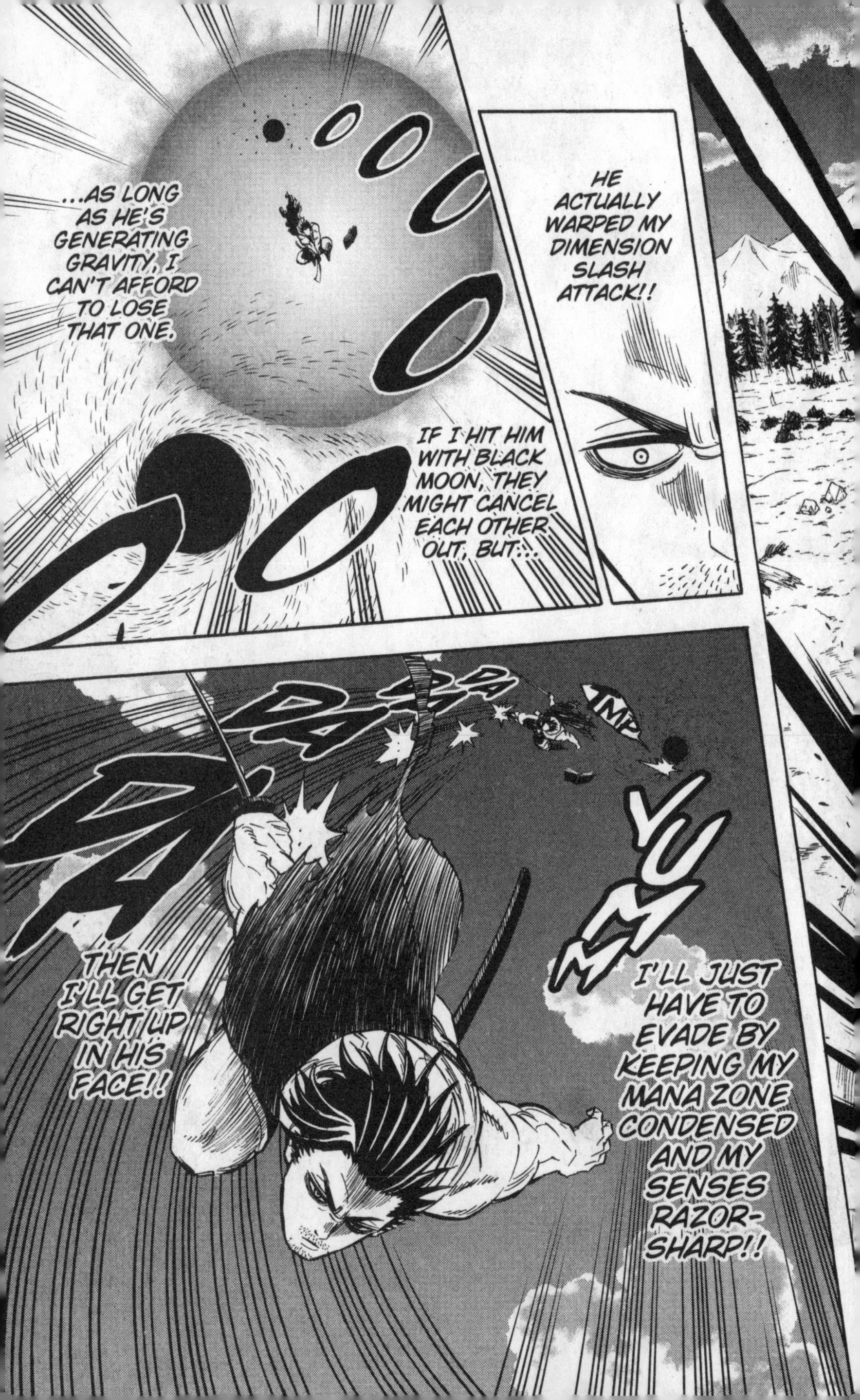
HE ACTUALLY WARPED MY DIMENSION SLASH ATTACK!!
...AS LONG AS HE'S GENERATING GRAVITY, I CAN'T AFFORD TO LOSE THAT ONE.
IF I HIT HIM WITH BLACK MOON, THEY MIGHT CANCEL EACH OTHER OUT, BUT...
TMP
DA DA DA DA
YUMM
I'LL JUST HAVE TO EVADE BY KEEPING MY MANA ZONE CONDENSED AND MY SENSES RAZOR-SHARP!!
THEN I'LL GET RIGHT UP IN HIS FACE!!

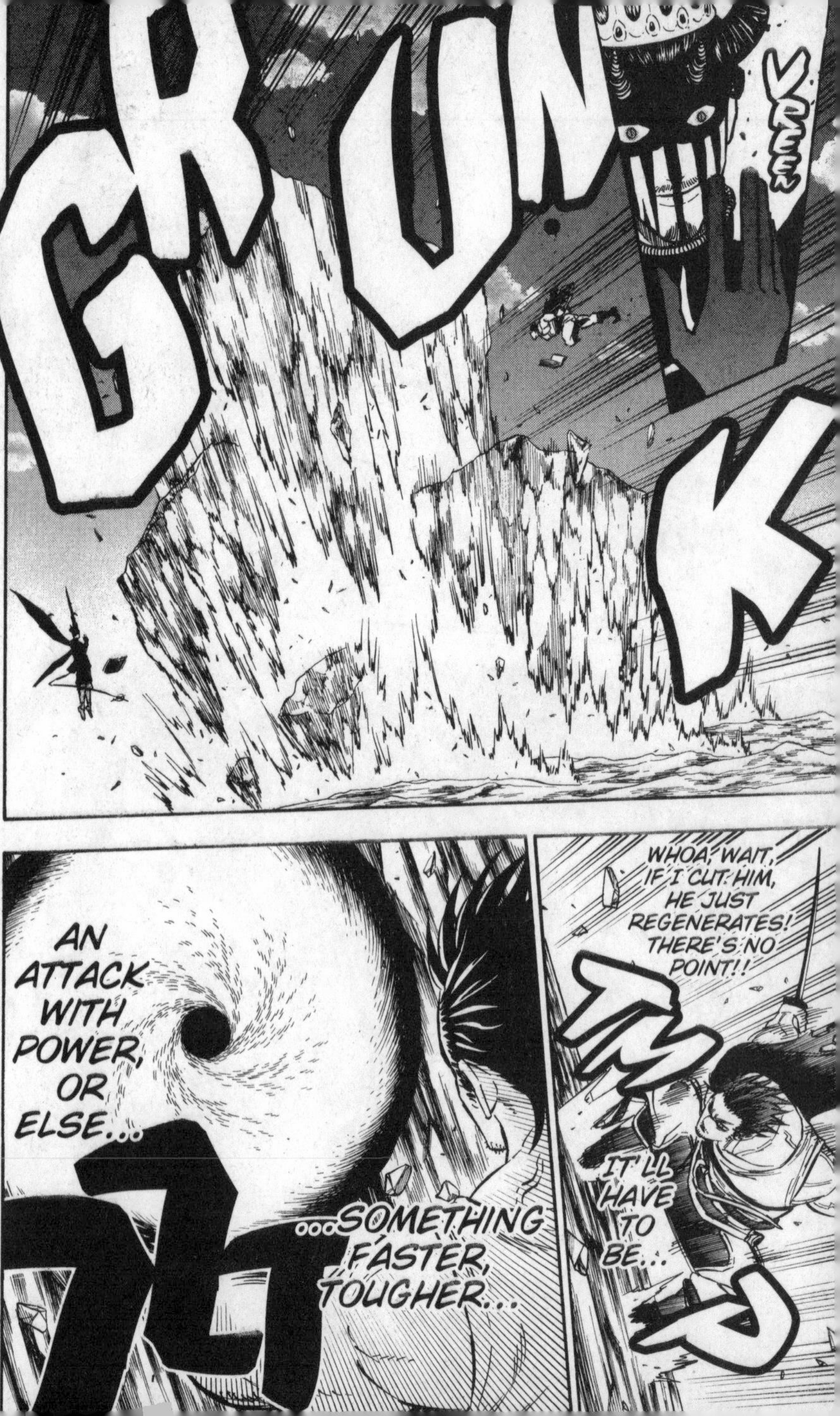
CRUNK
VREEN
WHOA, WAIT, IF I CUT HIM, HE JUST REGENERATES! THERE'S NO POINT!!
IT'LL HAVE TO BE...
AN ATTACK WITH POWER, OR ELSE...
...SOMETHING FASTER, TOUGHER...

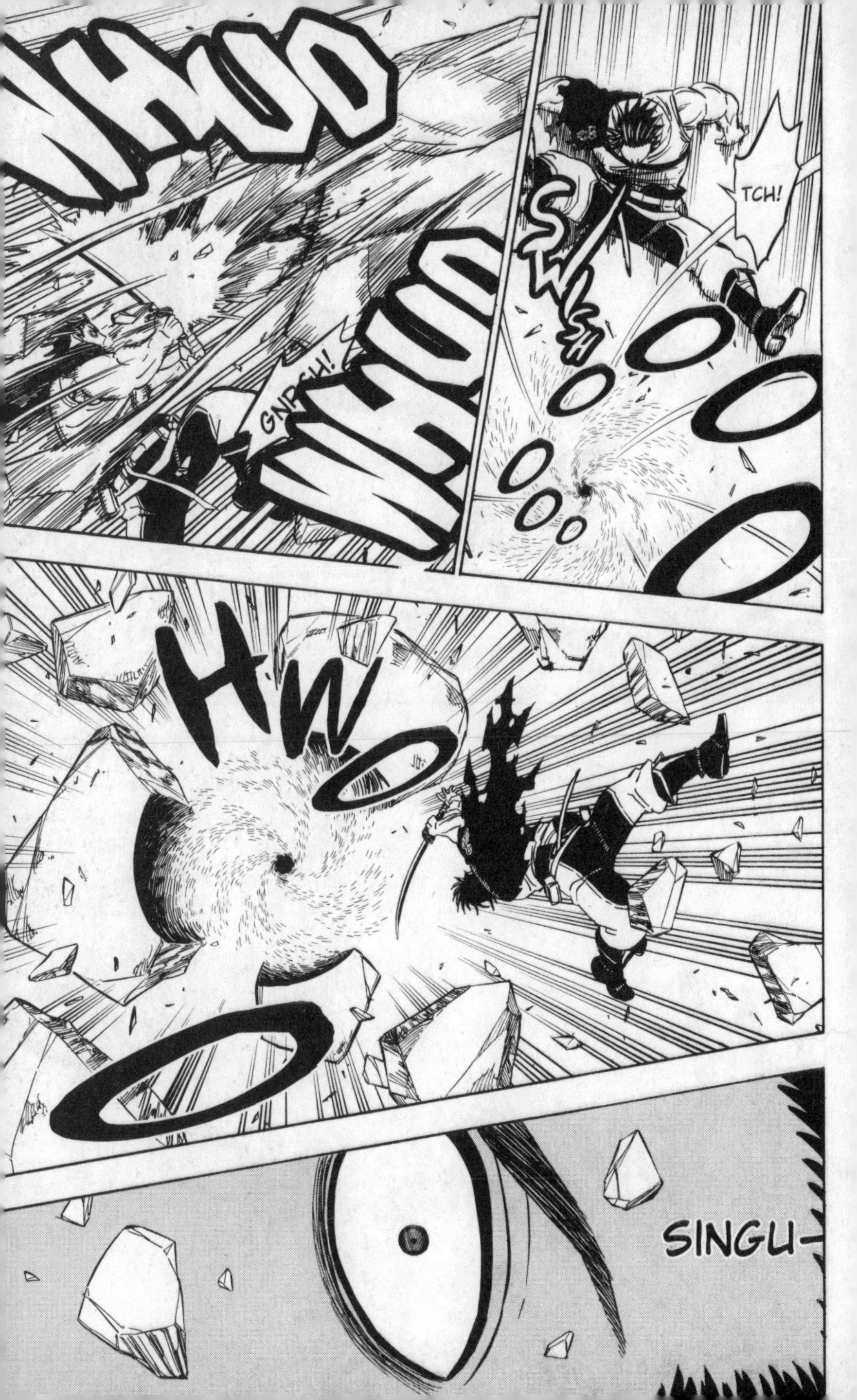
TCH!
SWISH
SINGU-

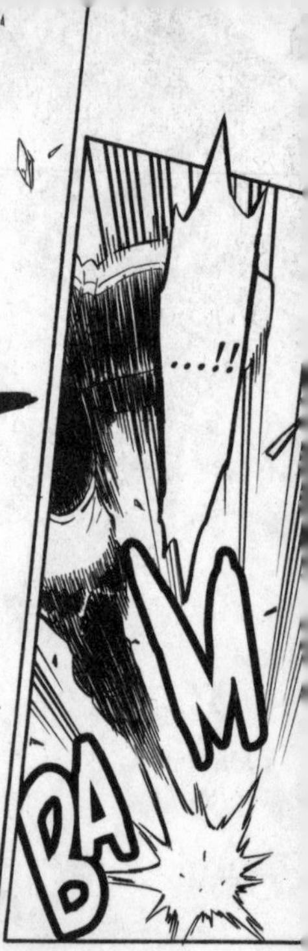
...!!
BAM

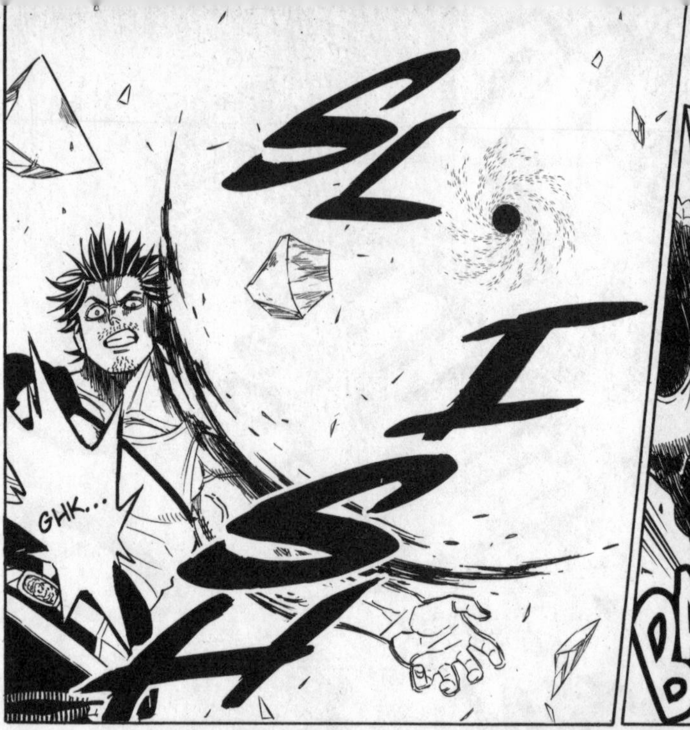
SLISH
GHK...

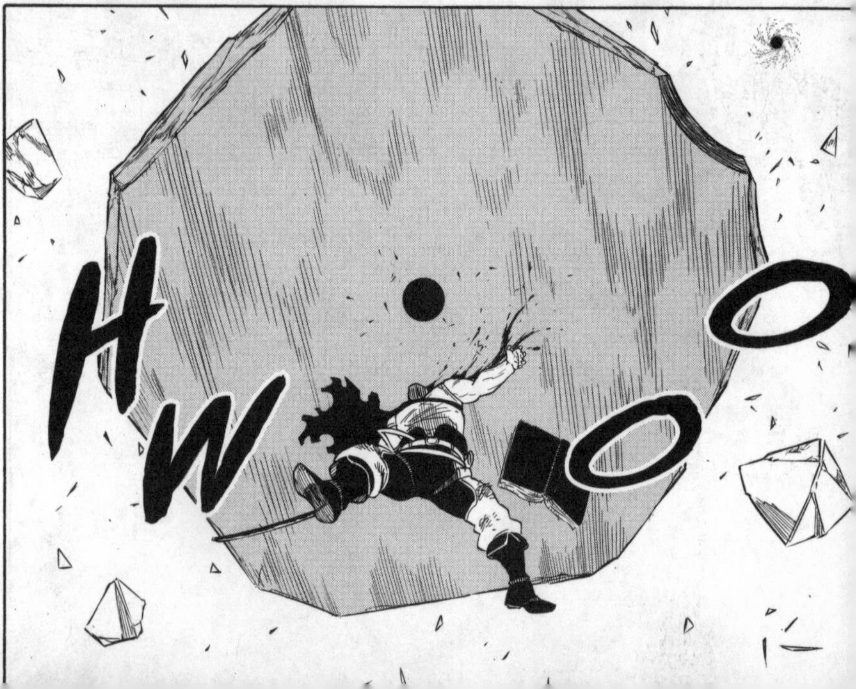
HWOOO

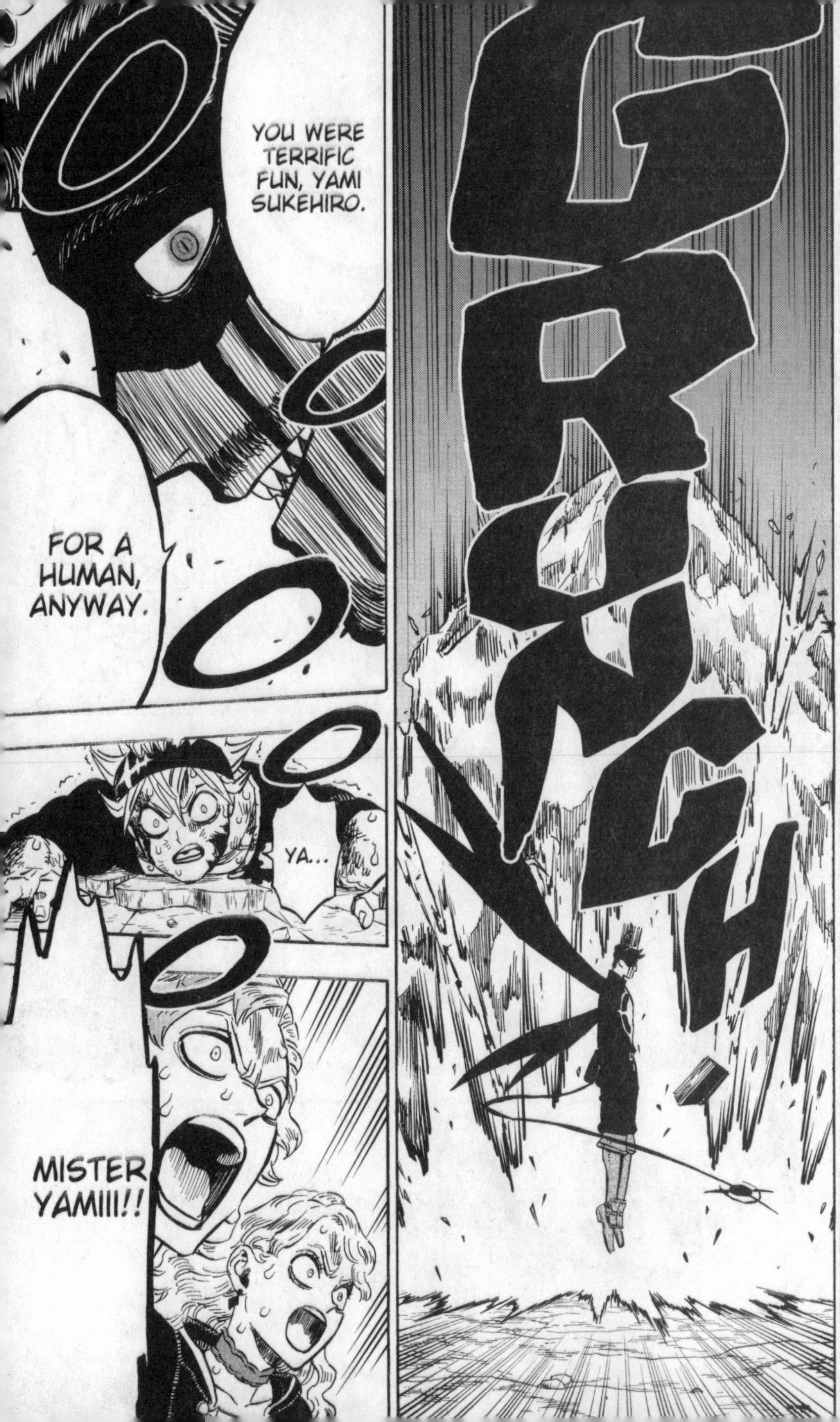
YOU WERE TERRIFIC FUN, YAMI SUKEHIRO.
FOR A HUMAN, ANYWAY.
YA...
MISTER YAMIIII!!

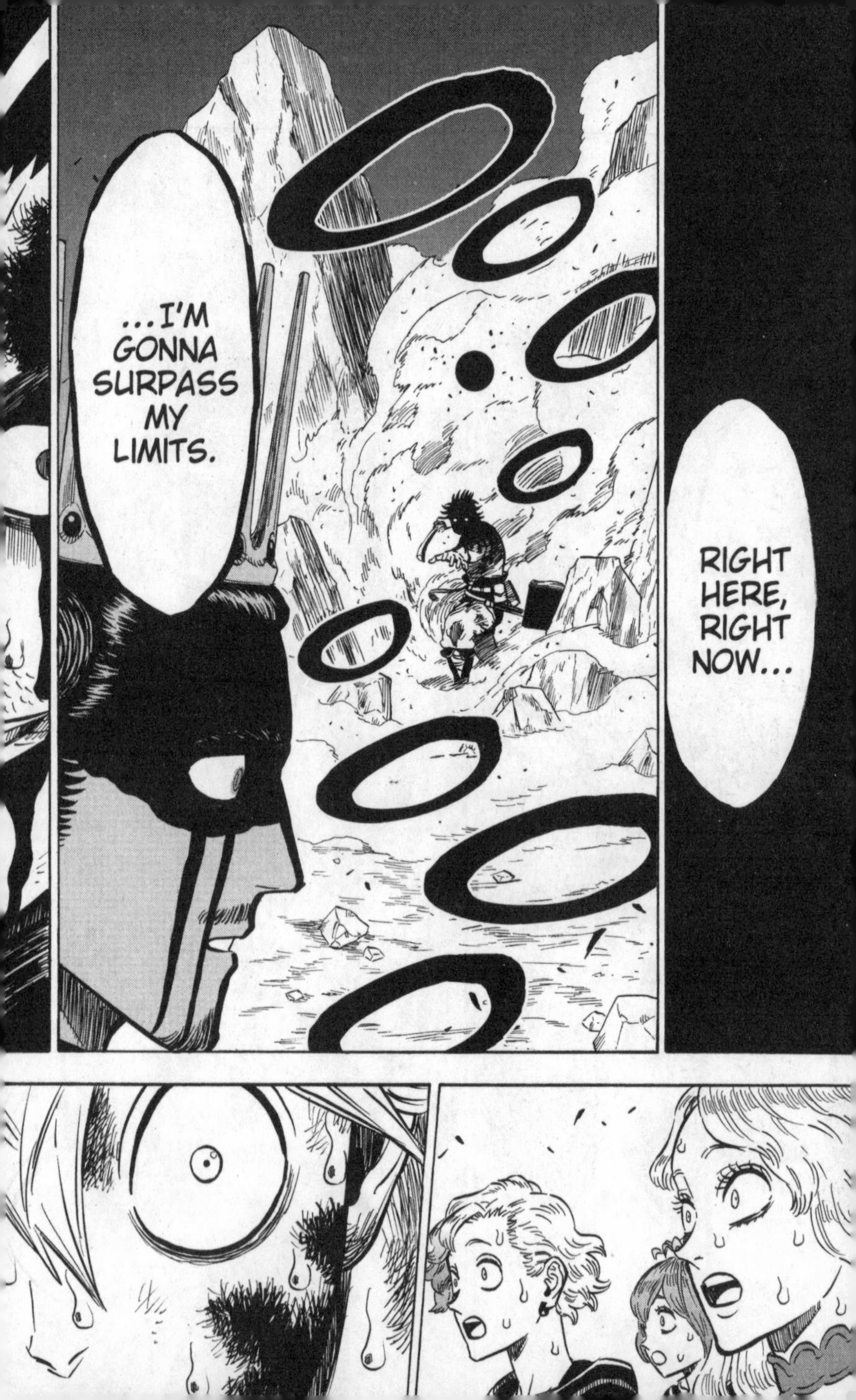
RIGHT HERE, RIGHT NOW...
...I'M GONNA SURPASS MY LIMITS.

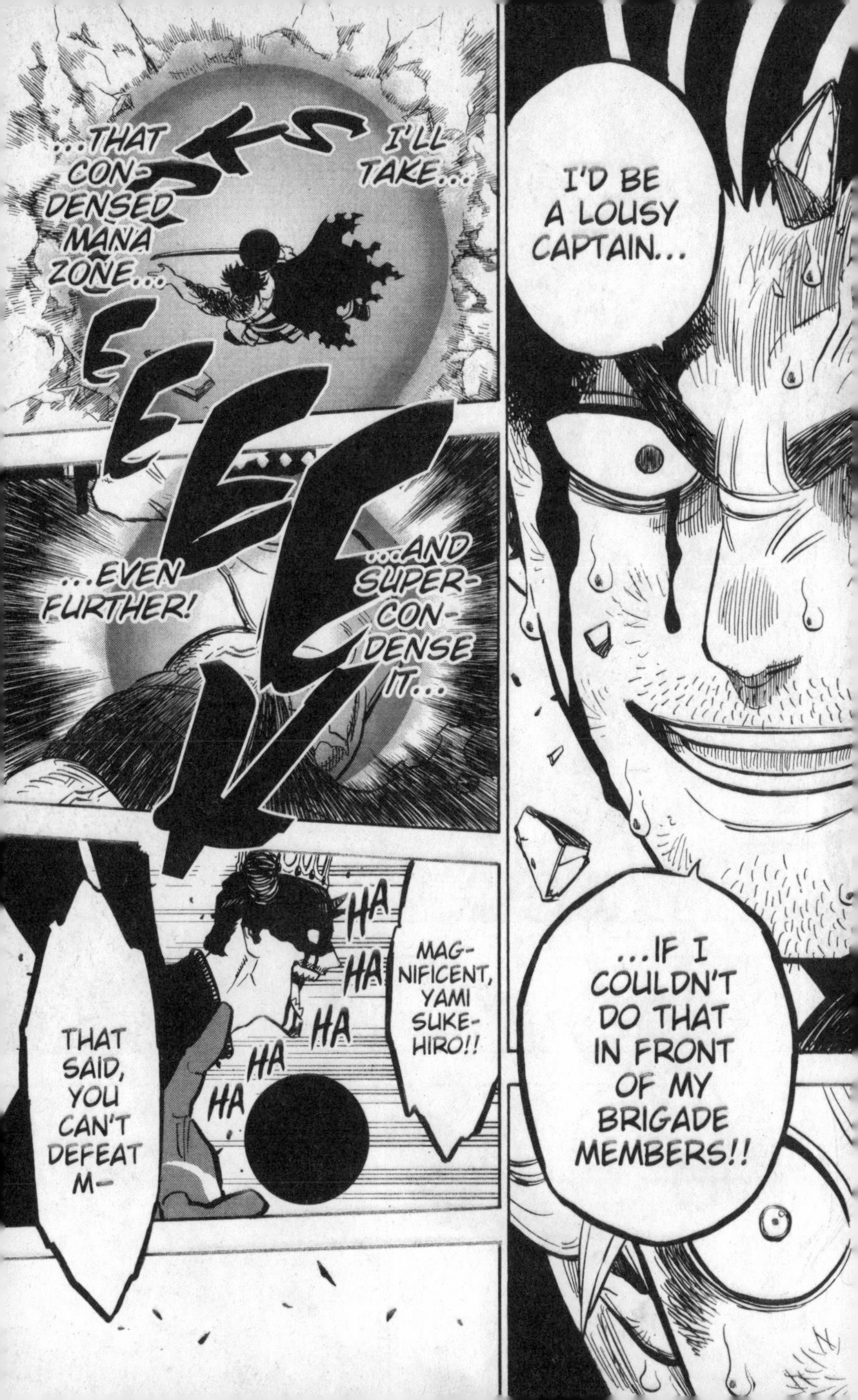
I'D BE A LOUSY CAPTAIN...
...IF I COULDN'T DO THAT IN FRONT OF MY BRIGADE MEMBERS!!
I'LL TAKE...
...THAT CONDENSED MANA ZONE...
...AND SUPER-CONDENSE IT...
...EVEN FURTHER!
MAGNIFICENT, YAMI SUKEHIRO!!
HA HA HA HA HA
THAT SAID, YOU CAN'T DEFEAT M—

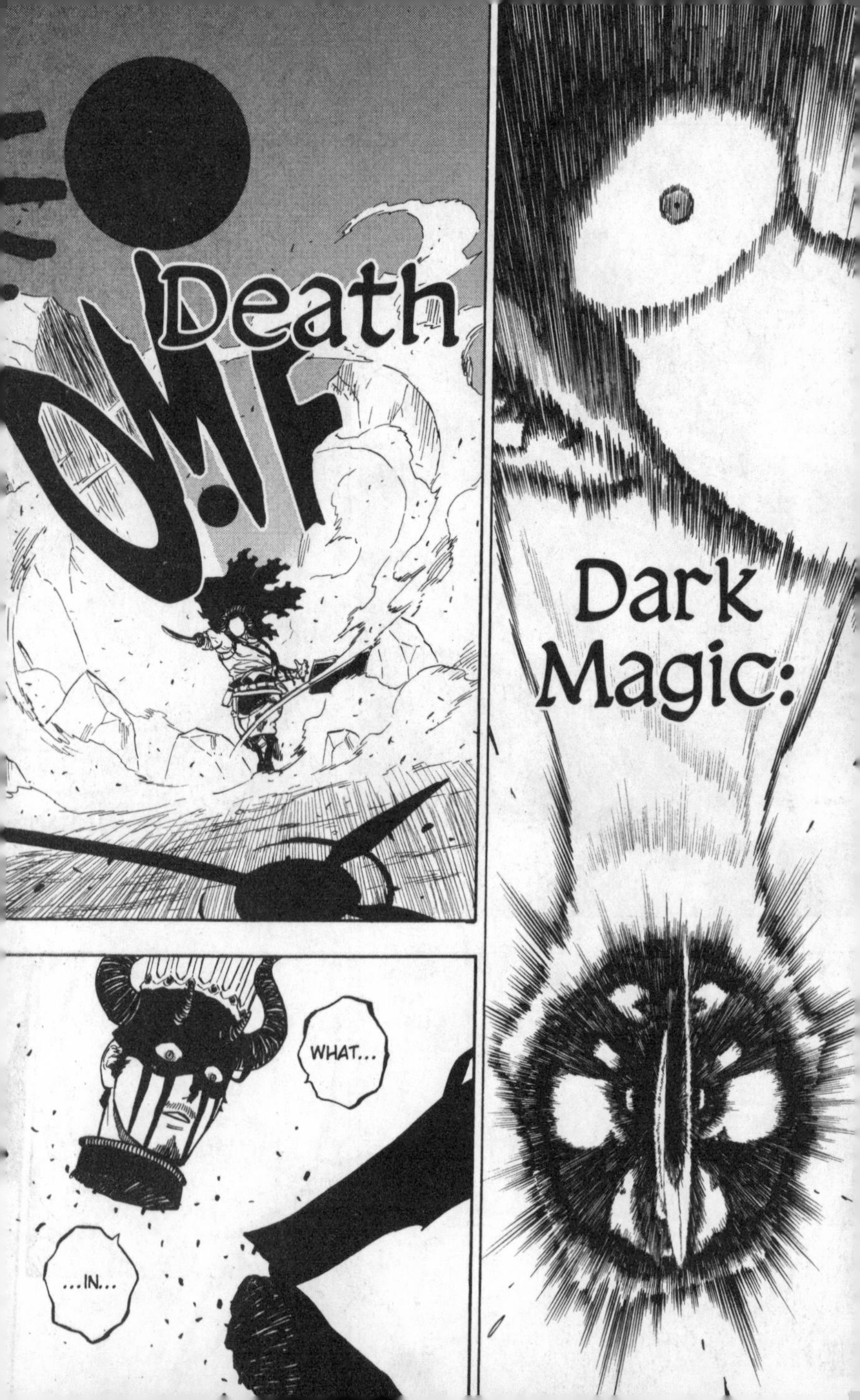
Dark Magic:
Death
WHAT...
...IN...

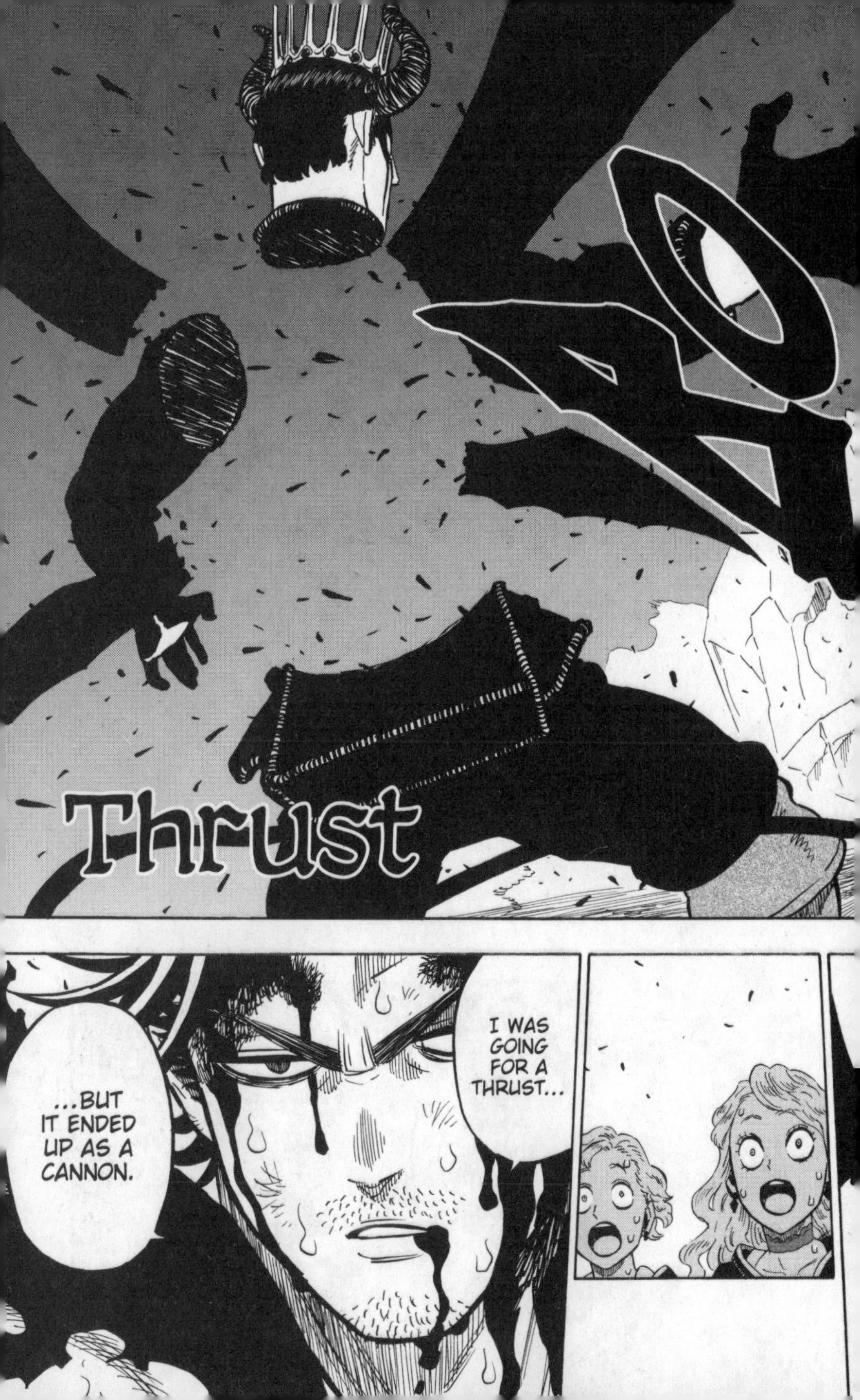
Thrust
I WAS GOING FOR A THRUST...
...BUT IT ENDED UP AS A CANNON.

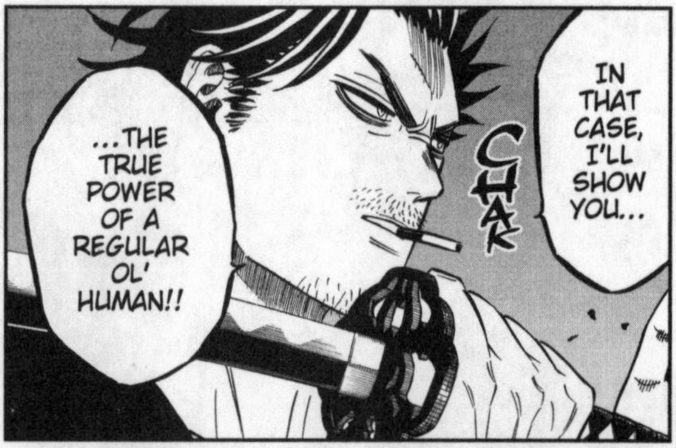
IN THAT CASE, I'LL SHOW YOU...
CHAK
...THE TRUE POWER OF A REGULAR OL' HUMAN!!

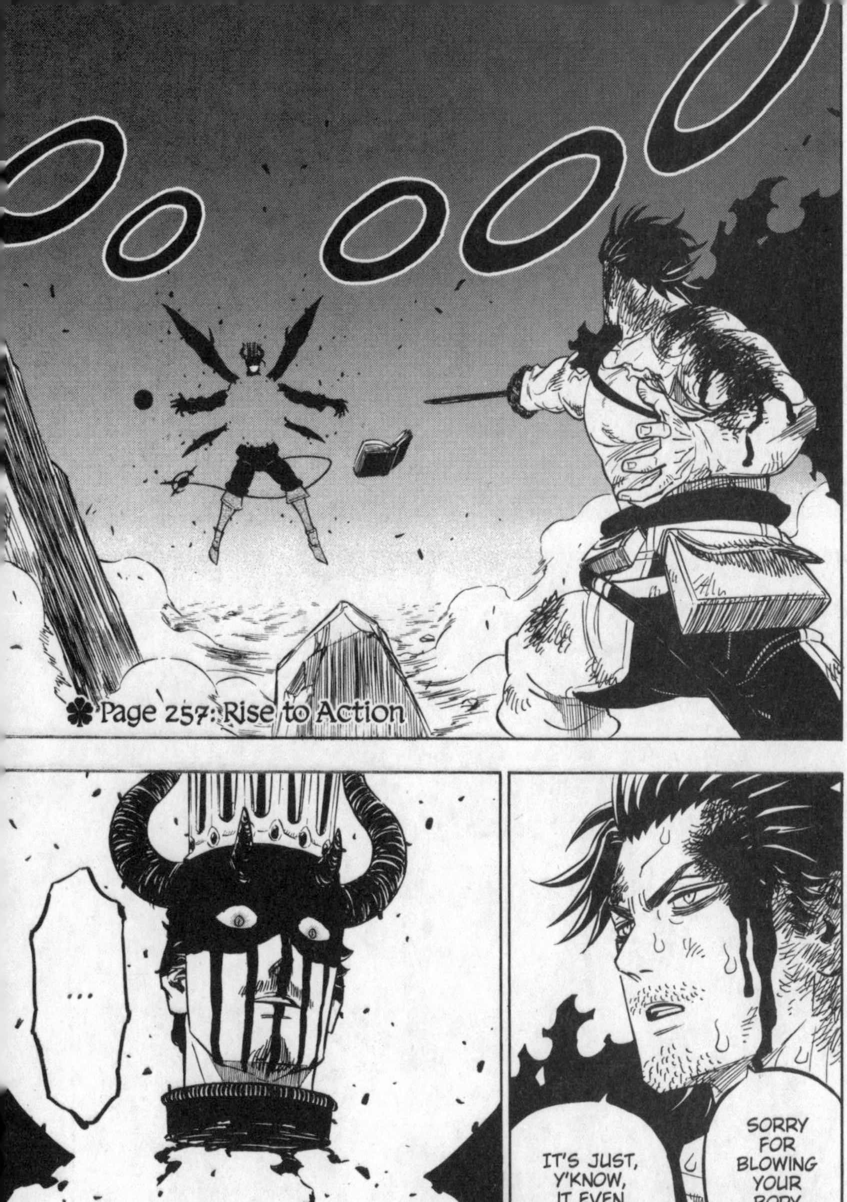
Page 257: Rise to Action
SORRY FOR BLOWING YOUR BODY AWAY LIKE THAT.
IT'S JUST, Y'KNOW, IT EVEN HAD THAT TARGET PATTERN ON IT AND ALL.
...

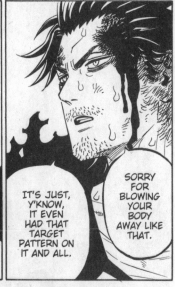

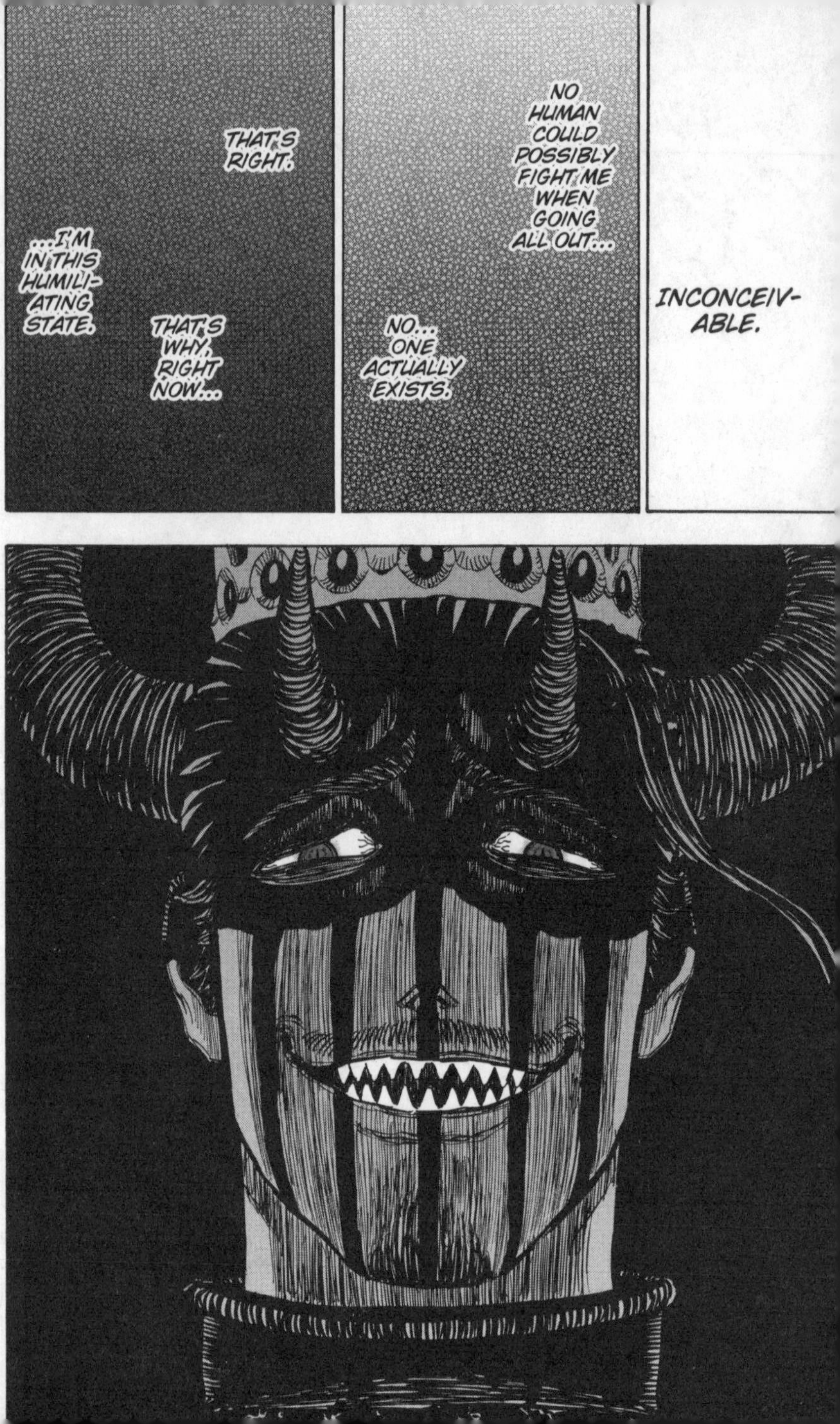
INCONCEIV-ABLE.
NO HUMAN COULD POSSIBLY FIGHT ME WHEN GOING ALL OUT...
NO... ONE ACTUALLY EXISTS.
THAT'S RIGHT.
THAT'S WHY, RIGHT NOW...
...I'M IN THIS HUMILI-ATING STATE.

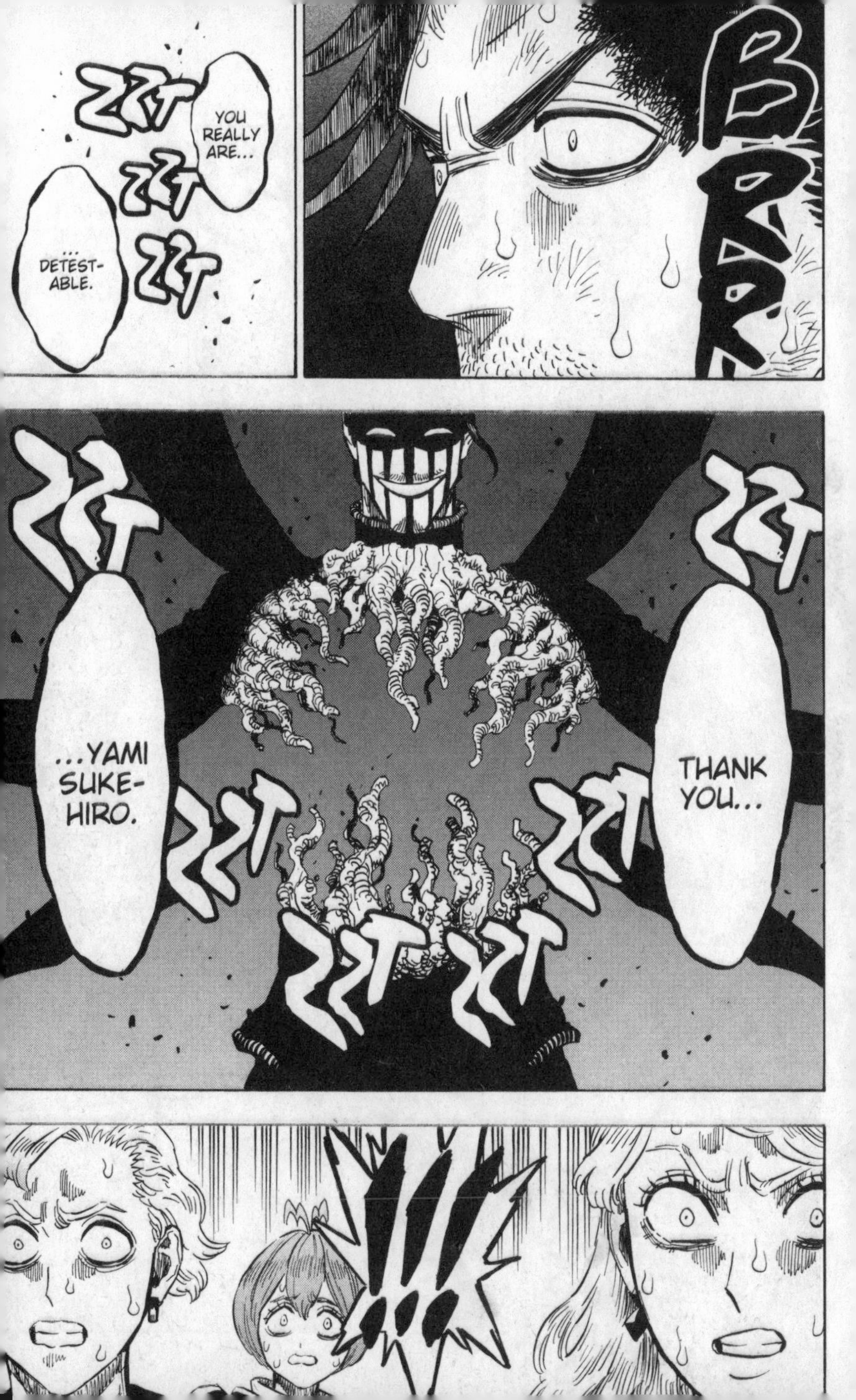
ZZT
YOU REALLY ARE...
ZZT
ZZT
...DETESTABLE.
ZZT
THANK YOU...
ZZT
ZZT
ZZT
...YAMI SUKEHIRO.
ZZT
!!!

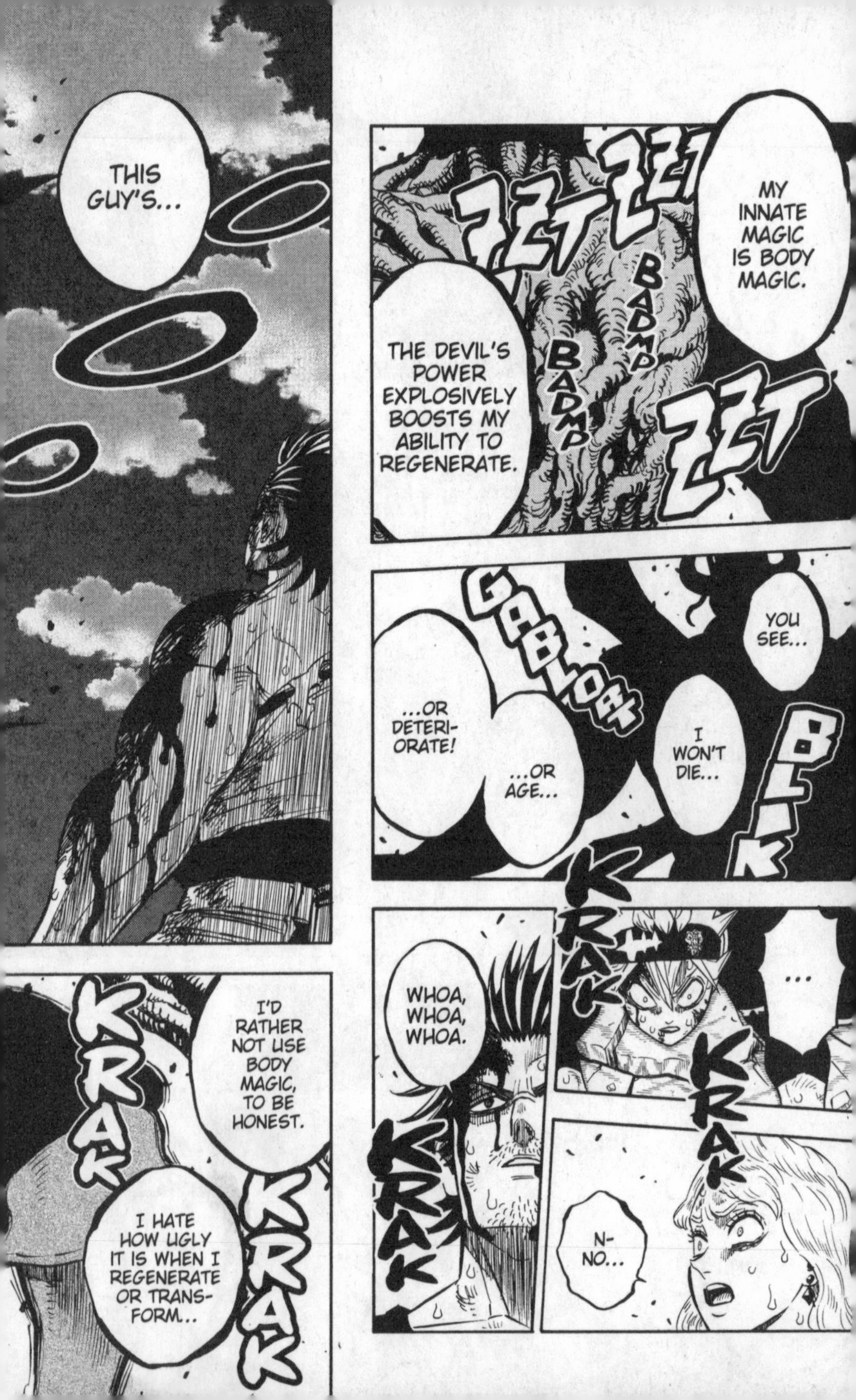
MY INNATE MAGIC IS BODY MAGIC.
ZZZT
ZZZT
BADMP
BADMP
THE DEVIL'S POWER EXPLOSIVELY BOOSTS MY ABILITY TO REGENERATE.
ZZZT
YOU SEE...
BLiK
I WON'T DIE...
...OR AGE...
GABLOOF
...OR DETERIORATE!
KRAK
...
KRAK
N-NO...
WHOA, WHOA, WHOA.
KRAK
THIS GUY'S...
KRAK
I'D RATHER NOT USE BODY MAGIC, TO BE HONEST.
KRAK
I HATE HOW UGLY IT IS WHEN I REGENERATE OR TRANSFORM...

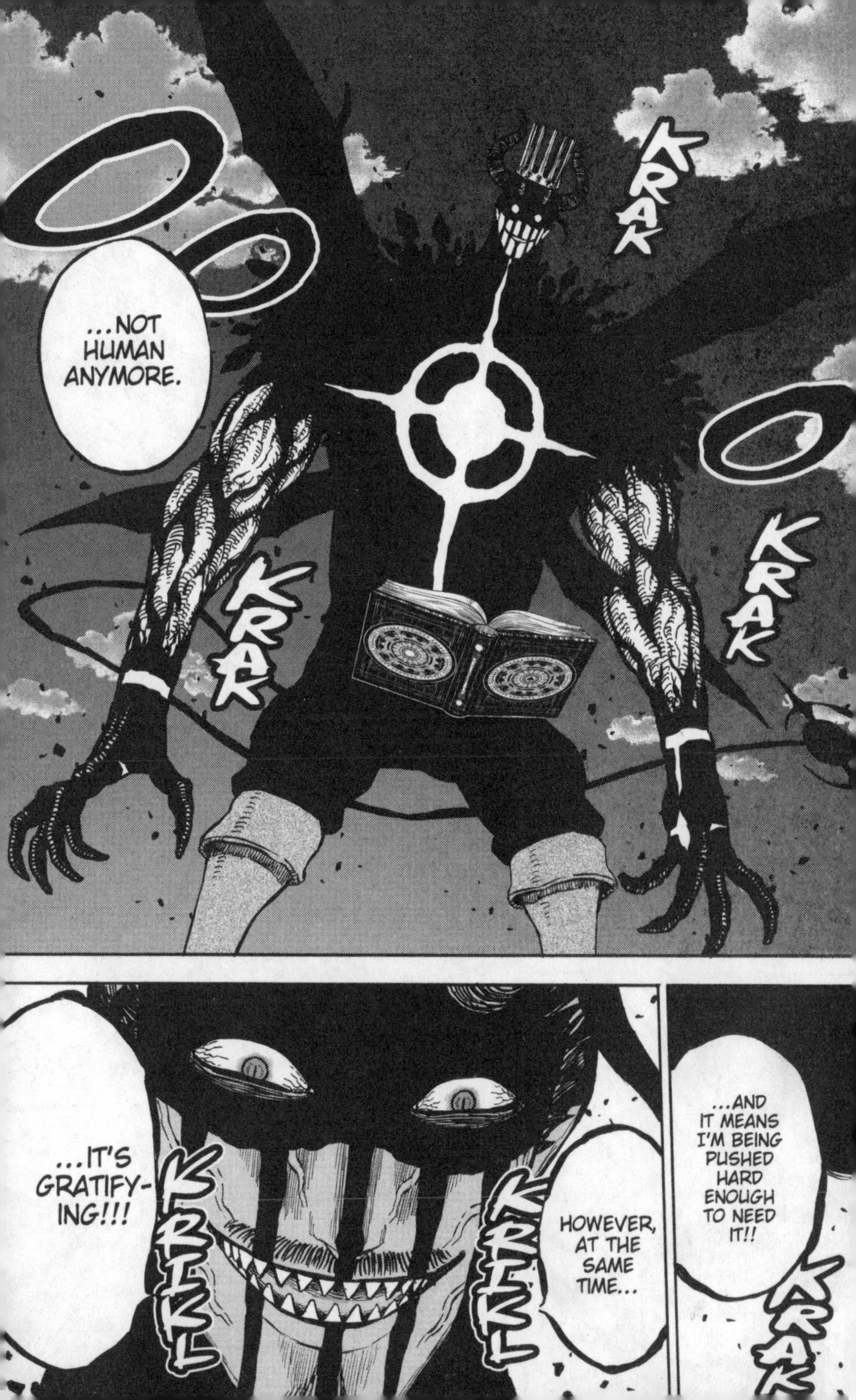
KRAK
...NOT HUMAN ANYMORE.
KRAK
KRAK
...AND IT MEANS I'M BEING PUSHED HARD ENOUGH TO NEED IT!!
KRAK
HOWEVER, AT THE SAME TIME...
KRIKL
...IT'S GRATIFY-ING!!!
KRIKL

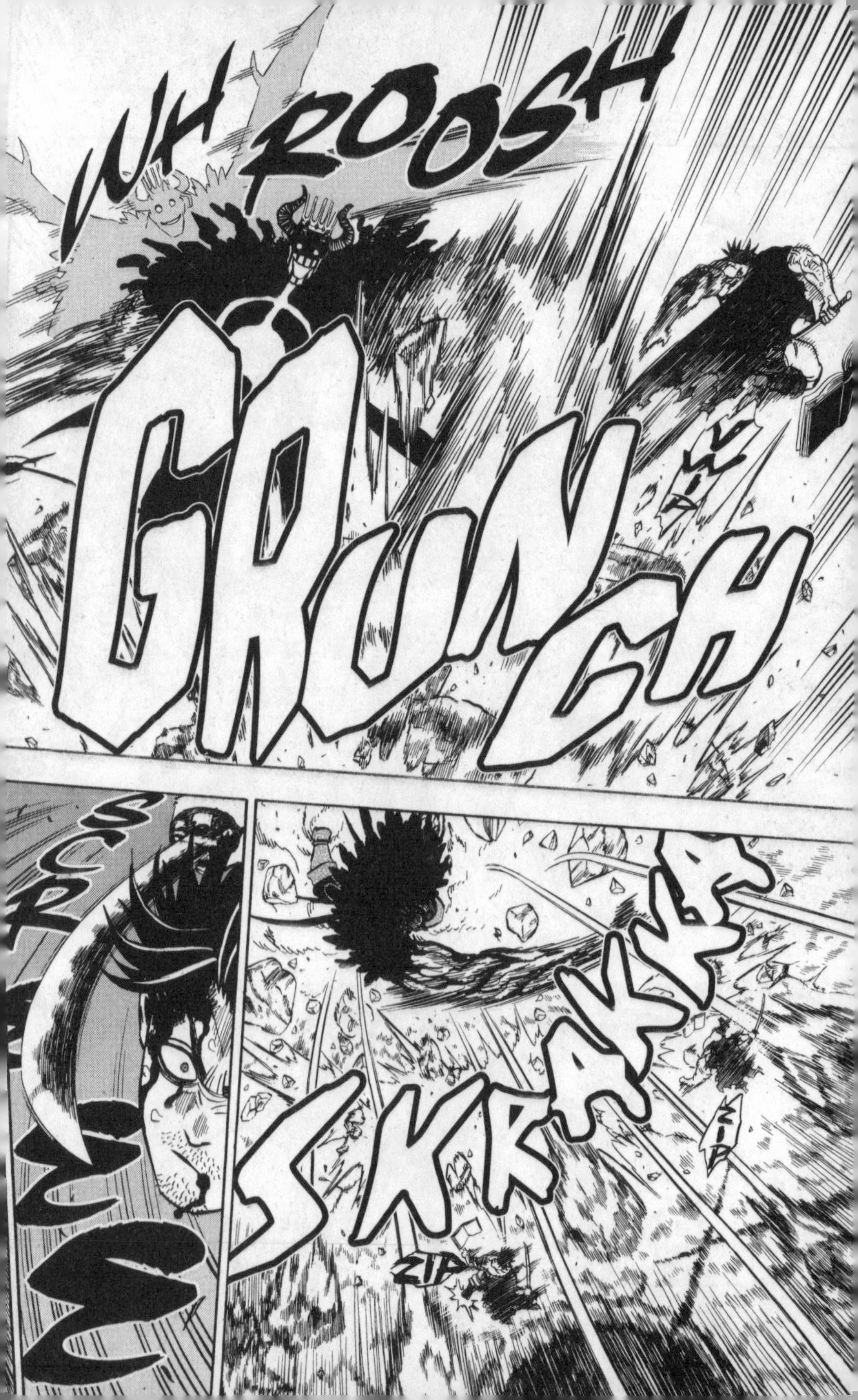
WH ROOSH
CRUNCH
SKRAKK
ZIP
ZIP

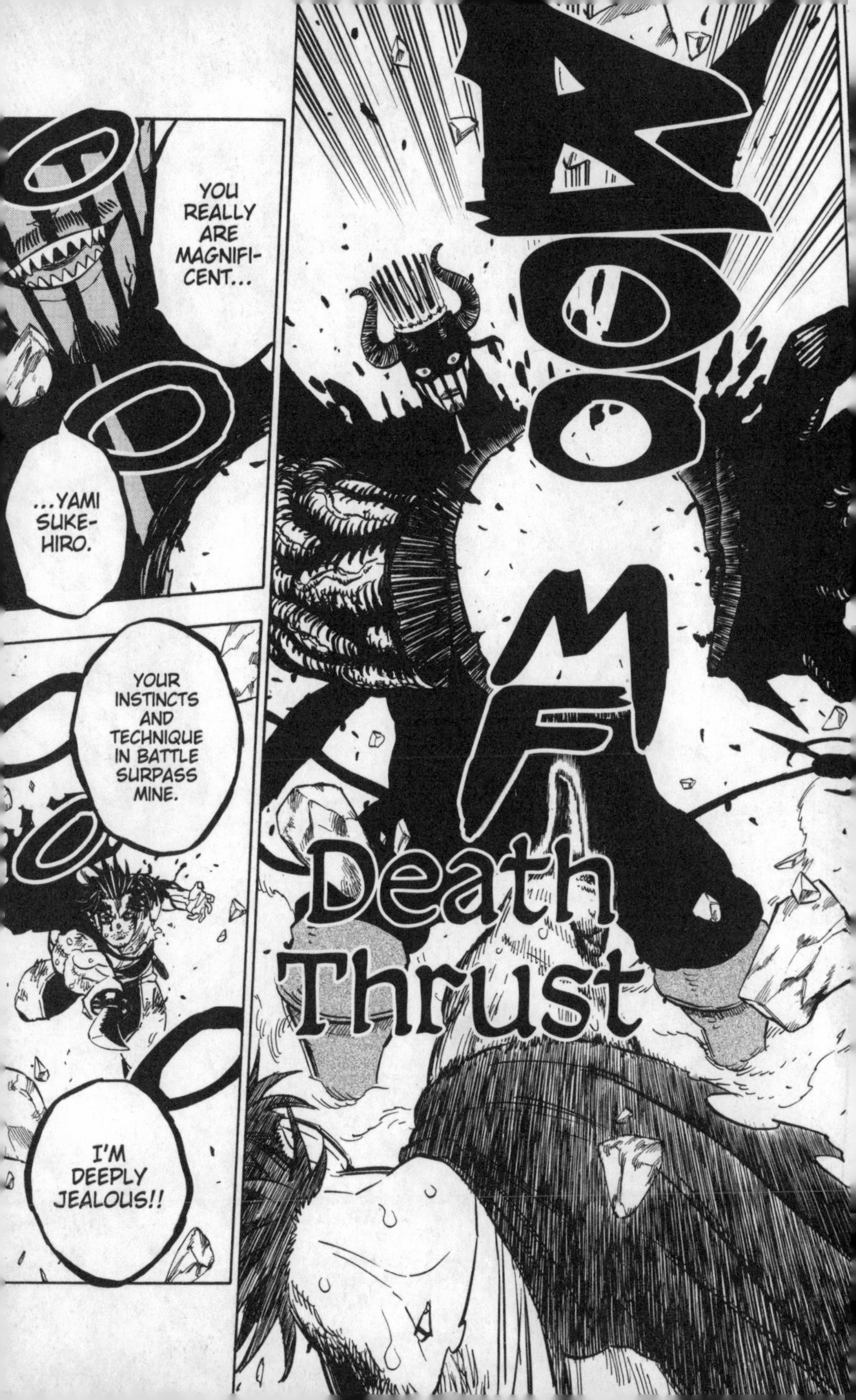
BOOMF
Death Thrust
YOU REALLY ARE MAGNIFICENT...
...YAMI SUKEHIRO.
YOUR INSTINCTS AND TECHNIQUE IN BATTLE SURPASS MINE.
I'M DEEPLY JEALOUS!!

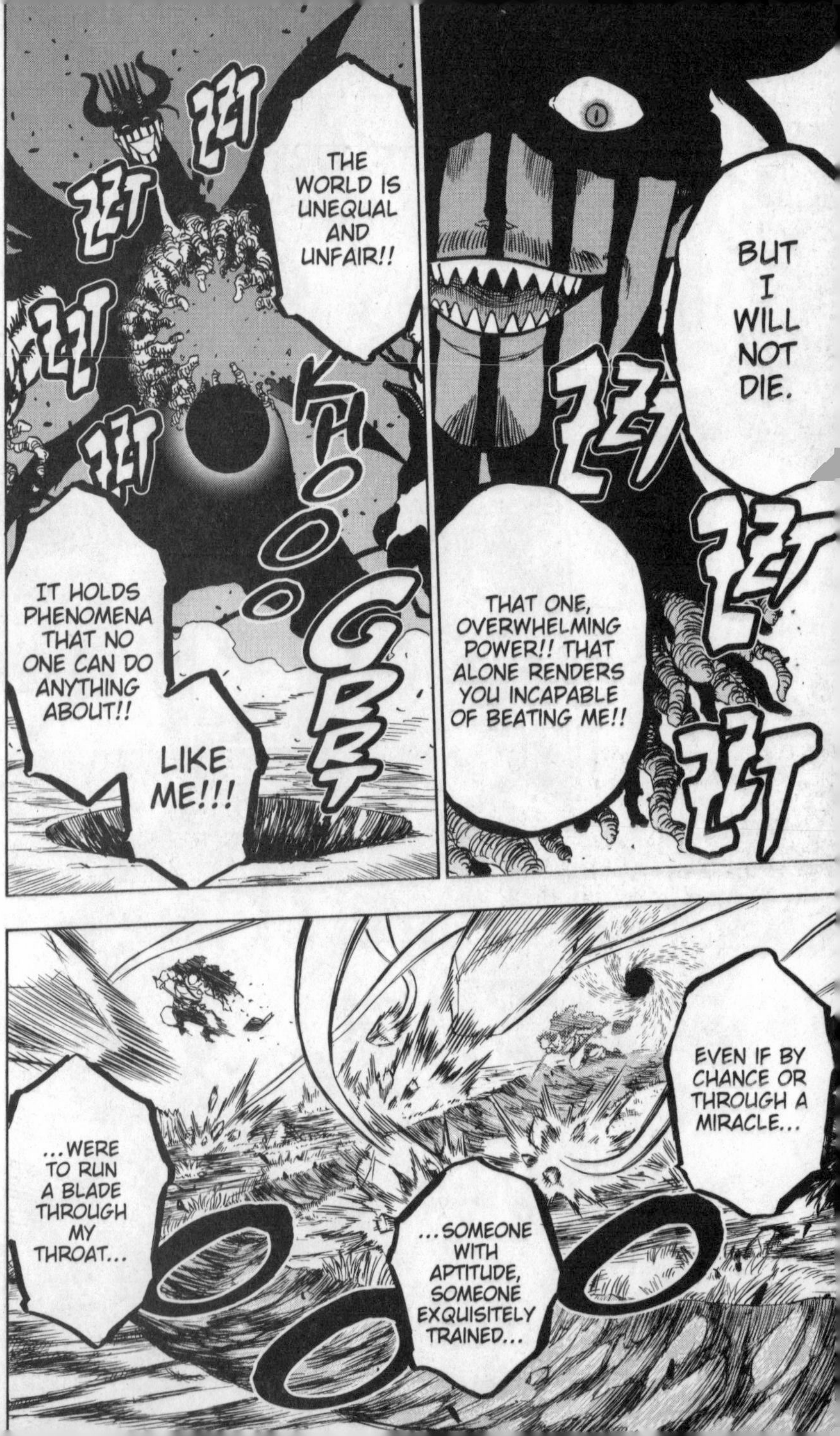
BUT I WILL NOT DIE.
ZZZT
ZZZT
ZZZT
THAT ONE, OVERWHELMING POWER!! THAT ALONE RENDERS YOU INCAPABLE OF BEATING ME!!
ZZZT
ZZZT
ZZZT
ZZZT
THE WORLD IS UNEQUAL AND UNFAIR!!
KHOOOOGRRT
IT HOLDS PHENOMENA THAT NO ONE CAN DO ANYTHING ABOUT!!
LIKE ME!!!
EVEN IF BY CHANCE OR THROUGH A MIRACLE...
...SOMEONE WITH APTITUDE, SOMEONE EXQUISITELY TRAINED...
...WERE TO RUN A BLADE THROUGH MY THROAT...

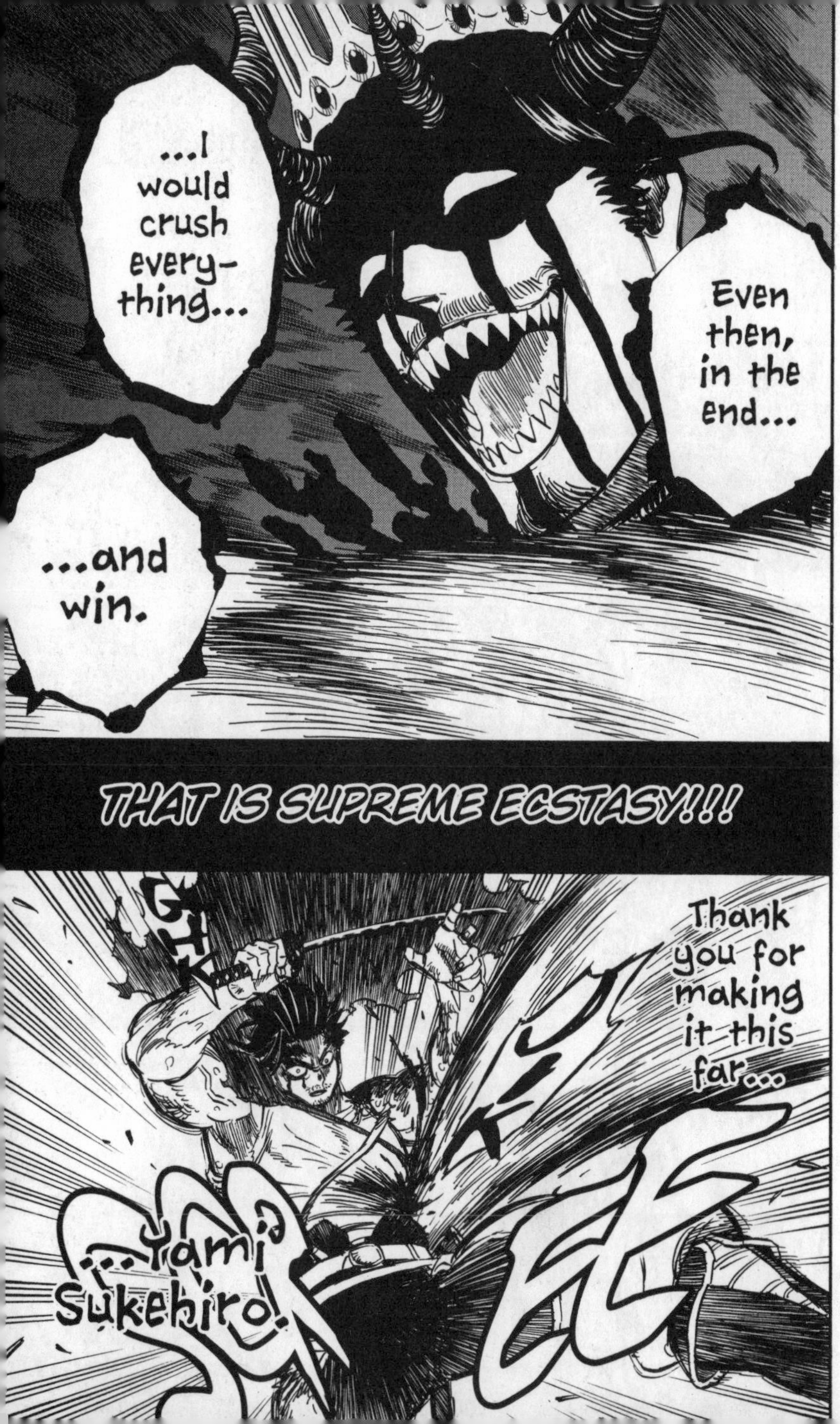
Even then, in the end...
...I would crush every-thing...
...and win.
THAT IS SUPREME ECSTASY!!!
Thank you for making it this far...
...Yami Sukehiro!

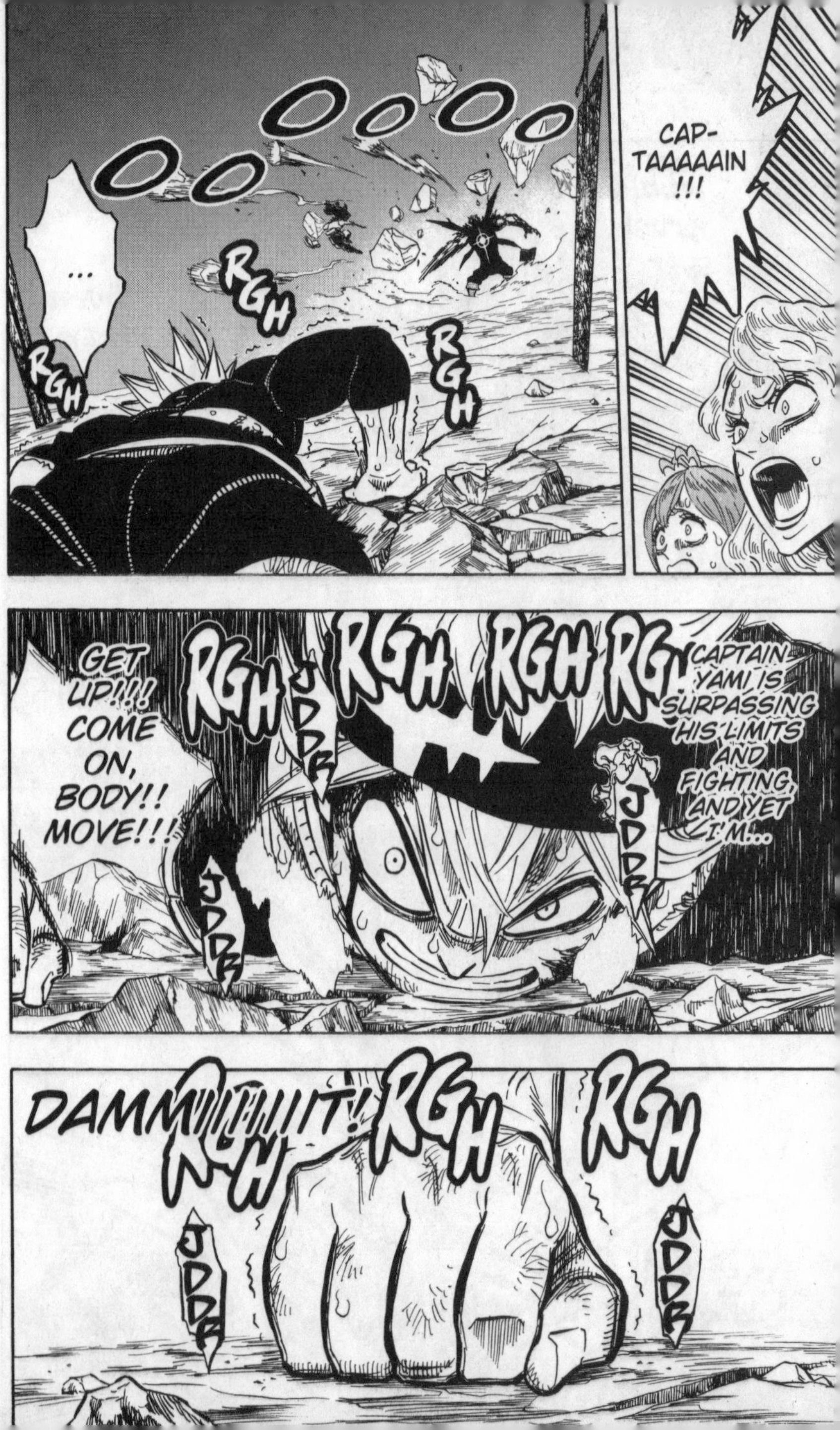

CAP-TAAAAAIN!!!
OOOOOOOO
...
RGH
RGH
RGH
CAPTAIN YAMI IS SURPASSING HIS LIMITS AND FIGHTING, AND YET I'M...
RGH RG
JDDR
RGH
JDDR
RGH
JDDR
GET UP!!! COME ON, BODY!! MOVE!!!
JDDR
RGH
RGH
DAMMIIIIIT!
RGH
JDDR
JDDR

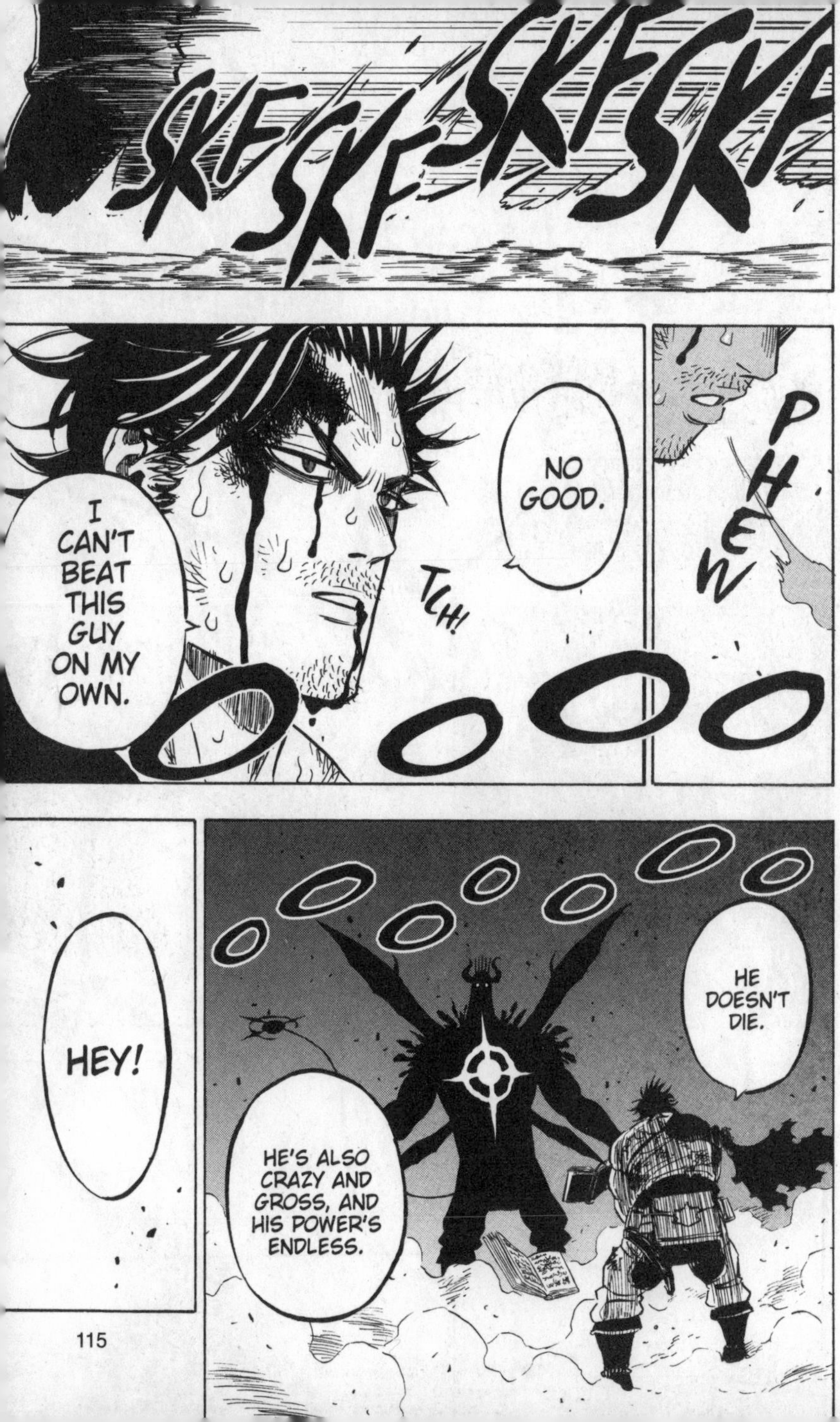
SKYF SKYF SKYF SKYF
PHEW
NO GOOD.
TCH!
I CAN'T BEAT THIS GUY ON MY OWN.
HE DOESN'T DIE.
HE'S ALSO CRAZY AND GROSS, AND HIS POWER'S ENDLESS.
HEY!

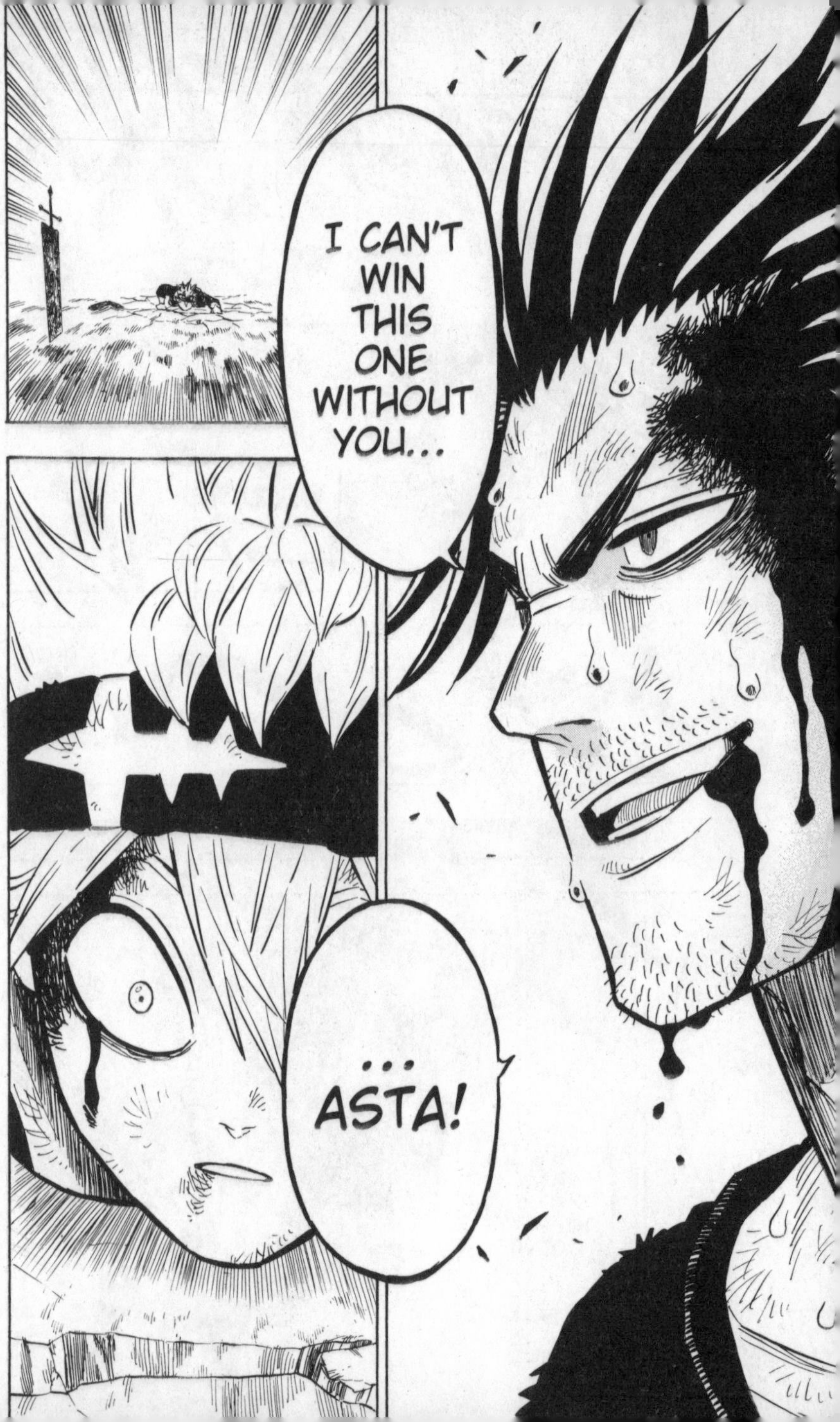
I CAN'T WIN THIS ONE WITHOUT YOU...
... ASTA!

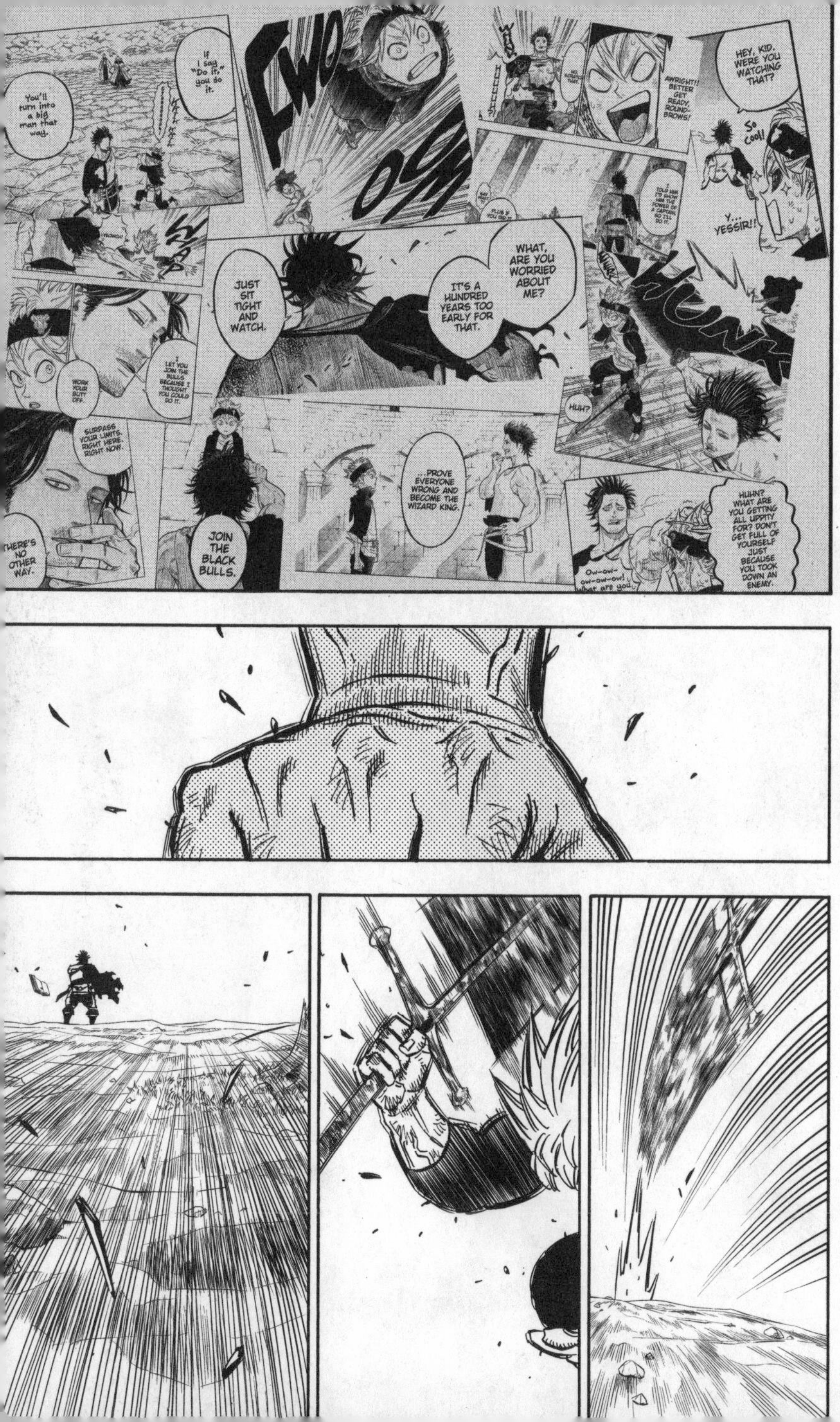
HEY, KID. WERE YOU WATCHING THAT?
So cool!
Y... YESSIR!!
AWRIGHT!! BETTER GET READY, ROUND-BROWS!
NO, SCRATCH THAT.
HUUUUH?!
I TOLD HIM I'D SHOW HIM THE POWER OF A CAPTAIN, SO I'LL DO IT.
FWOOOM
If I say "Do it," you do it.
You'll turn into a big man that way.
WHAT, ARE YOU WORRIED ABOUT ME?
IT'S A HUNDRED YEARS TOO EARLY FOR THAT.
JUST SIT TIGHT AND WATCH.
I LET YOU JOIN THE BULLS BECAUSE I THOUGHT YOU COULD DO IT.
WORK YOUR BUTT OFF.
SURPASS YOUR LIMITS. RIGHT HERE. RIGHT NOW.
THERE'S NO OTHER WAY.
HUH?
HUHN? WHAT ARE YOU GETTING ALL UPPITY FOR? DON'T GET FULL OF YOURSELF JUST BECAUSE YOU TOOK DOWN AN ENEMY.
Ow-ow-ow-ow-ow! What are you
...PROVE EVERYONE WRONG AND BECOME THE WIZARD KING.
JOIN THE BLACK BULLS.

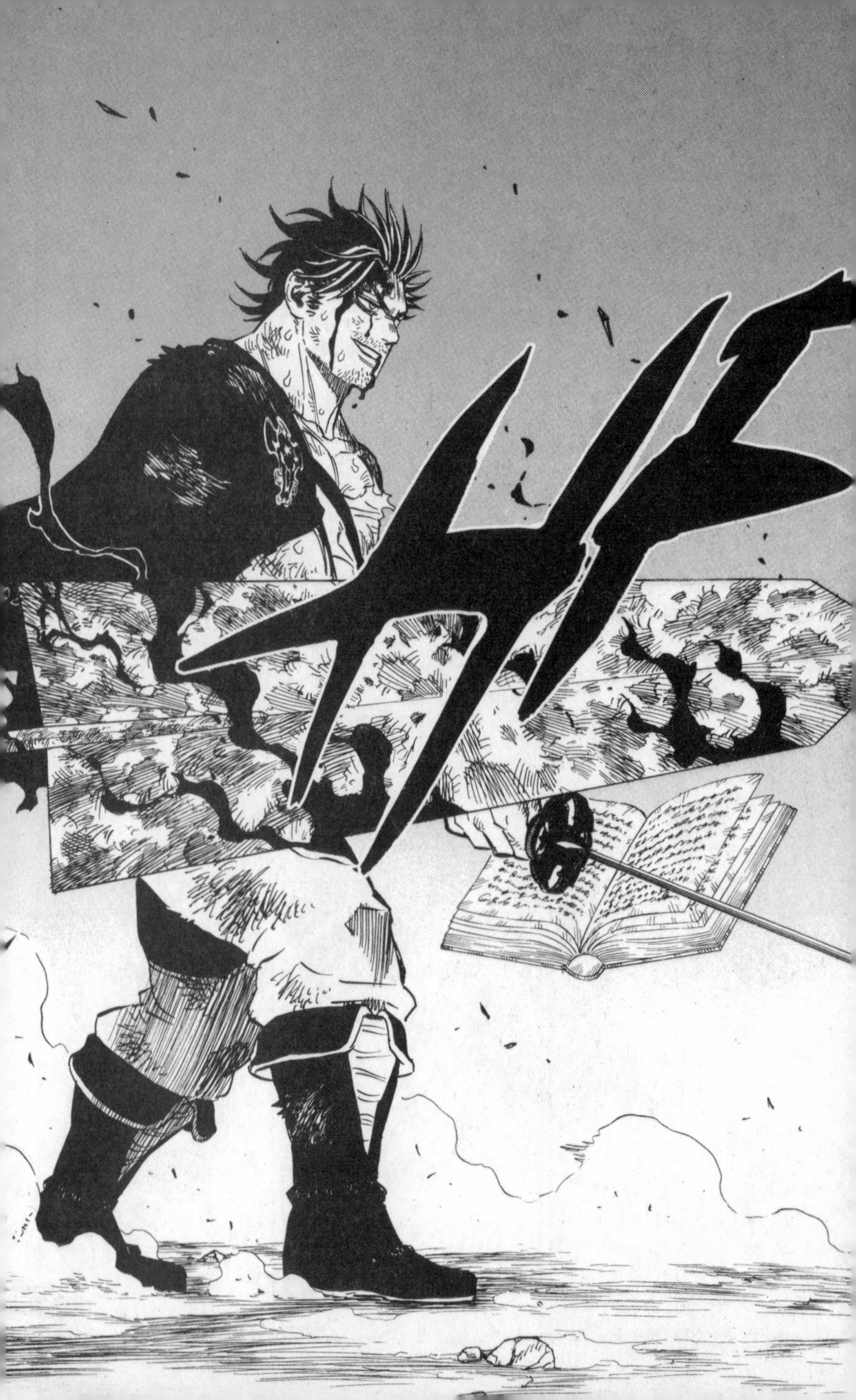

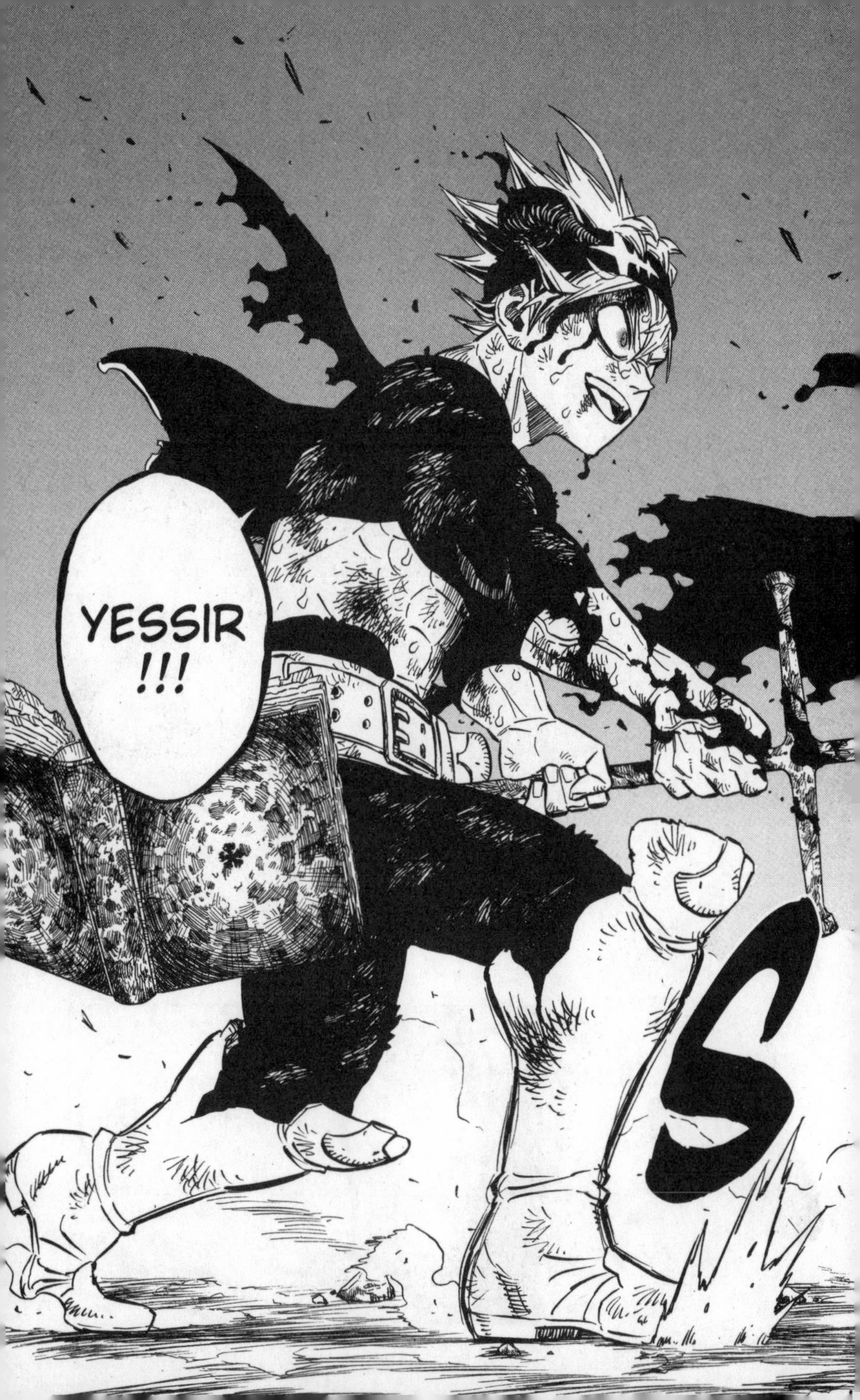
YESSIR !!!
S

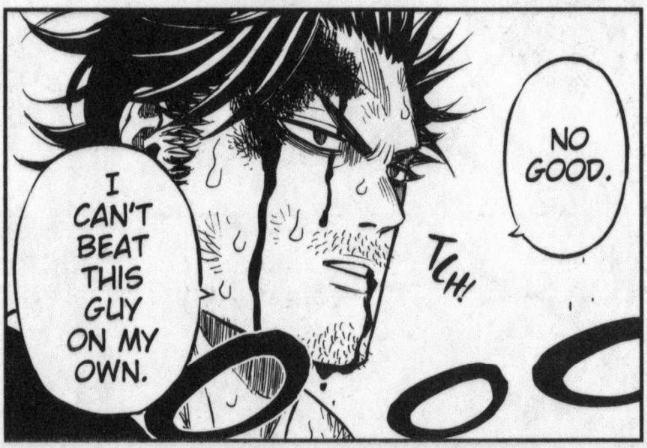
NO GOOD.
TCH!
I CAN'T BEAT THIS GUY ON MY OWN.

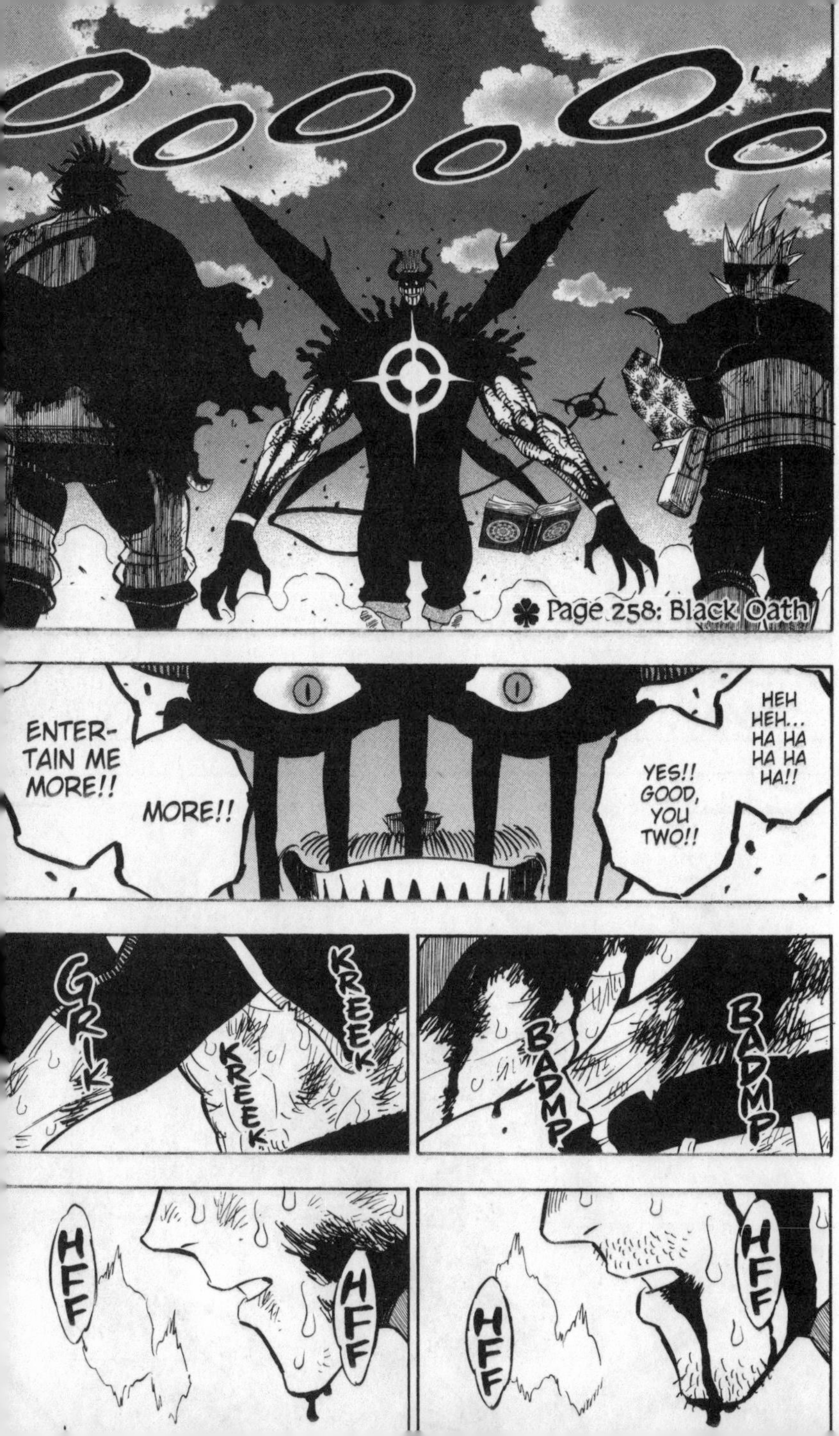
Page 258: Black Oath
HEH HEH... HA HA HA HA HA!!
YES!! GOOD, YOU TWO!!
ENTER-TAIN ME MORE!!
MORE!!
BADMP
BADMP
KREEK
KREEK
GRIK
HFF
HFF
HFF
HFF

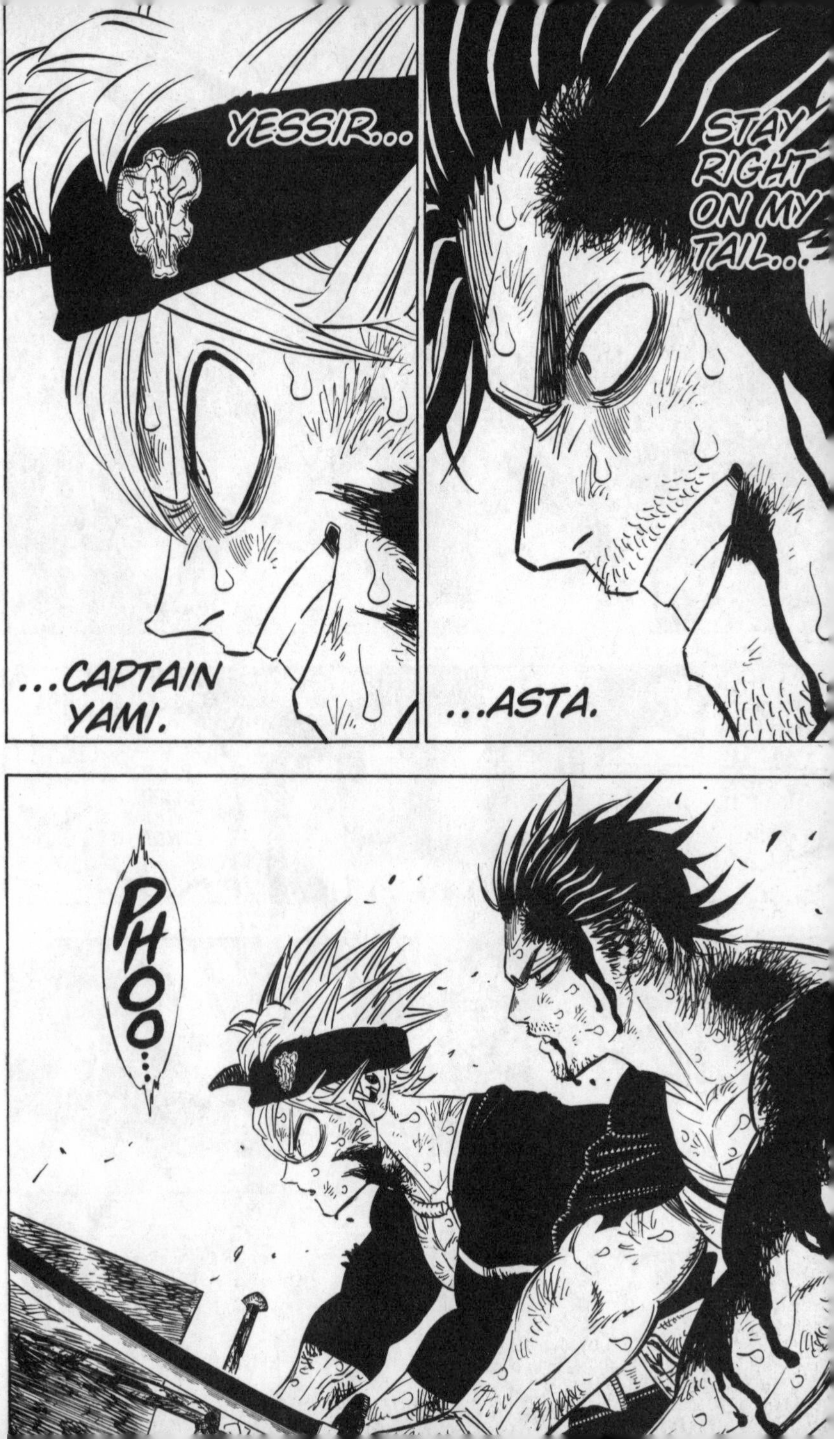
STAY RIGHT ON MY TAIL...
...ASTA.
YESSIR...
...CAPTAIN YAMI.
PHOO...

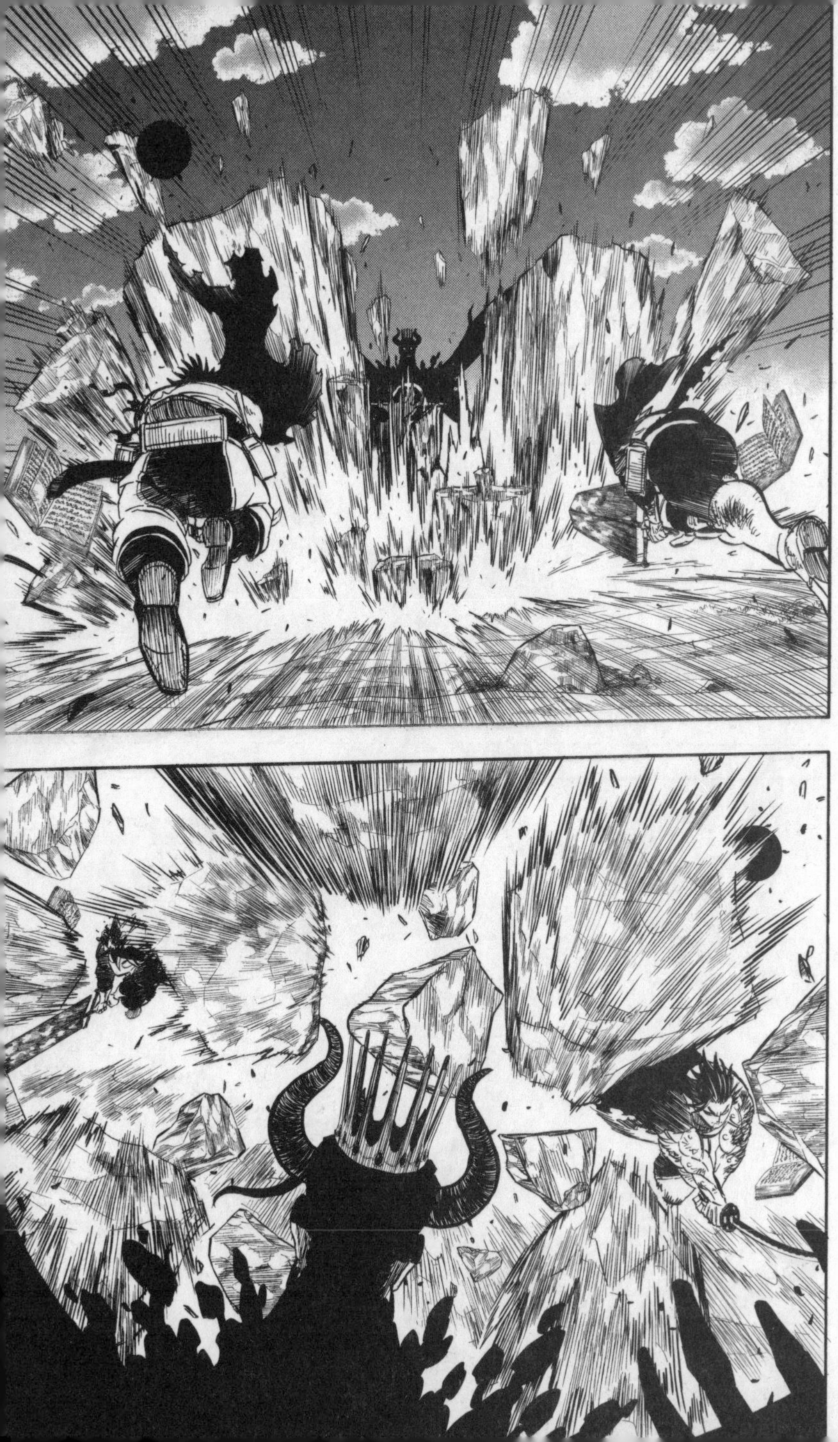

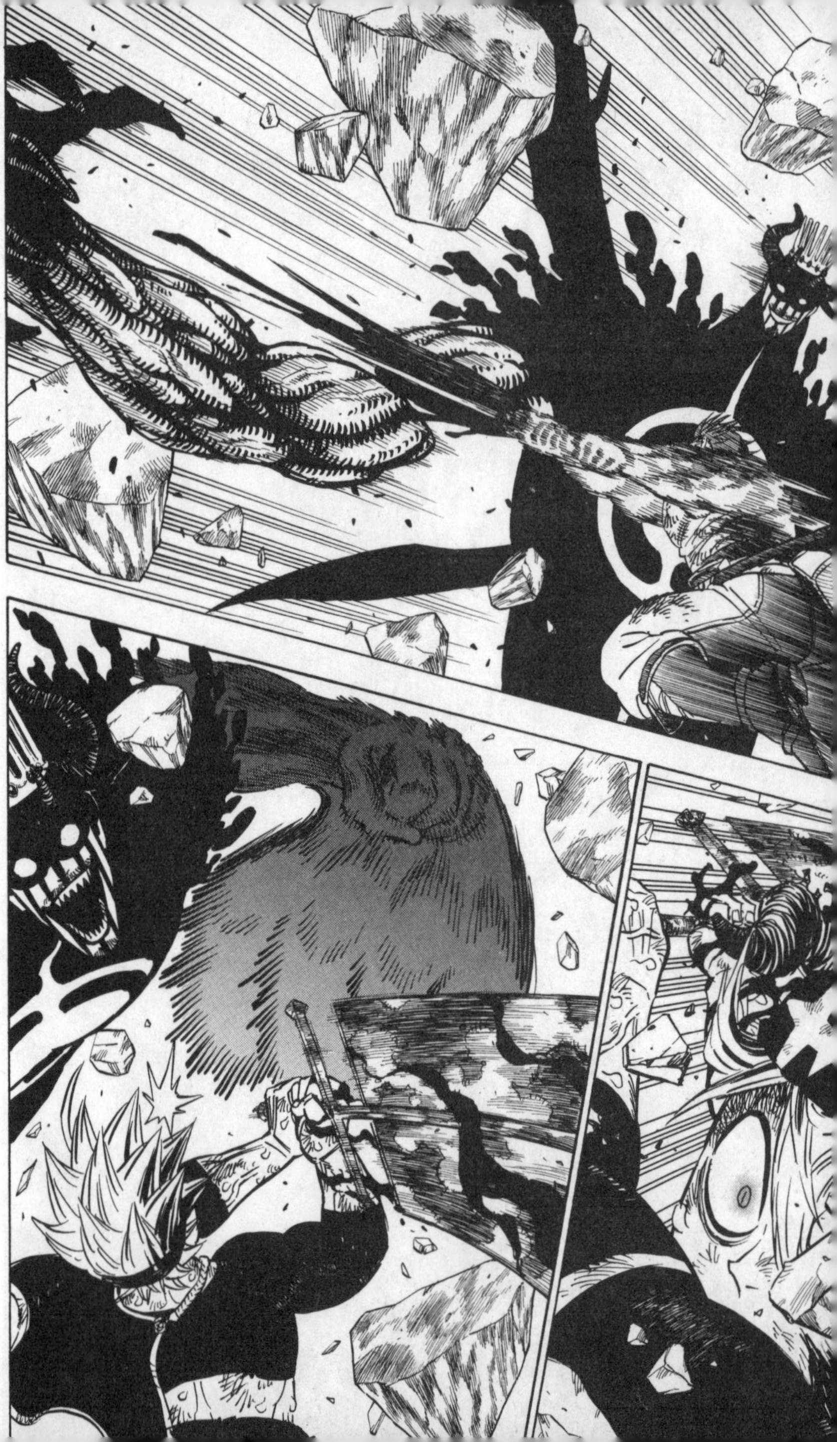

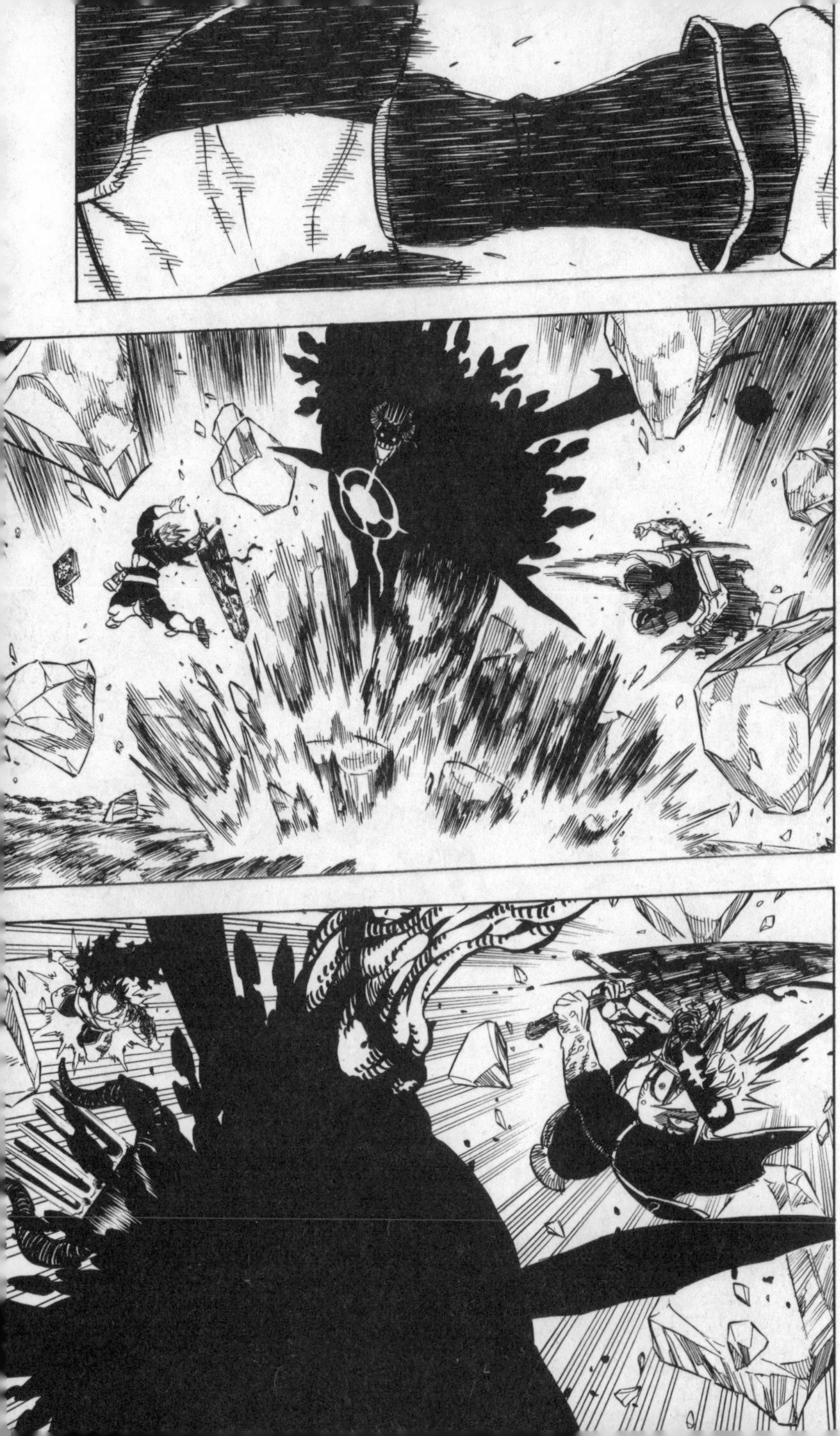

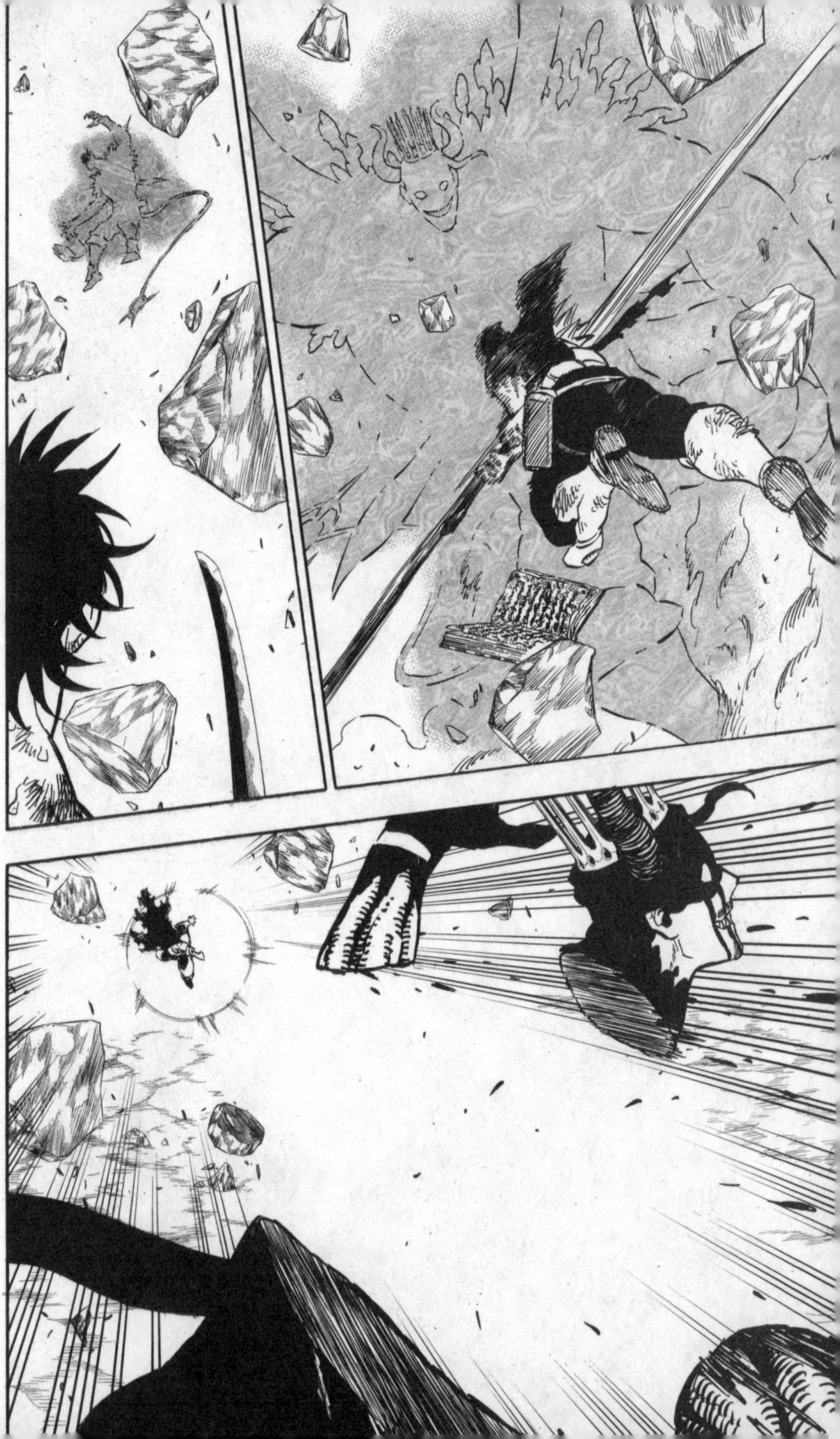

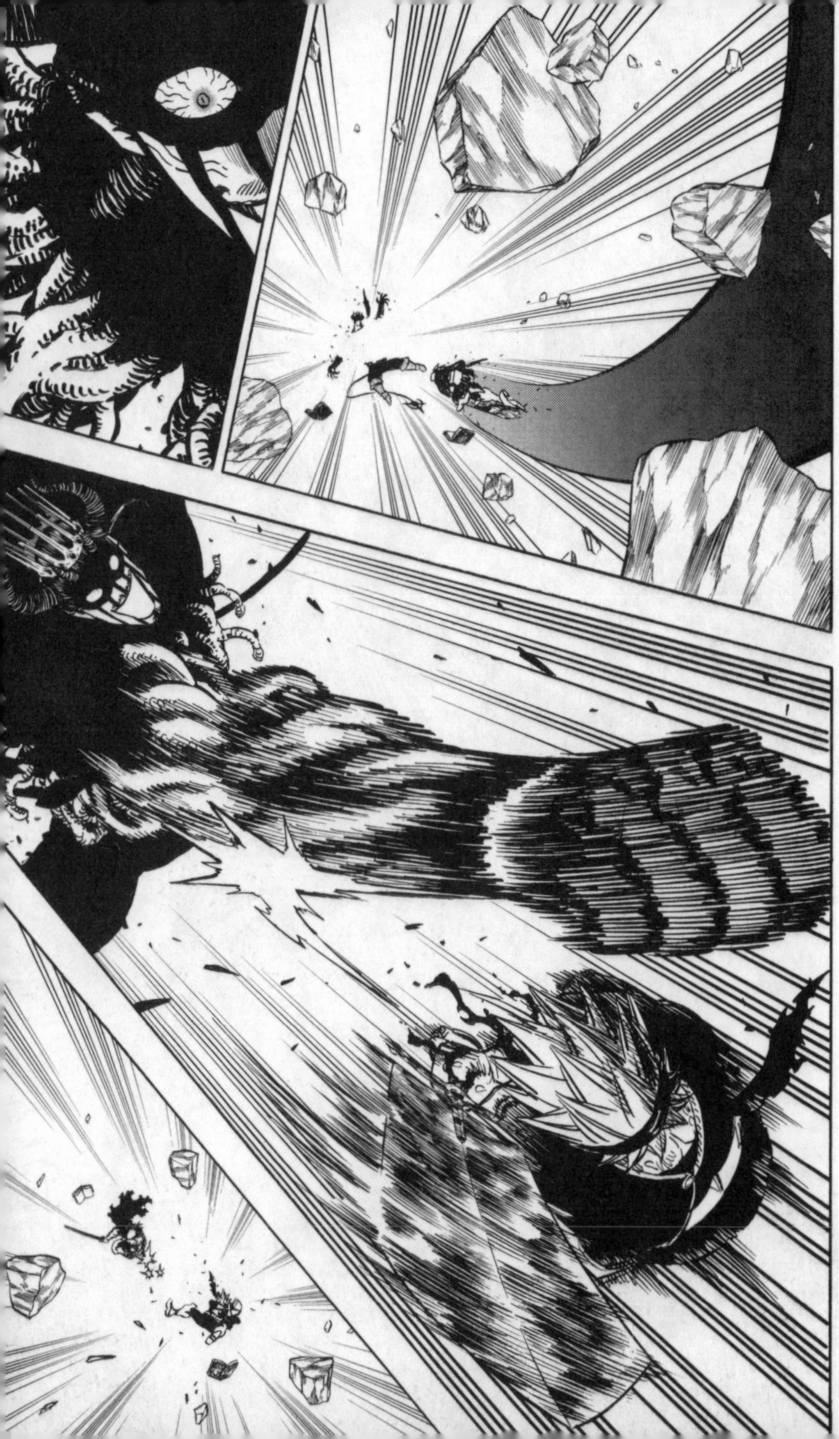

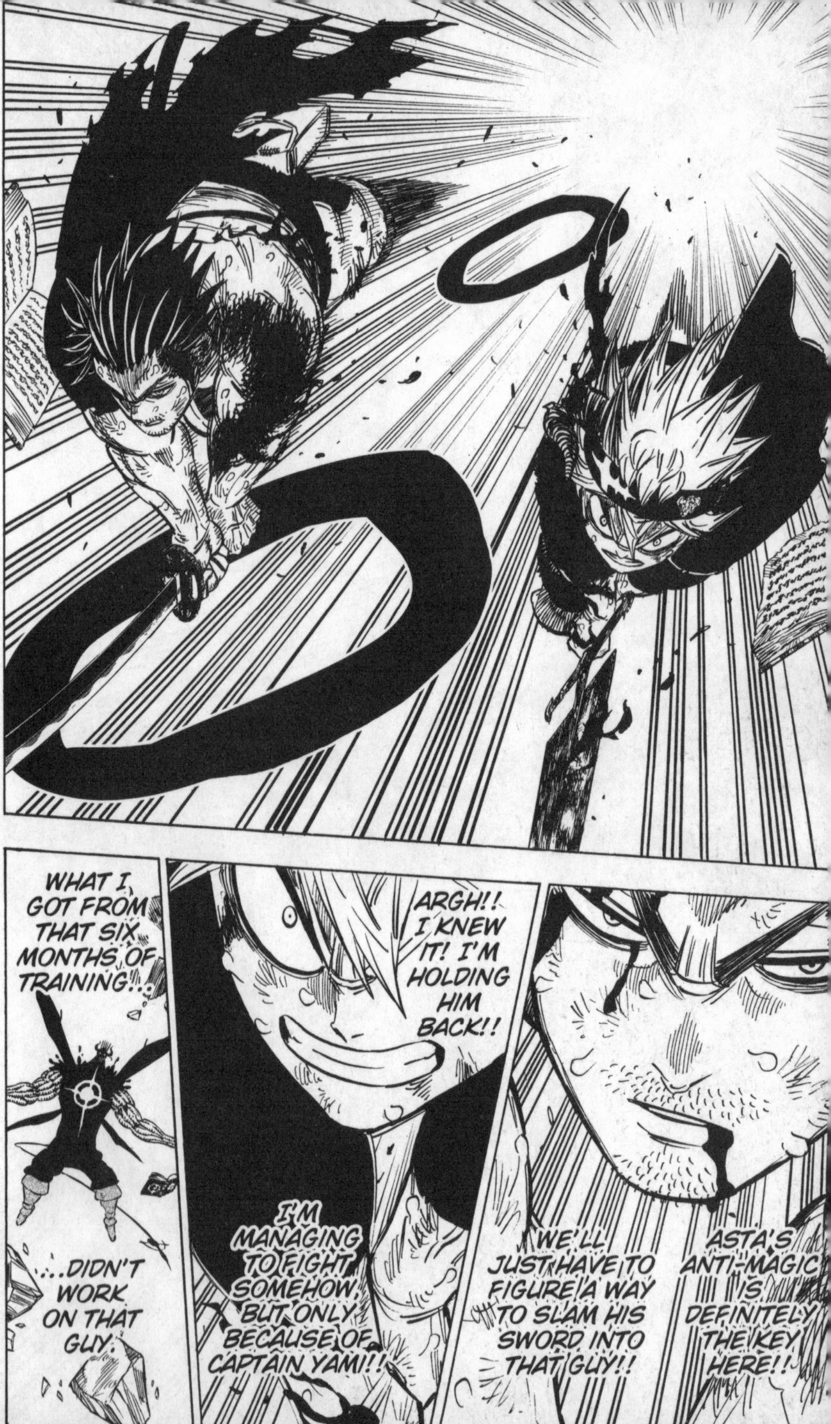
ASTA'S ANTI-MAGIC IS DEFINITELY THE KEY HERE!!
WE'LL JUST HAVE TO FIGURE A WAY TO SLAM HIS SWORD INTO THAT GUY!!
ARGH!! I KNEW IT! I'M HOLDING HIM BACK!!
I'M MANAGING TO FIGHT SOMEHOW, BUT ONLY BECAUSE OF CAPTAIN YAMI!!
WHAT I GOT FROM THAT SIX MONTHS OF TRAINING...
...DIDN'T WORK ON THAT GUY.

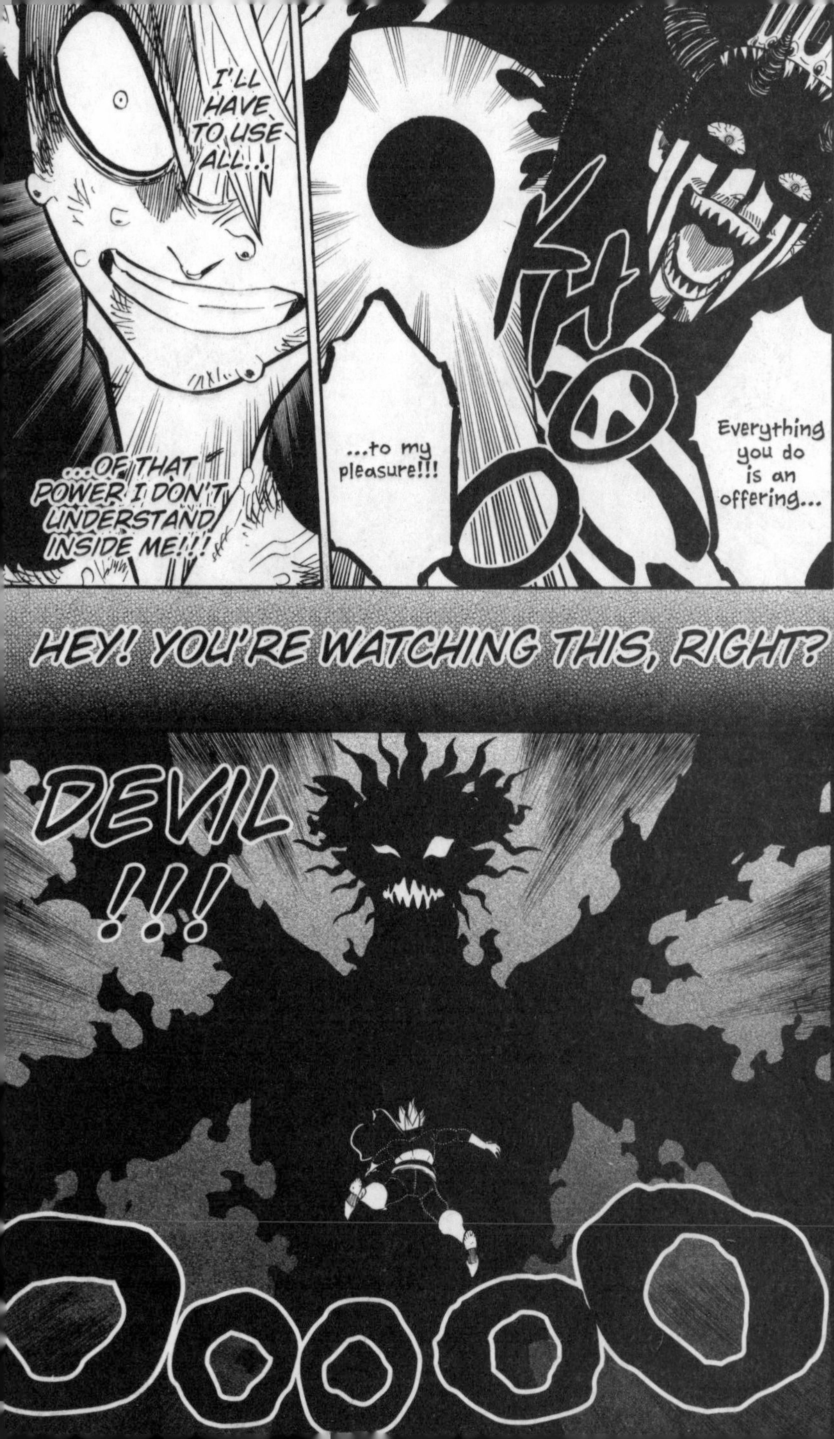
Everything you do is an offering...
...to my pleasure!!!
I'LL HAVE TO USE ALL...
...OF THAT POWER I DON'T UNDERSTAND INSIDE ME!!!
HEY! YOU'RE WATCHING THIS, RIGHT?
DEVIL !!!

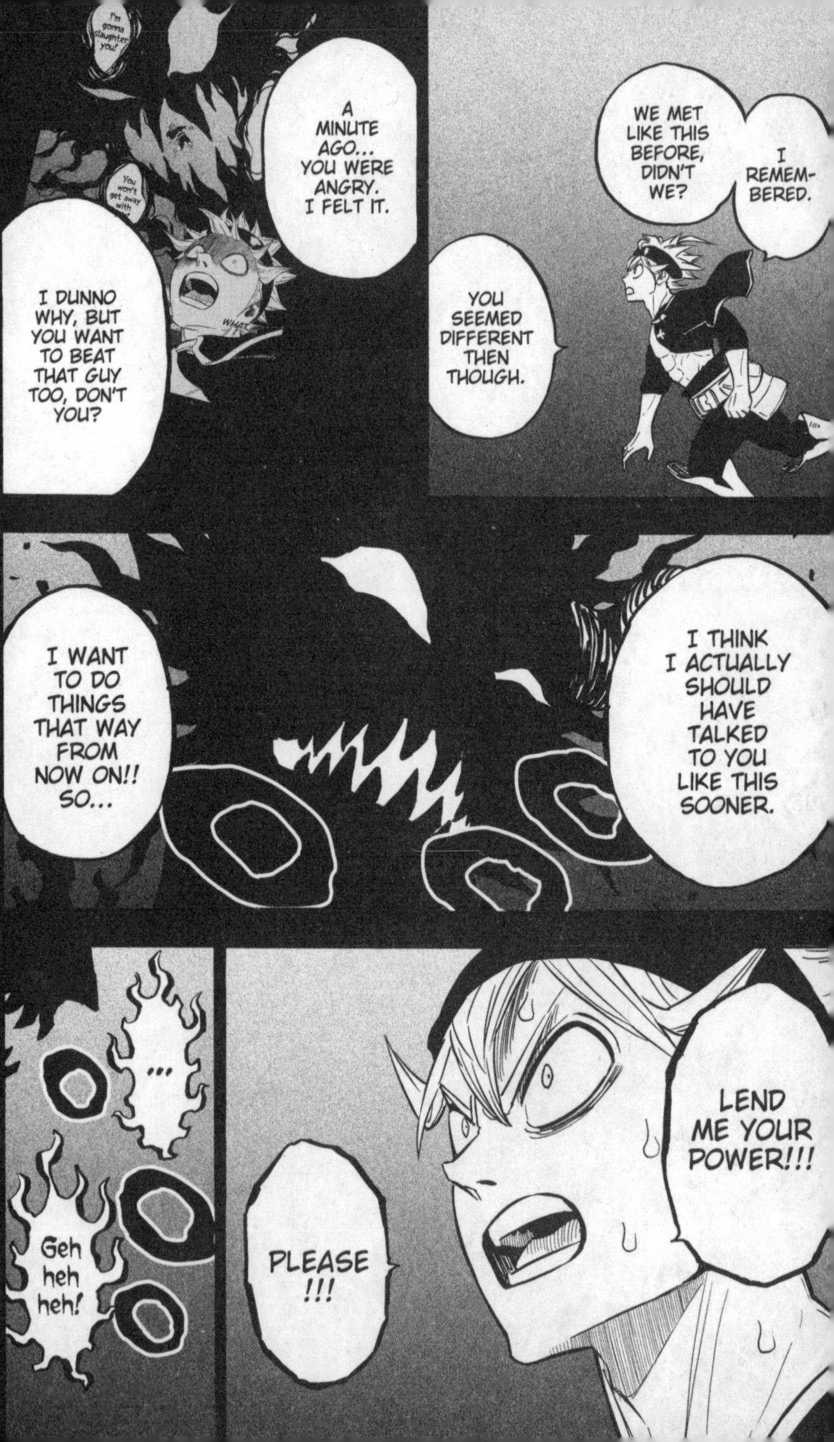
I REMEMBERED.
WE MET LIKE THIS BEFORE, DIDN'T WE?
YOU SEEMED DIFFERENT THEN THOUGH.
A MINUTE AGO... YOU WERE ANGRY. I FELT IT.
I'm gonna slaughter you!
You won't get away with
WHAT
I DUNNO WHY, BUT YOU WANT TO BEAT THAT GUY TOO, DON'T YOU?
I THINK I ACTUALLY SHOULD HAVE TALKED TO YOU LIKE THIS SOONER.
I WANT TO DO THINGS THAT WAY FROM NOW ON!! SO...
LEND ME YOUR POWER!!!
PLEASE!!!
...
Geh heh heh!

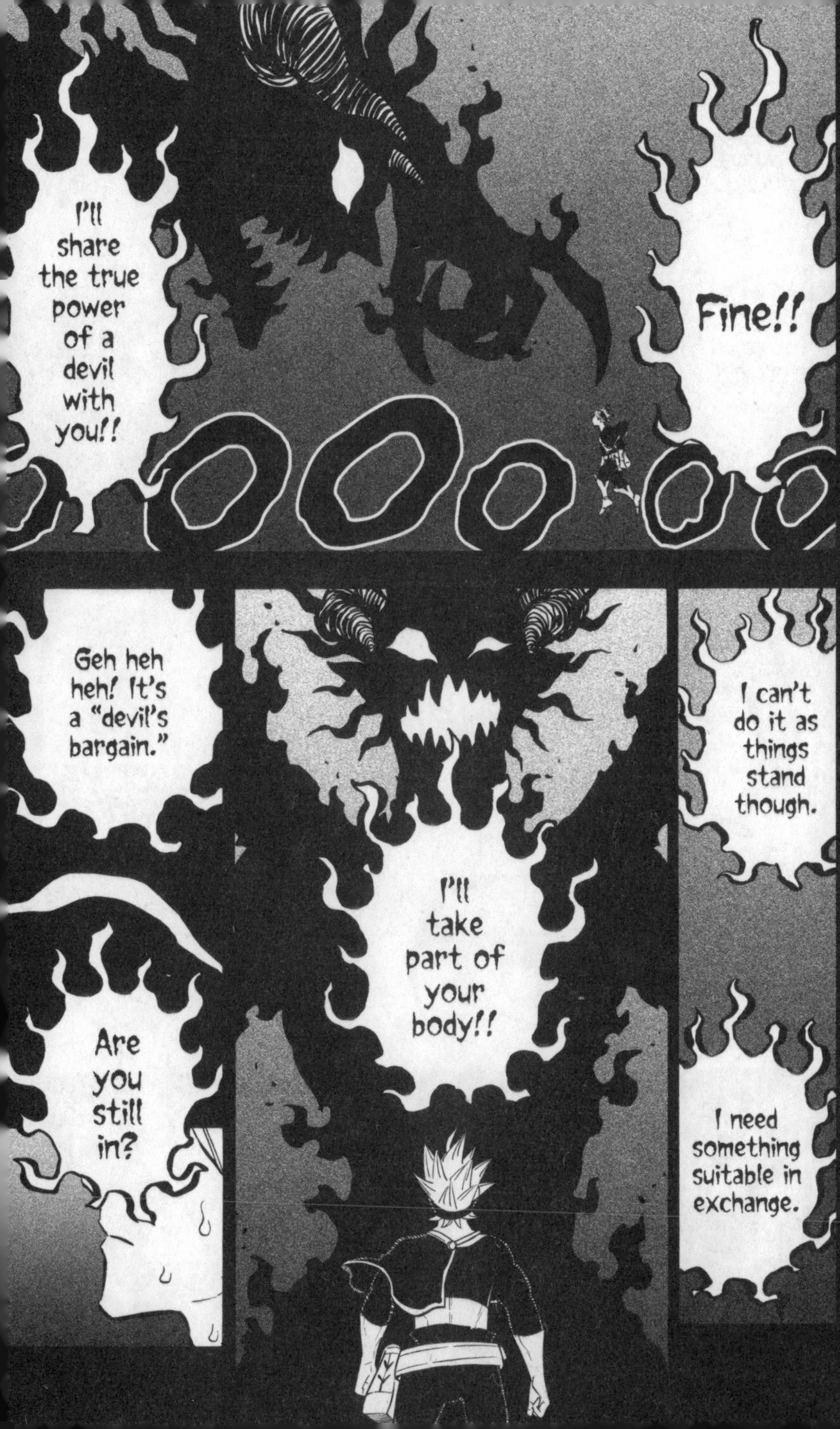
Fine!!
I'll share the true power of a devil with you!!
I can't do it as things stand though.
I need something suitable in exchange.
I'll take part of your body!!
Geh heh heh! It's a "devil's bargain."
Are you still in?

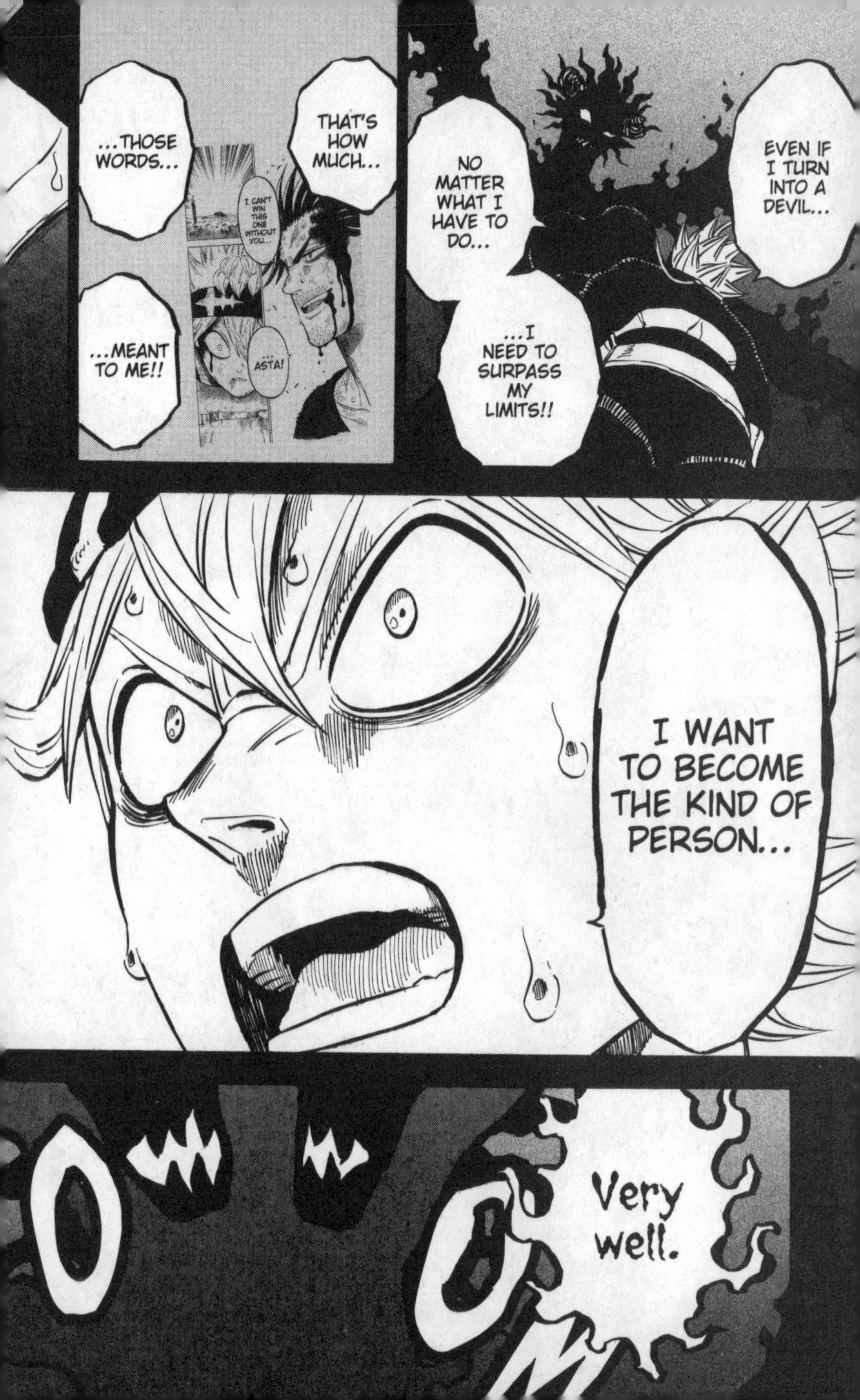
EVEN IF I TURN INTO A DEVIL...
NO MATTER WHAT I HAVE TO DO...
...I NEED TO SURPASS MY LIMITS!!
THAT'S HOW MUCH...
...THOSE WORDS...
I CAN'T WIN THIS ONE WITHOUT YOU...
...ASTA!
...MEANT TO ME!!
I WANT TO BECOME THE KIND OF PERSON...
Very well.

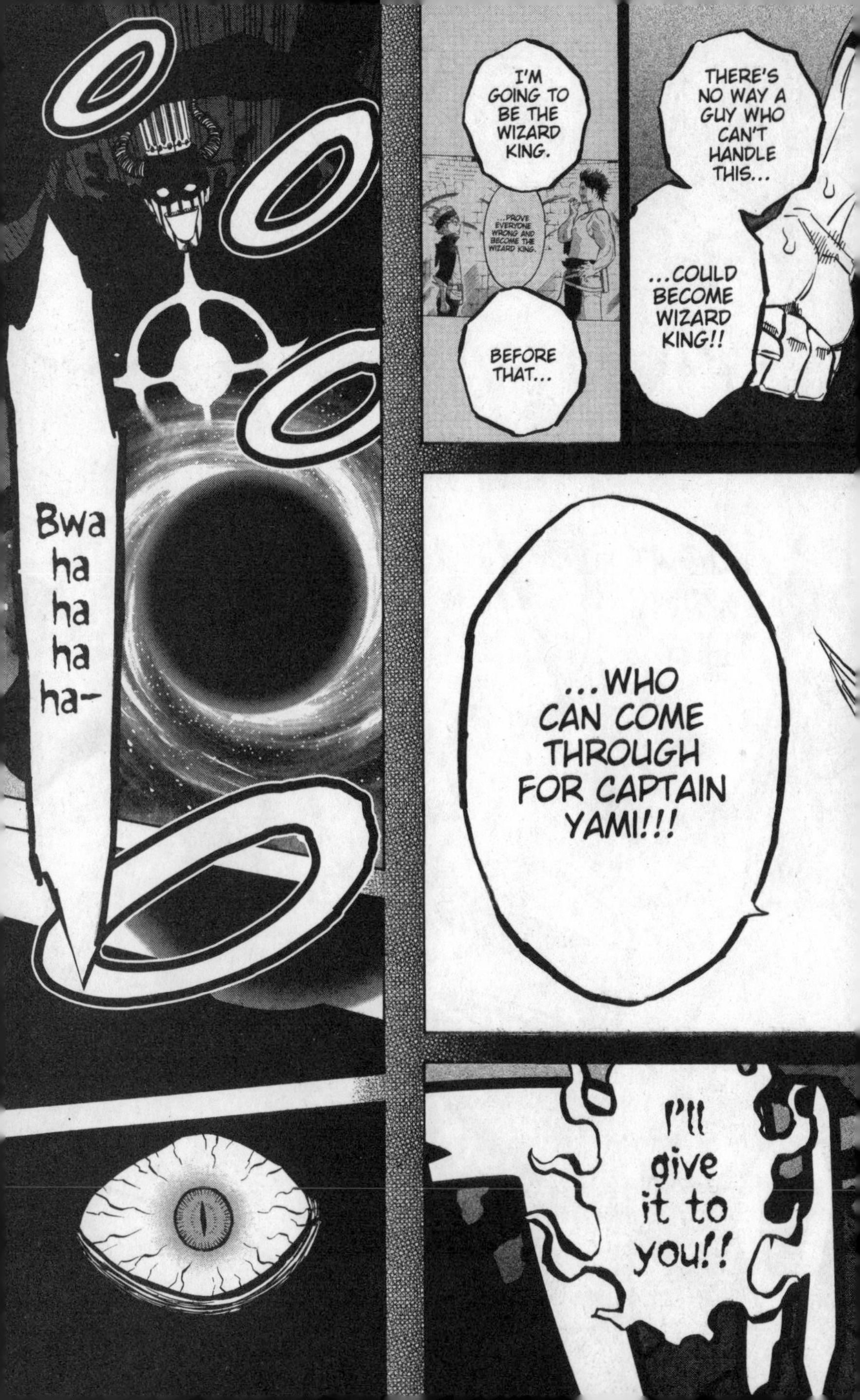
THERE'S NO WAY A GUY WHO CAN'T HANDLE THIS...
...COULD BECOME WIZARD KING!!
I'M GOING TO BE THE WIZARD KING.
...PROVE EVERYONE WRONG AND BECOME THE WIZARD KING.
BEFORE THAT...
...WHO CAN COME THROUGH FOR CAPTAIN YAMI!!!
I'll give it to you!!
Bwa ha ha ha ha-

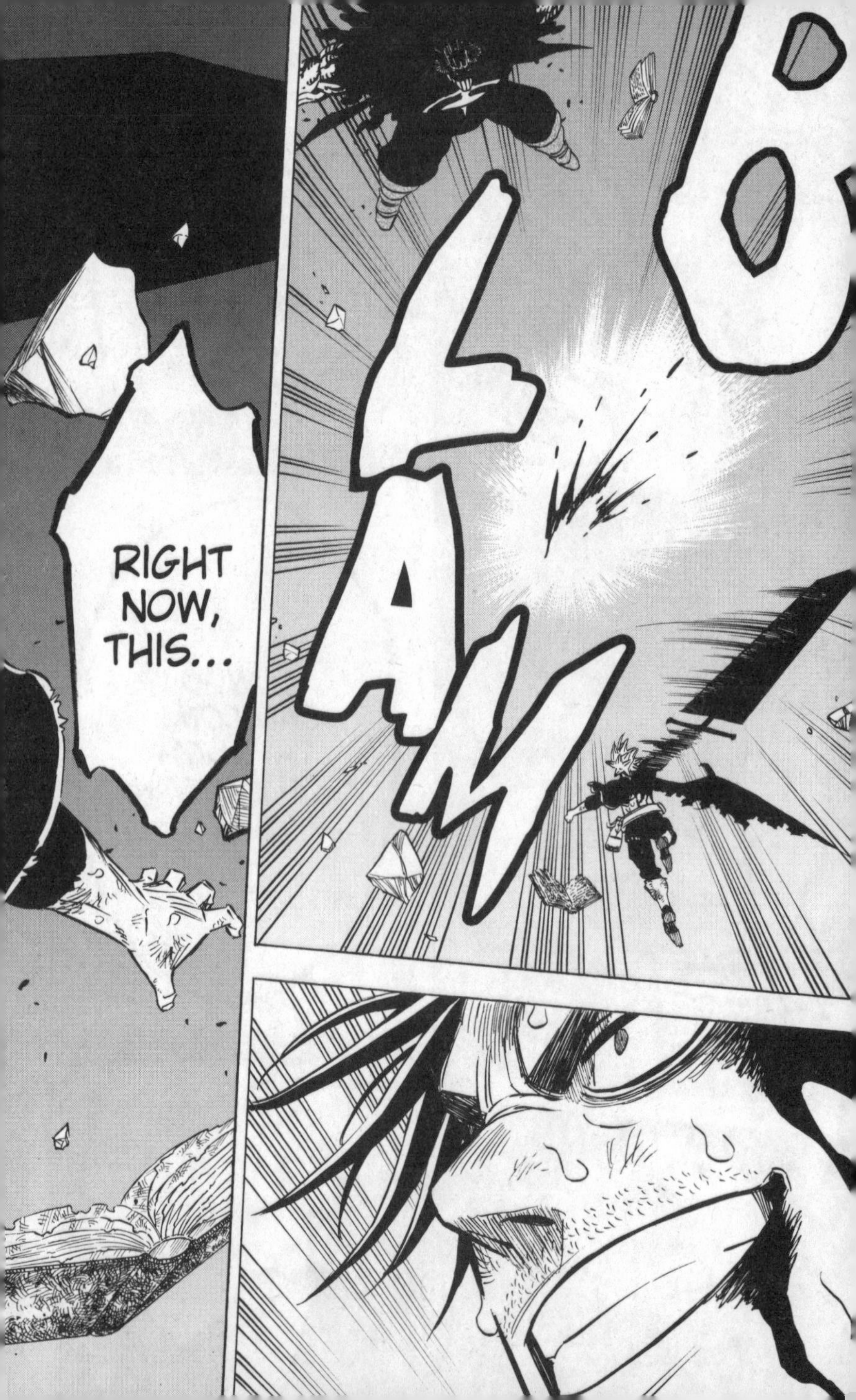
RIGHT NOW, THIS...

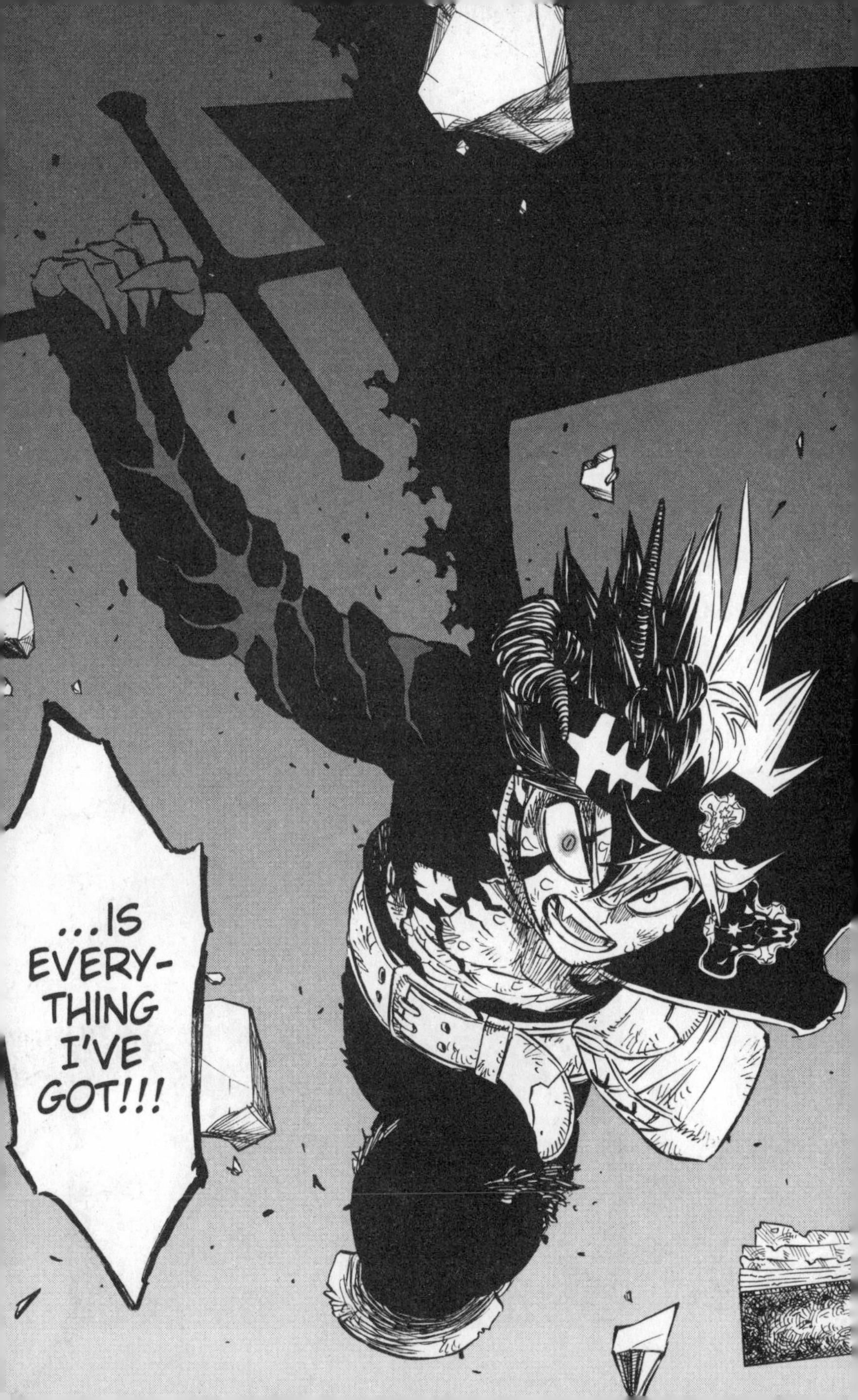
...IS EVERY-THING I'VE GOT!!!

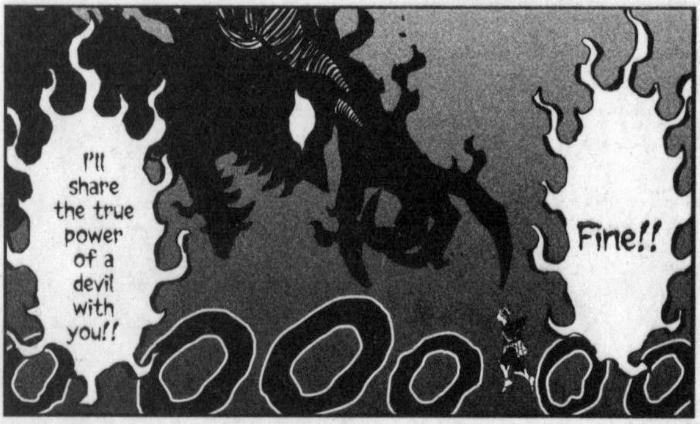
Fine!!
I'll share the true power of a devil with you!!

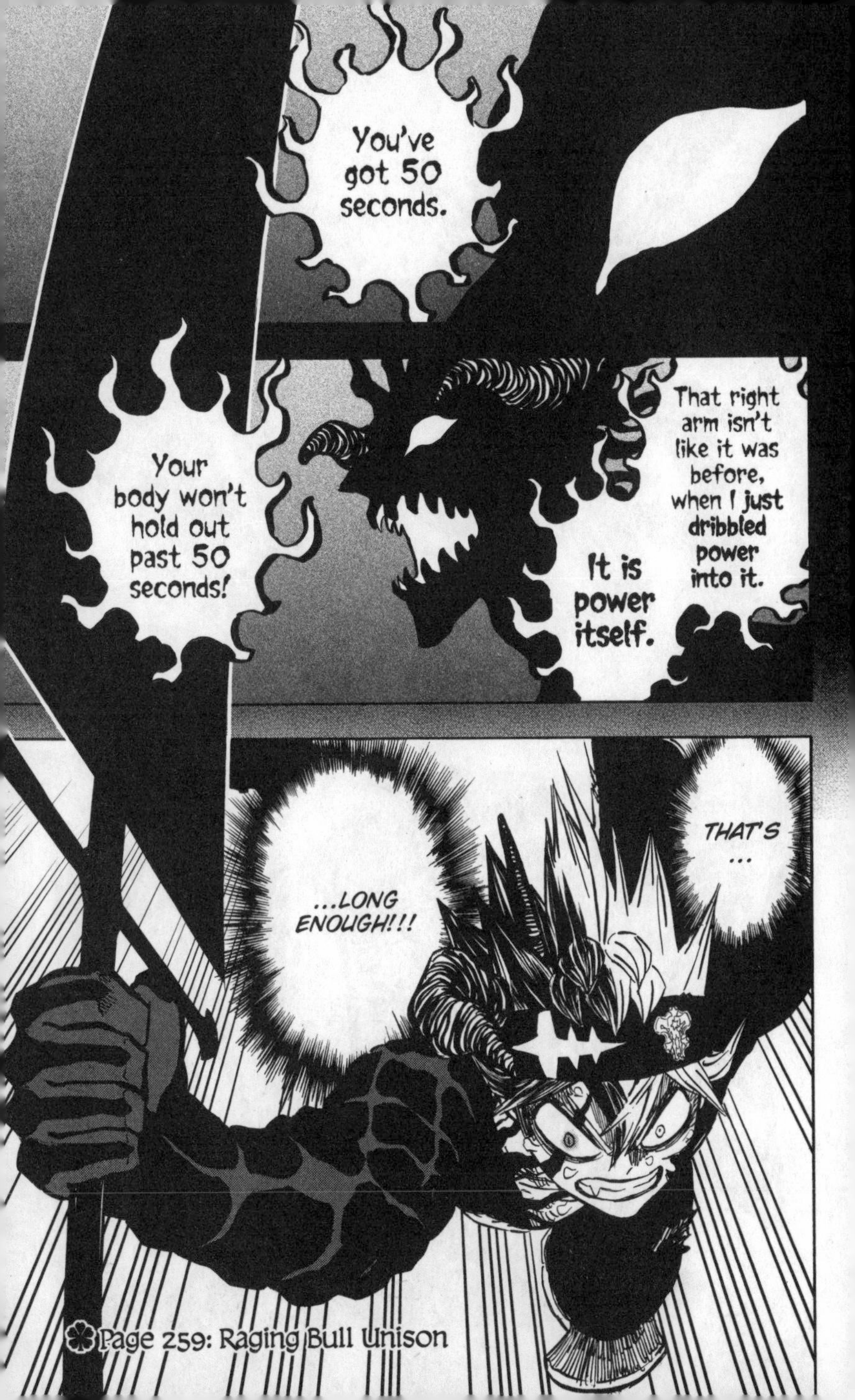
You've got 50 seconds.
That right arm isn't like it was before, when I just dribbled power into it.
It is power itself.
Your body won't hold out past 50 seconds!
THAT'S ...
...LONG ENOUGH!!!

Page 259: Raging Bull Unison

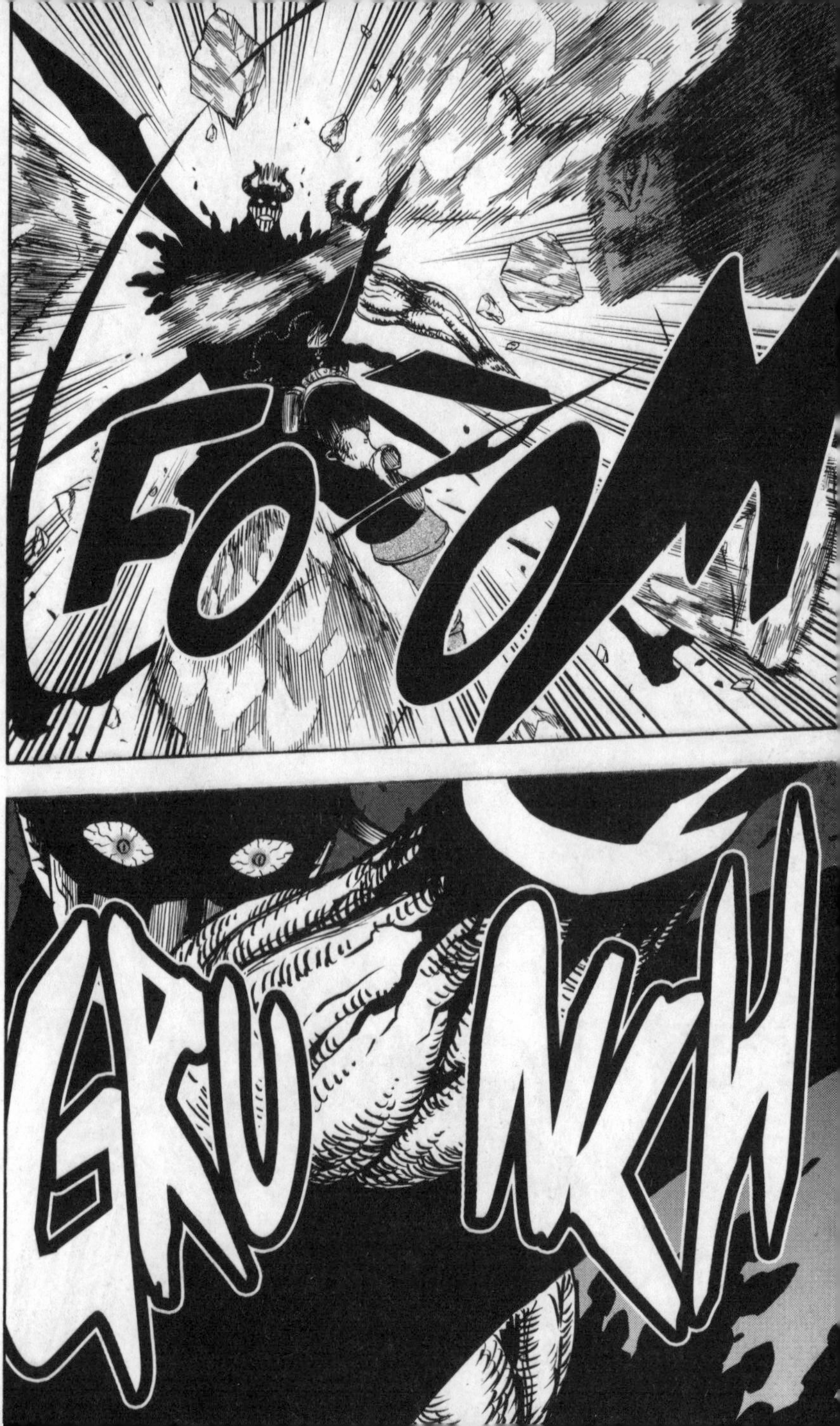
FOOM
CRUNCH

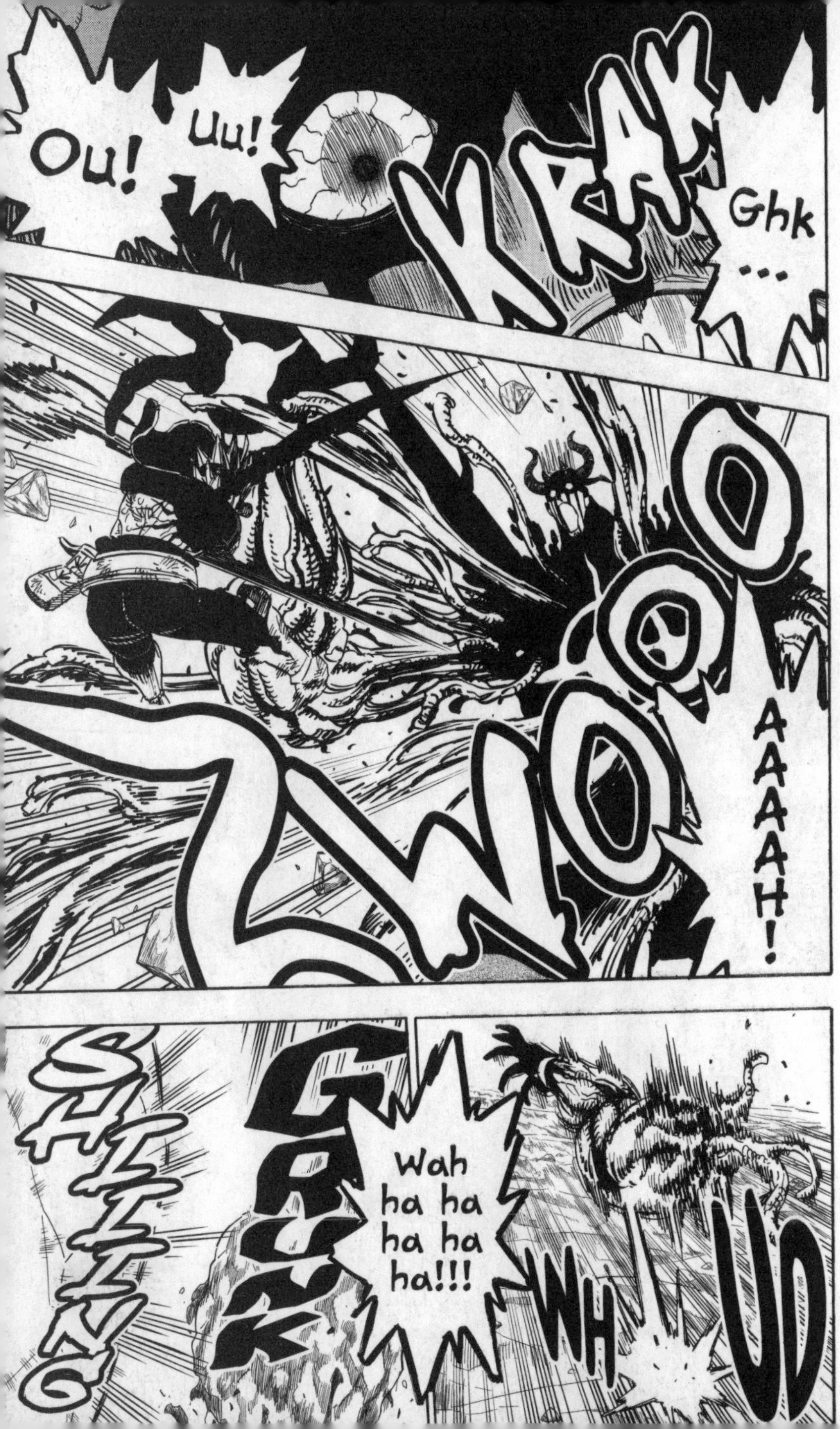
Ghk ...
KRAK
Uu!
Ou!
WAAAAH!
WOOO
WHUD
Wah ha ha ha ha ha!!!
GRACK
SHIIING

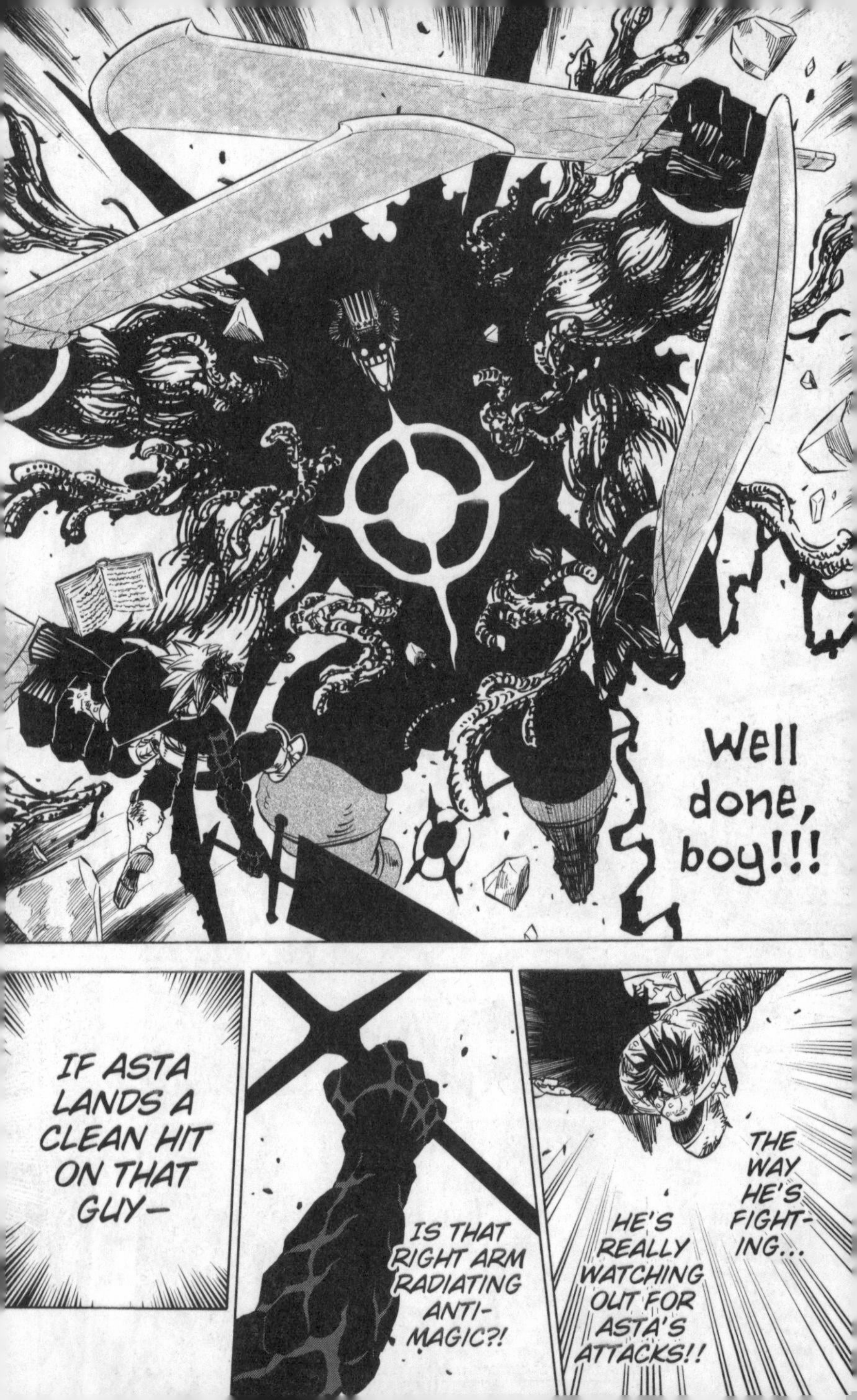
Well done, boy!!!
THE WAY HE'S FIGHTING...
HE'S REALLY WATCHING OUT FOR ASTA'S ATTACKS!!
IS THAT RIGHT ARM RADIATING ANTI-MAGIC?!
IF ASTA LANDS A CLEAN HIT ON THAT GUY—

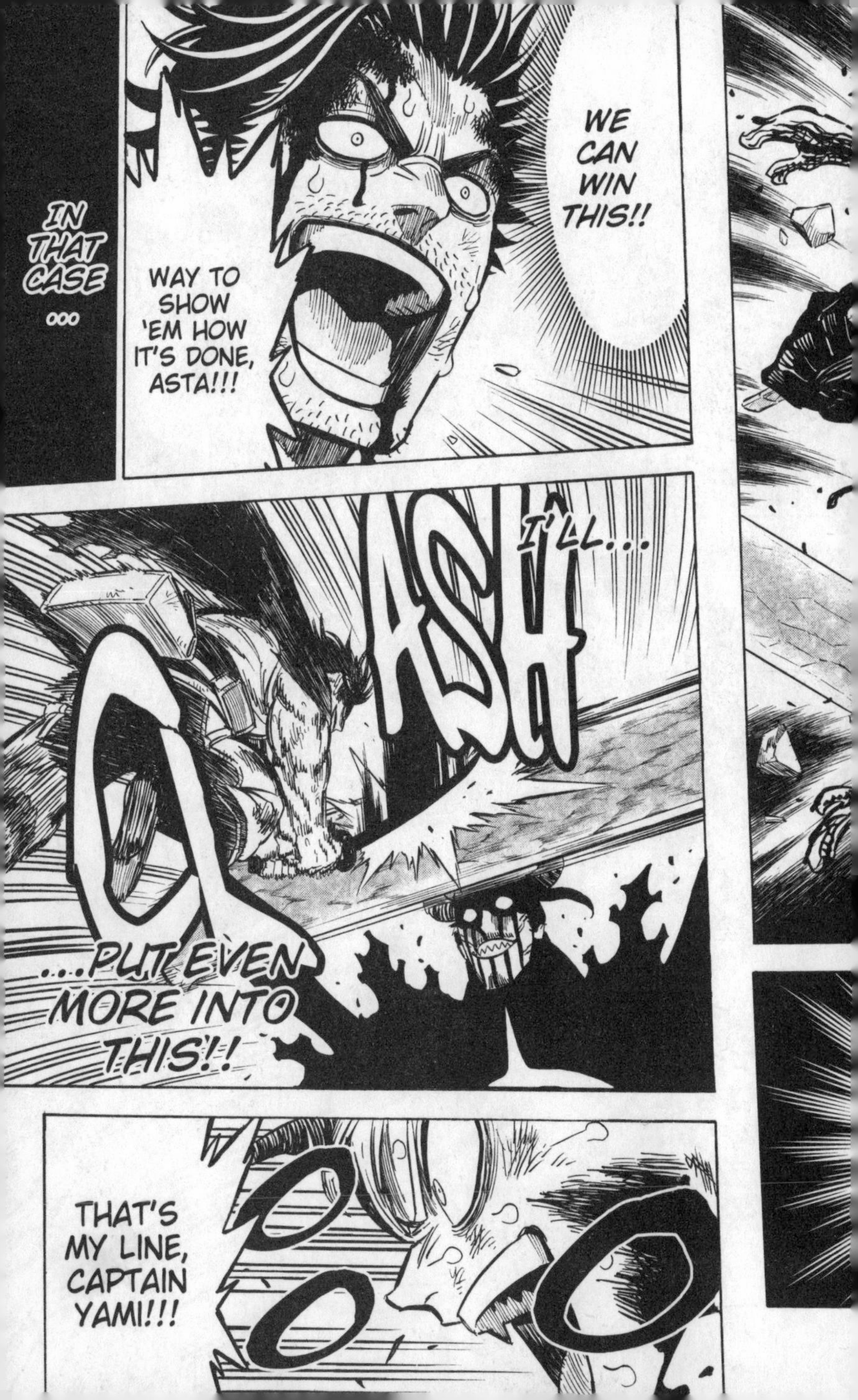
WE CAN WIN THIS!!
WAY TO SHOW 'EM HOW IT'S DONE, ASTA!!!
IN THAT CASE...
I'LL...
ASH
...PUT EVEN MORE INTO THIS!!
THAT'S MY LINE, CAPTAIN YAMI!!!

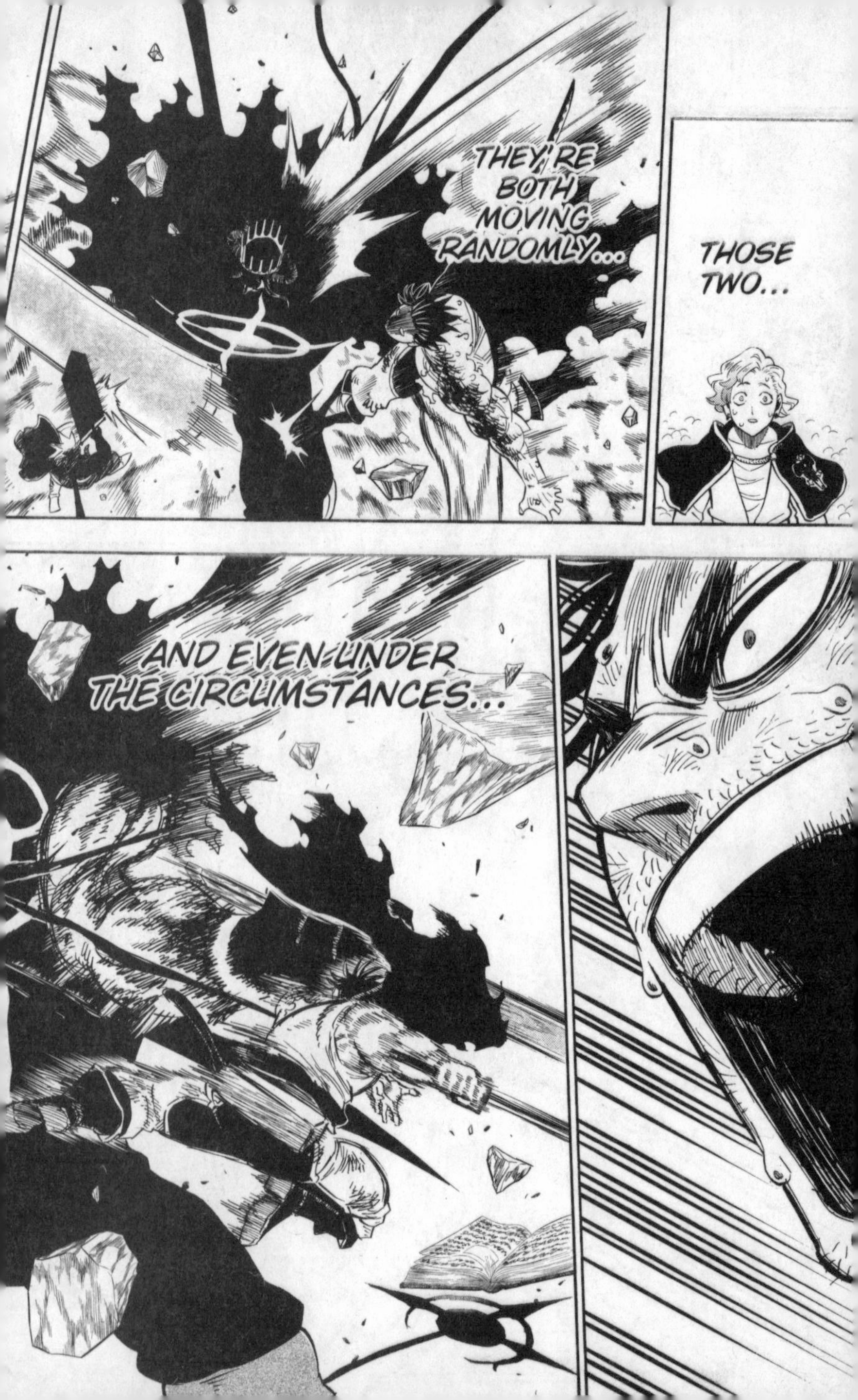
THOSE TWO...
THEY'RE BOTH MOVING RANDOMLY...
AND EVEN UNDER THE CIRCUMSTANCES...

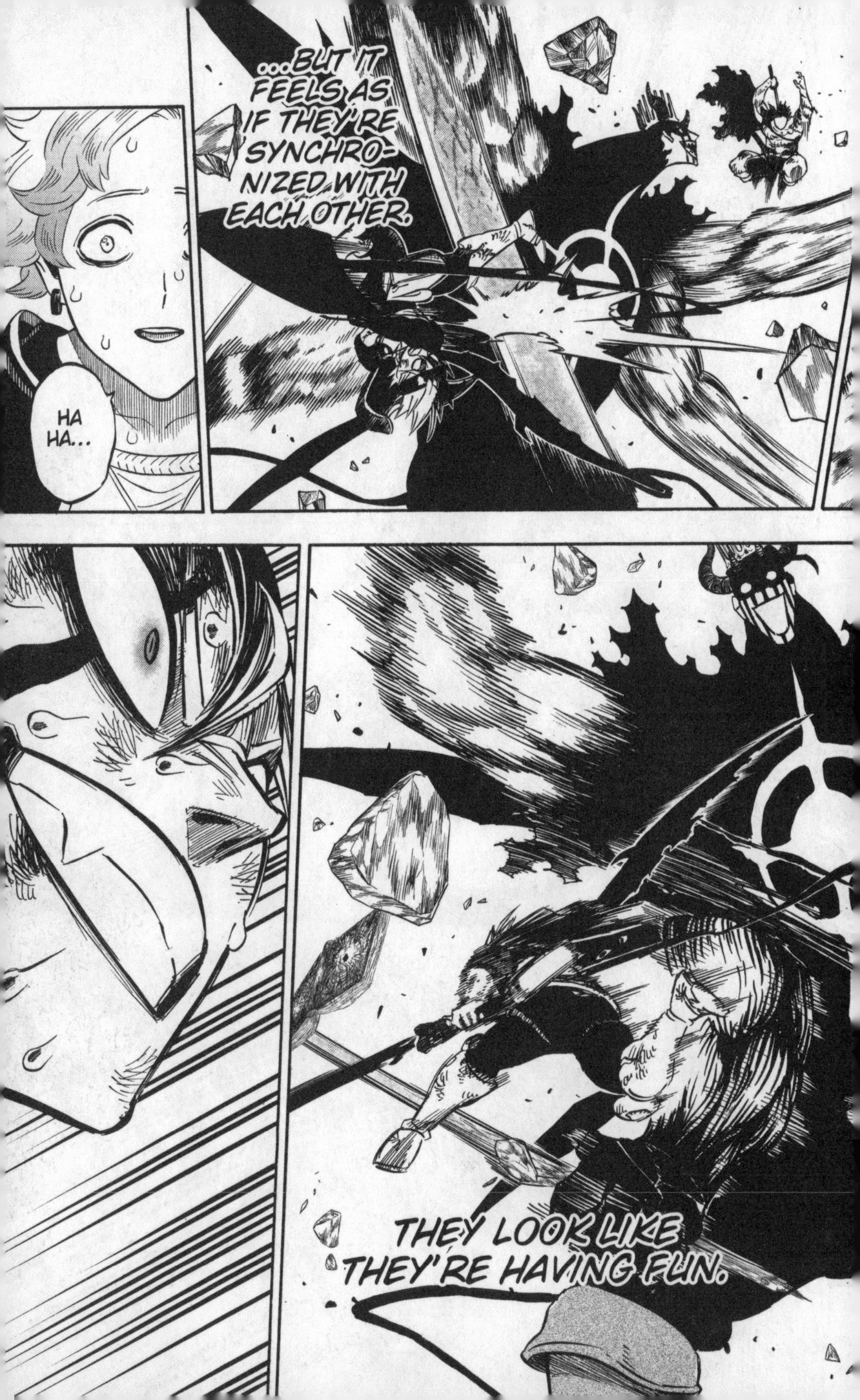
...BUT IT FEELS AS IF THEY'RE SYNCHRO-NIZED WITH EACH OTHER.
HA HA...
THEY LOOK LIKE THEY'RE HAVING FUN.

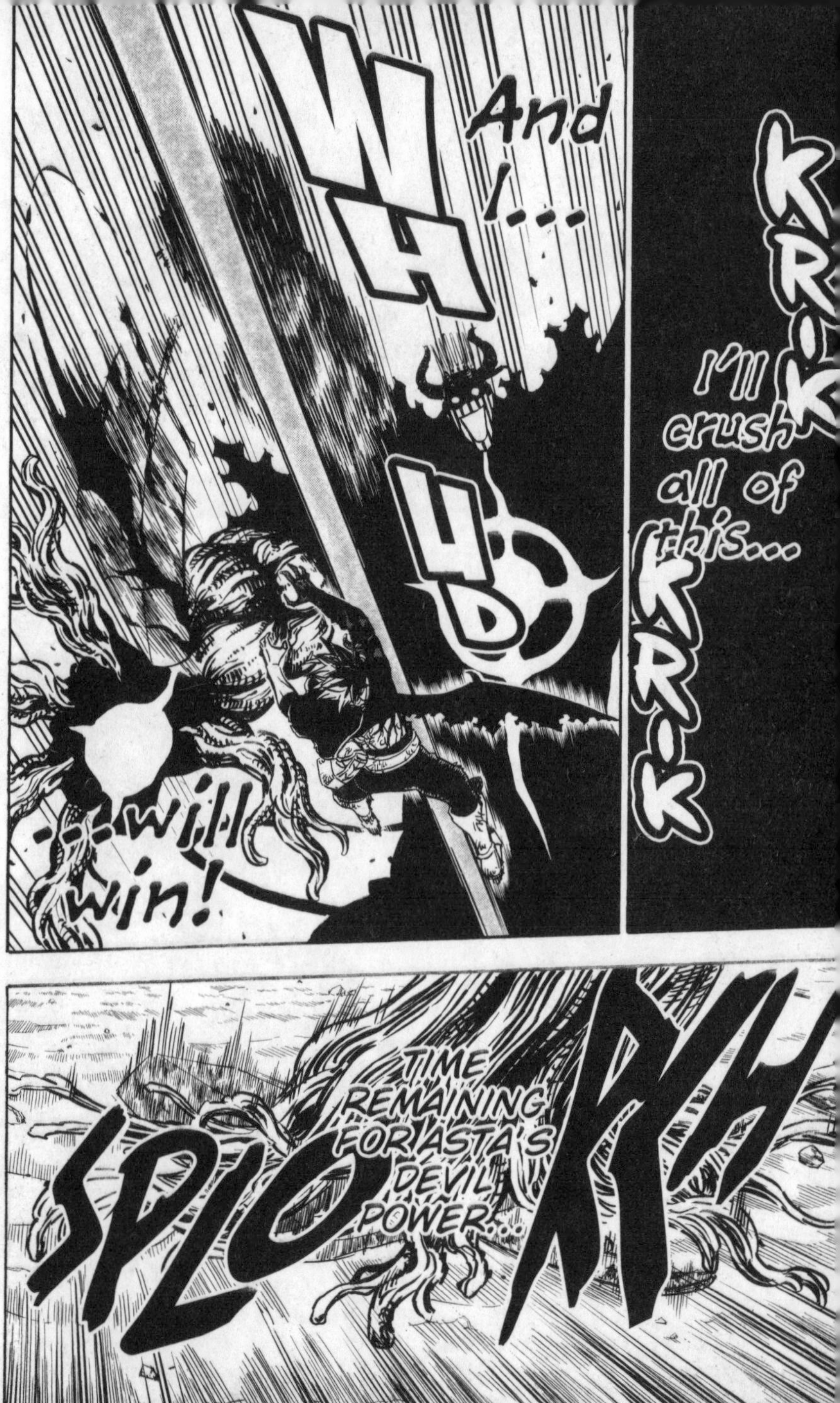
KRIK
I'll crush all of this...
KRIK
And I...
WHUD
...will win!
TIME REMAINING FOR ASTA'S DEVIL POWER...

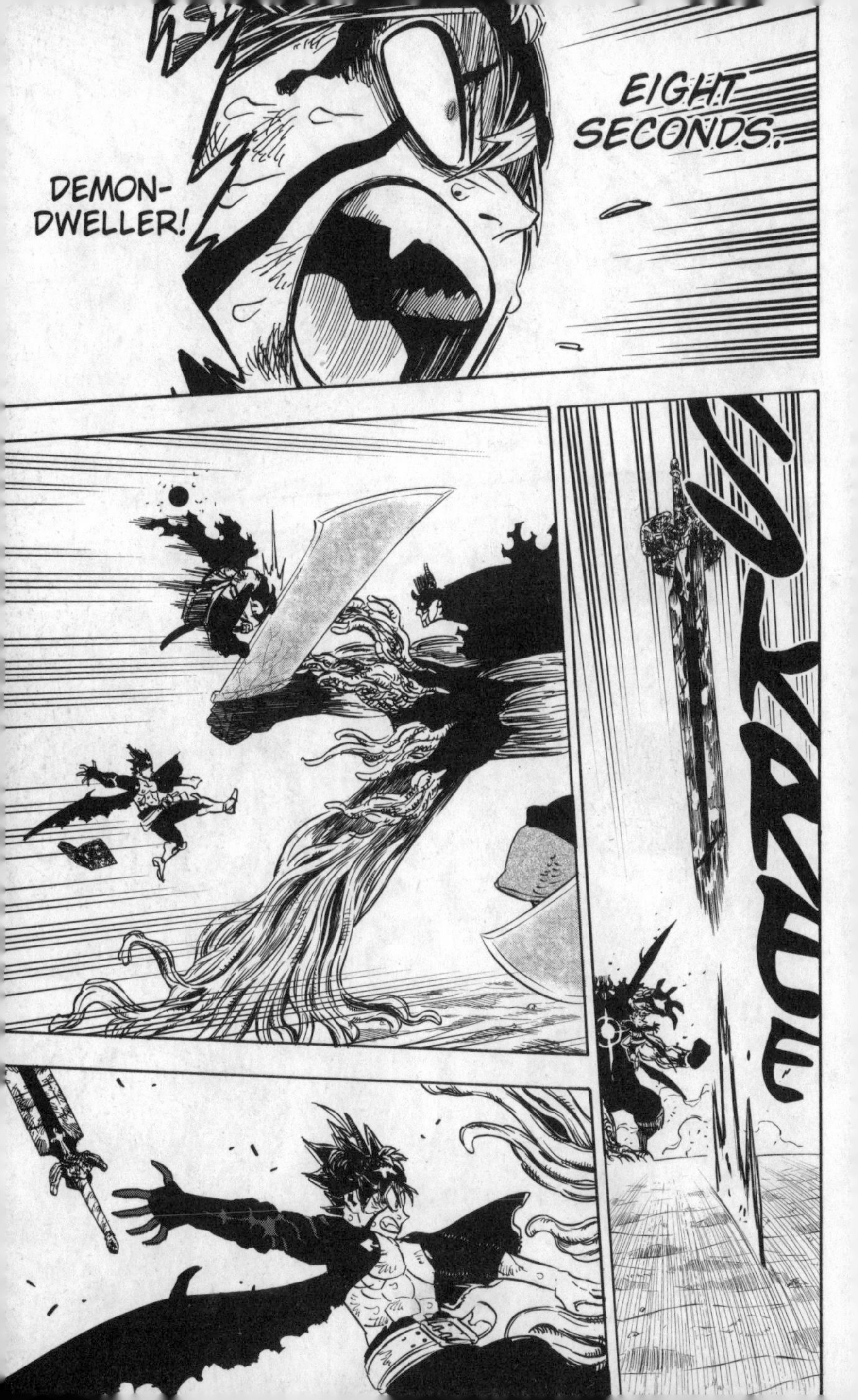
EIGHT SECONDS.
DEMON-DWELLER!

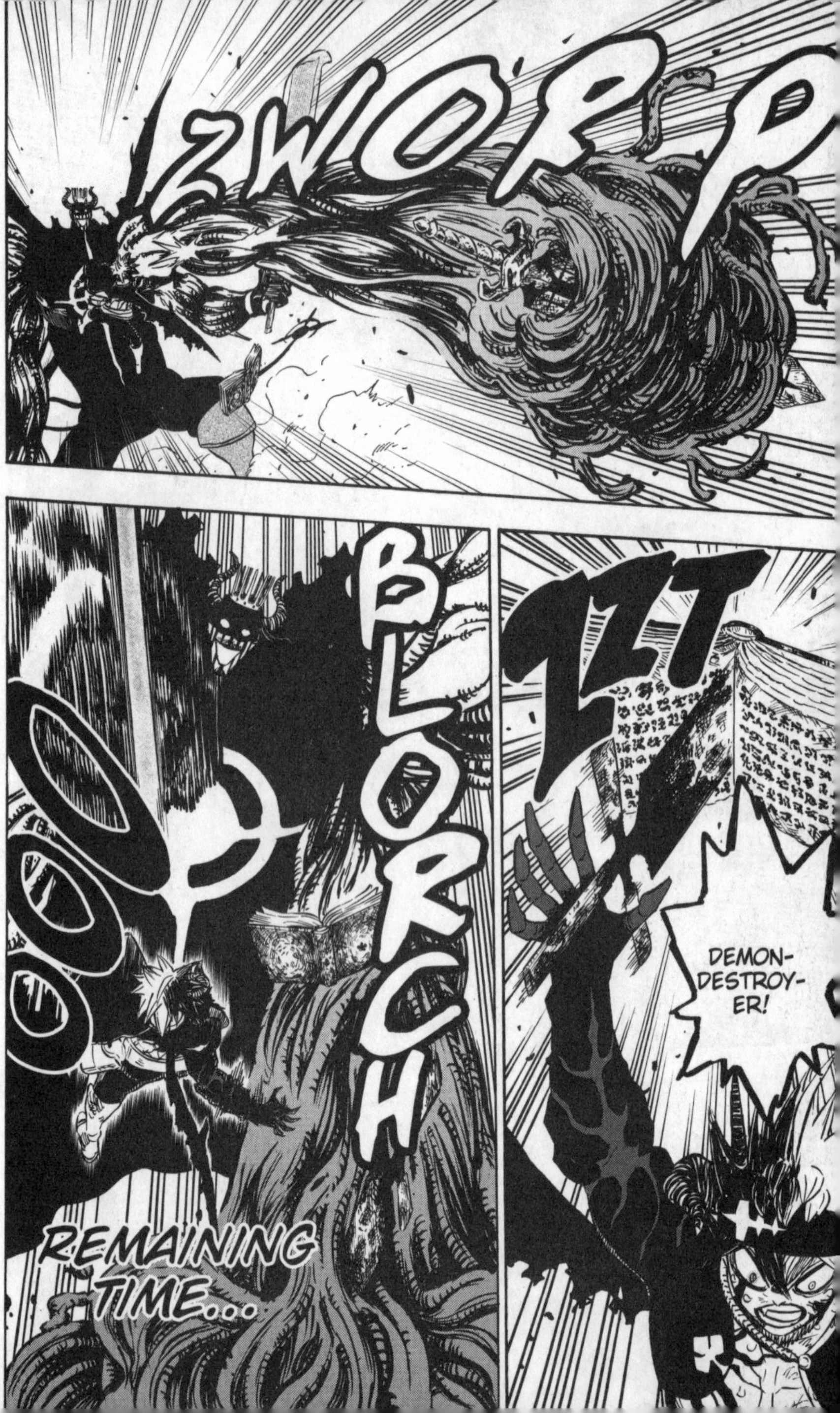
ZWOPP
DEMON-DESTROYER!
BLORCH
REMAINING TIME...

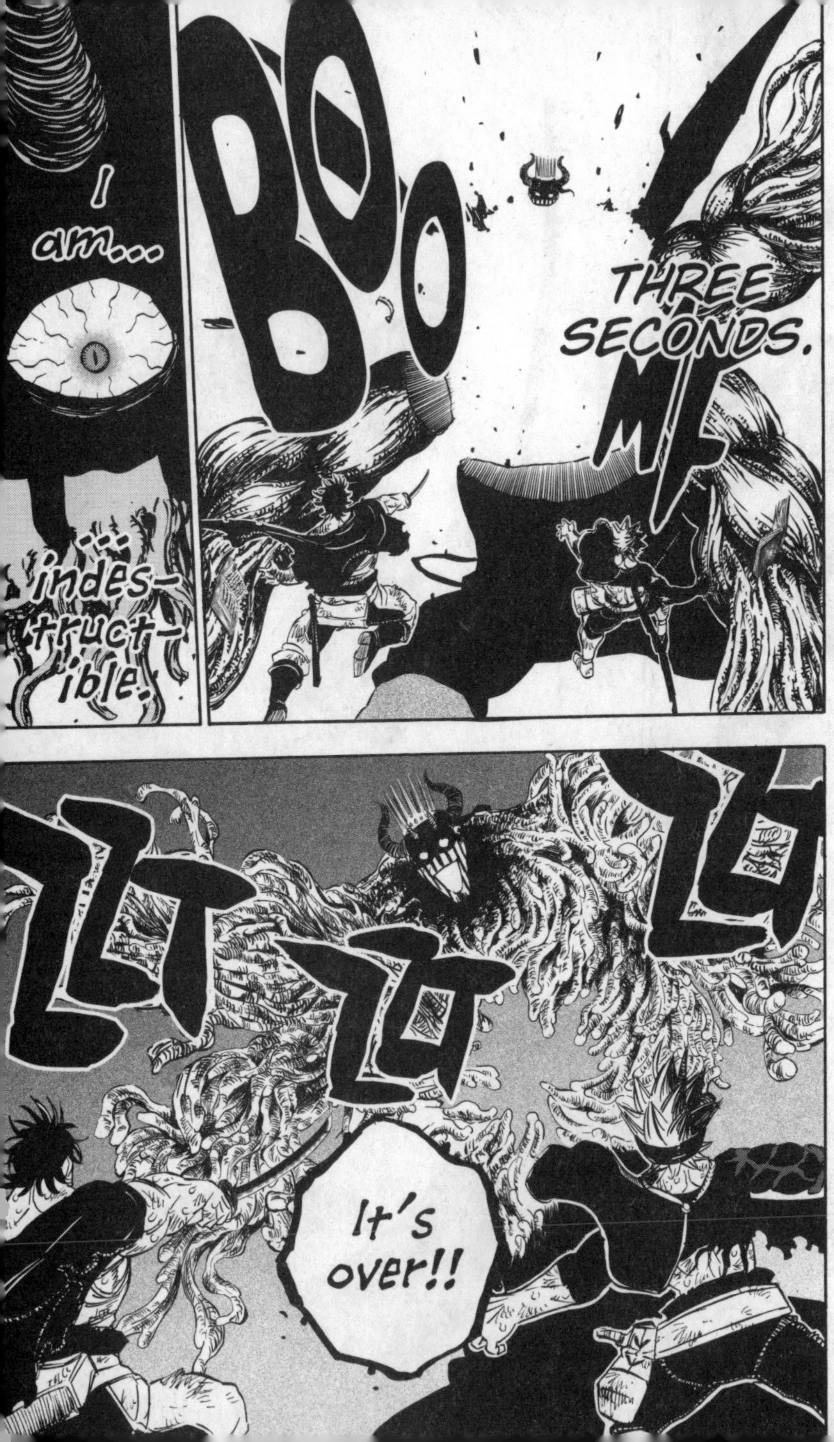
THREE SECONDS.
BOOM
I am...
...indestructible.
It's over!!

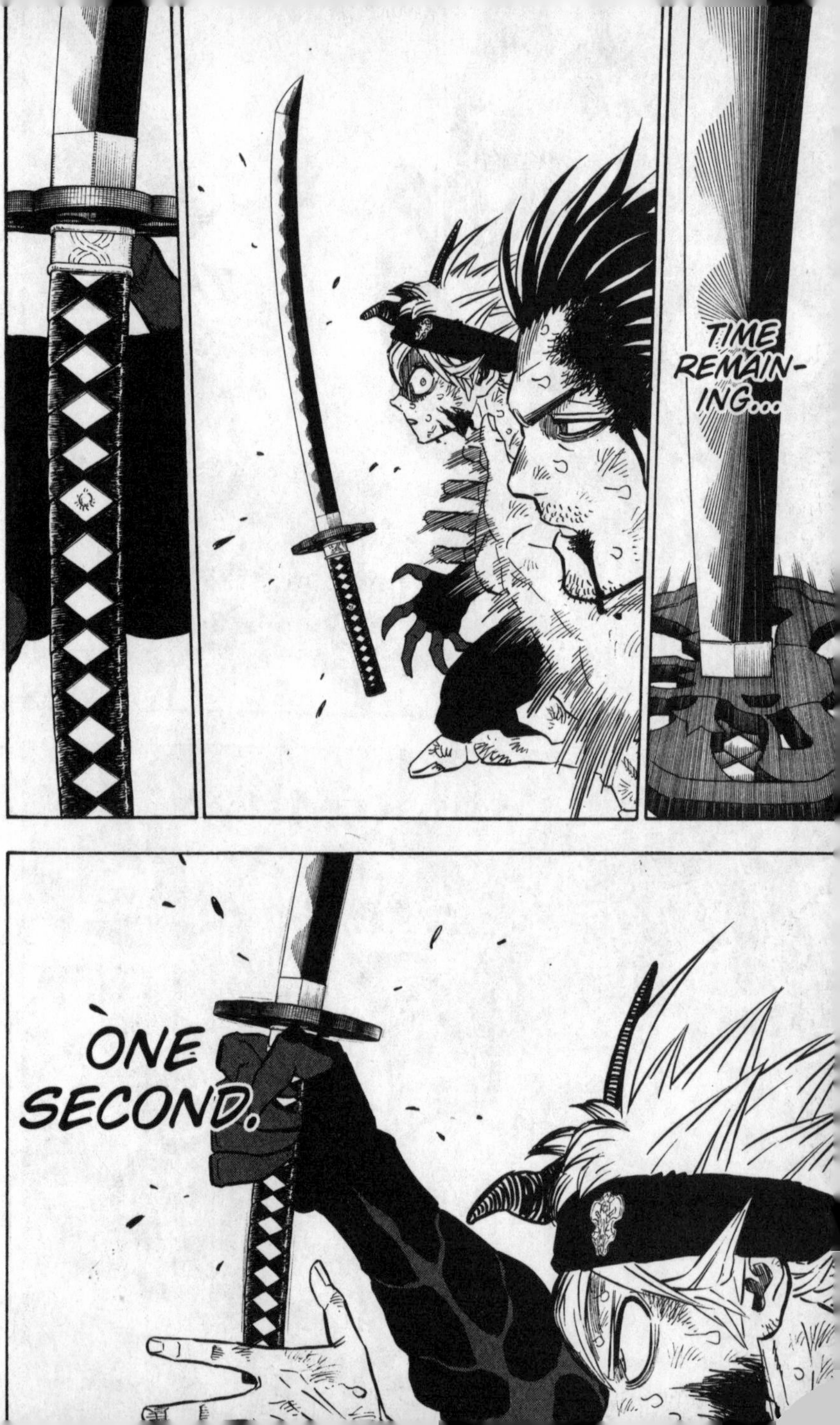
TIME REMAINING...
ONE SECOND.

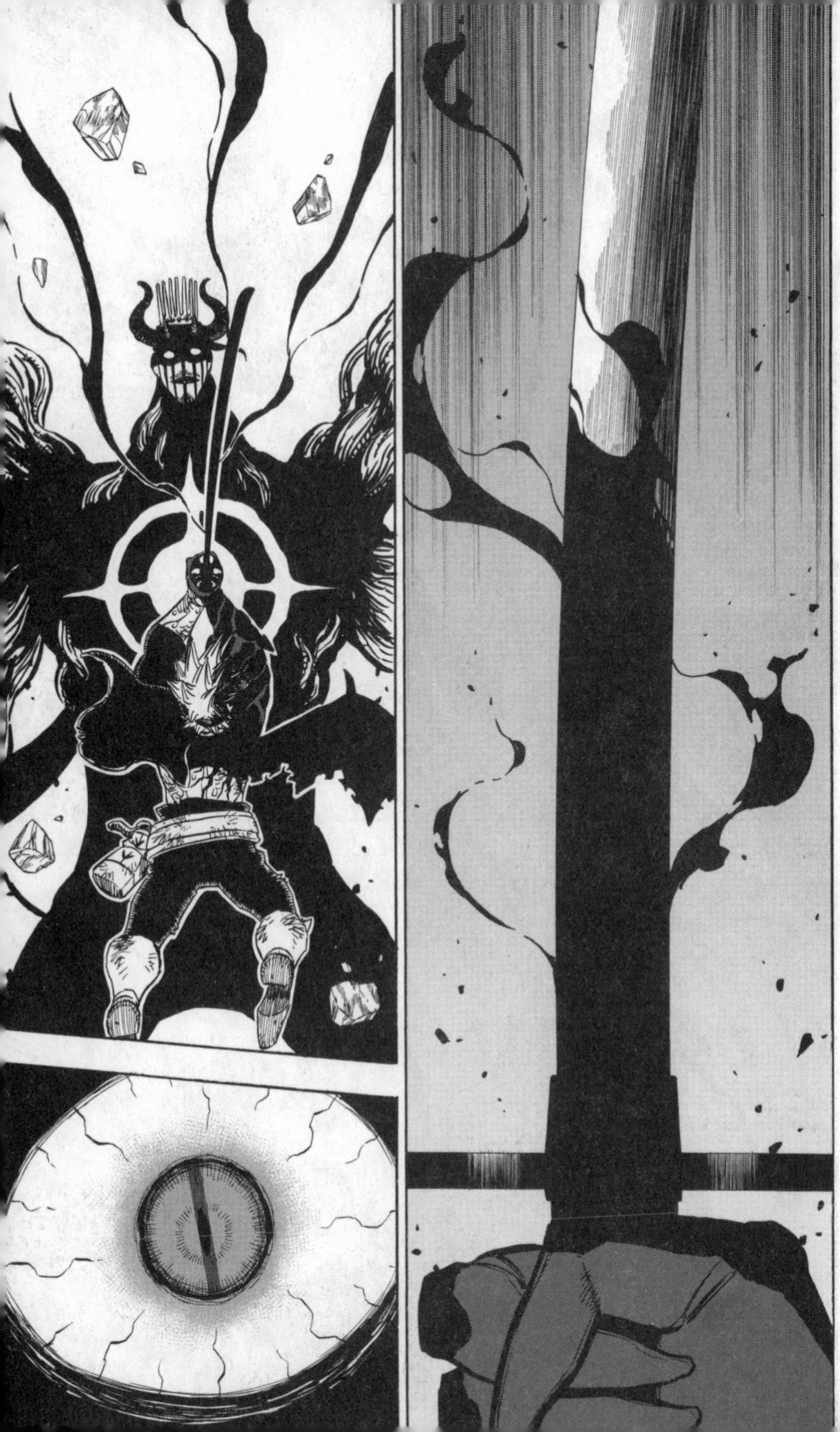

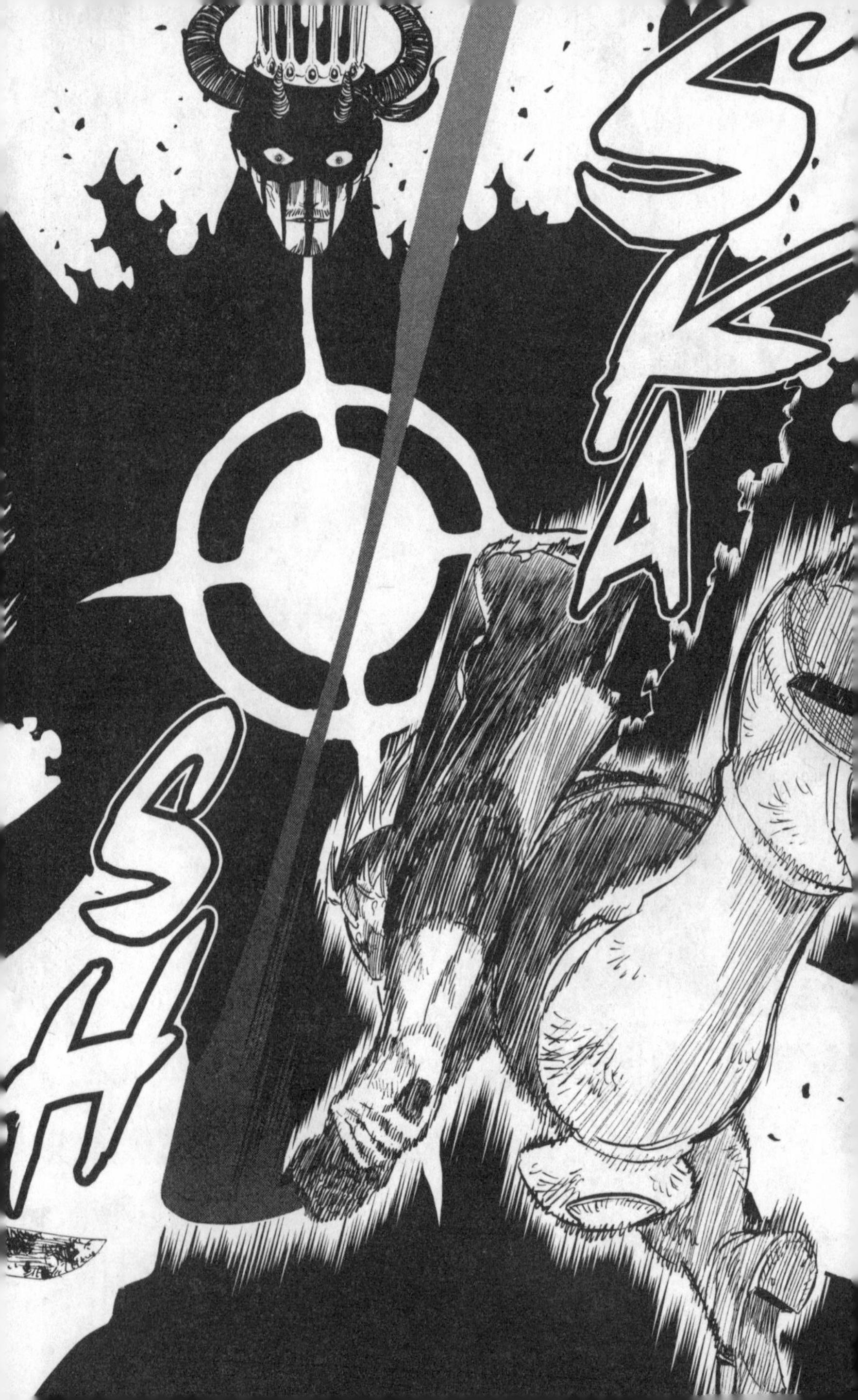
SKA
SH

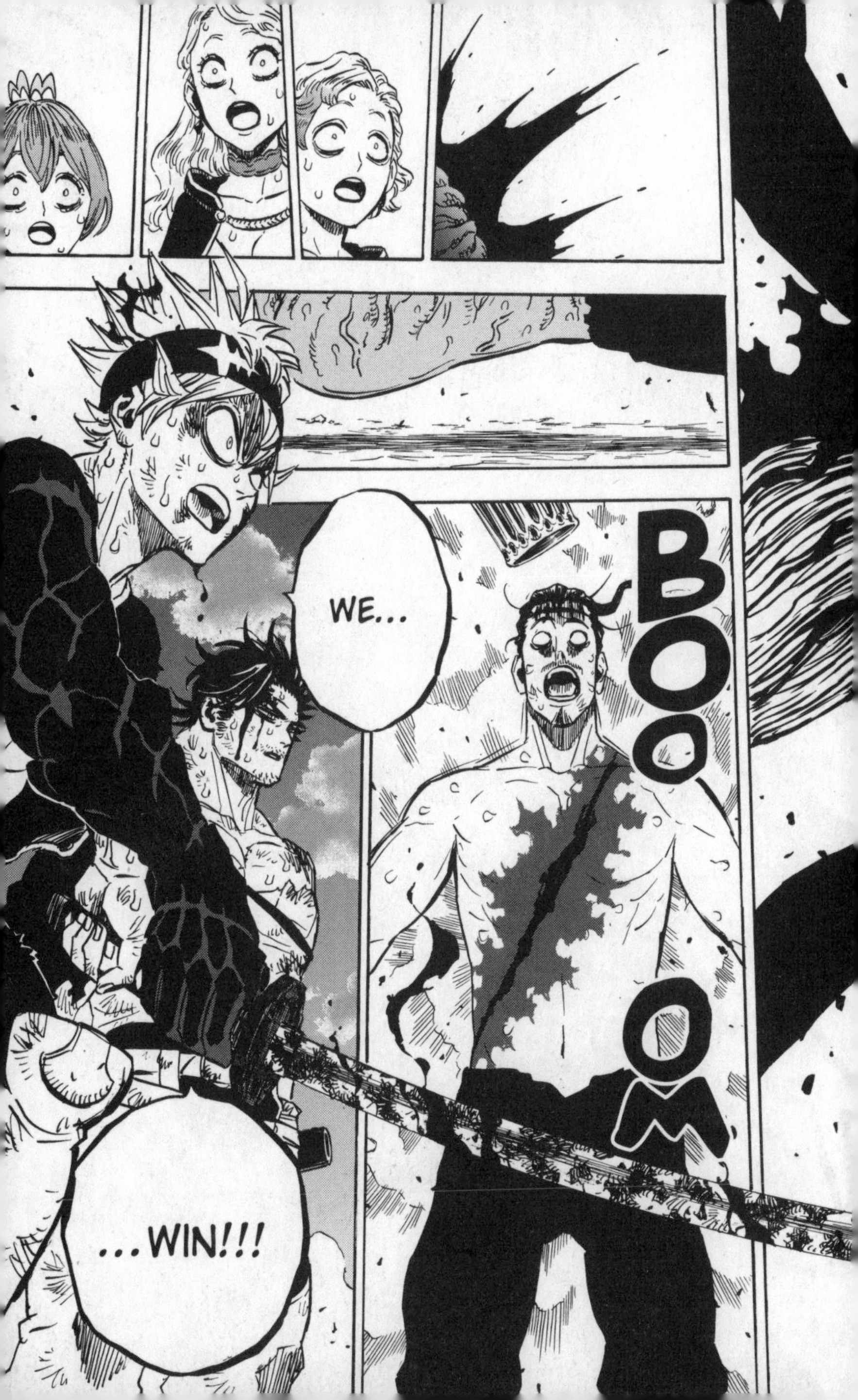
WE...
BOOOM
...WIN!!!

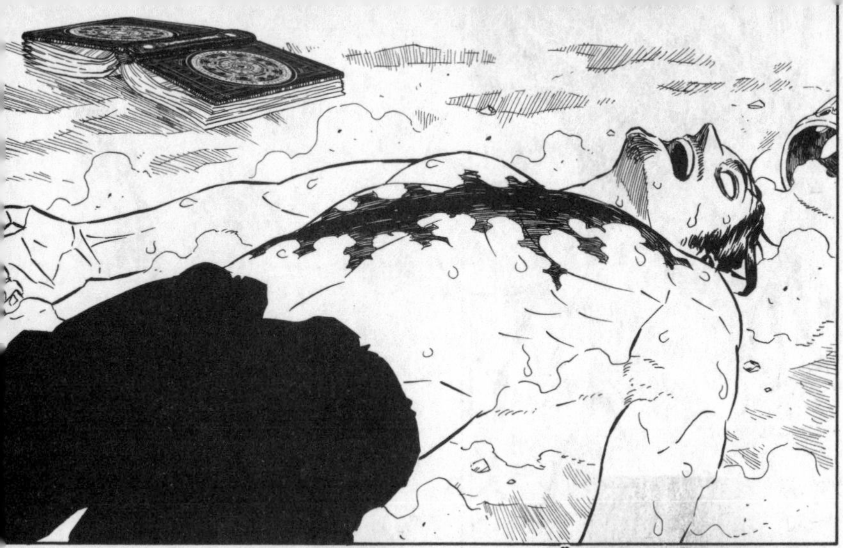

Page 260: Dark Out

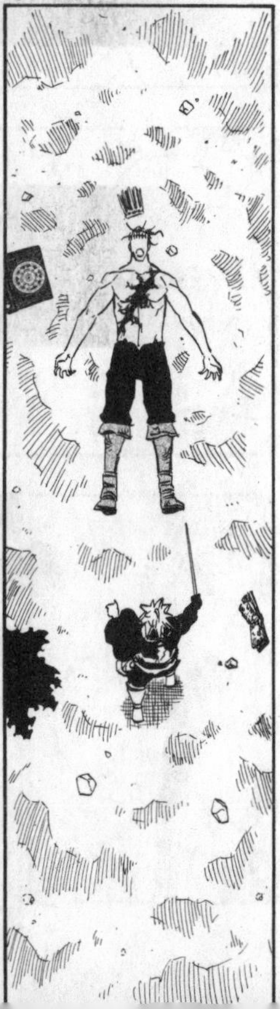

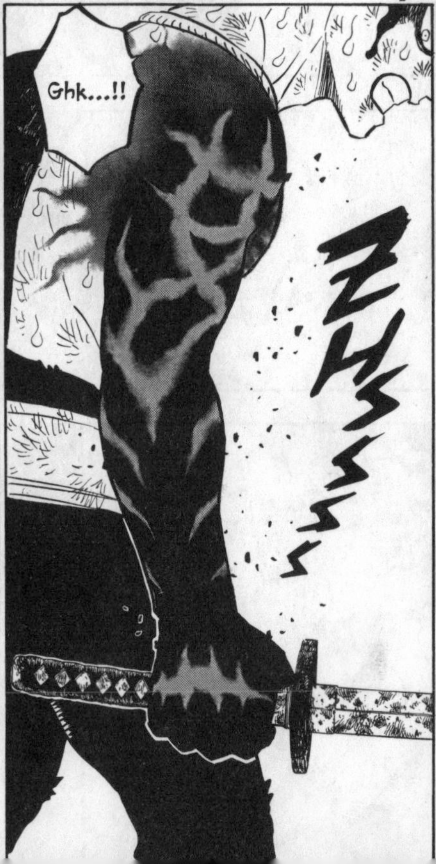
Ghk...!!
ZZHSSSS

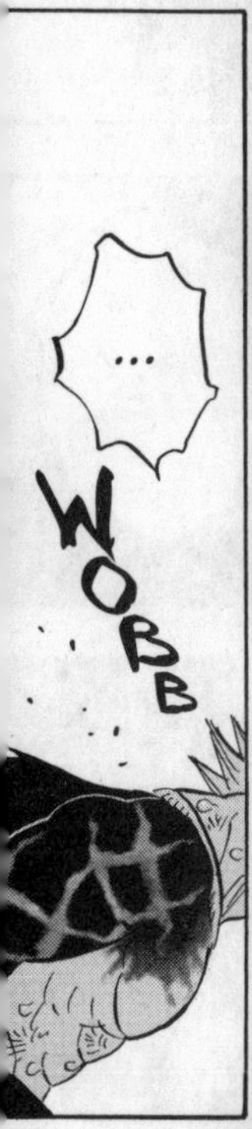
...
WOBB

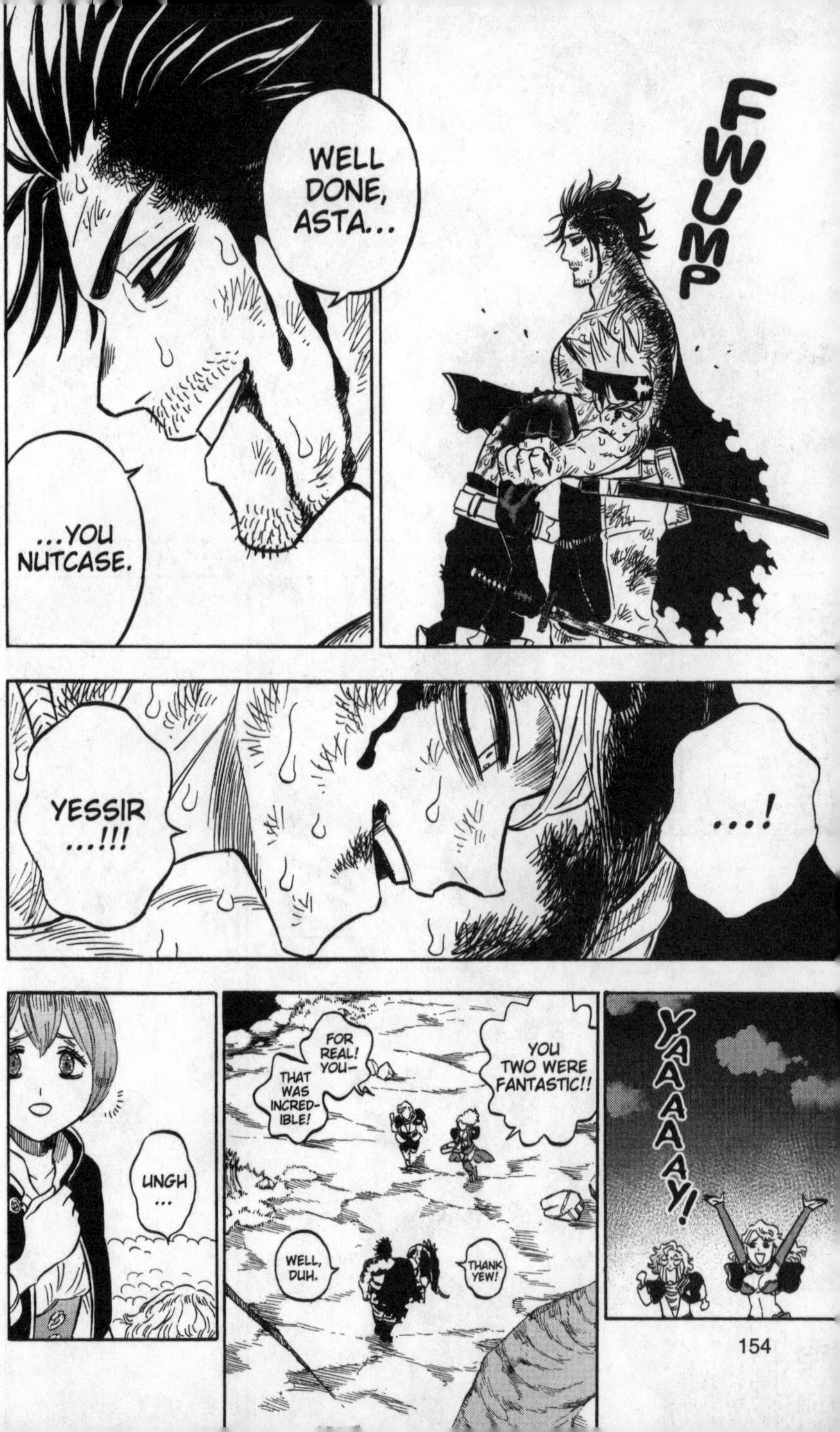
FWUMP
WELL DONE, ASTA...
...YOU NUTCASE.
...!
YESSIR ...!!!
YAAAAAY!
YOU TWO WERE FANTASTIC!!
FOR REAL! YOU-
THAT WAS INCRED-IBLE!
THANK YEW!
WELL, DUH.
UNGH ...

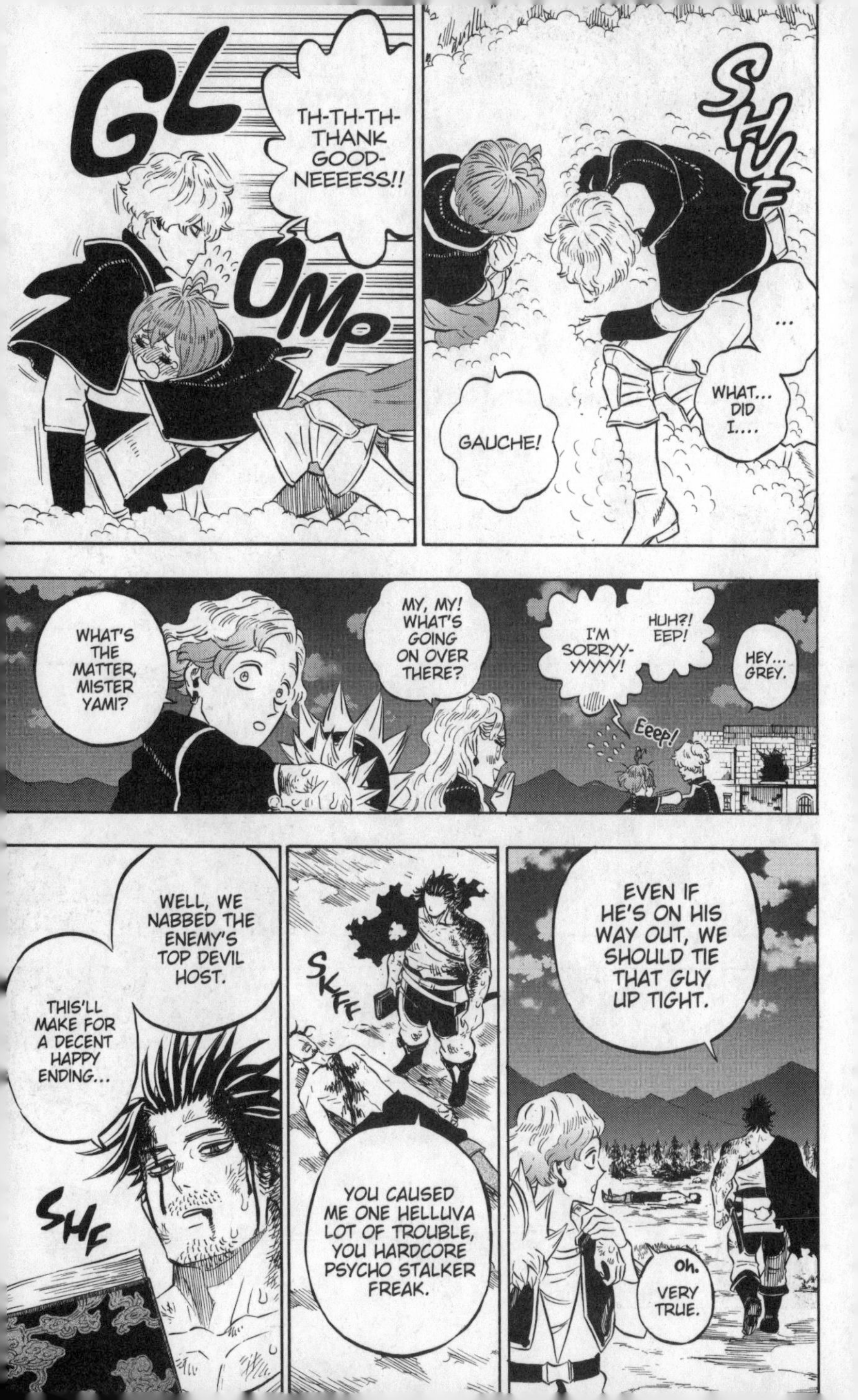
SHUF
...
WHAT... DID I....
GAUCHE!
TH-TH-TH-THANK GOOD-NEEEEESS!!
GLOMP
HEY... GREY.
HUH?! EEP!
I'M SORRYY-YYYYY!
Eeep!
MY, MY! WHAT'S GOING ON OVER THERE?
WHAT'S THE MATTER, MISTER YAMI?
EVEN IF HE'S ON HIS WAY OUT, WE SHOULD TIE THAT GUY UP TIGHT.
Oh.
VERY TRUE.
SKFF
YOU CAUSED ME ONE HELLUVA LOT OF TROUBLE, YOU HARDCORE PSYCHO STALKER FREAK.
WELL, WE NABBED THE ENEMY'S TOP DEVIL HOST.
THIS'LL MAKE FOR A DECENT HAPPY ENDING...
SHF

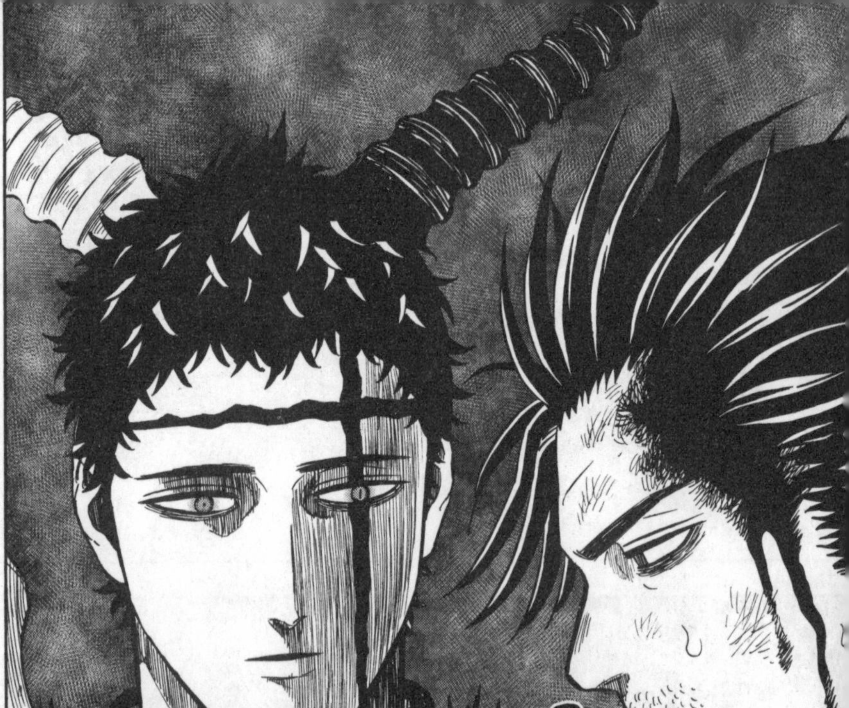
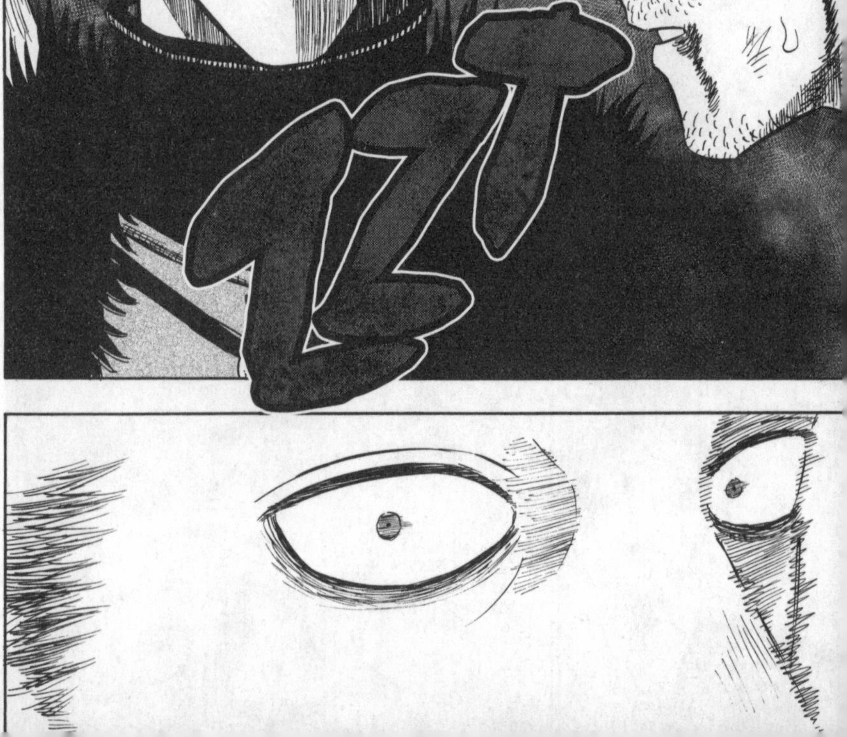

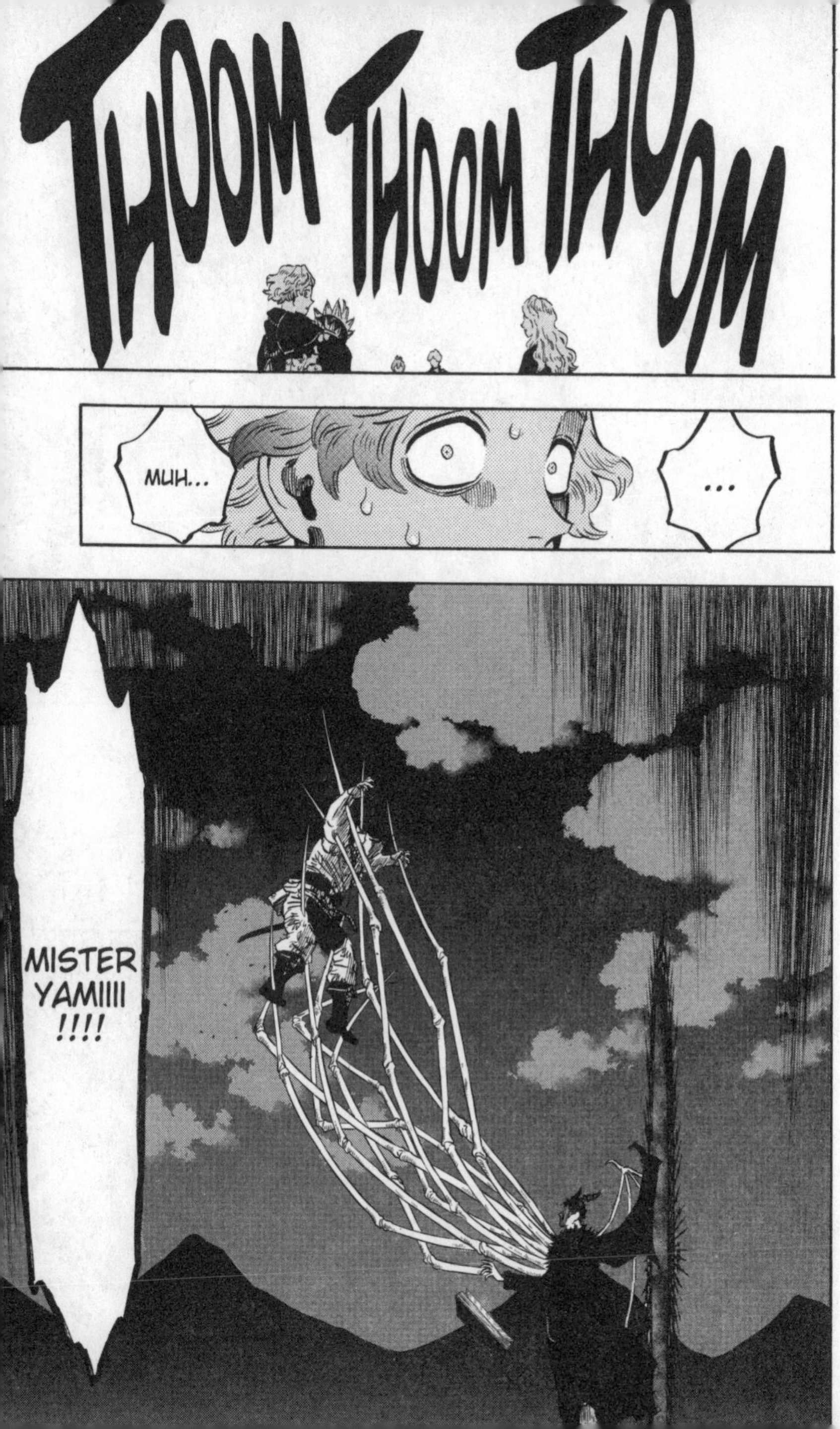
THOOM THOOM THOOM
...
MUH...
MISTER YAMIIIII !!!!

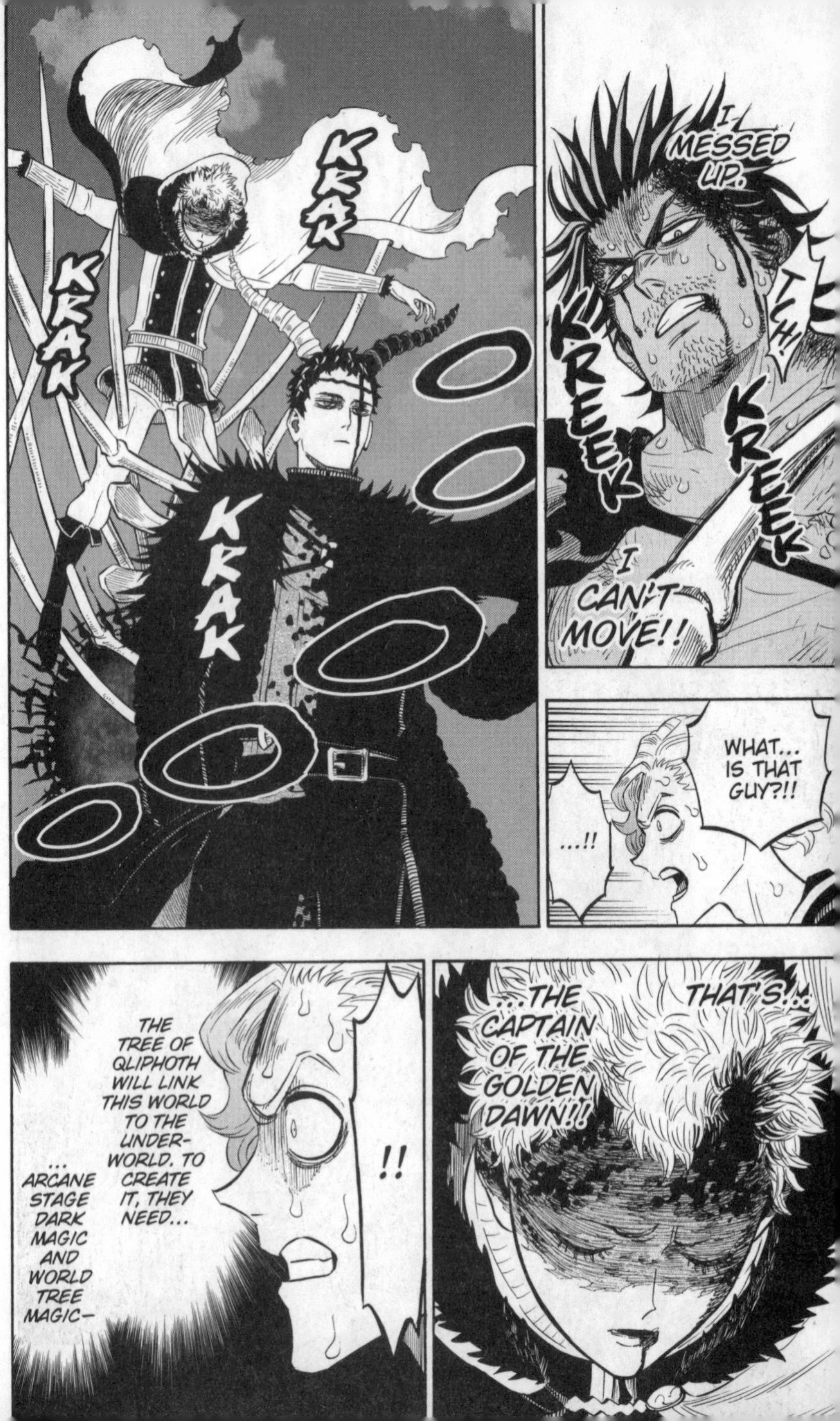
I MESSED UP.
TCH!
KREEEK
KREEEK
I CAN'T MOVE!!
WHAT... IS THAT GUY?!!
...!!
KRAK
KRAK
KRAK
THAT'S...
...THE CAPTAIN OF THE GOLDEN DAWN!!
!!
THE TREE OF QLIPHOTH WILL LINK THIS WORLD TO THE UNDER-WORLD. TO CREATE IT, THEY NEED...
...ARCANE STAGE DARK MAGIC AND WORLD TREE MAGIC—

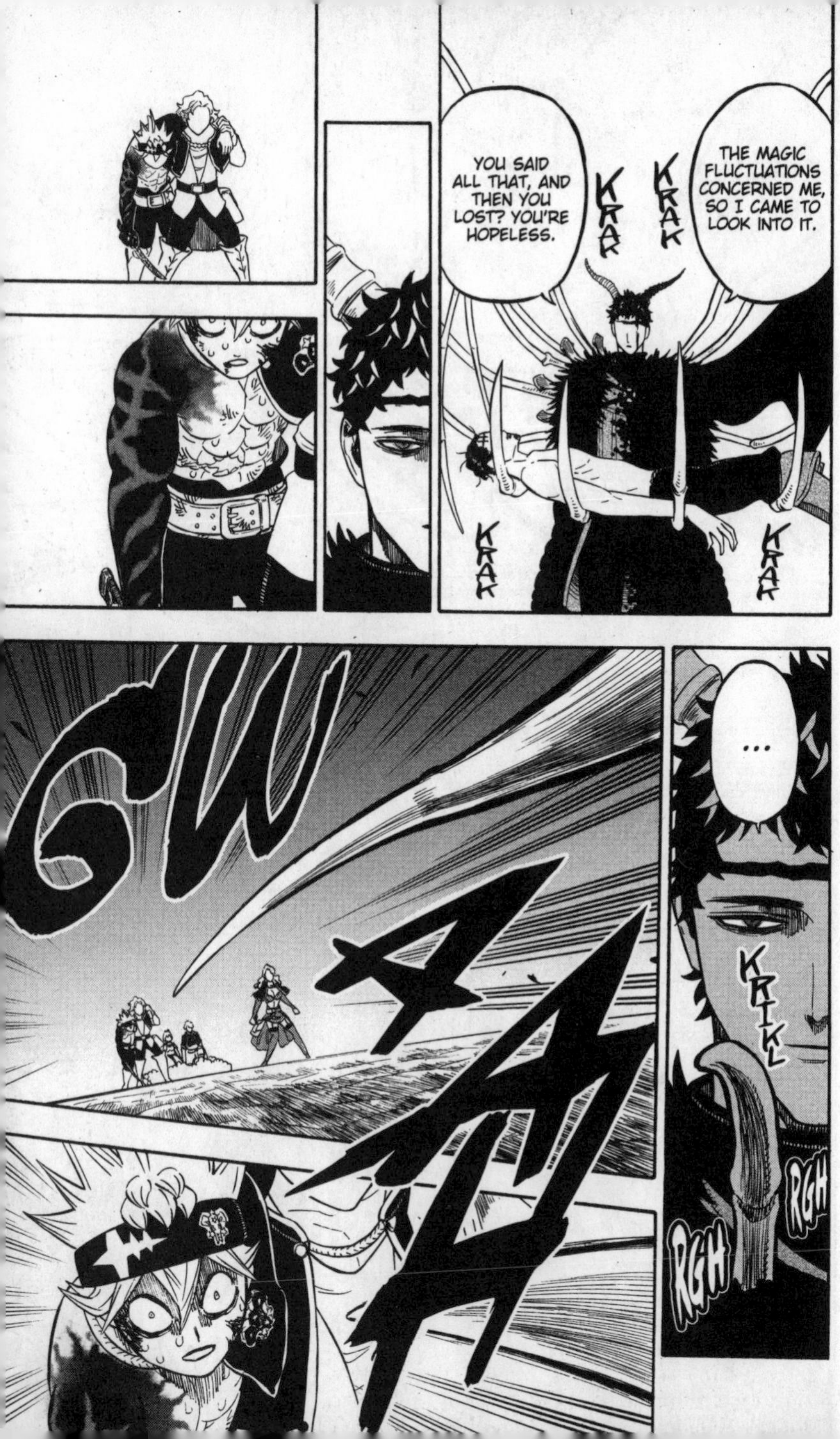
THE MAGIC FLUCTUATIONS CONCERNED ME, SO I CAME TO LOOK INTO IT.
KRAK
YOU SAID ALL THAT, AND THEN YOU LOST? YOU'RE HOPELESS.
KRAK
KRAK
KRAK
...
KRIKL
RGH
RGH
GWWAAAH

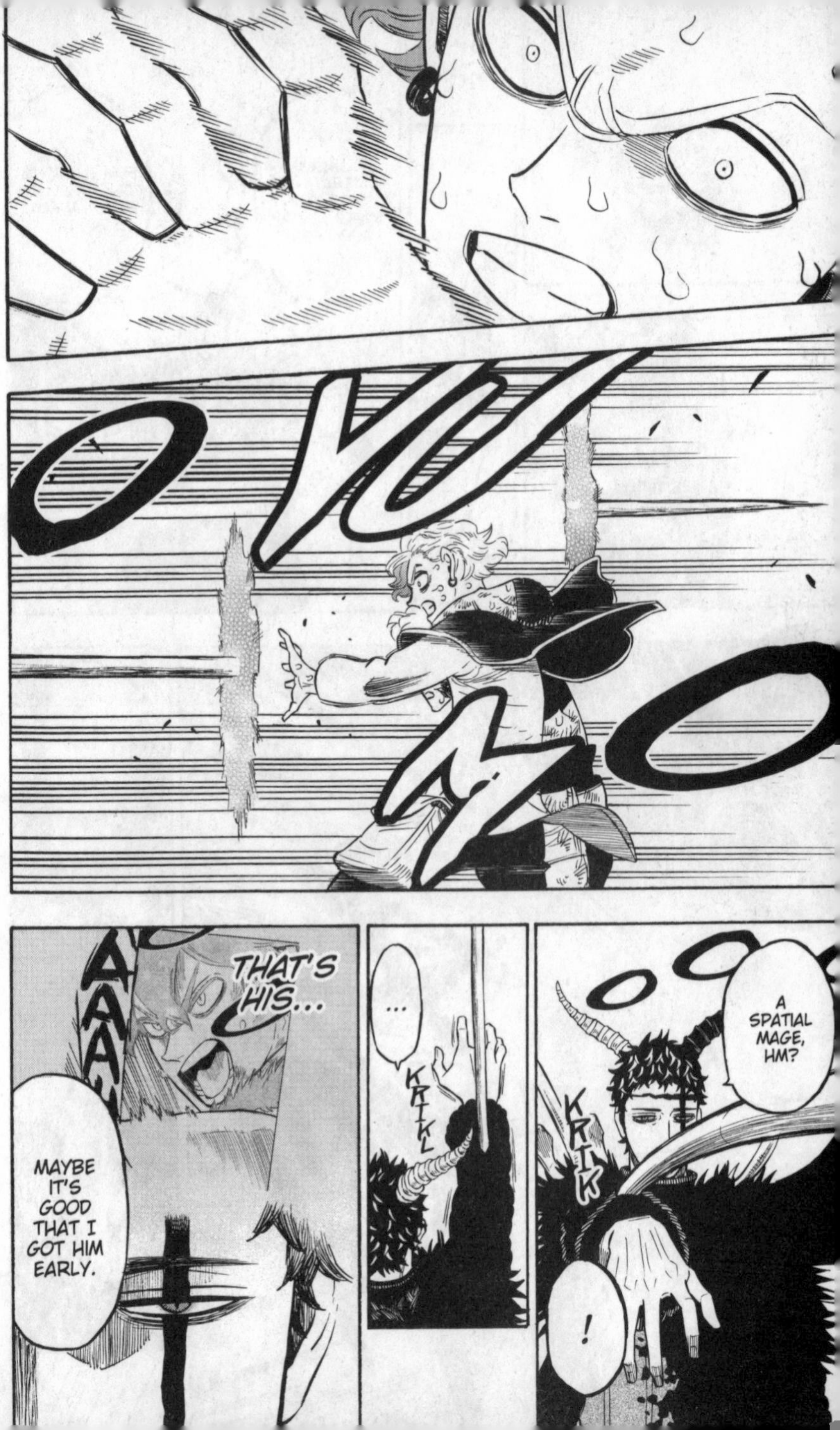
OYUOO
A SPATIAL MAGE, HM?
KRIK
!
KRIKL
...
AAA
THAT'S HIS...
MAYBE IT'S GOOD THAT I GOT HIM EARLY.

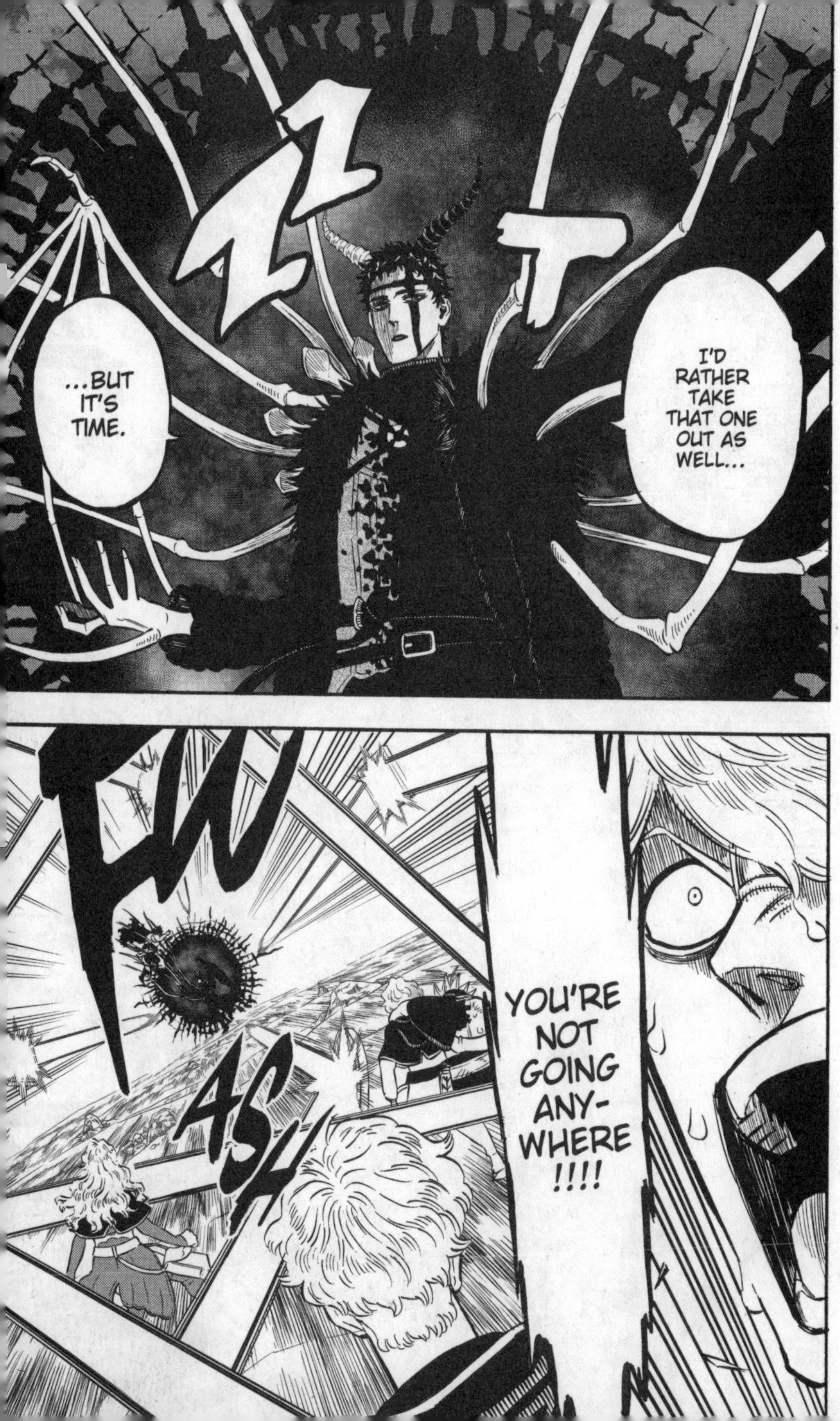
I'D RATHER TAKE THAT ONE OUT AS WELL...
...BUT IT'S TIME.
YOU'RE NOT GOING ANYWHERE!!!!

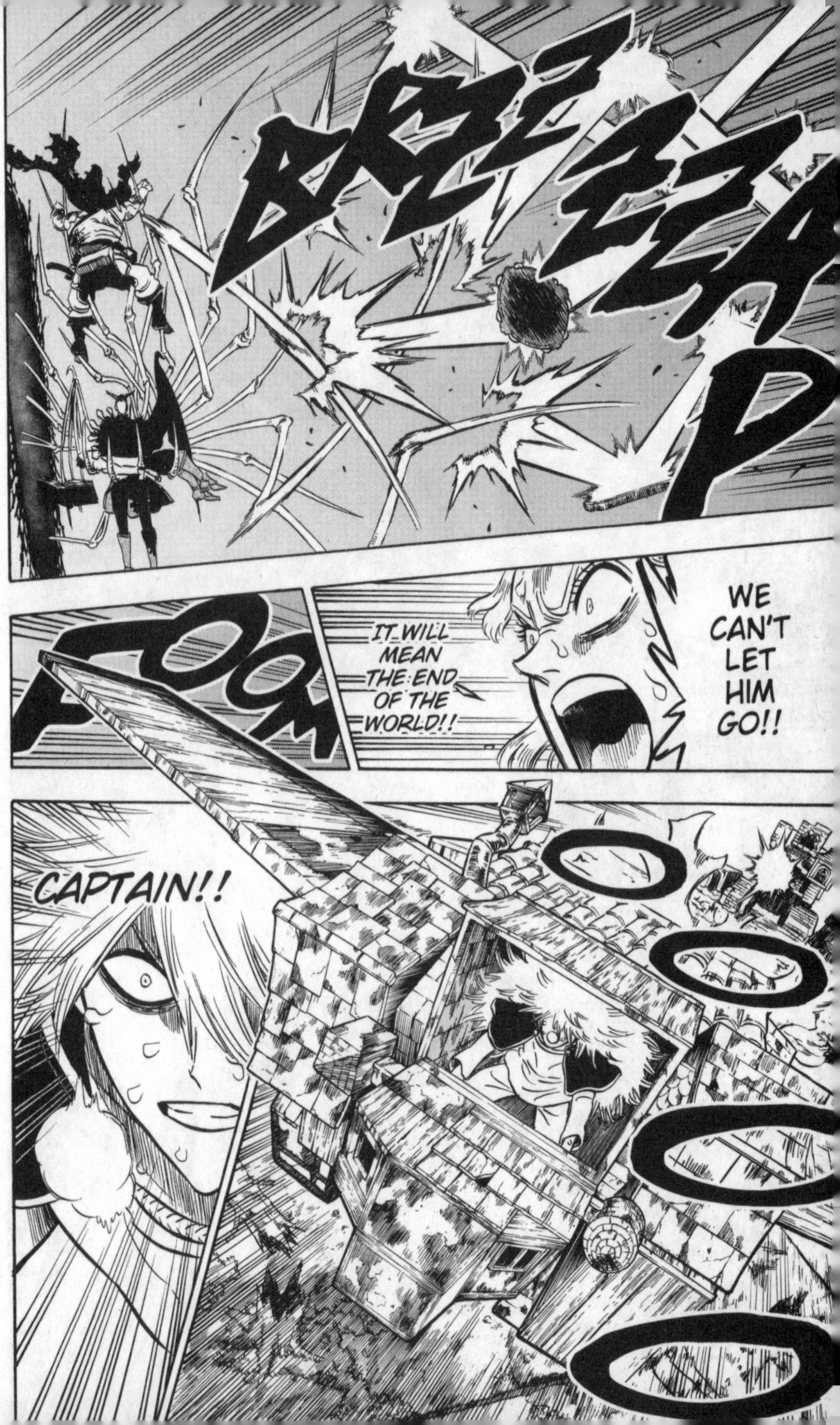
BRZZAP
WE CAN'T LET HIM GO!!
IT WILL MEAN THE END OF THE WORLD!!
FOOM
CAPTAIN!!

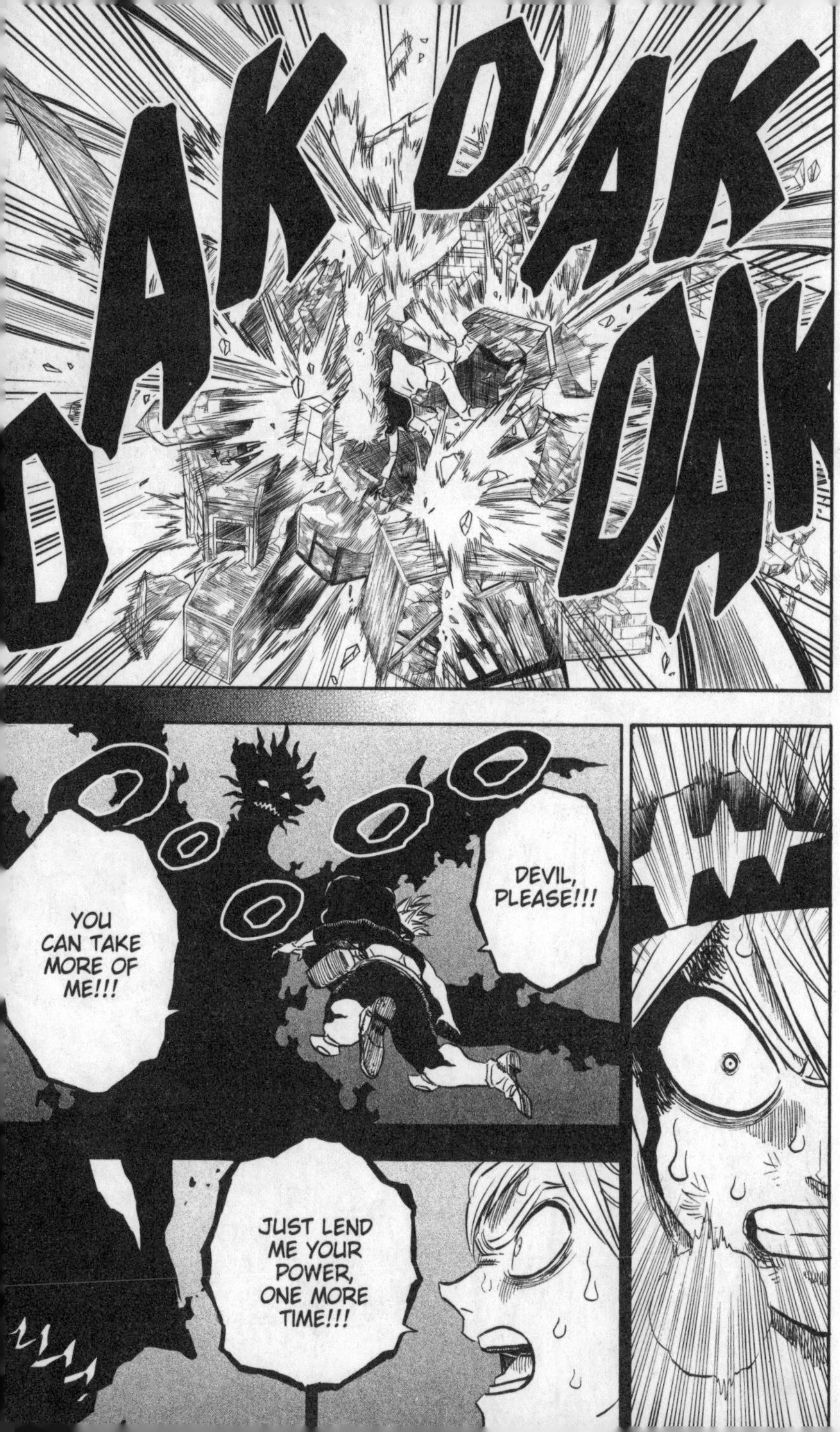
DAK DAK DAK
DEVIL, PLEASE!!!
YOU CAN TAKE MORE OF ME!!!
JUST LEND ME YOUR POWER, ONE MORE TIME!!!

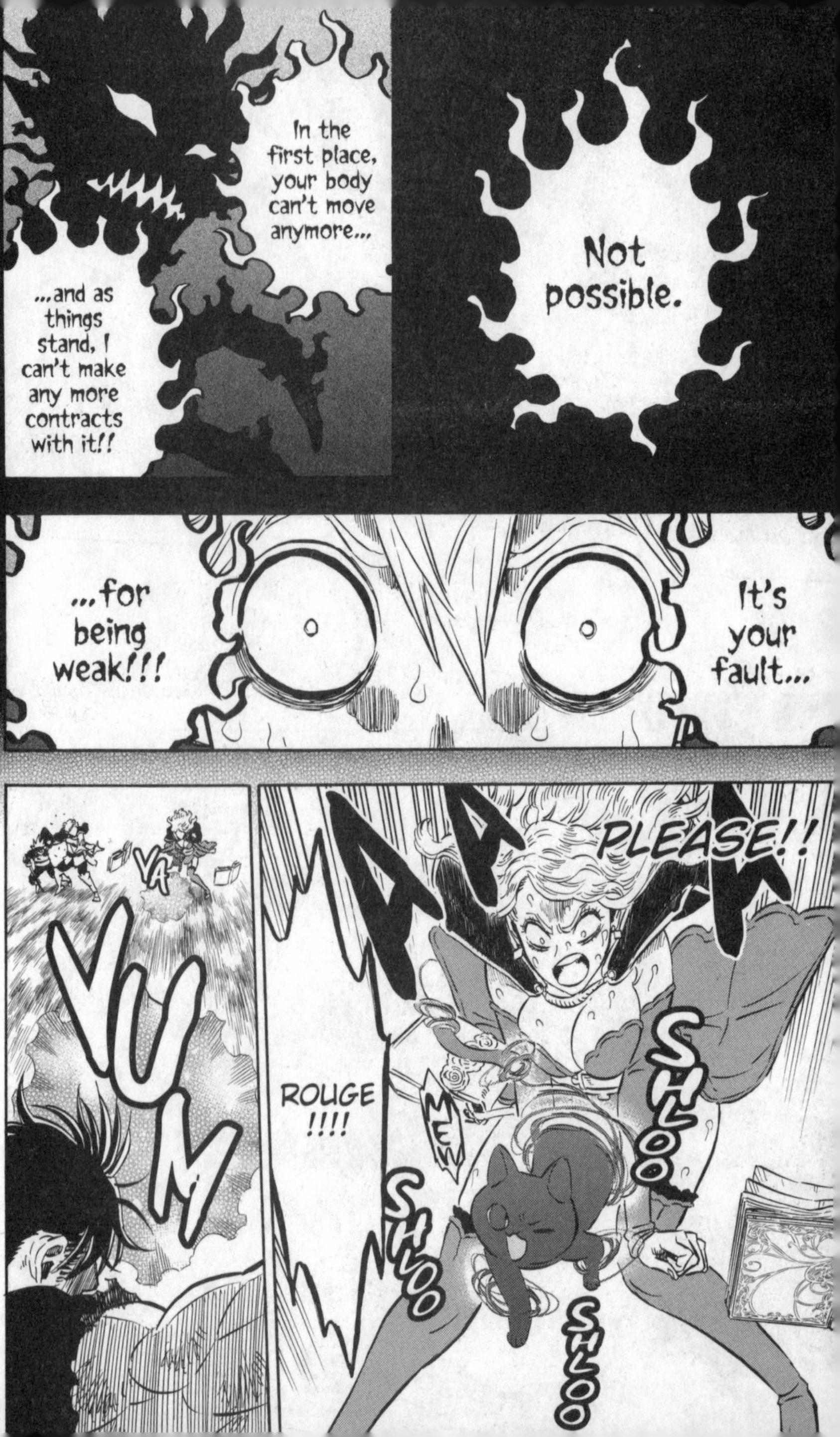
Not possible.
In the first place, your body can't move anymore...
...and as things stand, I can't make any more contracts with it!!
It's your fault...
...for being weak!!!
AA
PLEASE!!
SHLOO
MEW
ROUGE !!!!
SHLOO
SHLOO
YA
VUM

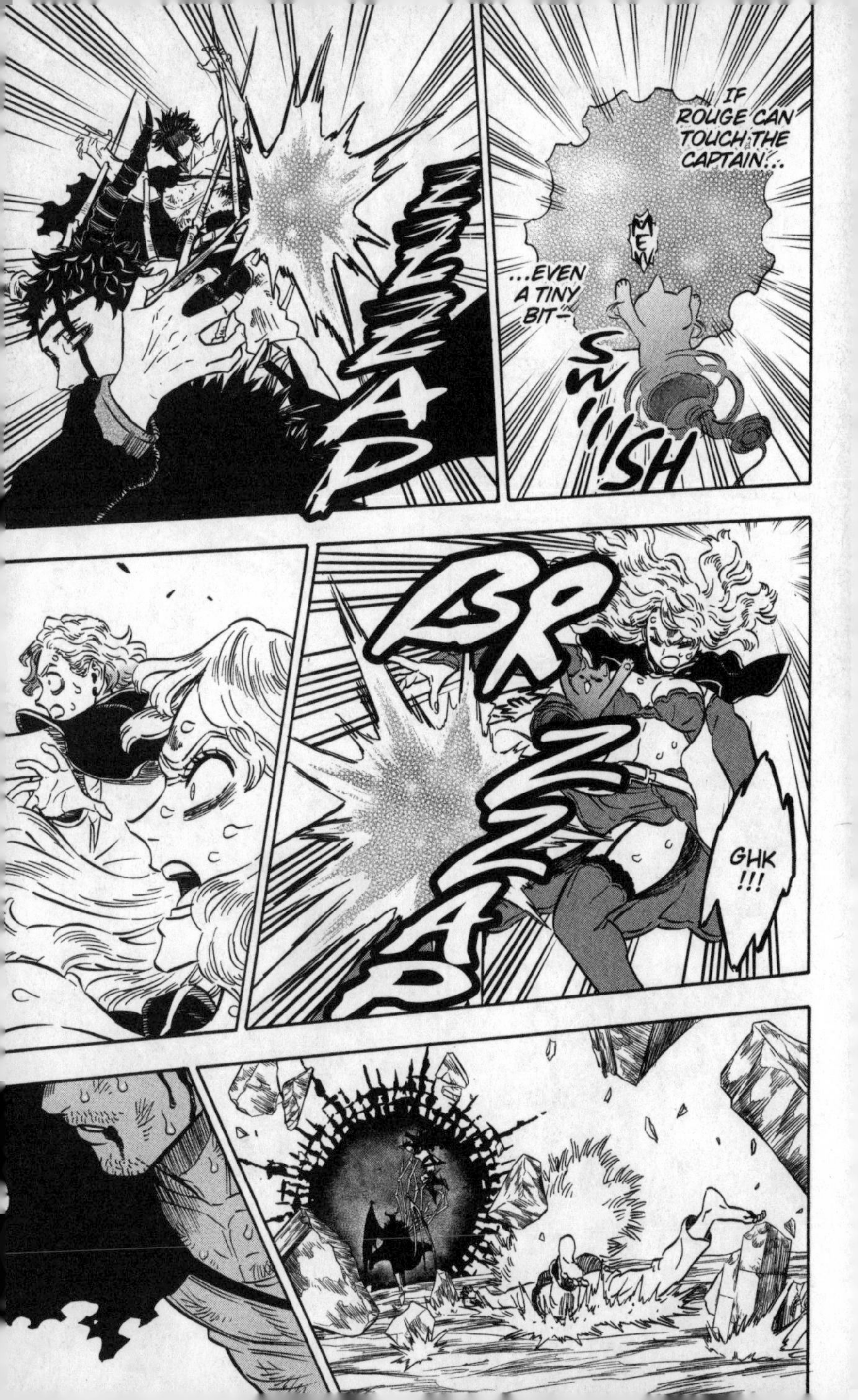
IF ROUGE CAN TOUCH THE CAPTAIN...
MEW
...EVEN A TINY BIT—
SWIISH
ZZZZZAP
BZZZAP
GHK!!!

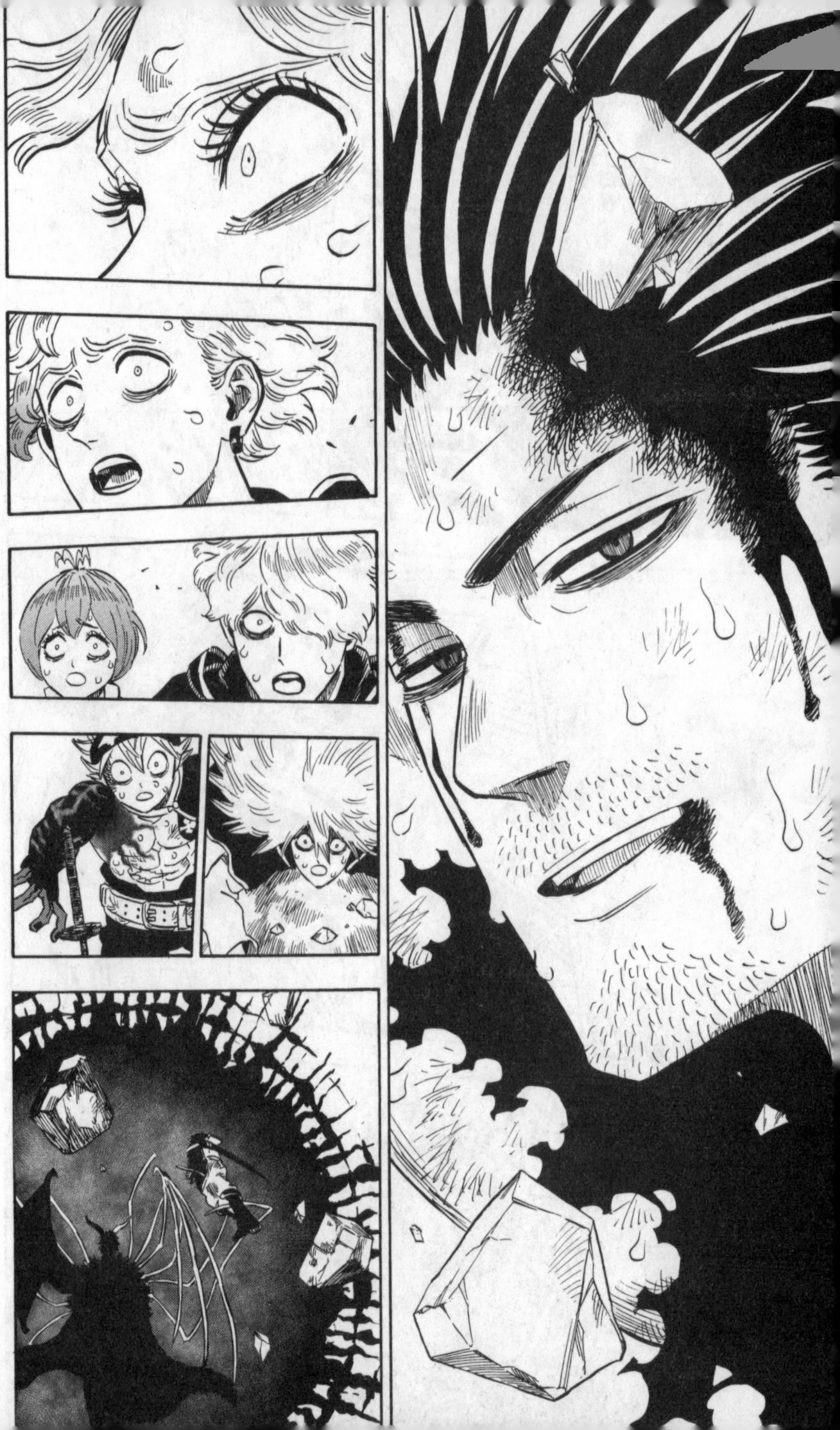

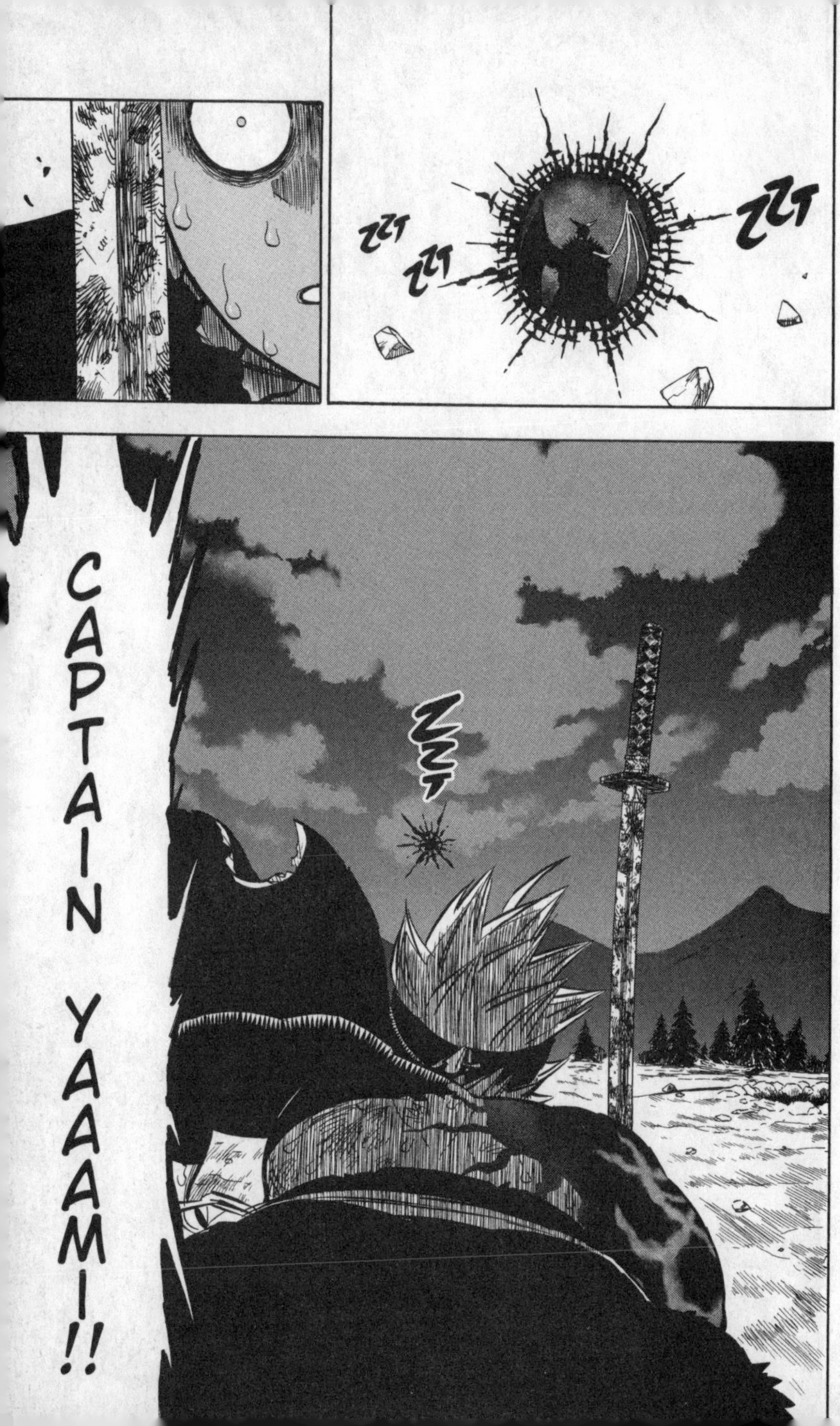
ZZT
ZZT
ZZT
ZZZT
CAPTAIN YAAAMI!!

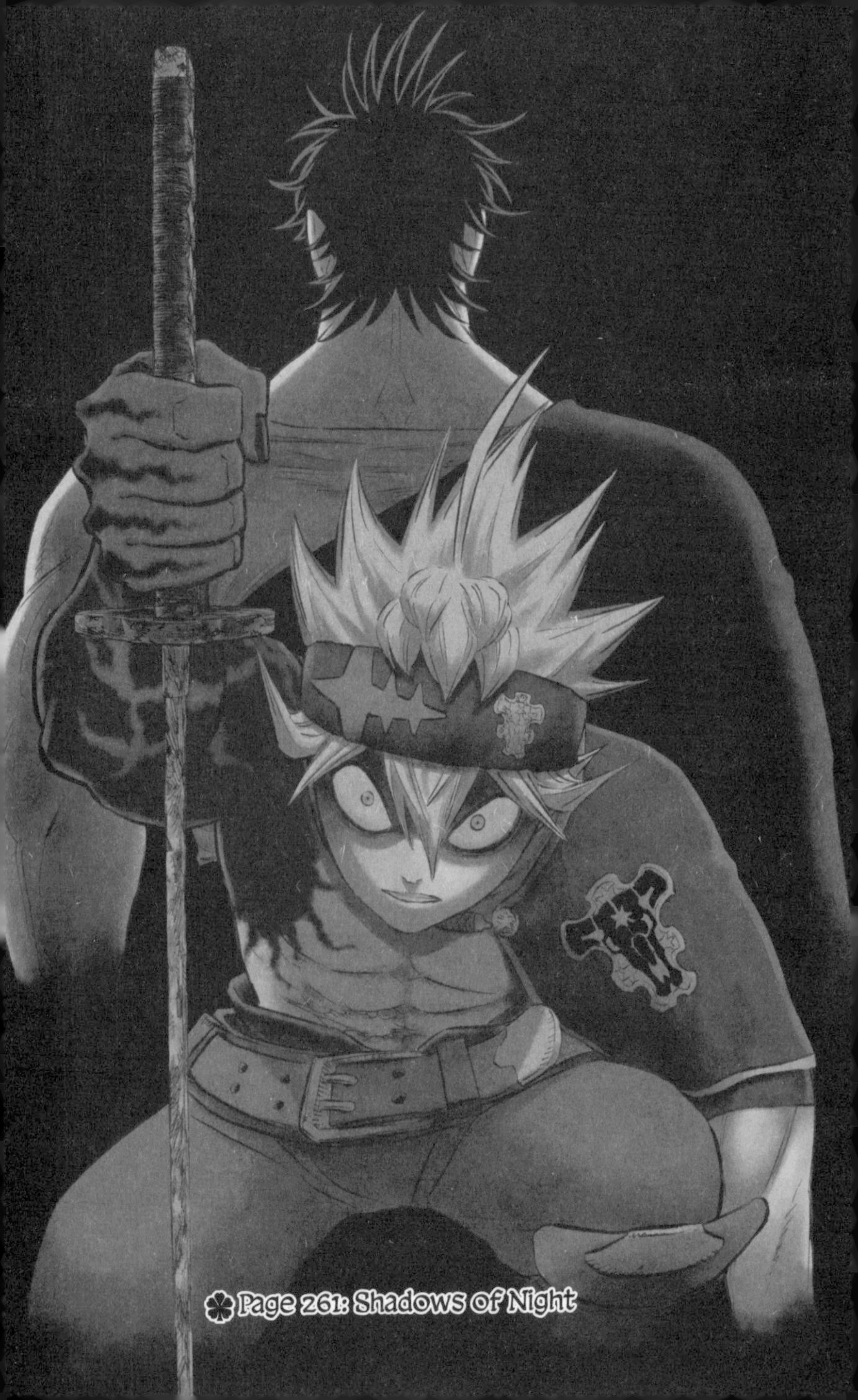
Page 261: Shadows of Night

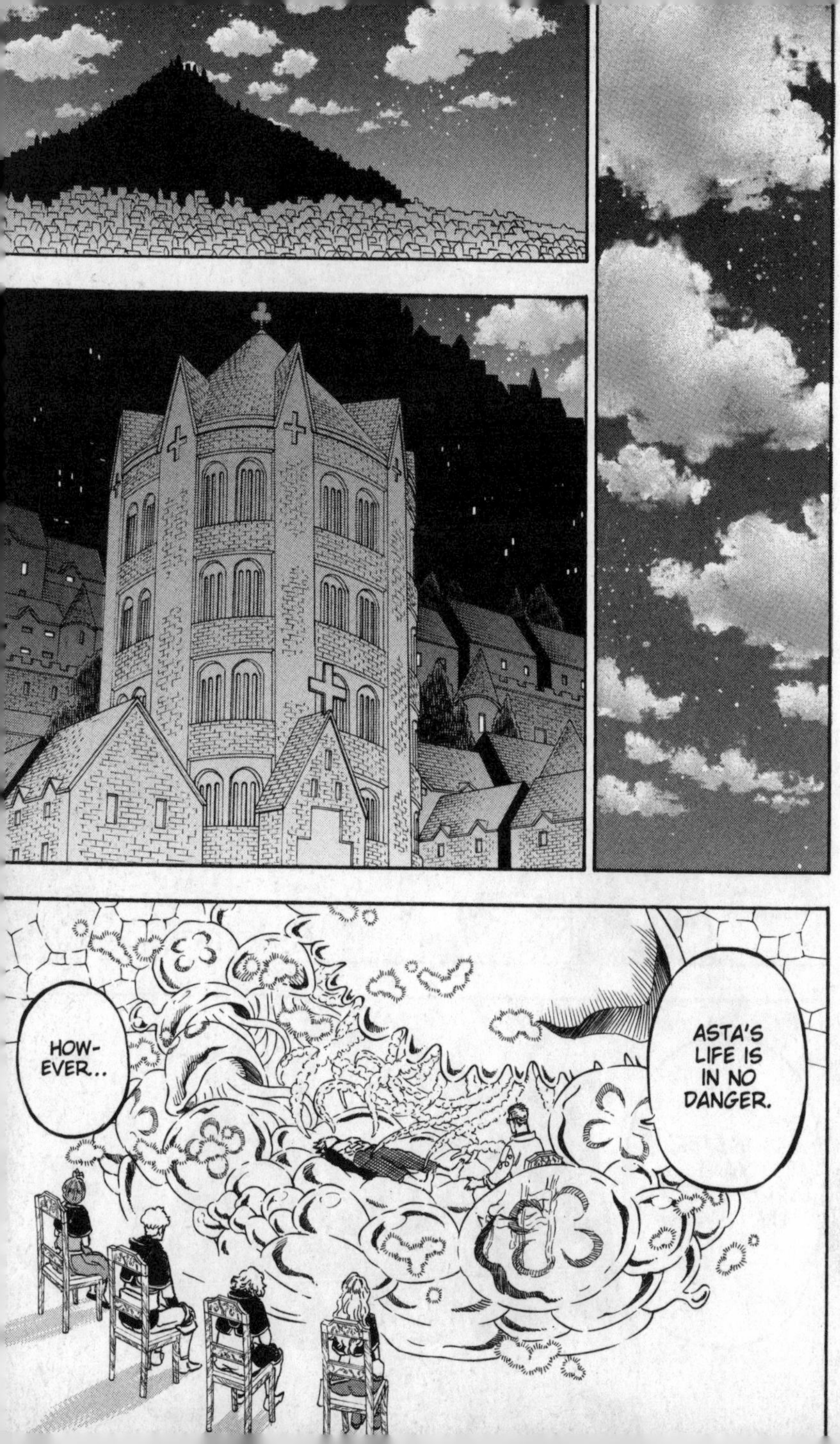
ASTA'S LIFE IS IN NO DANGER.
HOW-EVER...

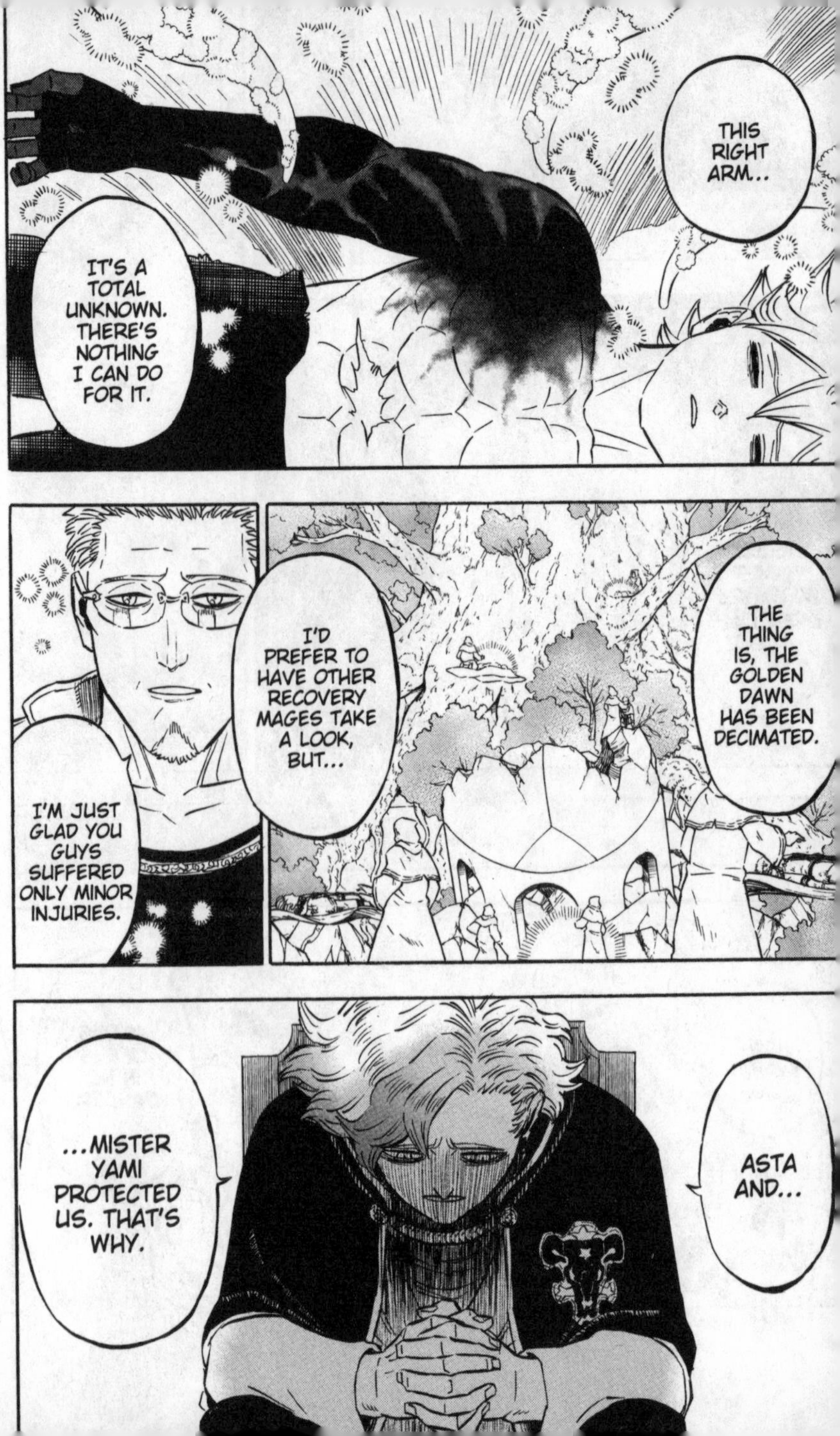
THIS RIGHT ARM...
IT'S A TOTAL UNKNOWN. THERE'S NOTHING I CAN DO FOR IT.
THE THING IS, THE GOLDEN DAWN HAS BEEN DECIMATED.
I'D PREFER TO HAVE OTHER RECOVERY MAGES TAKE A LOOK, BUT...
I'M JUST GLAD YOU GUYS SUFFERED ONLY MINOR INJURIES.
ASTA AND...
...MISTER YAMI PROTECTED US. THAT'S WHY.

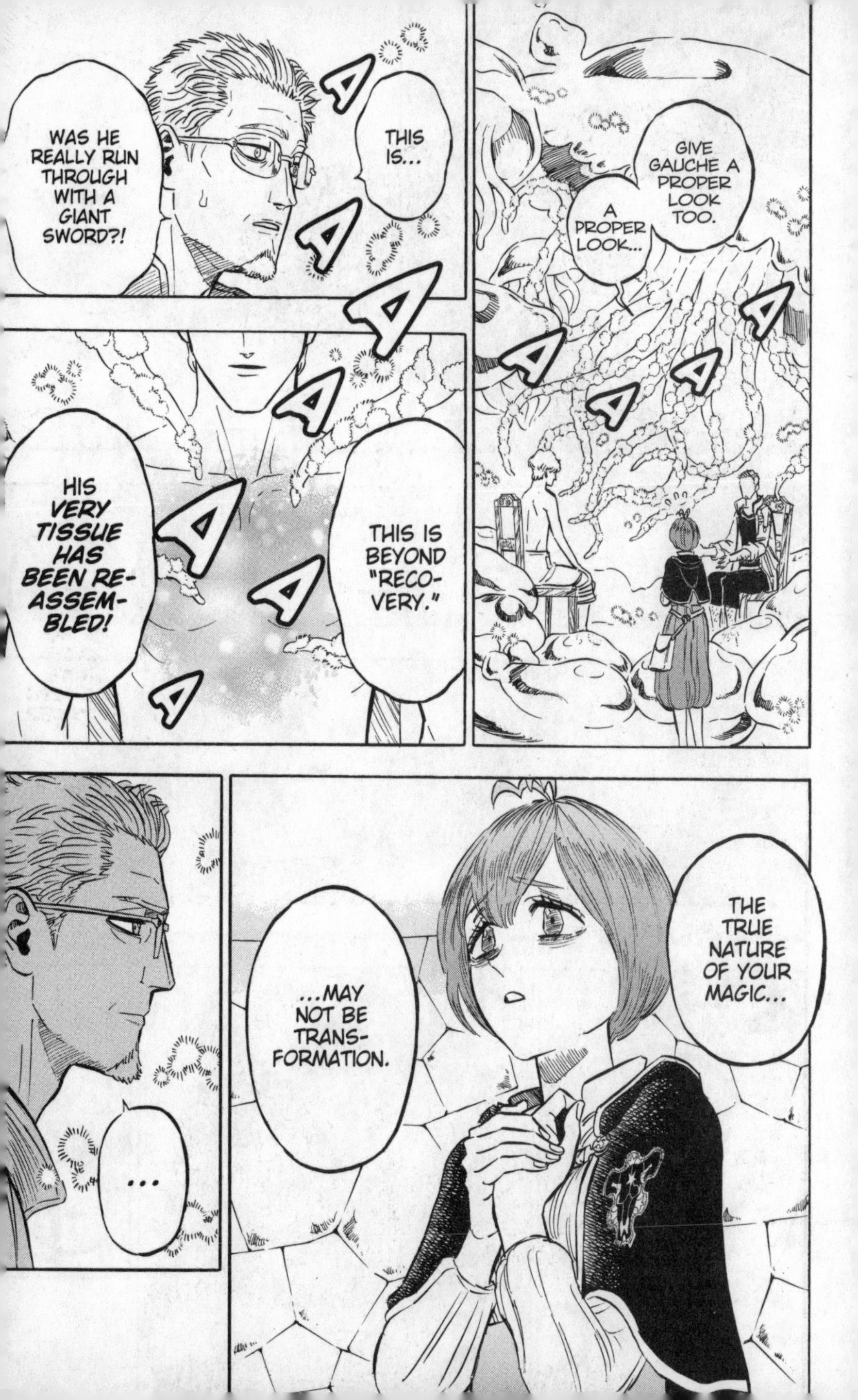
GIVE GAUCHE A PROPER LOOK TOO.
A PROPER LOOK...
THIS IS...
WAS HE REALLY RUN THROUGH WITH A GIANT SWORD?!
THIS IS BEYOND "RECOVERY."
HIS *VERY TISSUE HAS BEEN REASSEMBLED!*
THE TRUE NATURE OF YOUR MAGIC...
...MAY NOT BE TRANSFORMATION.
...

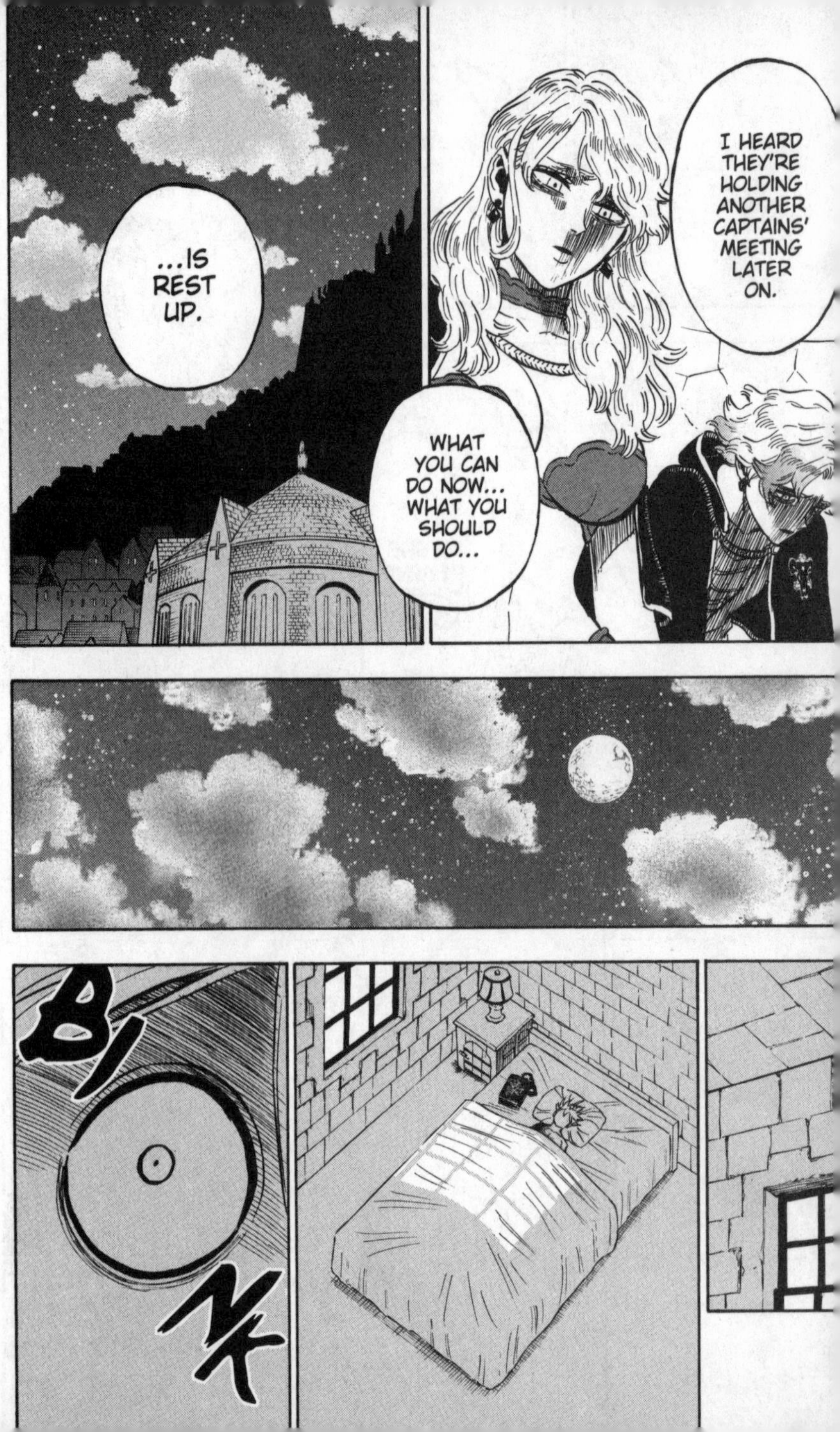
I HEARD THEY'RE HOLDING ANOTHER CAPTAINS' MEETING LATER ON.
WHAT YOU CAN DO NOW... WHAT YOU SHOULD DO...
...IS REST UP.
BONK

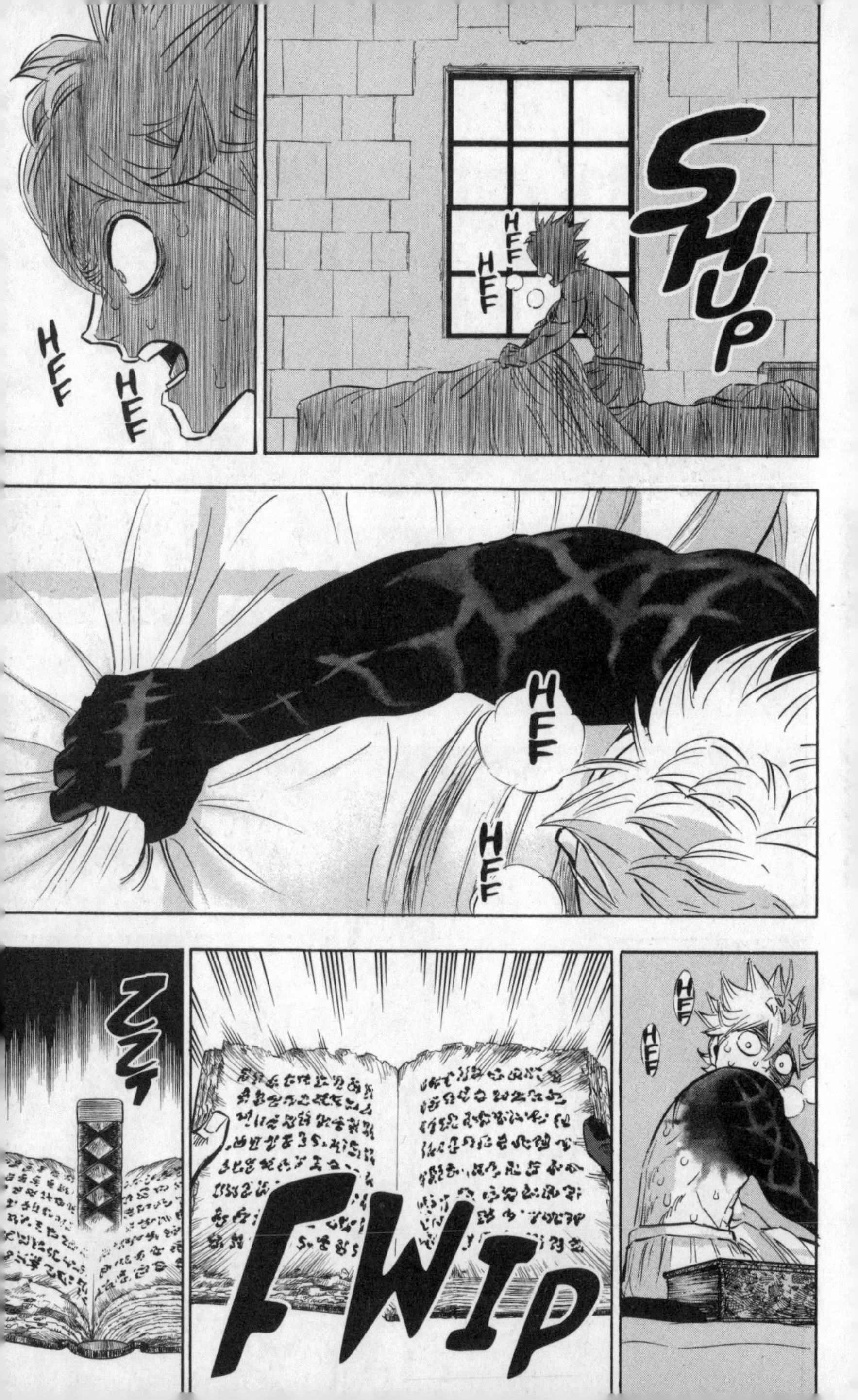
SHUP
HEF HEF
HEF HEF
HEF HEF
HEF
HEF
HEF
HEF
FWIP
ZZZT

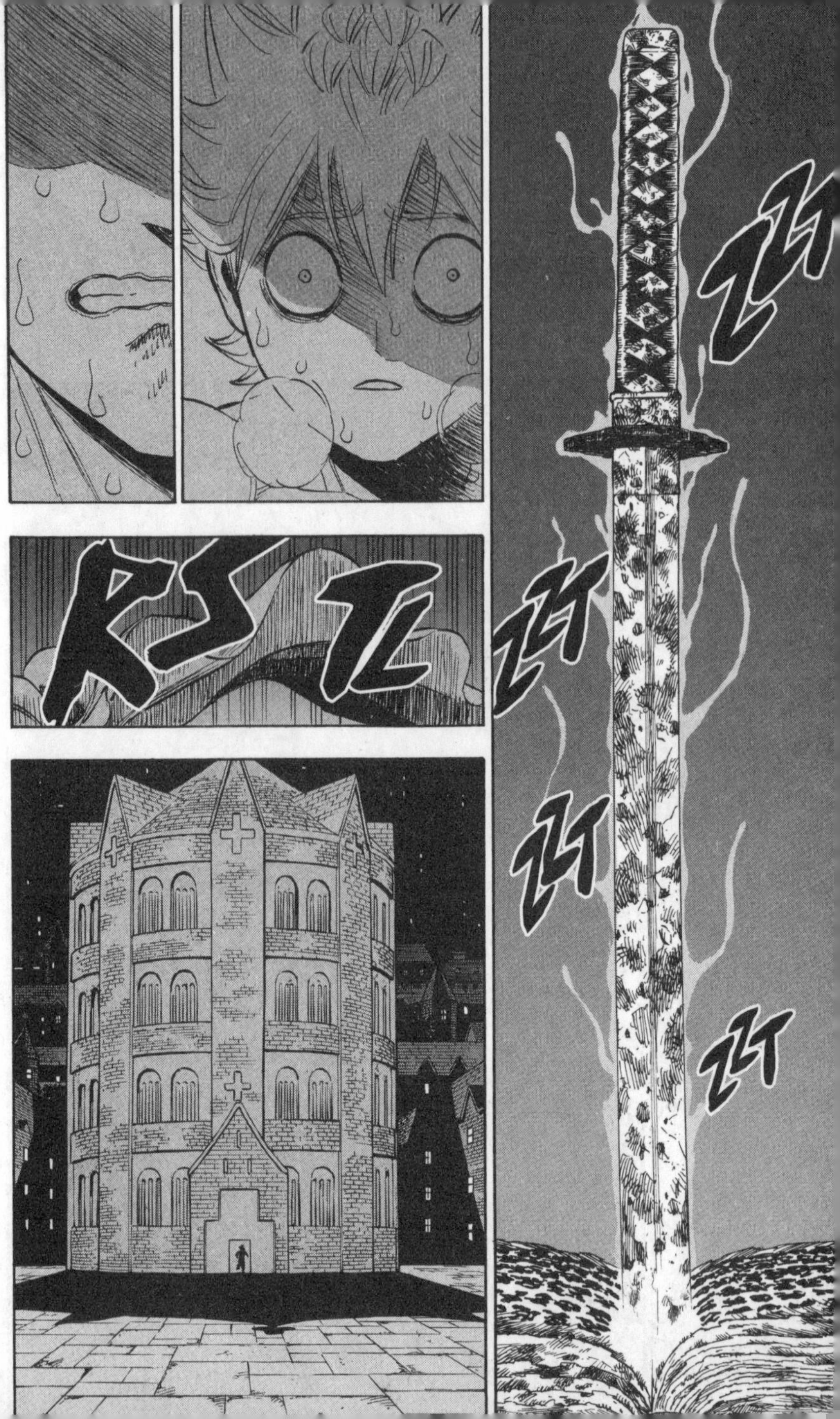
ZZZT
ZZZT
ZZT
ZZT
RSTL

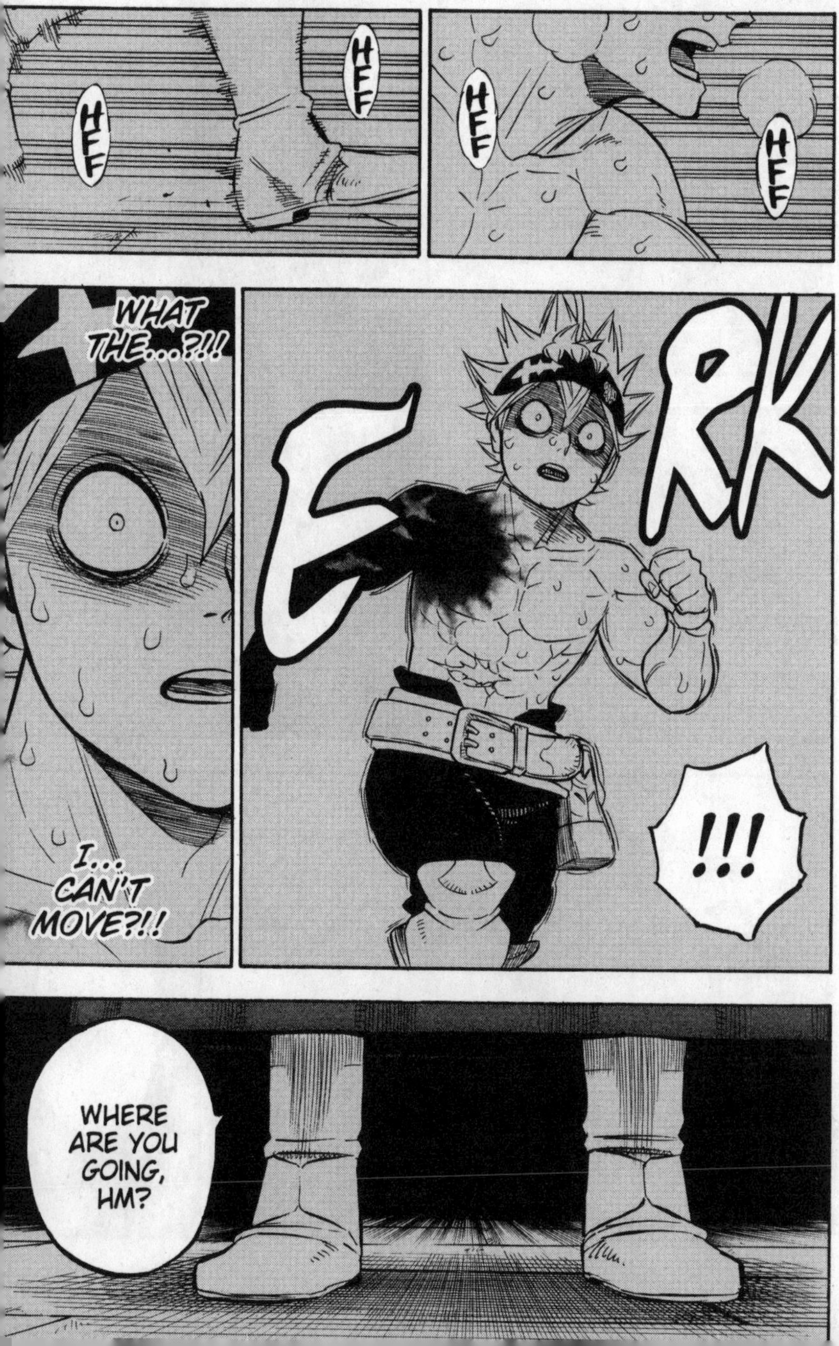
HFF
HFF
HFF
HFF
ERK
!!!
WHAT THE...?!!
I... CAN'T MOVE?!!
WHERE ARE YOU GOING, HM?

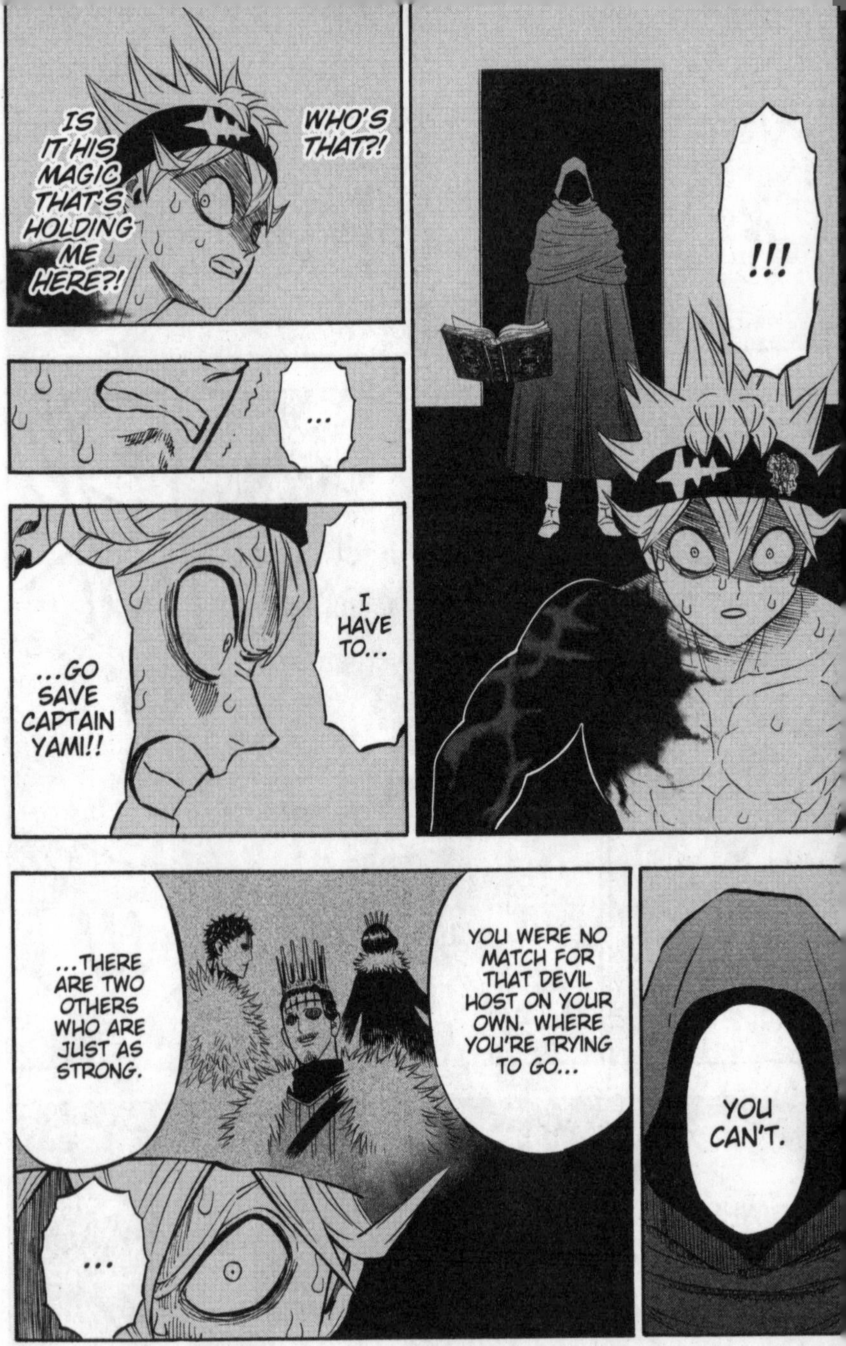
!!!
WHO'S THAT?!
IS IT HIS MAGIC THAT'S HOLDING ME HERE?!
...
I HAVE TO...
...GO SAVE CAPTAIN YAMI!!
YOU CAN'T.
YOU WERE NO MATCH FOR THAT DEVIL HOST ON YOUR OWN. WHERE YOU'RE TRYING TO GO...
...THERE ARE TWO OTHERS WHO ARE JUST AS STRONG.
...

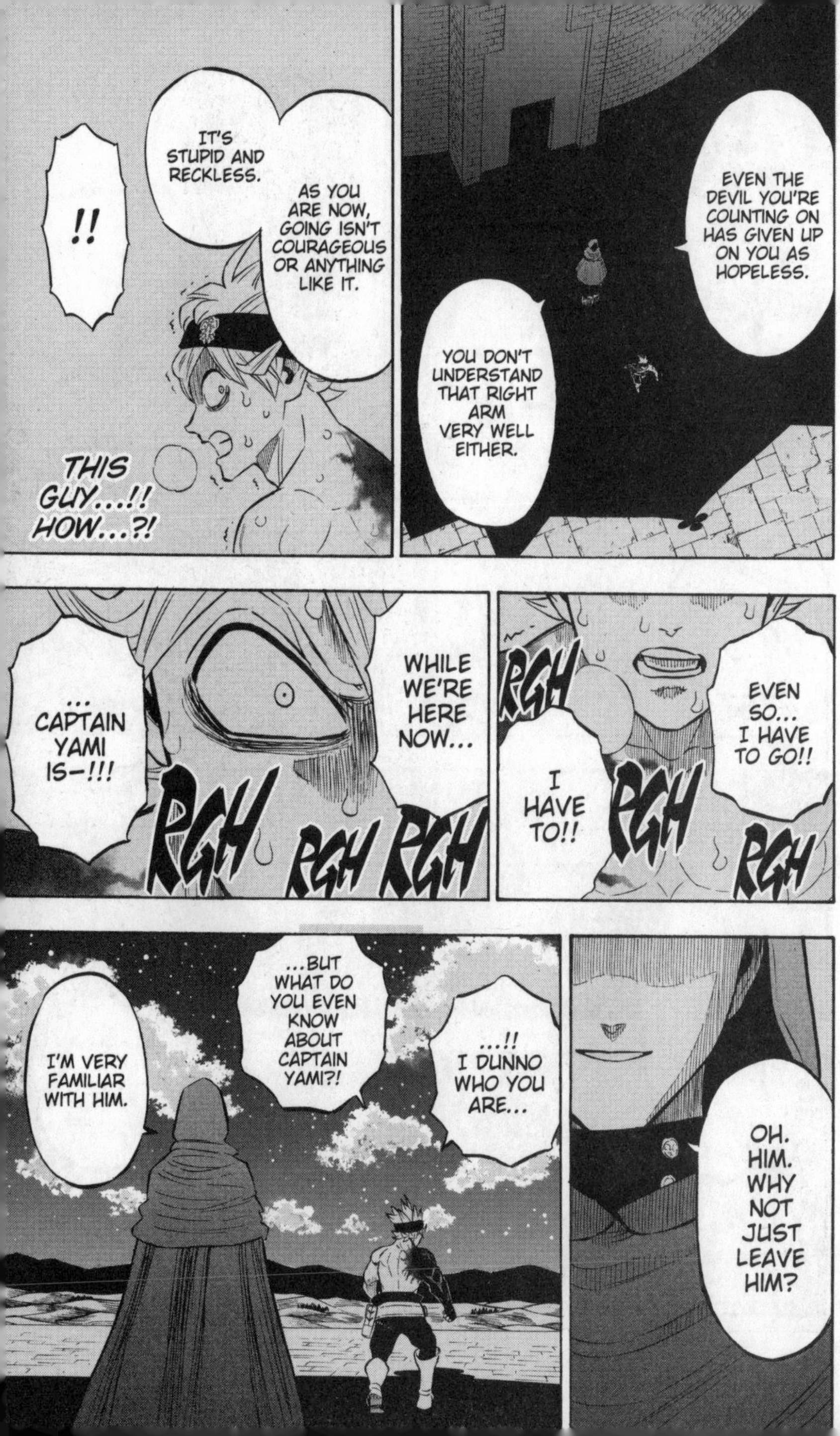
EVEN THE DEVIL YOU'RE COUNTING ON HAS GIVEN UP ON YOU AS HOPELESS.
YOU DON'T UNDERSTAND THAT RIGHT ARM VERY WELL EITHER.
IT'S STUPID AND RECKLESS.
AS YOU ARE NOW, GOING ISN'T COURAGEOUS OR ANYTHING LIKE IT.
!!
THIS GUY...!! HOW...?!
EVEN SO... I HAVE TO GO!!
RGH
I HAVE TO!!
RGH
RGH
WHILE WE'RE HERE NOW...
... CAPTAIN YAMI IS-!!!
RGH
RGH RGH
OH. HIM. WHY NOT JUST LEAVE HIM?
...!! I DUNNO WHO YOU ARE...
...BUT WHAT DO YOU EVEN KNOW ABOUT CAPTAIN YAMI?!
I'M VERY FAMILIAR WITH HIM.

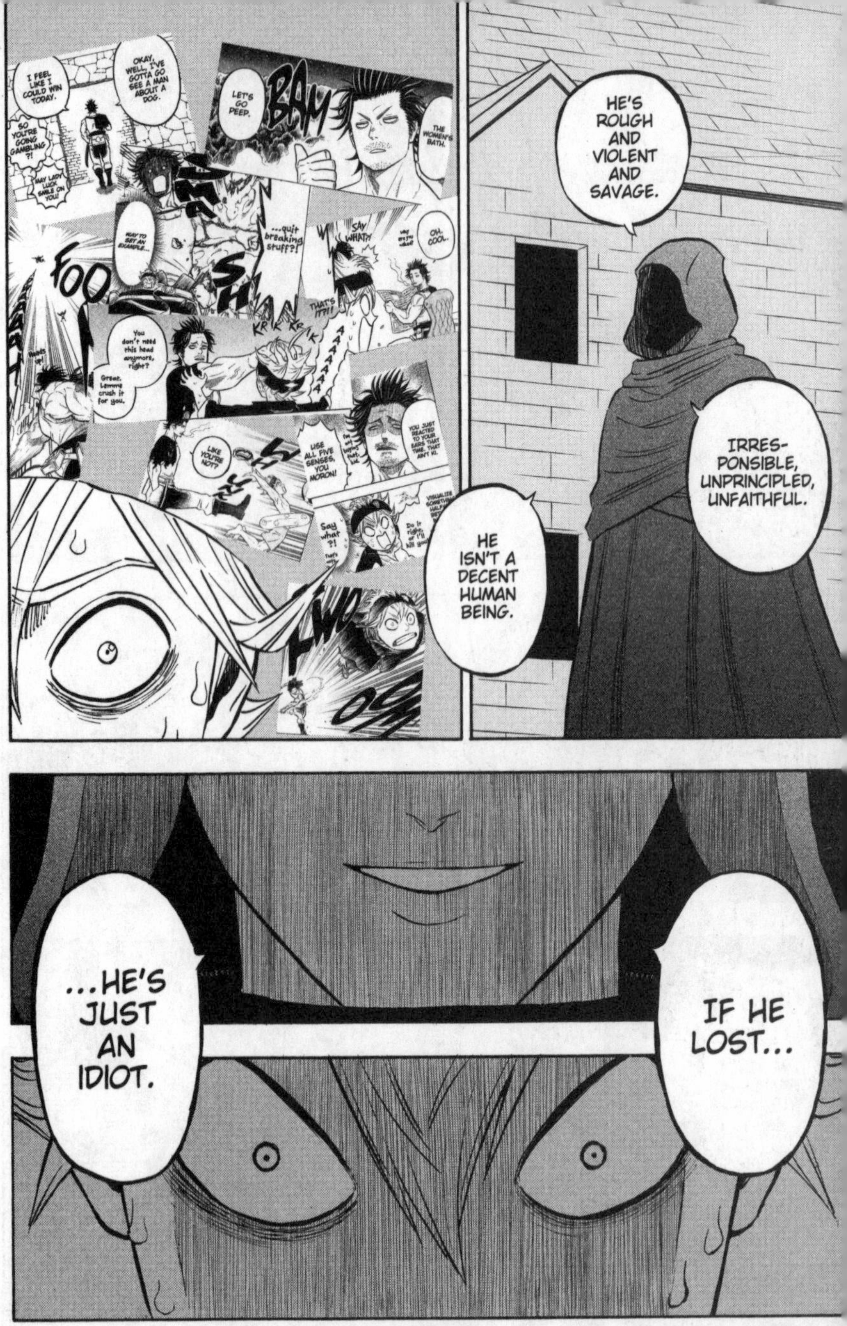
HE'S ROUGH AND VIOLENT AND SAVAGE.
IRRES-PONSIBLE, UNPRINCIPLED, UNFAITHFUL.
HE ISN'T A DECENT HUMAN BEING.
THE WOMEN'S BATH.
BAM
LET'S GO PEEP.
OKAY, WELL, I'VE GOTTA GO SEE A MAN ABOUT A DOG.
I FEEL LIKE I COULD WIN TODAY.
SO YOU'RE GOING GAMBLING?!
MAY LADY LUCK SMILE ON YOU!
OH, COOL.
SAY WHAT?!
...quit breaking stuff?!
THAT'S IT?!
FOO
You don't need this head anymore, right?
Great. Lemme crush it for you.
USE ALL FIVE SENSES, YOU MORON!
LIKE YOU'RE NOT?
Say what?!
IF HE LOST...
...HE'S JUST AN IDIOT.

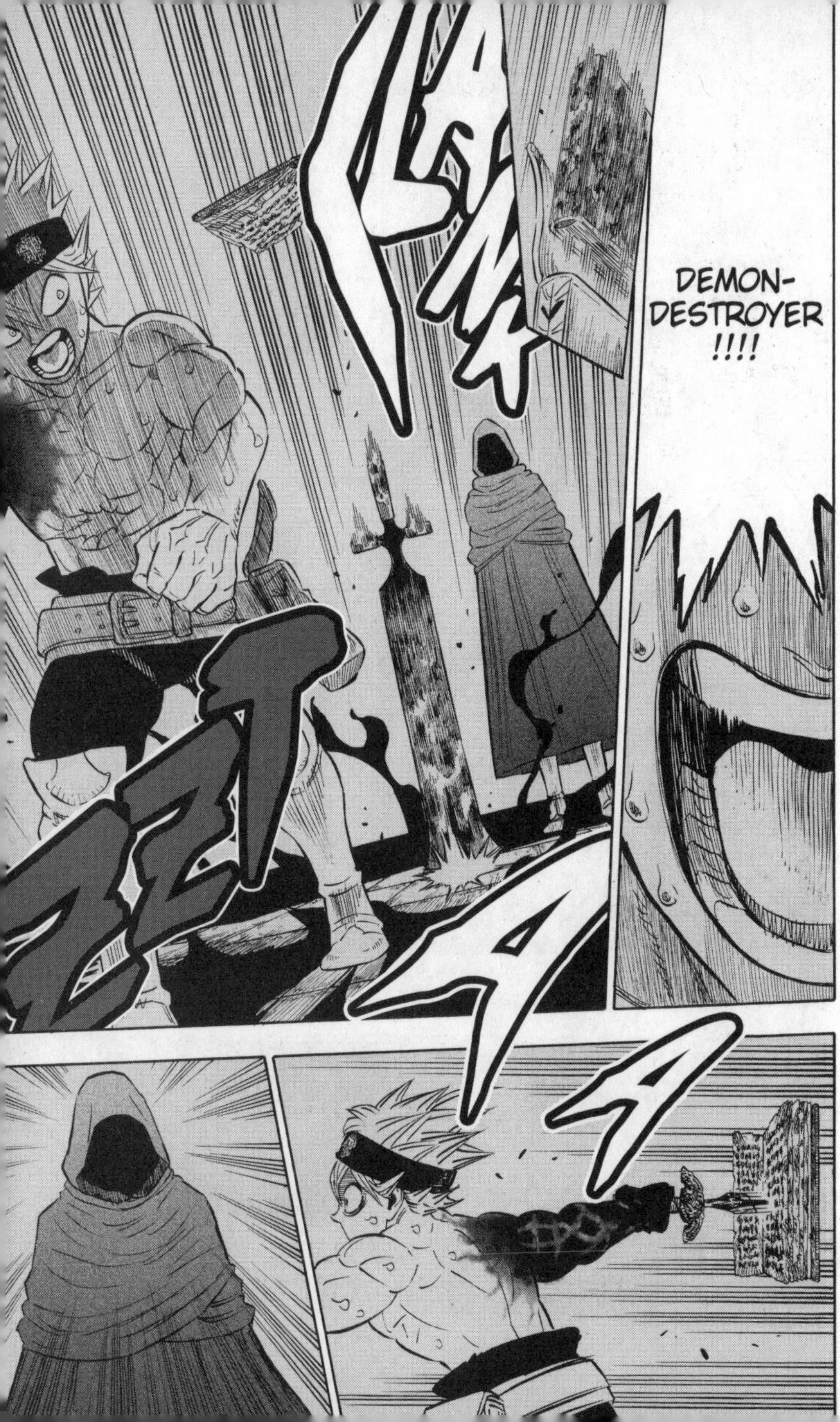
DEMON-DESTROYER !!!!

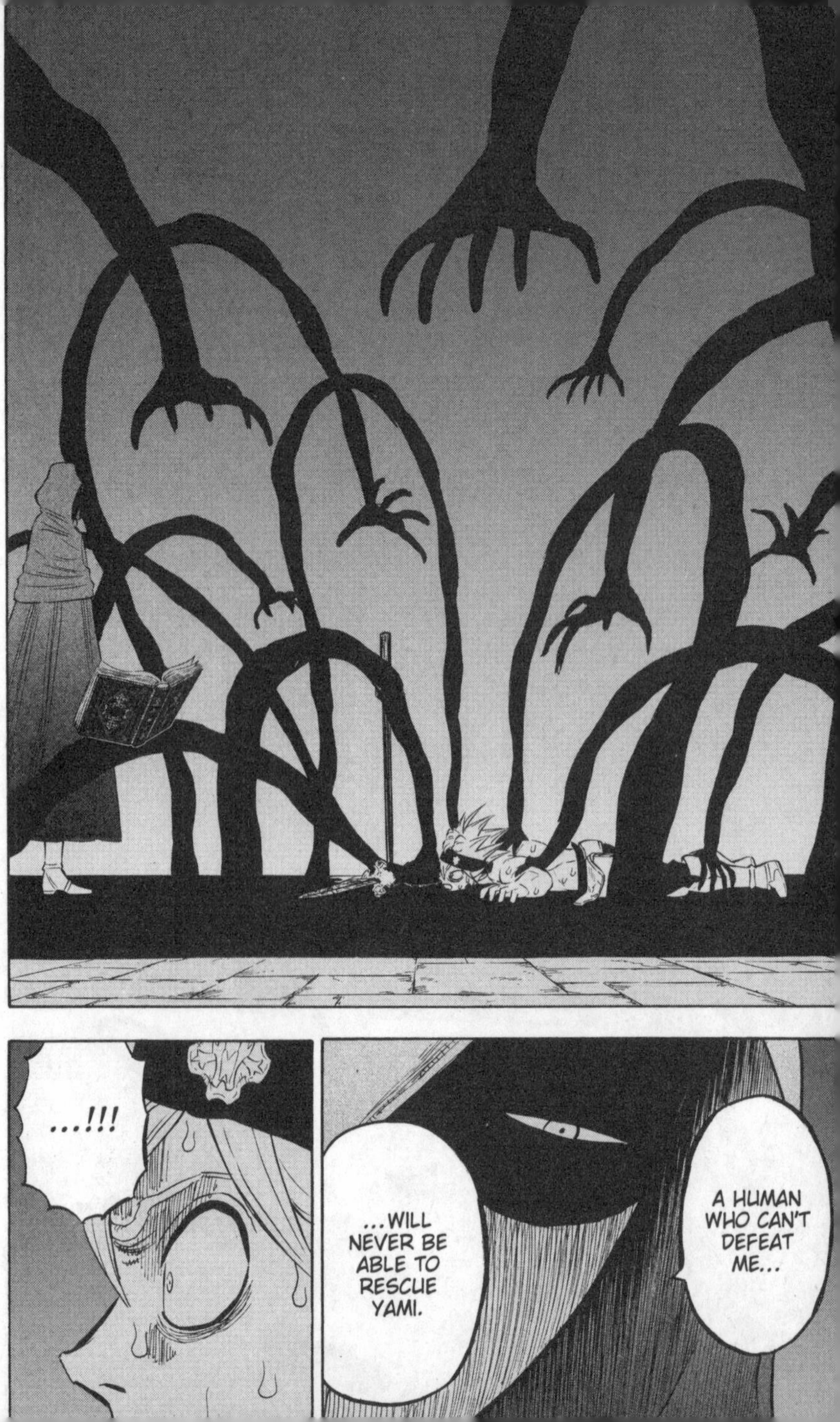
A HUMAN WHO CAN'T DEFEAT ME...
...WILL NEVER BE ABLE TO RESCUE YAMI.
...!!!

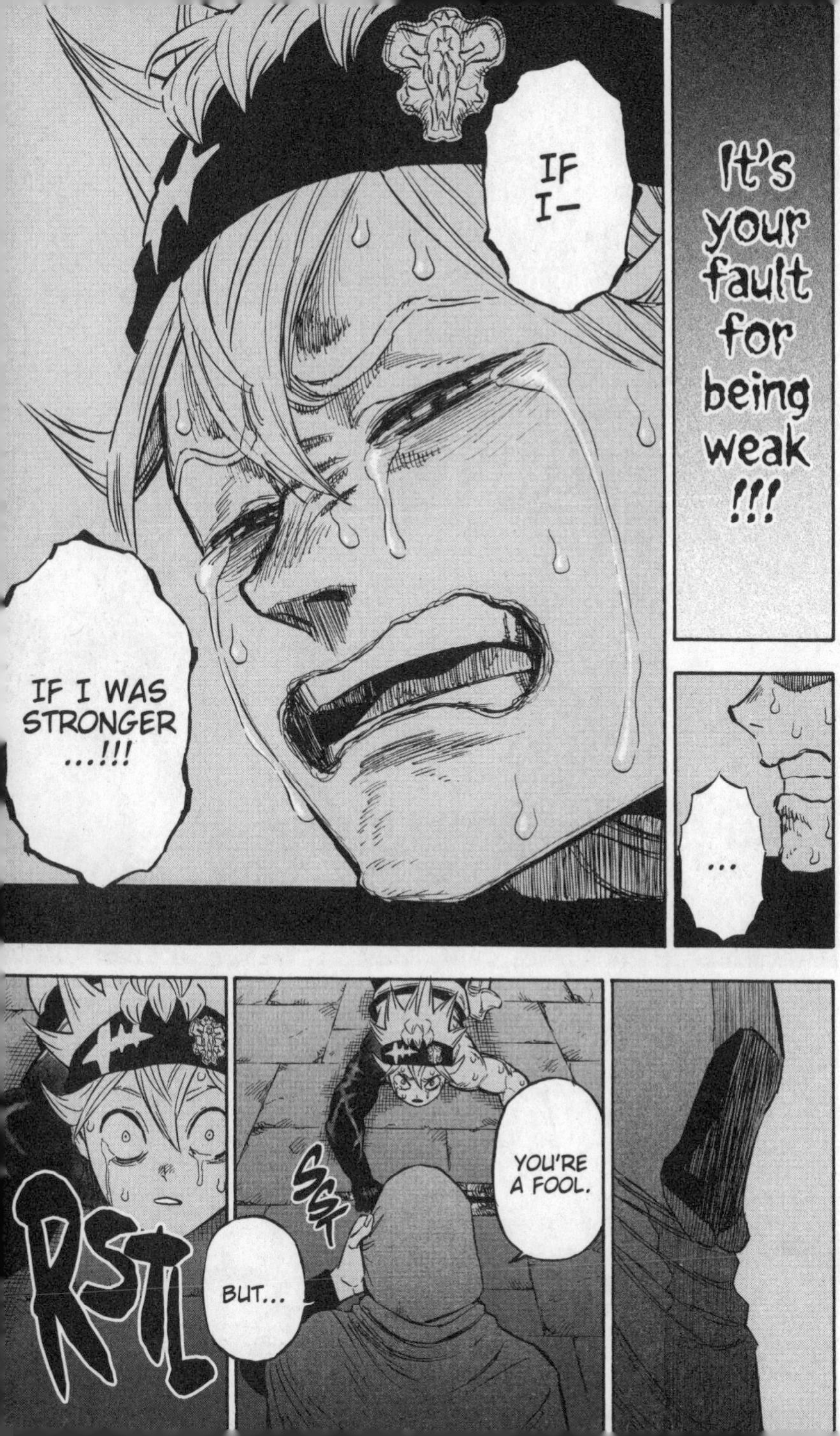

It's your fault for being weak!!!
...
IF I—
IF I WAS STRONGER ...!!!
YOU'RE A FOOL.
SSK
BUT...
RSTL

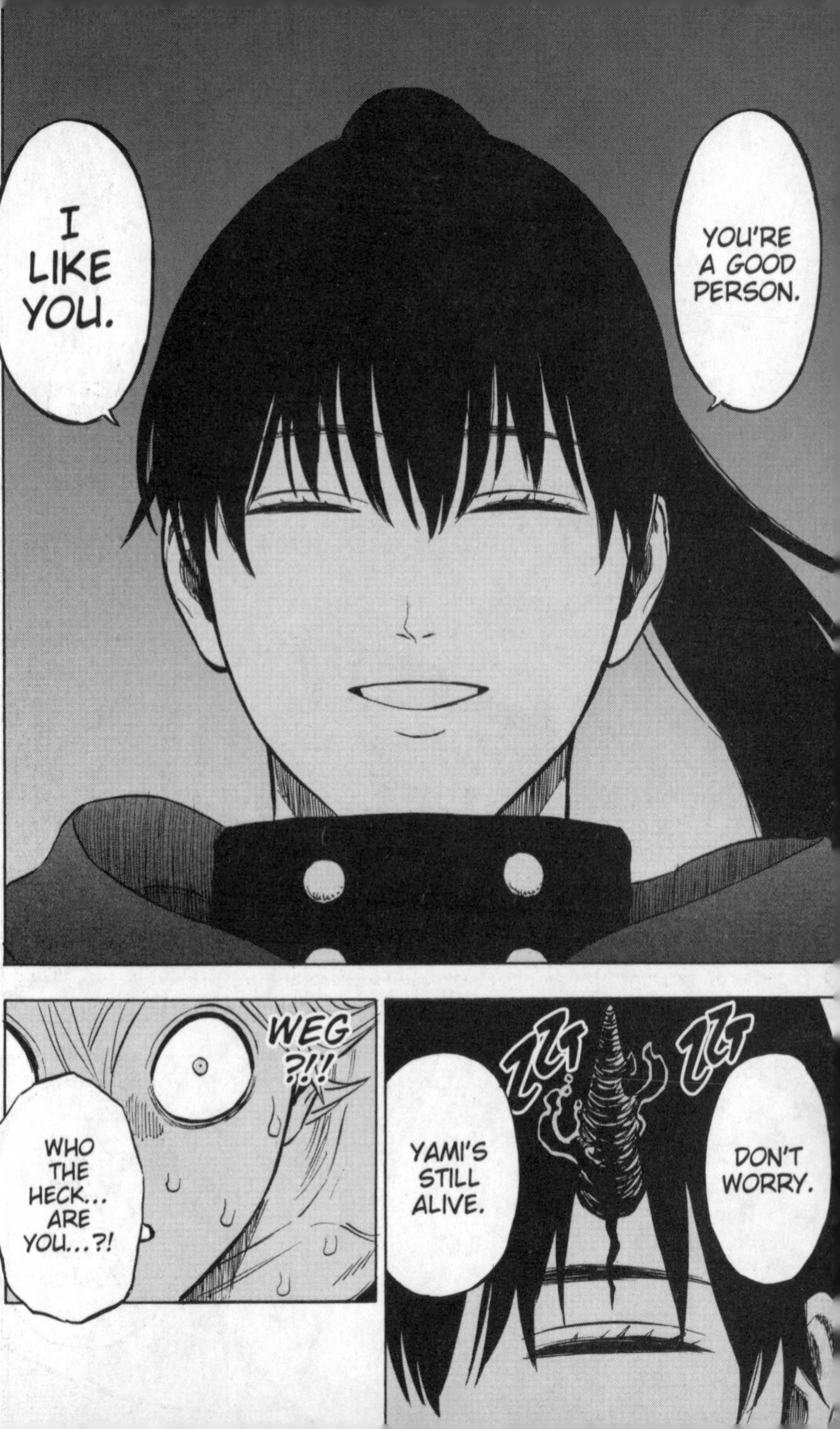
YOU'RE A GOOD PERSON.
I LIKE YOU.
ZZT
ZZT
DON'T WORRY.
YAMI'S STILL ALIVE.
WEG ?!!
WHO THE HECK... ARE YOU...?!

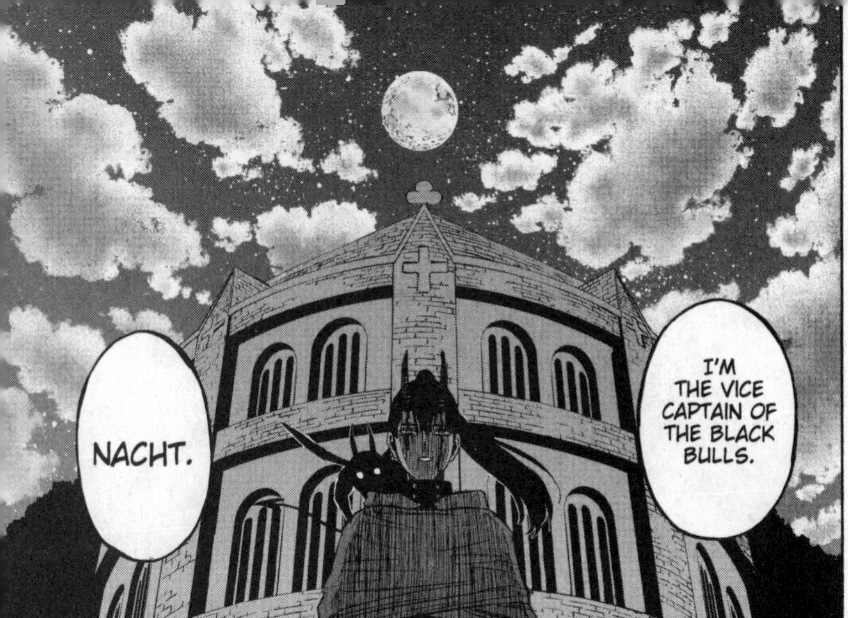
I'M THE VICE CAPTAIN OF THE BLACK BULLS.
NACHT.

TO BE CONTINUED IN VOLUME 27!

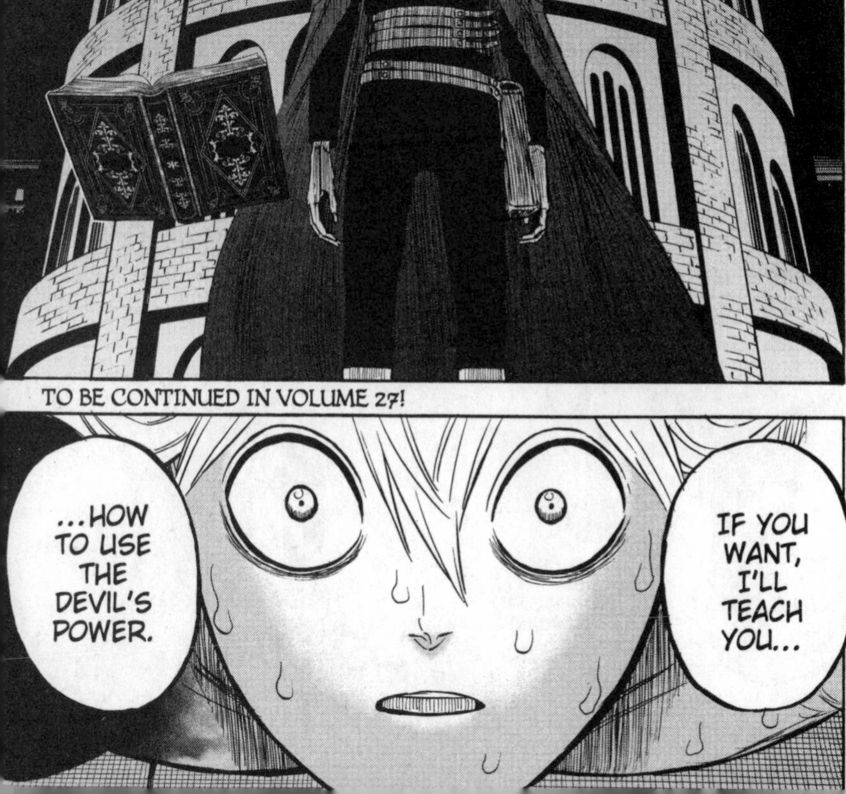
IF YOU WANT, I'LL TEACH YOU...
...HOW TO USE THE DEVIL'S POWER.

The Blank Page Brigade

This volume's topic: Something that made you think "Compared to who I used to be, I've grown."

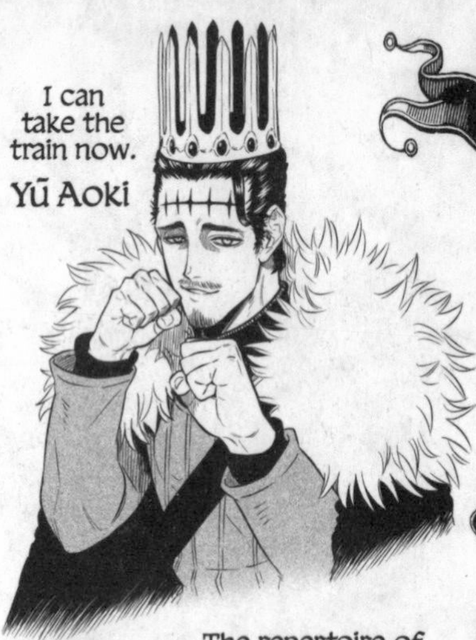

I can take the train now.

Yū Aoki

My stomach...

Hayato Gotō

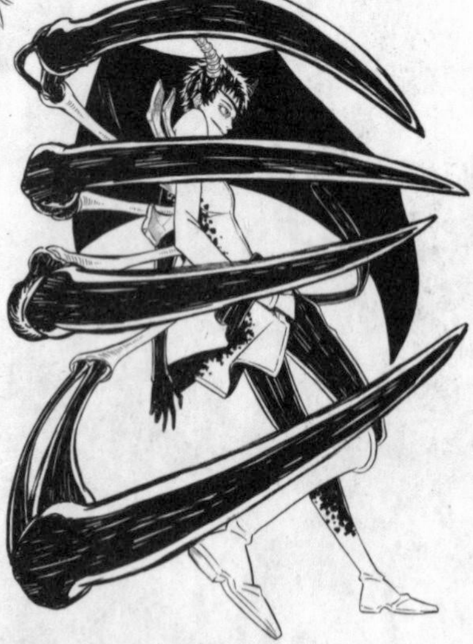

The repertoire of recipes I can make is bigger.

Sōta Hishikawa

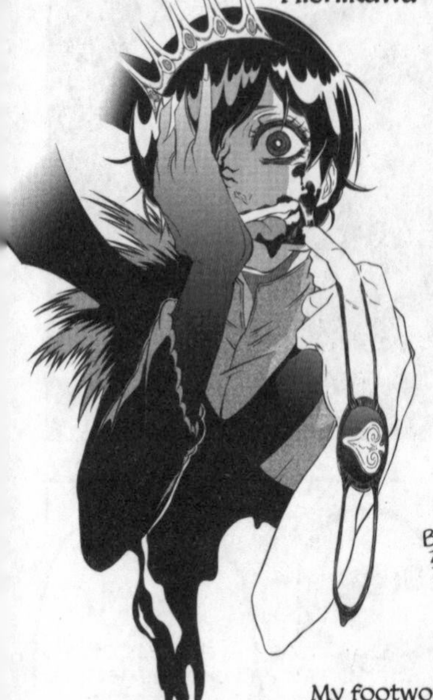

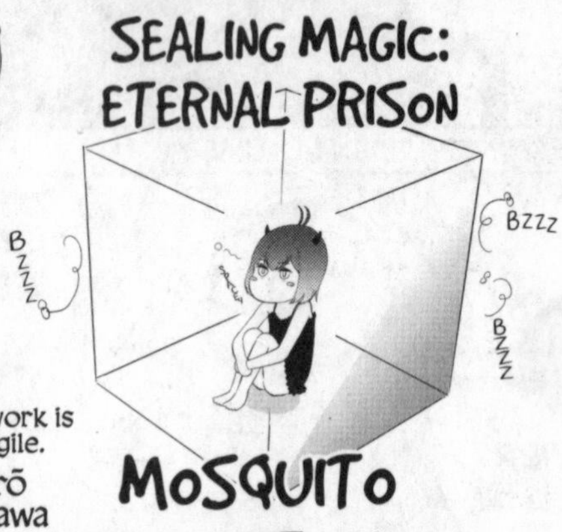
SEALING MAGIC: ETERNAL PRISON
BZZZ
BZZZ
BZZZ
MOSQUITO NET

My footwork is more agile.

Yōtarō Hayakawa

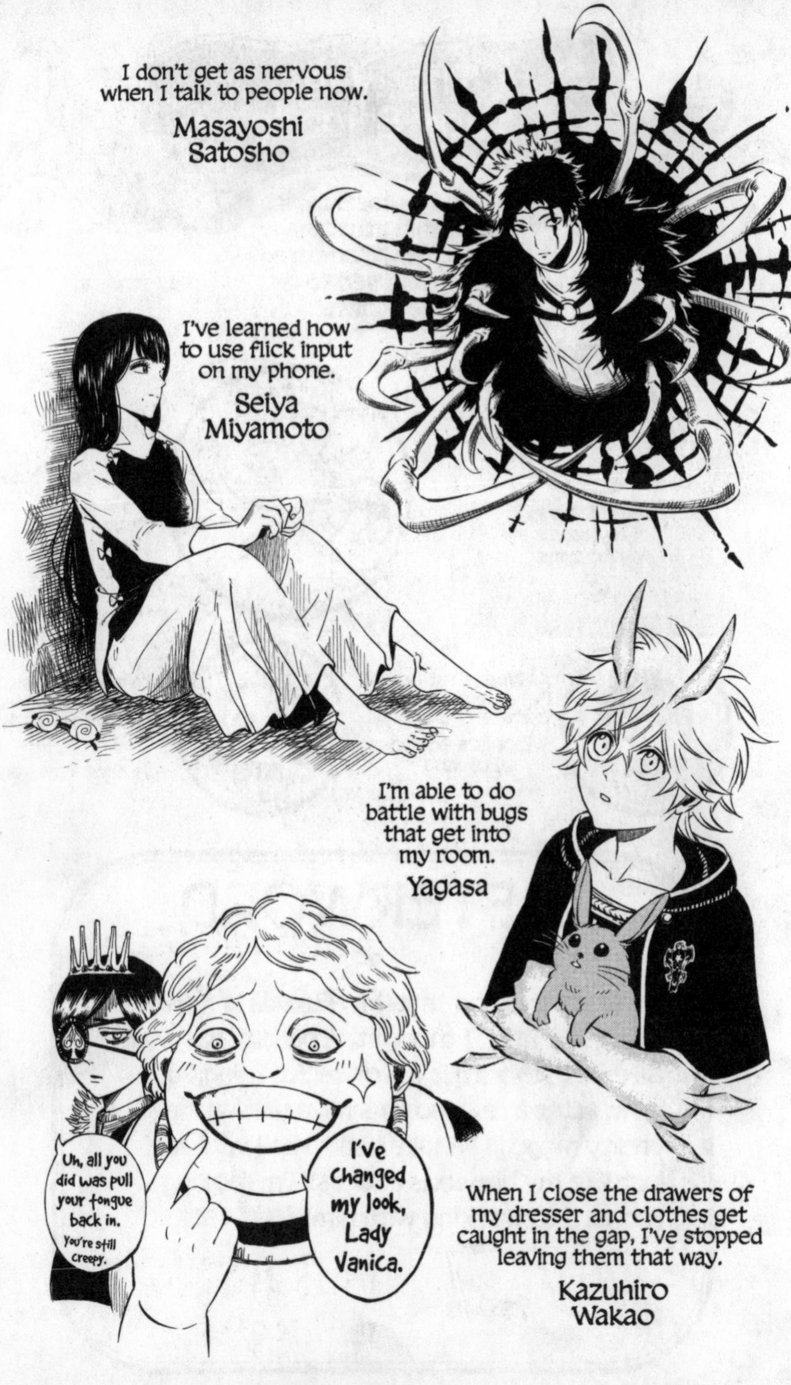
I don't get as nervous when I talk to people now.
Masayoshi Satosho
I've learned how to use flick input on my phone.
Seiya Miyamoto
I'm able to do battle with bugs that get into my room.
Yagasa
When I close the drawers of my dresser and clothes get caught in the gap, I've stopped leaving them that way.
Kazuhiro Wakao
I've changed my look, Lady Vanica.
Uh, all you did was pull your tongue back in.
You're still creepy.

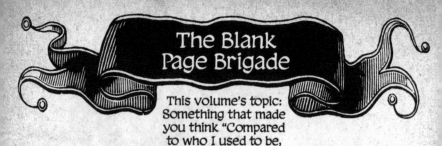

The Blank Page Brigade

This volume's topic: Something that made you think "Compared to who I used to be, I've grown."

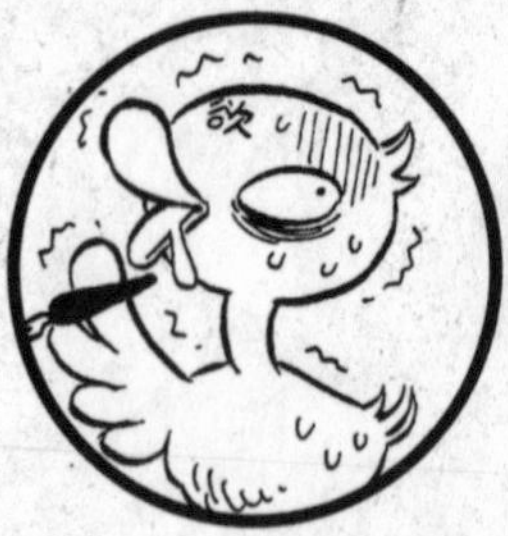

I'm now capable of booting up a computer.

Captain Tabata

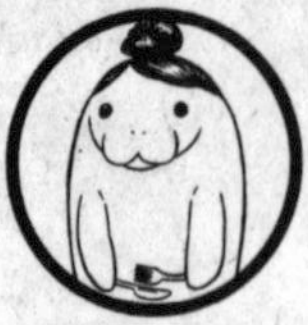

The thickness of my calves. My fat arms.

©

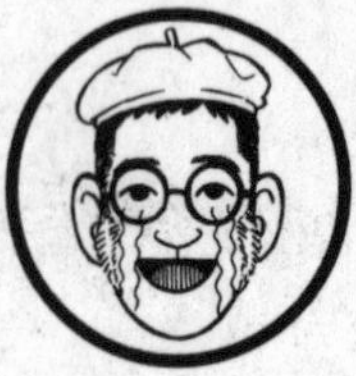

During my physical this year, I turned out to be exactly 170 cm tall.

Editor Fukuda

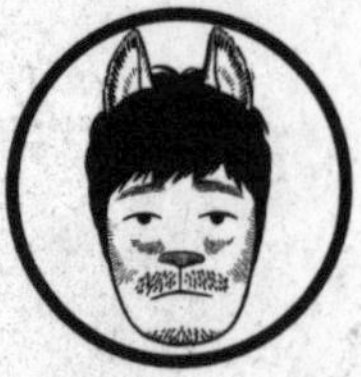

When I eat out, I've stopped ordering extra-large portions.

Comics editor Fujiwara

AFTERWORD

Between this and that, Mr. Fukuda is now my editor! At first, I thought, "This guy has a lot of energy. Youth is a wonderful thing," but now, after a few months have passed, he's pretty ragged!! I'll take him to hell with me, just like my previous editors!! I'm looking forward to working with him!!

 Special Bonus Material!

The elite who defend the Heart Kingdom.

 FIRE SPIRIT GUARDIAN

Floga

EARTH SPIRIT GUARDIAN

Sarado

WIND SPIRIT GUARDIAN

Smurik

DEMON SLAYER
KIMETSU NO YAIBA

Story and Art by
KOYOHARU GOTOUGE

In Taisho-era Japan, kindhearted Tanjiro Kamado makes a living selling charcoal. But his peaceful life is shattered when a demon slaughters his entire family. His little sister Nezuko is the only survivor, but she has been transformed into a demon herself! Tanjiro sets out on a dangerous journey to find a way to return his sister to normal and destroy the demon who ruined his life.

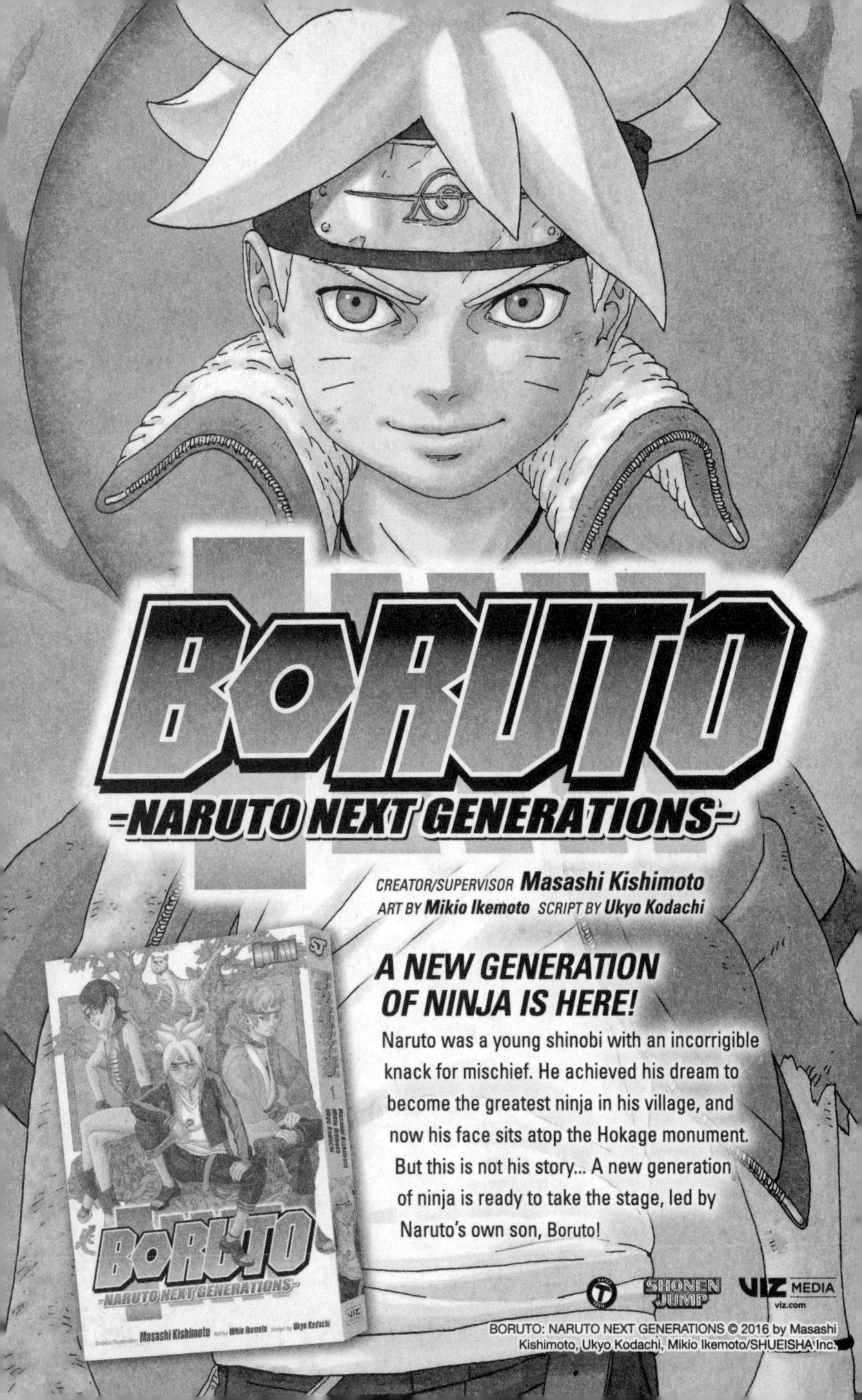
BORUTO
-NARUTO NEXT GENERATIONS-
CREATOR/SUPERVISOR Masashi Kishimoto
ART BY Mikio Ikemoto SCRIPT BY Ukyo Kodachi
A NEW GENERATION OF NINJA IS HERE!
Naruto was a young shinobi with an incorrigible knack for mischief. He achieved his dream to become the greatest ninja in his village, and now his face sits atop the Hokage monument. But this is not his story... A new generation of ninja is ready to take the stage, led by Naruto's own son, Boruto!
BORUTO
-NARUTO NEXT GENERATIONS-
Masashi Kishimoto
SHONEN JUMP
VIZ MEDIA
viz.com
BORUTO: NARUTO NEXT GENERATIONS © 2016 by Masashi Kishimoto, Ukyo Kodachi, Mikio Ikemoto/SHUEISHA Inc.

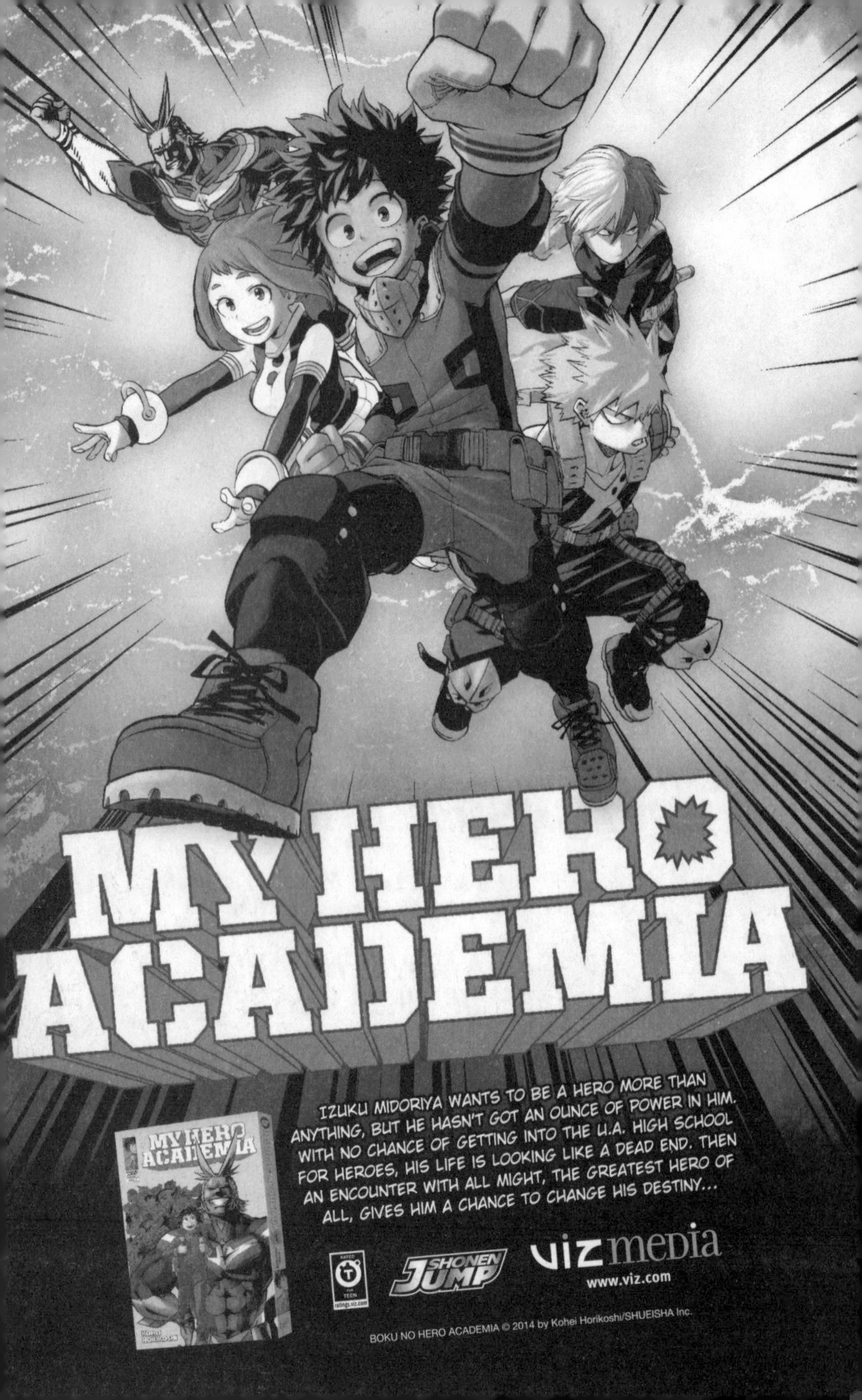
MY HERO ACADEMIA
IZUKU MIDORIYA WANTS TO BE A HERO MORE THAN ANYTHING, BUT HE HASN'T GOT AN OUNCE OF POWER IN HIM. WITH NO CHANCE OF GETTING INTO THE U.A. HIGH SCHOOL FOR HEROES, HIS LIFE IS LOOKING LIKE A DEAD END. THEN AN ENCOUNTER WITH ALL MIGHT, THE GREATEST HERO OF ALL, GIVES HIM A CHANCE TO CHANGE HIS DESTINY...
MY HERO ACADEMIA
SHONEN JUMP
viz media
www.viz.com
BOKU NO HERO ACADEMIA © 2014 by Kohei Horikoshi/SHUEISHA Inc.

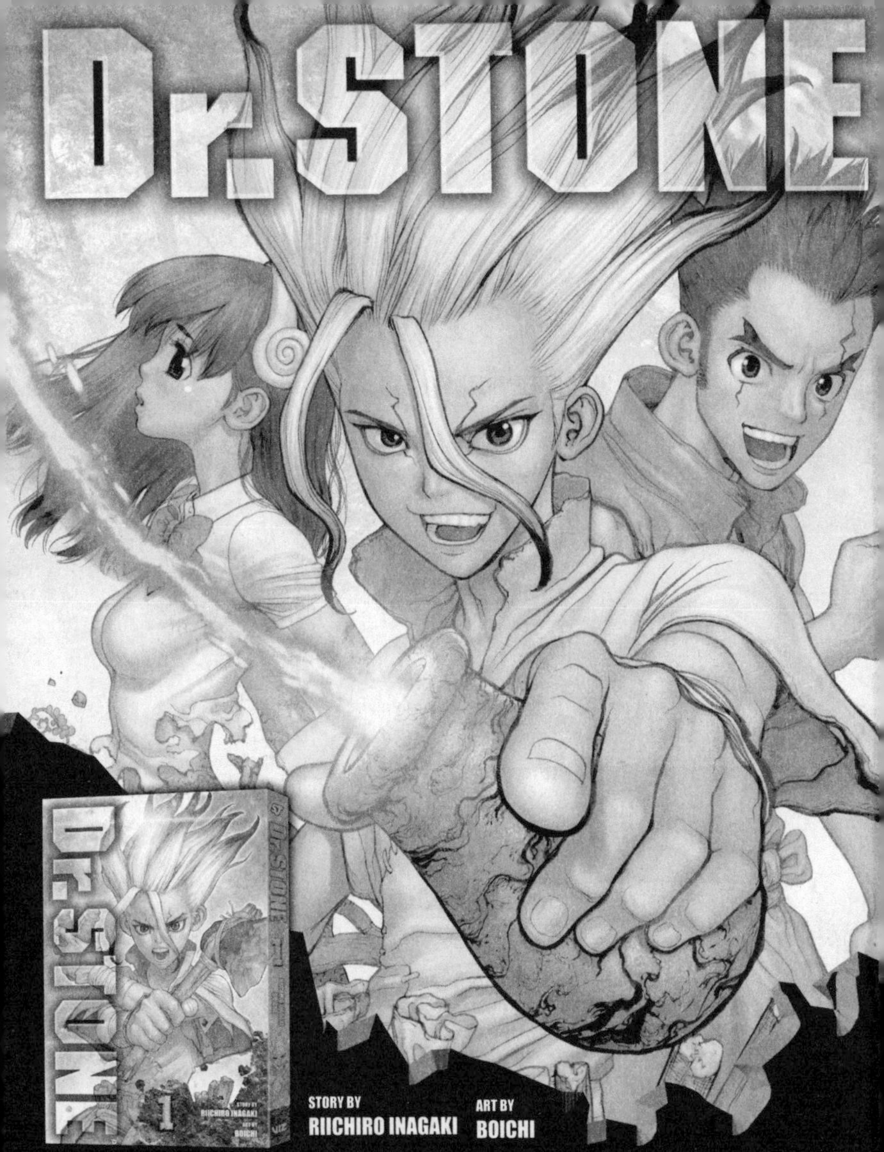

Dr. STONE

STORY BY
RIICHIRO INAGAKI

ART BY
BOICHI

One fateful day, all of humanity turned to stone. Many millennia later, Taiju frees himself from petrification and finds himself surrounded by statues. The situation looks grim—until he runs into his science-loving friend Senku! Together they plan to restart civilization with the power of science!

Stop

YOU'RE READING
THE WRONG WAY!

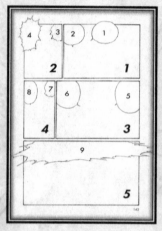

BLACK CLOVER

reads from right to left, starting
in the upper-right corner. Japanese
is read from right to left, meaning
that action, sound effects, and
word-balloon order are completely
reversed from English order.